IDIN ARCHITECTS
Integrating Design Into Nature

IDIN ARCHITECTS
Integrating Design Into Nature

Published in Australia in 2021 by
The Images Publishing Group Pty Ltd
ABN 89 059 734 431

Offices

Melbourne
6 Bastow Place
Mulgrave, Victoria 3170
Australia
Tel: +61 3 9561 5544

New York
6 West 18th Street 4B
New York City, NY 10011
United States
Tel: +1 212 645 1111

Shanghai
6F, Building C, 838 Guangji Road
Hongkou District, Shanghai 200434
China
Tel: +86 021 31260822

books@imagespublishing.com
www.imagespublishing.com

Copyright © IDIN Architects 2021
The Images Publishing Group Reference Number: 1596

All rights reserved. Apart from any fair dealing for the purposes of private study, research, criticism or review as permitted under the Copyright Act, no part of this publication may be reproduced, stored in a retrieval system or transmitted in any form by any means, electronic, mechanical, photocopying, recording or otherwise, without the written permission of the publisher.

All photography is attributed in the Project Credits on page 199, unless otherwise noted.
Endpapers: Spaceshift Studio (detail of Arize Hotel lobby ceiling); Page 198: courtesy of IDIN Architects; page 200: Ketsiree Wongwan (IDIN Architects office).

 A catalogue record for this book is available from the National Library of Australia

Title: IDIN Architects: Integrating Design Into Nature // IDIN Architects
ISBN: 9781864709032

This title was commissioned in IMAGES' Melbourne office and produced as follows: *Editorial* Chandranie, Georgia (Gina) Tsarouhas, *Graphic design* Ryan Marshall, *Production* Nicole Boehringer

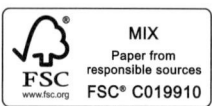

Printed on 140gsm Sun woodfree paper by Artron Art (Group) Co., Ltd, in China
Prepress by A&S Press, Singapore

IMAGES has included on its website a page for special notices in relation to this and its other publications. Please visit www.imagespublishing.com

Every effort has been made to trace the original source of copyright material contained in this book. The publishers would be pleased to hear from copyright holders to rectify any errors or omissions.

The information and illustrations in this publication have been prepared and supplied by IDIN Architects and the participants. While all reasonable efforts have been made to ensure accuracy, the publishers do not, under any circumstances, accept responsibility for errors, omissions and representations express or implied.

CONTENTS

6   INTRODUCTION

8   IDIN ARCHITECTS OFFICE

30 CHOUI FONG TEA CAFÉ

46 CHOUI FONG TEA CAFÉ 2

68 JB HOUSE

84 SIRI HOUSE

100 KA HOUSE

114 PA PRANK

130 LIMA DUVA

144 TARA VILLA

166 ARIZE HOTEL

192 OTHER PROJECTS

196 AWARDS

198 TEAM IDIN ARCHITECTS

199 PROJECT CREDITS

INTRODUCTION

IDIN Architects Co., Ltd. was founded in 2004. "IDIN" is the acronym for "Integrating Design Into Nature," and it reflects our philosophy in both English and Thai. In English, it portrays our raison d'être—merging architecture with nature in different ways, and why that matters. In Thai, "I-DIN" refers to the beautiful scent that emanates after rainfall, perfectly implying the tropical climate of Thailand, the firm's home, and birthplace. The name also ties in with my personal inspiration, tropical design.

"Nature" can be defined largely as the ecology around us, the context, as well as the different personalities of our clients—the nature of an individual. The design philosophy of IDIN Architects is to merge surrounding nature with the architectural aesthetic. Our emphasis is placed not only on aesthetics, but on a dynamic *balance* between aesthetics and practicality. The end result is an architecture that is tailored to our hot and humid environment, as beautifully as it creates a meaningful experience.

After graduation, I worked those intial years with a firm where I focused on learning and gaining experience. I had also been receiving significant architectural awards in Thailand, which was a proud achievement for me. As my confidence and experience grew, I began to court the idea of pursuing my passion in tropical design by setting up my own architectural design company. The plan gradually took shape, and in 2004, I ventured out on my own and did it.

Like any other young company, IDIN Architects began its journey in the world of architectural design with a small team of architects. At that time, the public's interest in, and use of architectural design was still limited in Thailand. Private houses and small resorts were the categories of projects that we undertook in our earlier years, but thankfully, things picked up. Looking back through the years, it can be said that IDIN Architects set milestones and faced turning points in its journey every five years.

In 2010, IDIN Architects received an ASA Architectural Design Award issued by The Association of Siamese Architects under Royal Patronage for the project Phuket Gateway. It was an especially prestigious award for such a young firm. Our W House project was also completed that year; its unique character and concept had been noticed by local and international publications, and the project quickly gained recognition. IDIN Architects became well known after Phuket Gateway and W House, and we received more opportunities to broaden our portfolio with projects spanning a variety of categories.

Many of these new projects were completed in 2015, including KA House, SIRI House, Lima Duva, and Choui Fong Tea Café, which are featured here. They were well received and positively reviewed by several publications, winning awards in Thailand, as well as abroad. That was a successful year for IDIN Architects as our work had gained the appreciation of the public audience, despite us being a small company of fewer than 10 people. It was a significant change for IDIN Architects; the company was growing, gaining momentum, and ready to go further. From that stepping stone, IDIN Architects moved up the scale to take on larger projects.

The year 2020 proves to be another turning point for IDIN Architects as we publish our first monograph for an international audience. The 10 projects featured in this book span several building categories and scales, and include residential houses, resorts, a hotel, and public buildings. These selected works feature new builds, as well as renovation projects, and they are a lively expression of IDIN Architects' core value and philosophical concept. Each conveys a different response to the fundamental philosophy that underscores our work: how can the design be integrated into nature such that the idea of nature can be interpreted and interrelated with the project, its characteristics, and conditions?

To put it simply, the 10 projects perfectly describe IDIN's heart and mind—the places where our architectural passion resides.

Jeravej Hongsakul
Founder and Principal Architect,
IDIN Architects

Sutthisan, Bangkok, Thailand, 2018

IDIN ARCHITECTS OFFICE

The IDIN Architects office is a reflection of its core beliefs—the symbiotic relationship between man, building, and environment. The building accommodates a pleasant working space and nurtures an environment that is beneficial to both physical and mental wellbeing with a therapeutic green strip on the outside along the work area. This is created by integrating the greenery of the site with the original trees adjacent to the plot. This small nature belt also attracts birds and squirrels that make their home in the foliage. The initial idea was to compose a highly private and creative workspace for architects and other staff. From that, it shaped into constructing a building that has an almost invisible presence within its urban context.

In this office design, IDIN Architects steps away from the usual building front of most standalone office buildings. This passive design, independent of a main front, enables flexibility in orientation; the different office zones and entrances are positioned in line with the shifting sun to minimize the building's energy consumption.

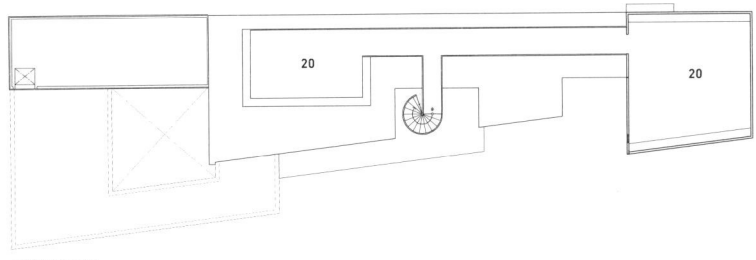

ROOF PLAN

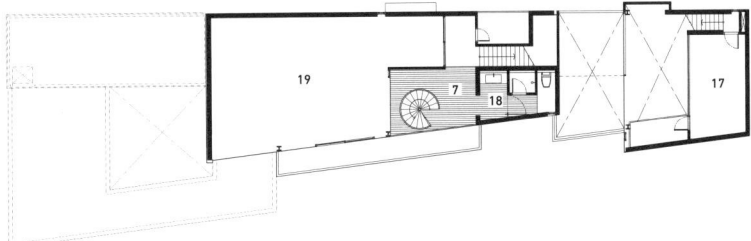

THIRD-FLOOR PLAN

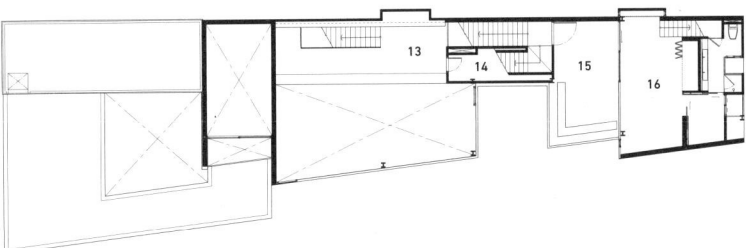

MEZZANINE FLOOR PLAN

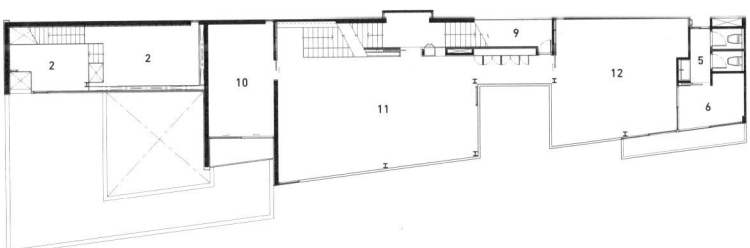

SECOND-FLOOR PLAN

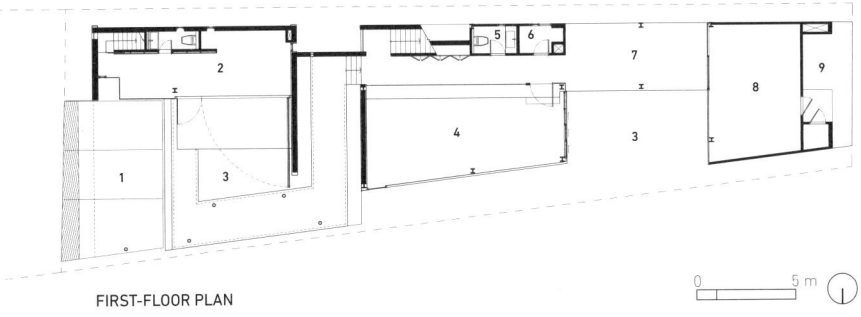

FIRST-FLOOR PLAN

1 PARKING
2 CAFÉ
3 COURTYARD
4 MEETING ROOM
5 RESTROOM
6 PANTRY
7 TERRACE
8 MATERIALS ROOM
9 SERVICE AREA
10 PRINCIPAL'S OFFICE
11 MAIN OFFICE AREA
12 COMMON AREA
13 OFFICE (MEZZANINE)
14 STORAGE
15 TERRACE
16 RESIDENCE
17 RESIDENCE (MEZZANINE)
18 BATHROOM
19 OFFICE FOR RENT
20 ROOF TERRACE

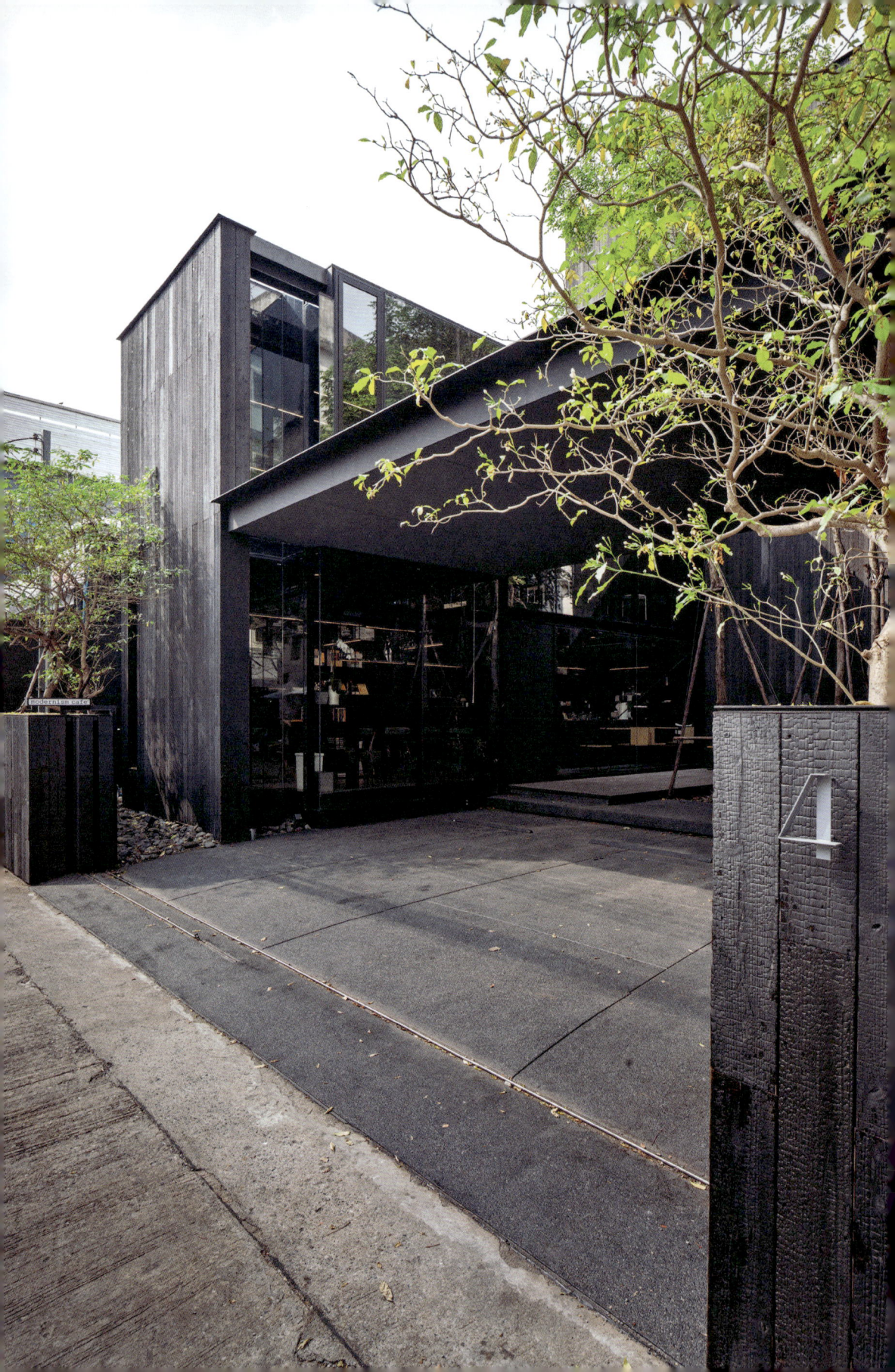

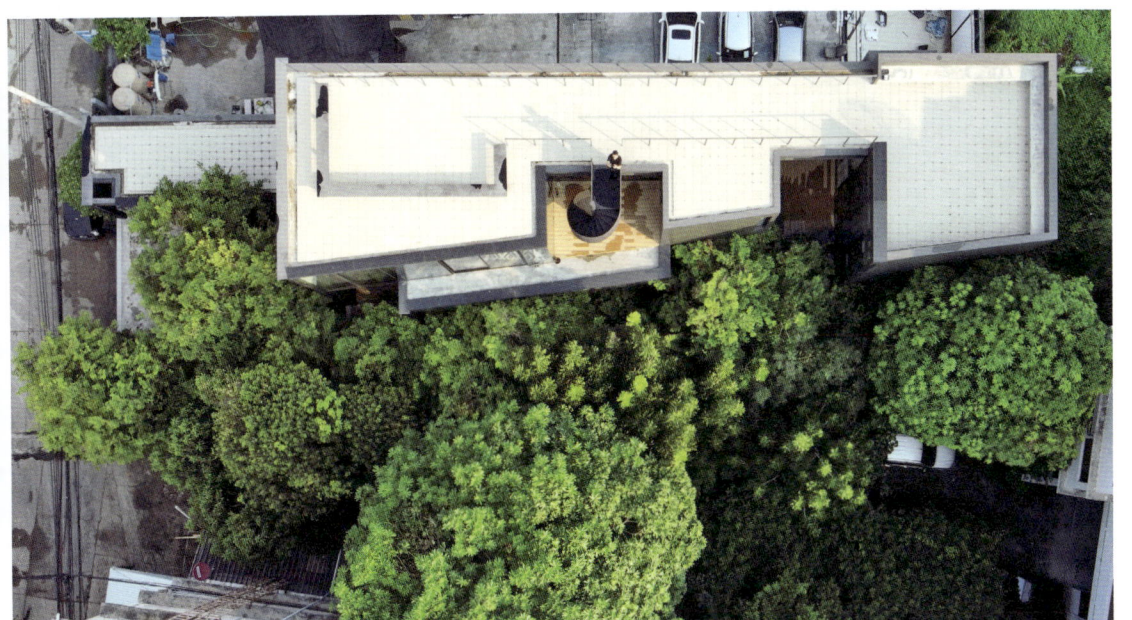

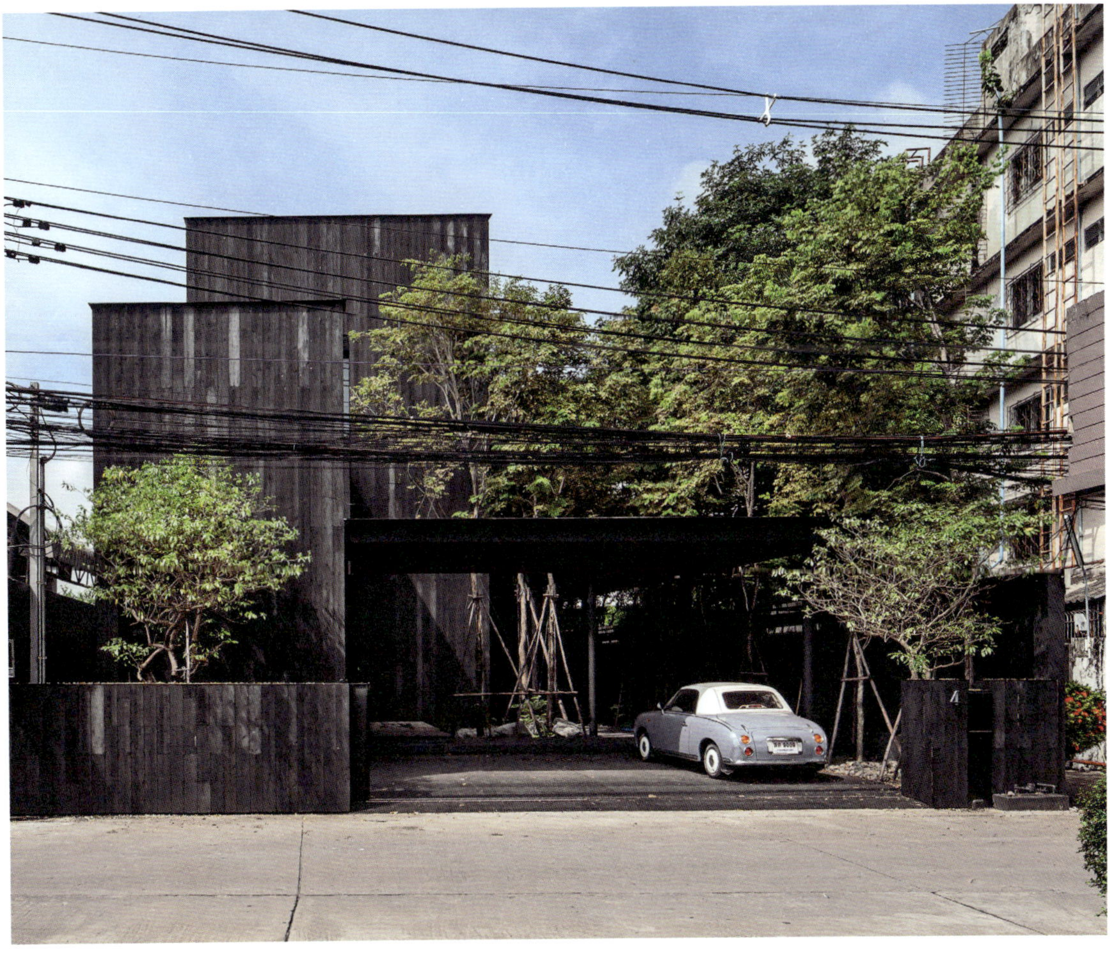

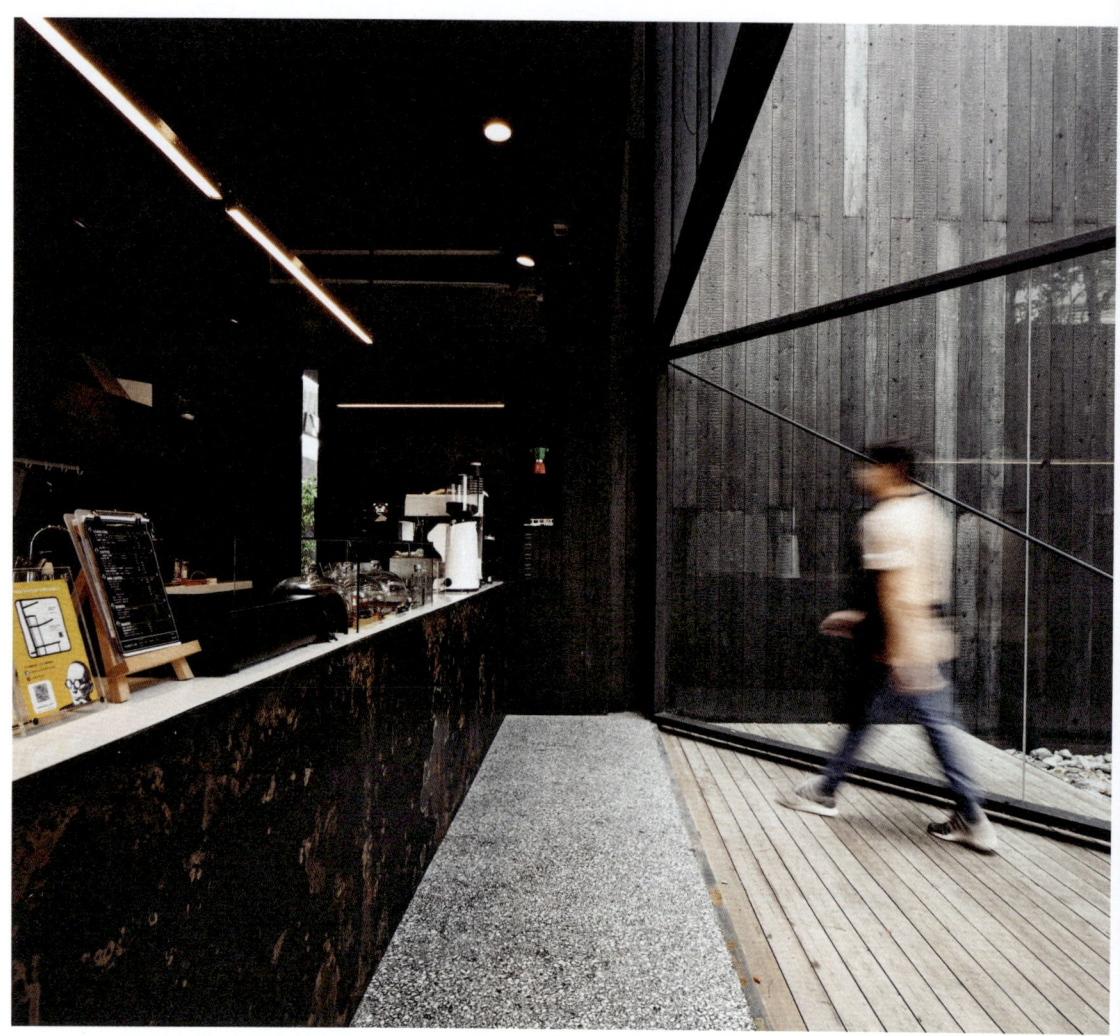

The IDIN Architects office exemplifies a private and creative workplace, situated on a small site in one of Bangkok's most bustling neighborhoods. The café at the front is often mistaken as being the complete extent of the space by many who visit the office and pass by, not realizing the full dimension of the building. As one enters further, the playful sequence is revealed, and the composition of the space gradually makes itself known, similar to how a book deliberately discloses the story to a reader with each line read. Each section features a different character, but still upholds the concept of the principal idea. Guest routes are filtered away from the work domain to ensure privacy and prevent disruption to the calmness and serenity of the workspace.

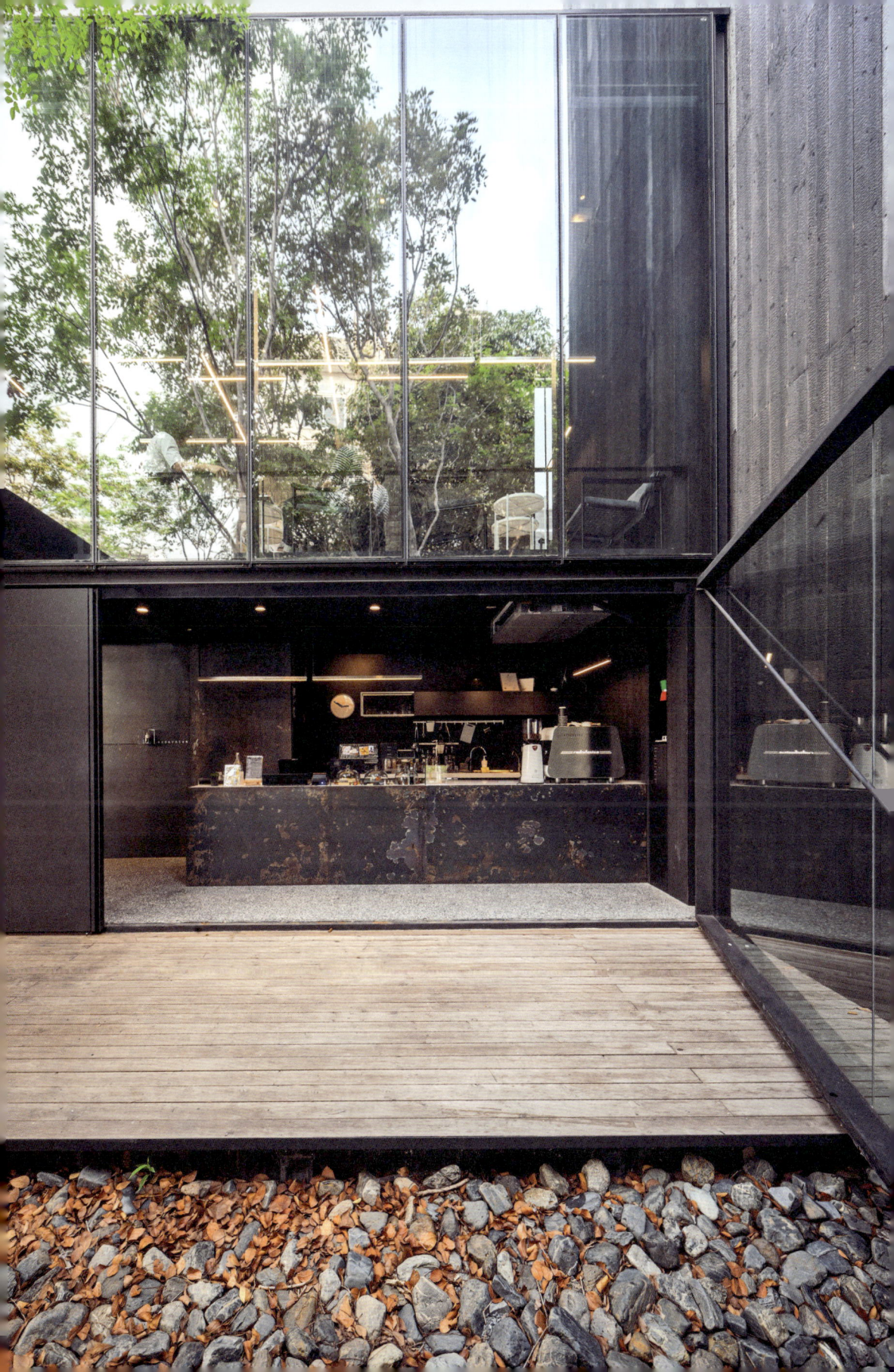

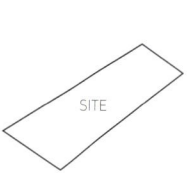
AN EXISTING NARROW LANDFORM

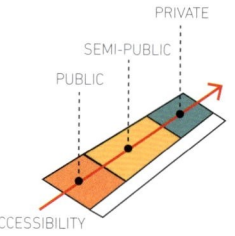
SEQUENCE OF SPACE FROM POINT OF ACCESSIBILITY IN HORIZONTAL DIRECTION

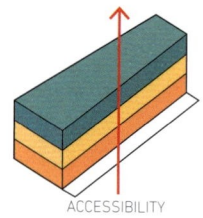
SEQUENCE OF SPACE FROM POINT OF ACCESSIBILITY IN VERTICAL DIRECTION

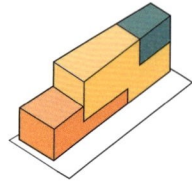
INTEGRATION BETWEEN VERTICAL AND HORIZONTAL SEQUENCES

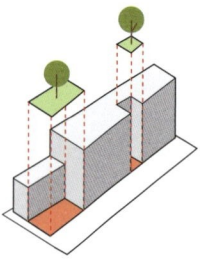
COURTYARDS INSERTED

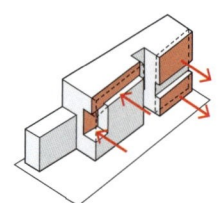
BUILDING FORM ADJUSTED TO REGULATION

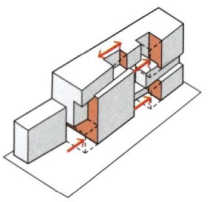
MASS EXPANDED TO CREATE TERRACES

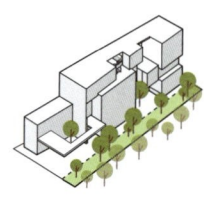
SITE GREENERY INTEGRATED WITH TREES IN ADJACENT PLOT

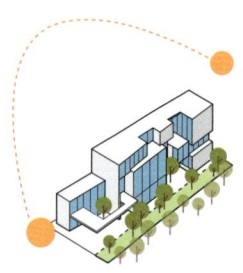
CURTAIN WALL FACING NORTH PROVIDES QUALITY LIGHT AND GREENERY VIEW

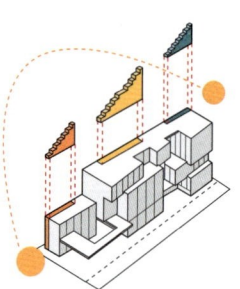
MAIN STAIRCASE ALIGNED ALONG SOUTH PREVENTS EXCESSIVE HEAT FROM ENTERING

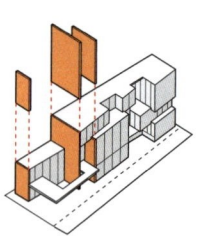
BURNT CEDAR INSTALLED AS MAIN FEATURE WALL

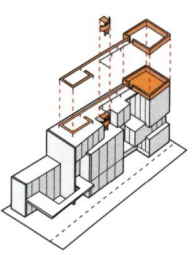
ROOFTOP TERRACE ACCESSED VIA SPIRAL STAIRCASE

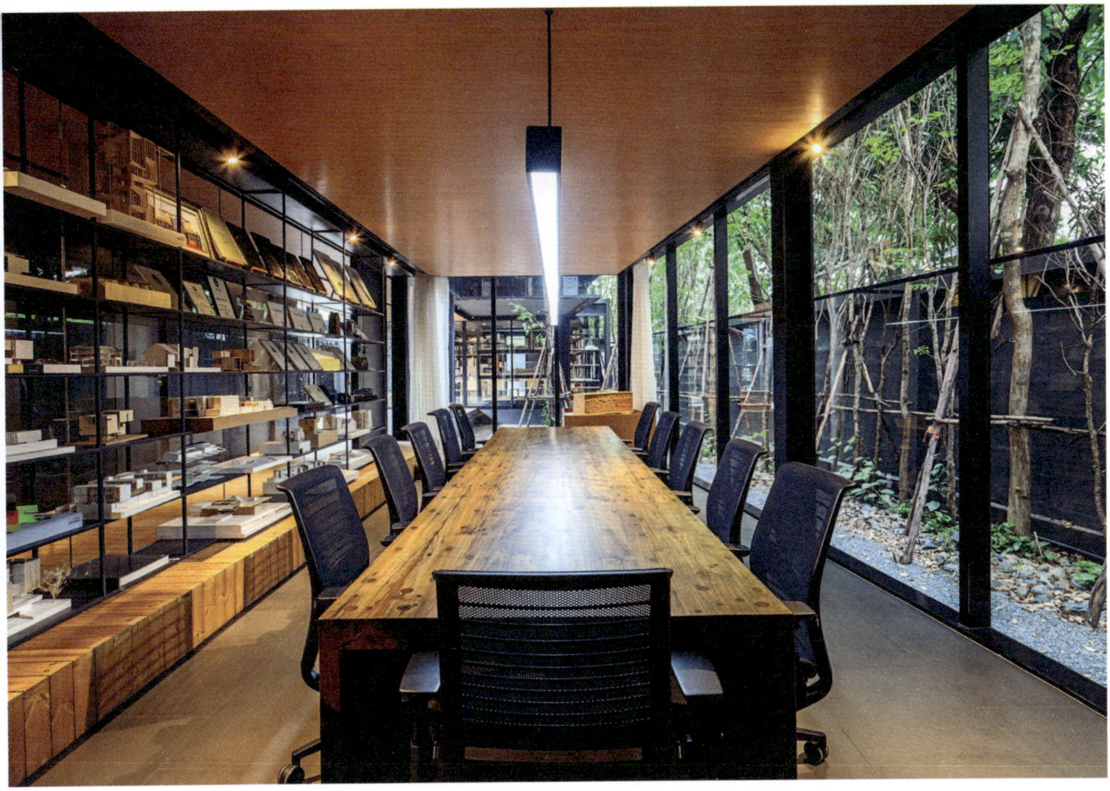

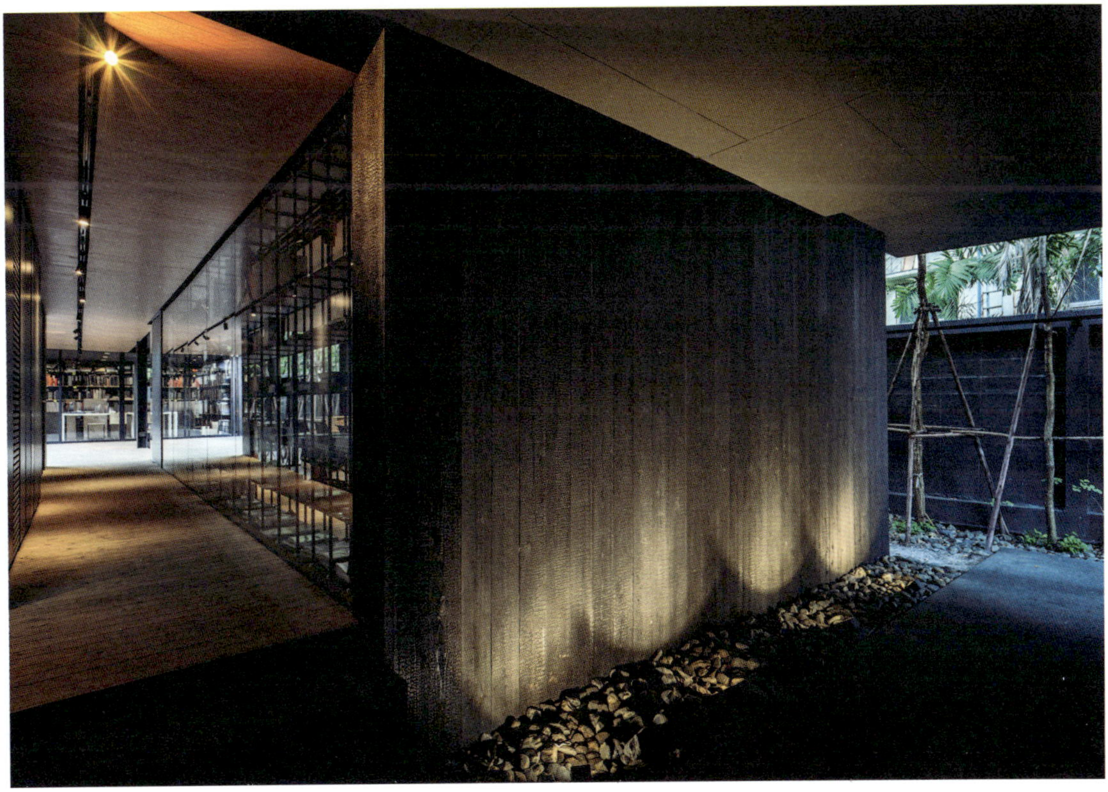

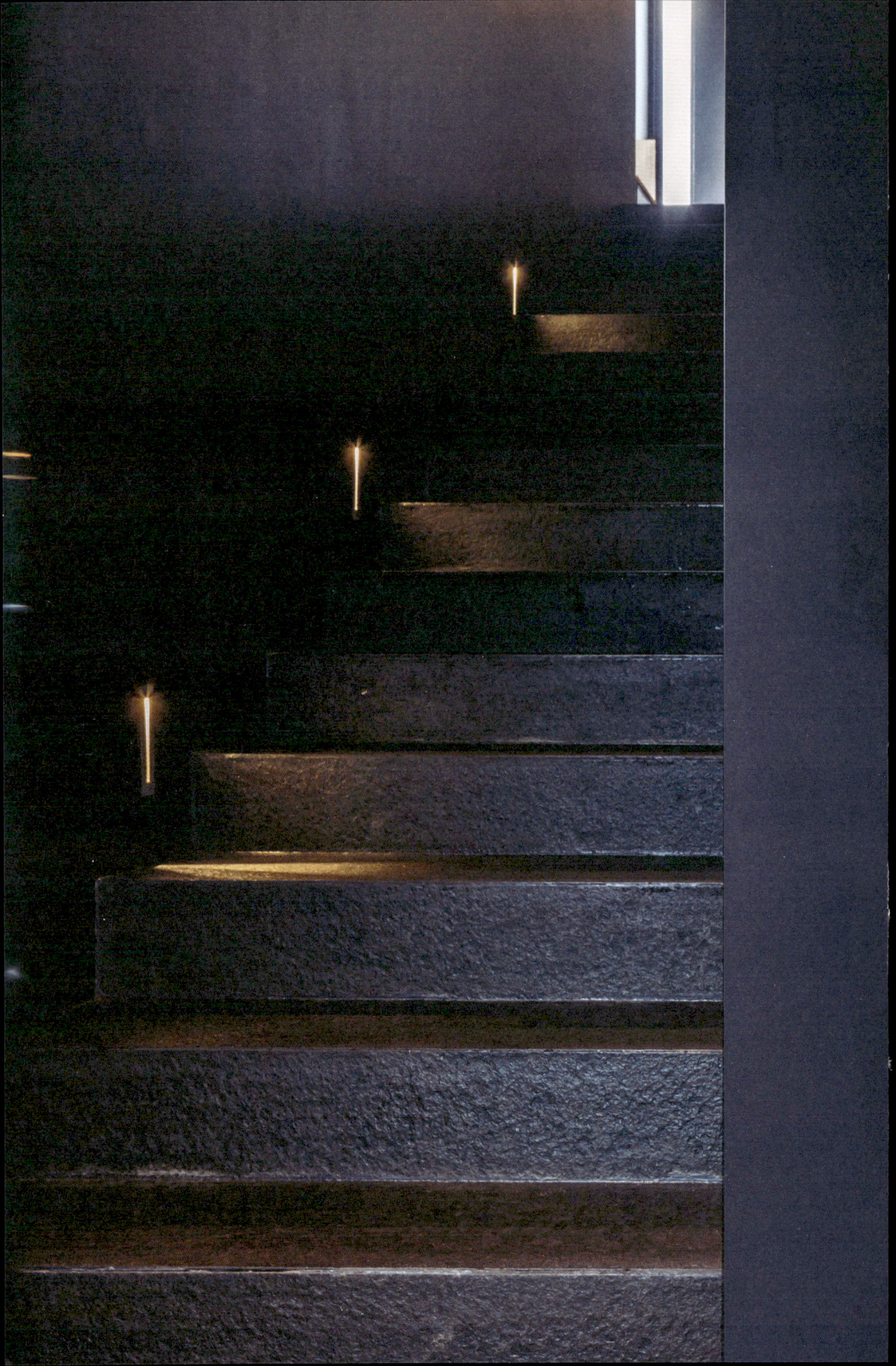

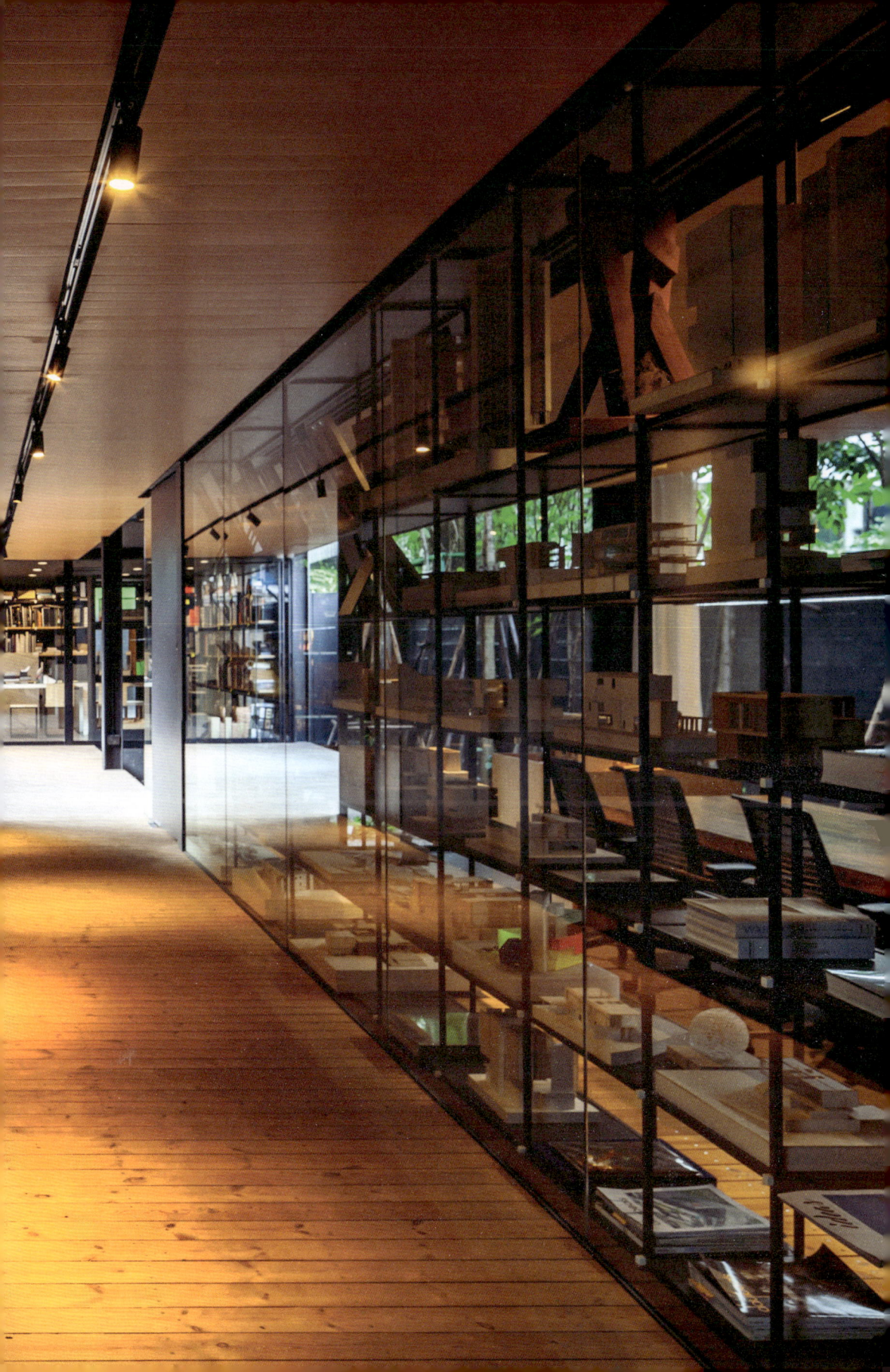

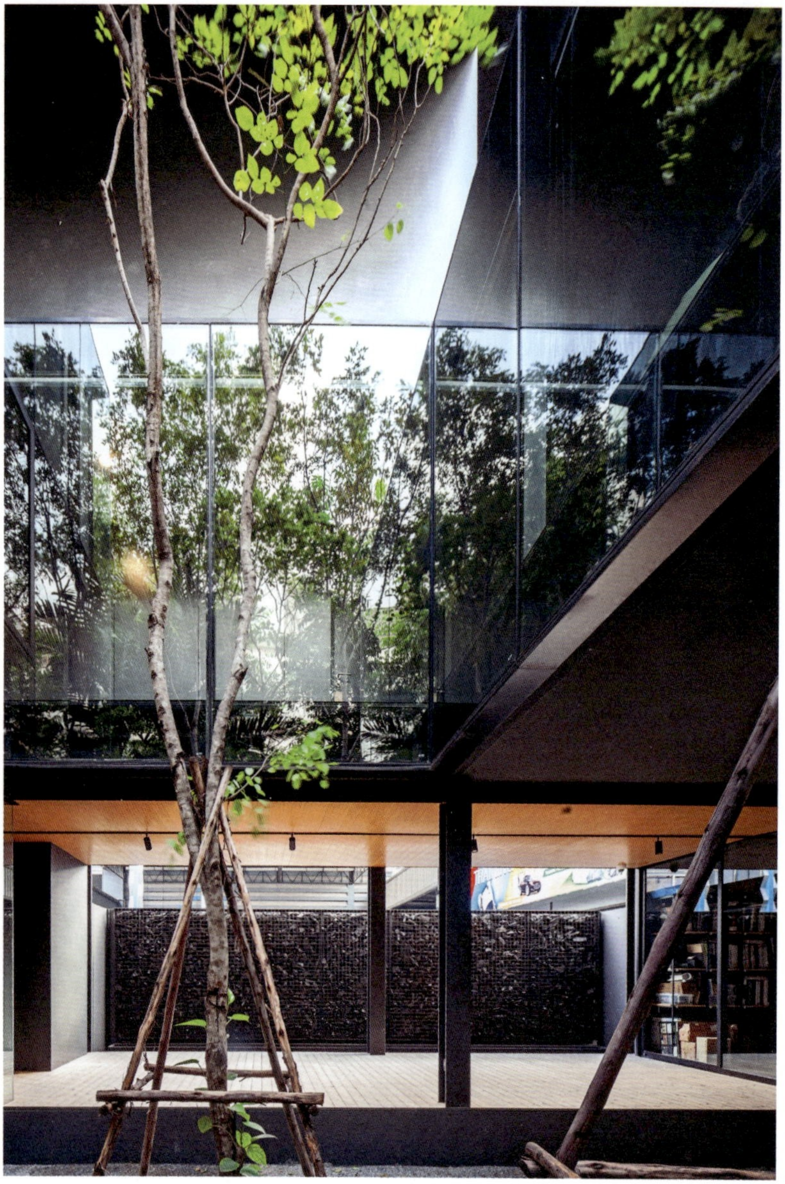

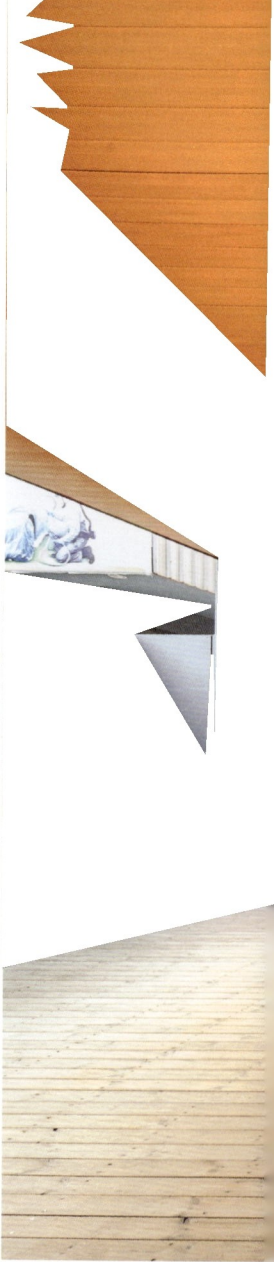

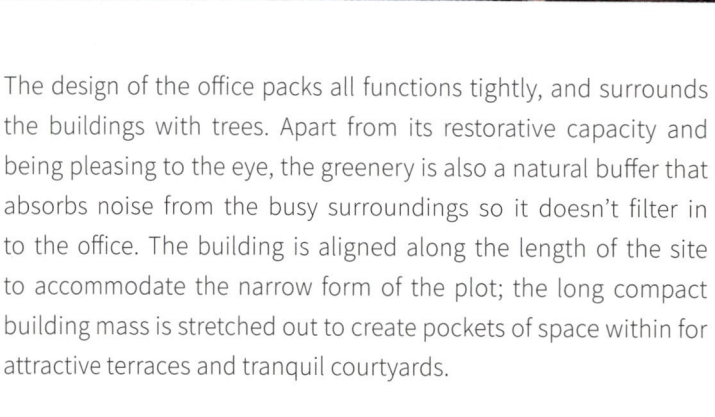

The design of the office packs all functions tightly, and surrounds the buildings with trees. Apart from its restorative capacity and being pleasing to the eye, the greenery is also a natural buffer that absorbs noise from the busy surroundings so it doesn't filter in to the office. The building is aligned along the length of the site to accommodate the narrow form of the plot; the long compact building mass is stretched out to create pockets of space within for attractive terraces and tranquil courtyards.

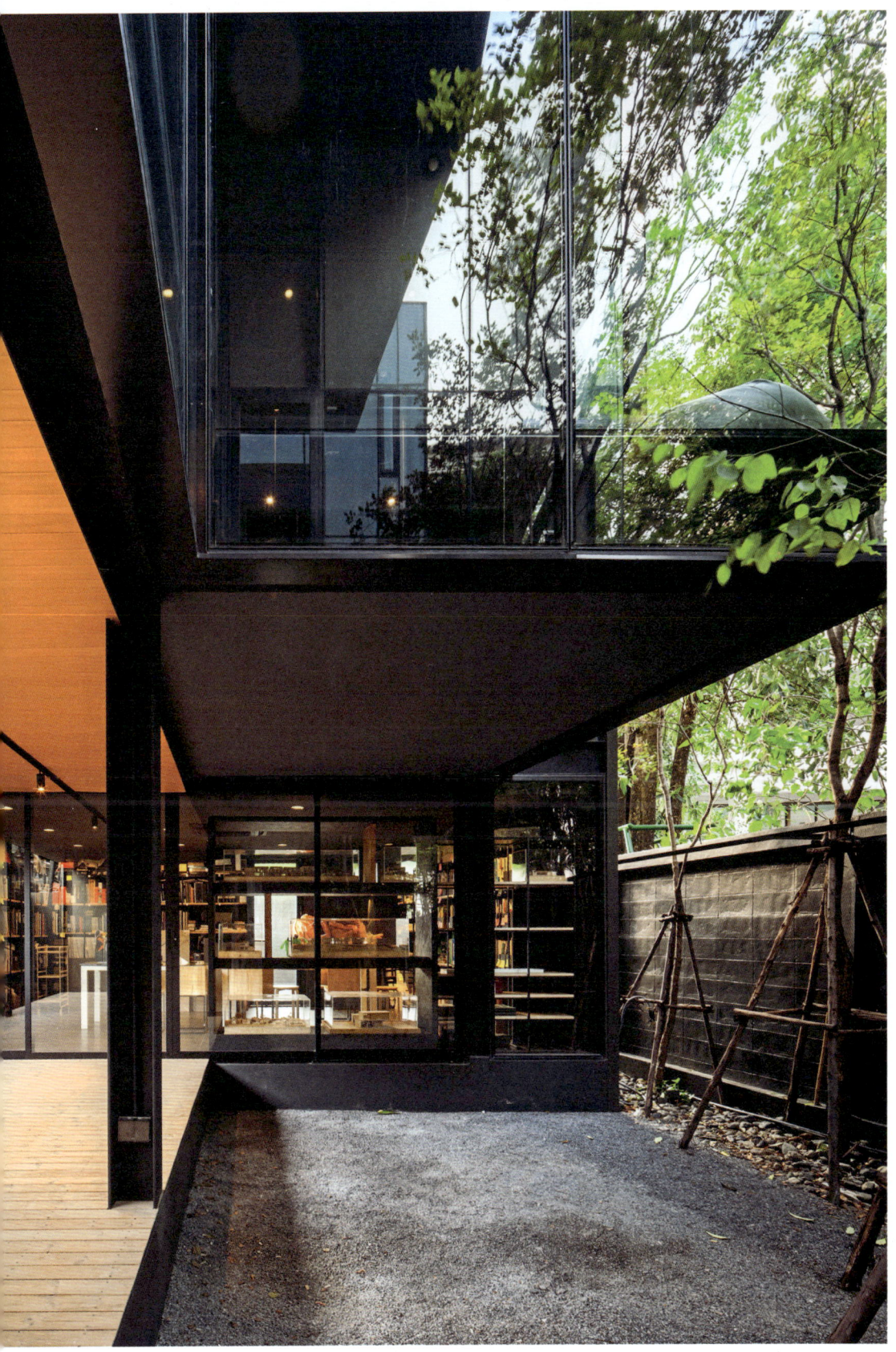

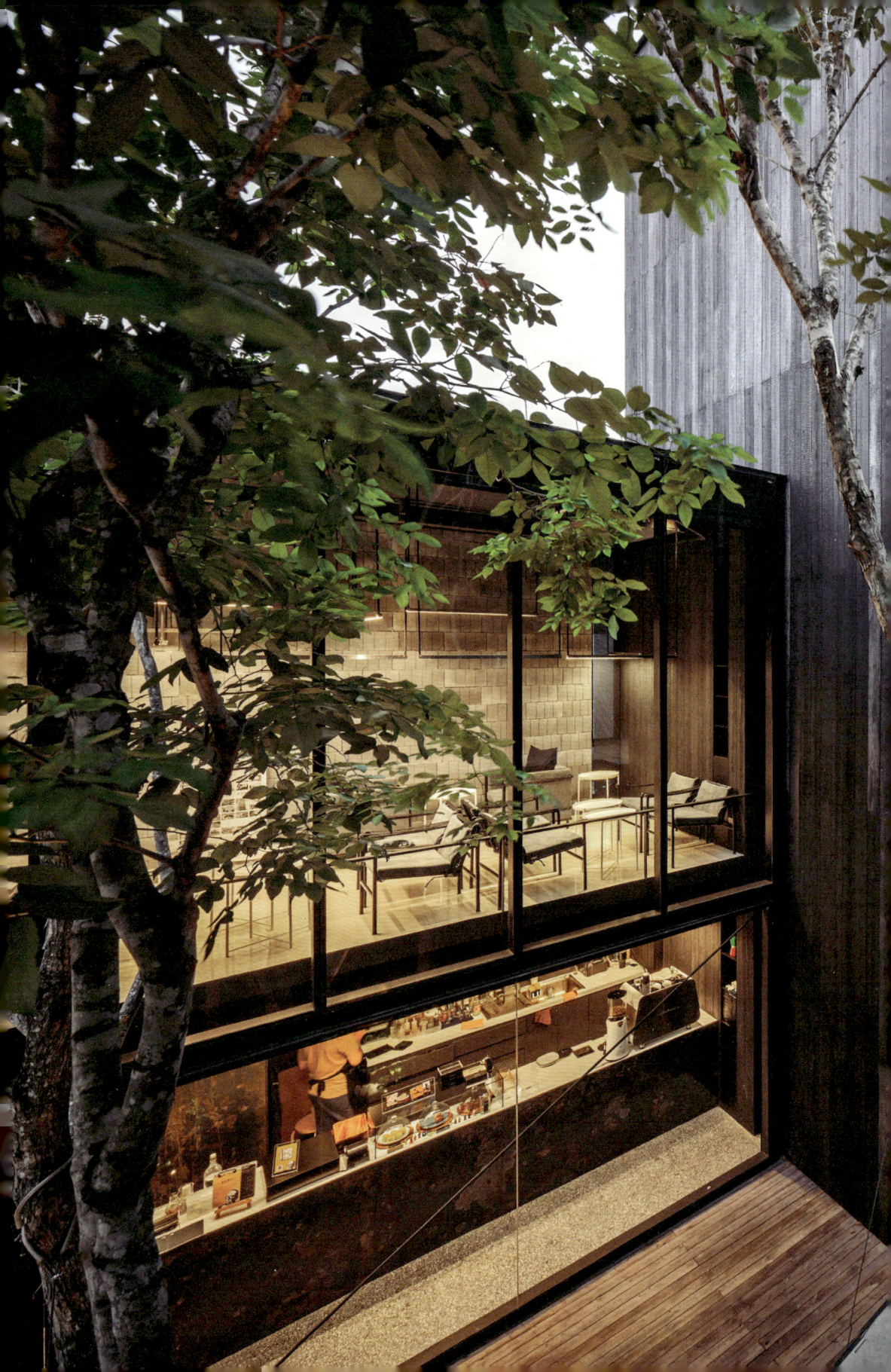

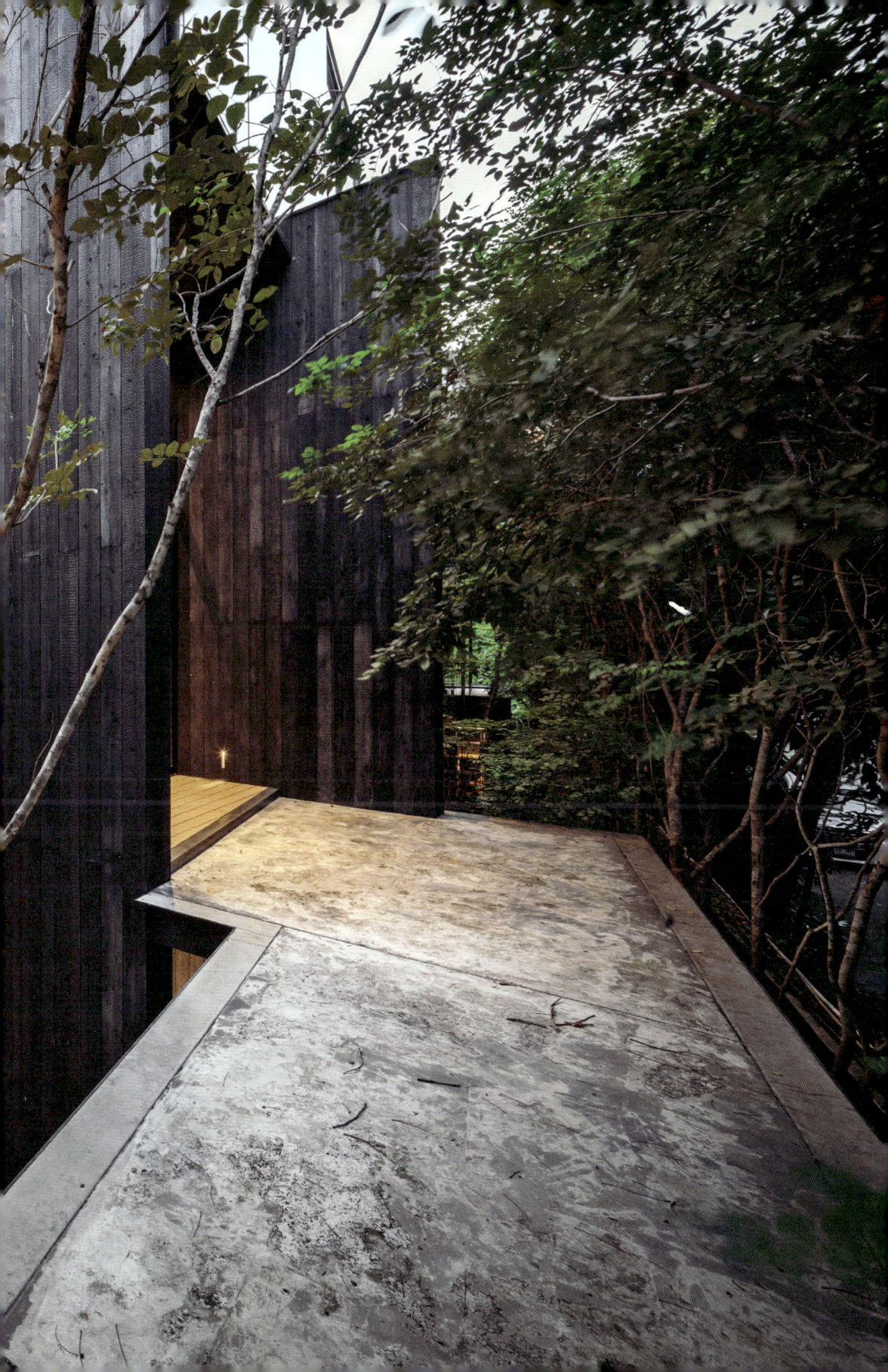

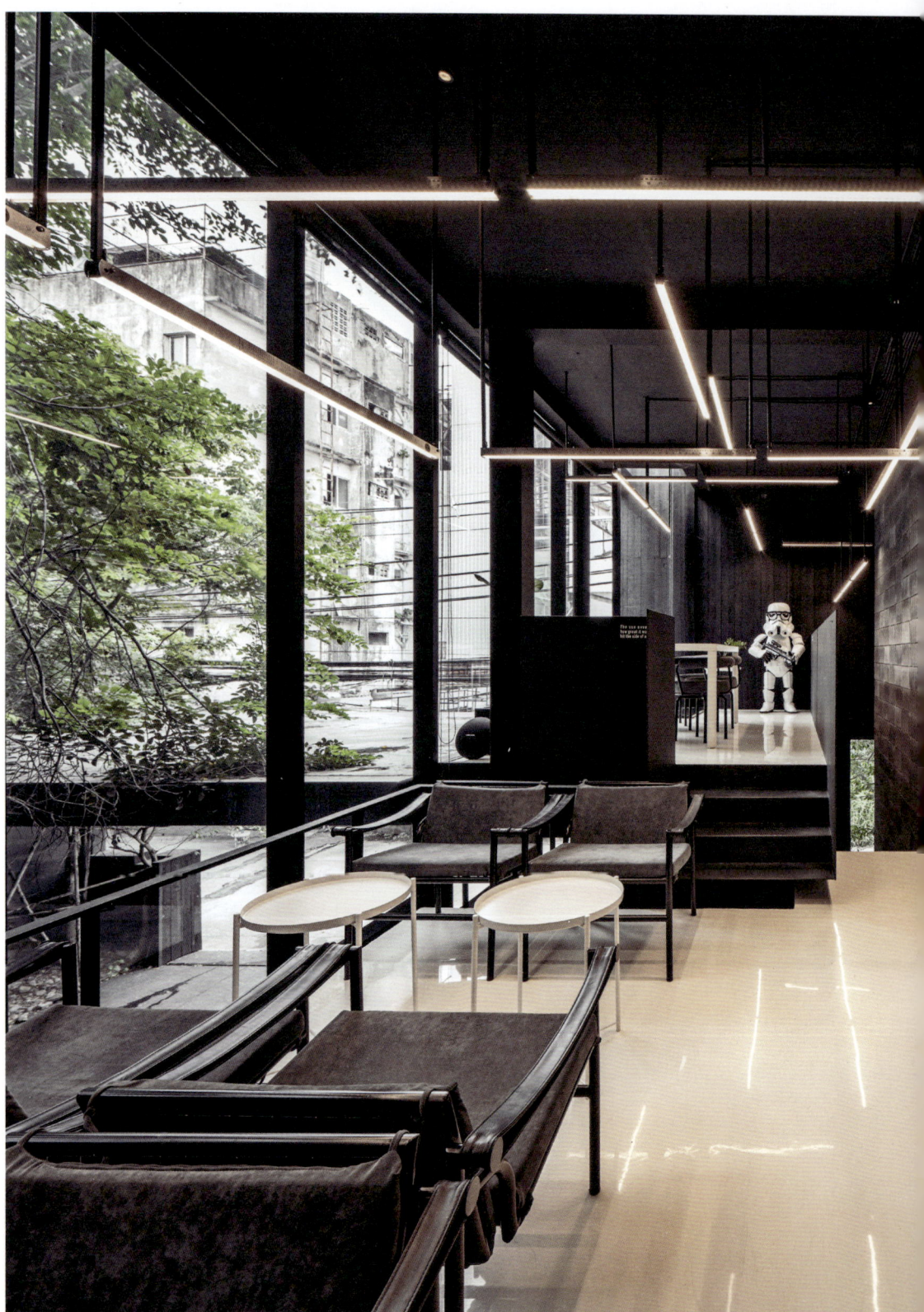

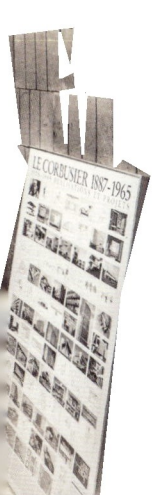

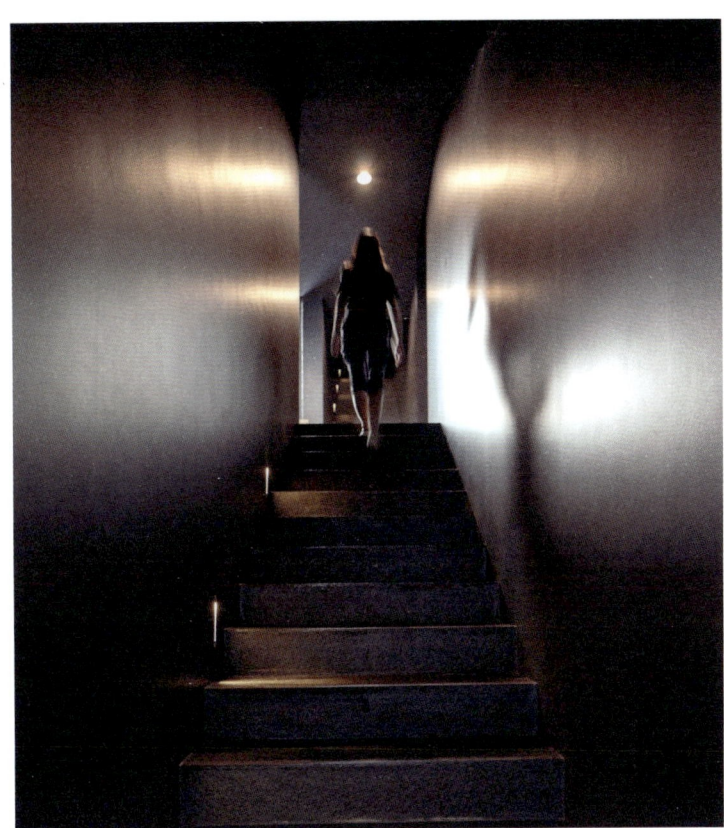

One of the main features of the office is its unique uniformity in tone, which is significant in the design and concept of the building. Burnt cedar planks fashion a solid exterior that flows seamlessly, almost undetected, to become interior walls, amplifying the element of continuity within the space; it also allows the building to blend in within itself, almost like a camouflage effect. The burnt cedar is also symbolic to IDIN Architects' credo; its distinctive black color and texture is not a result of painting or coloring, but a result of scorching the planks to protect them from fire damage and termites. This reflects IDIN Architects' belief that architecture should present as the solution in the problem-solving process, and the result should be unique, hold aesthetic appeal, and be beneficial to people, as well as better living for its occupants.

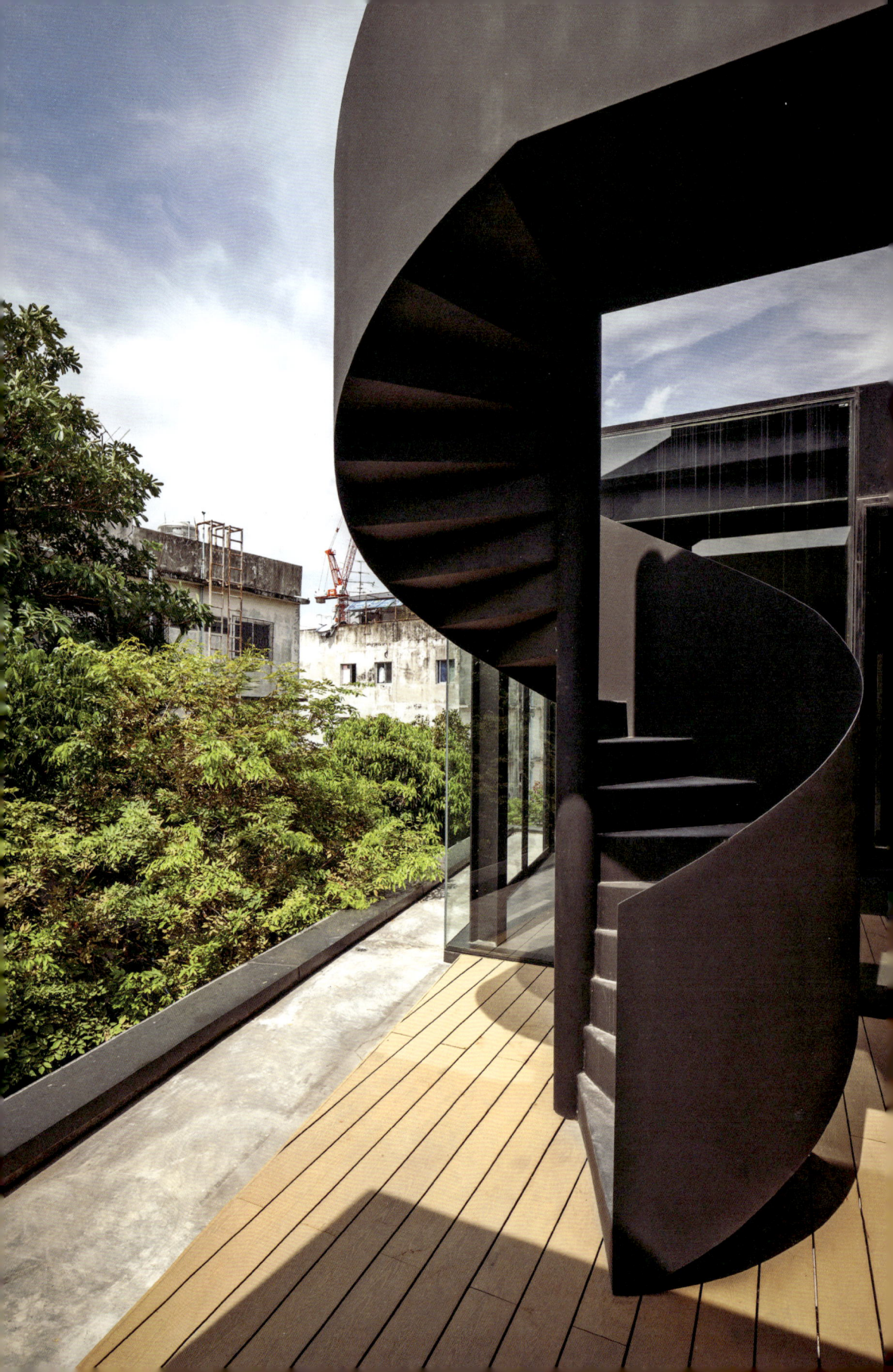

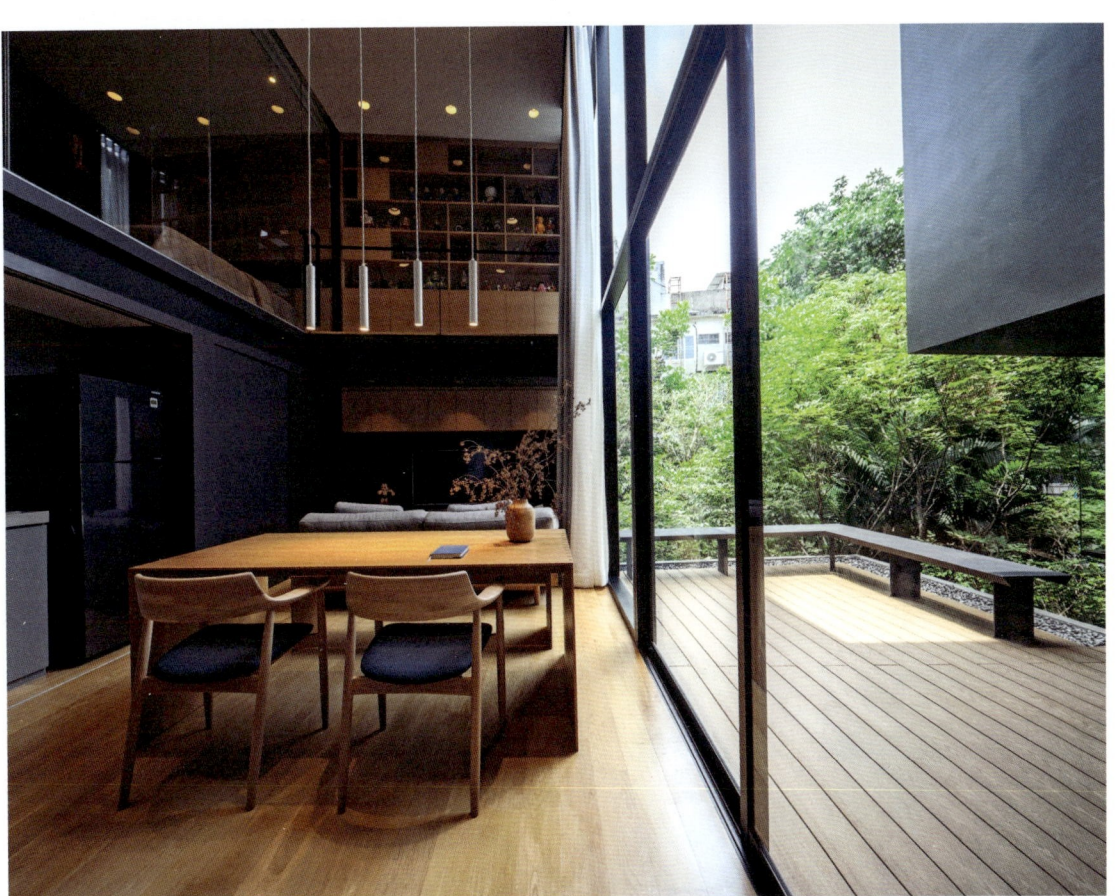

The building is organized into three zones: public, semi-public, and private, and the hierarchical relationships develop in both vertical and horizontal directions. The public zone is located on the first floor and is composed of a café and a meeting room to host meetings and visitors. The café is the only exposed function that can be seen from the street, and it welcomes anyone who'd enjoy a cuppa, while also serving as a reception area for visitors and clients. It also functions as a recreation area for staff during the day. The semi-public zone on the second floor contains all workspaces and takes up most of the building's plan. The innermost part of the building houses a private residential area for the company's principal.

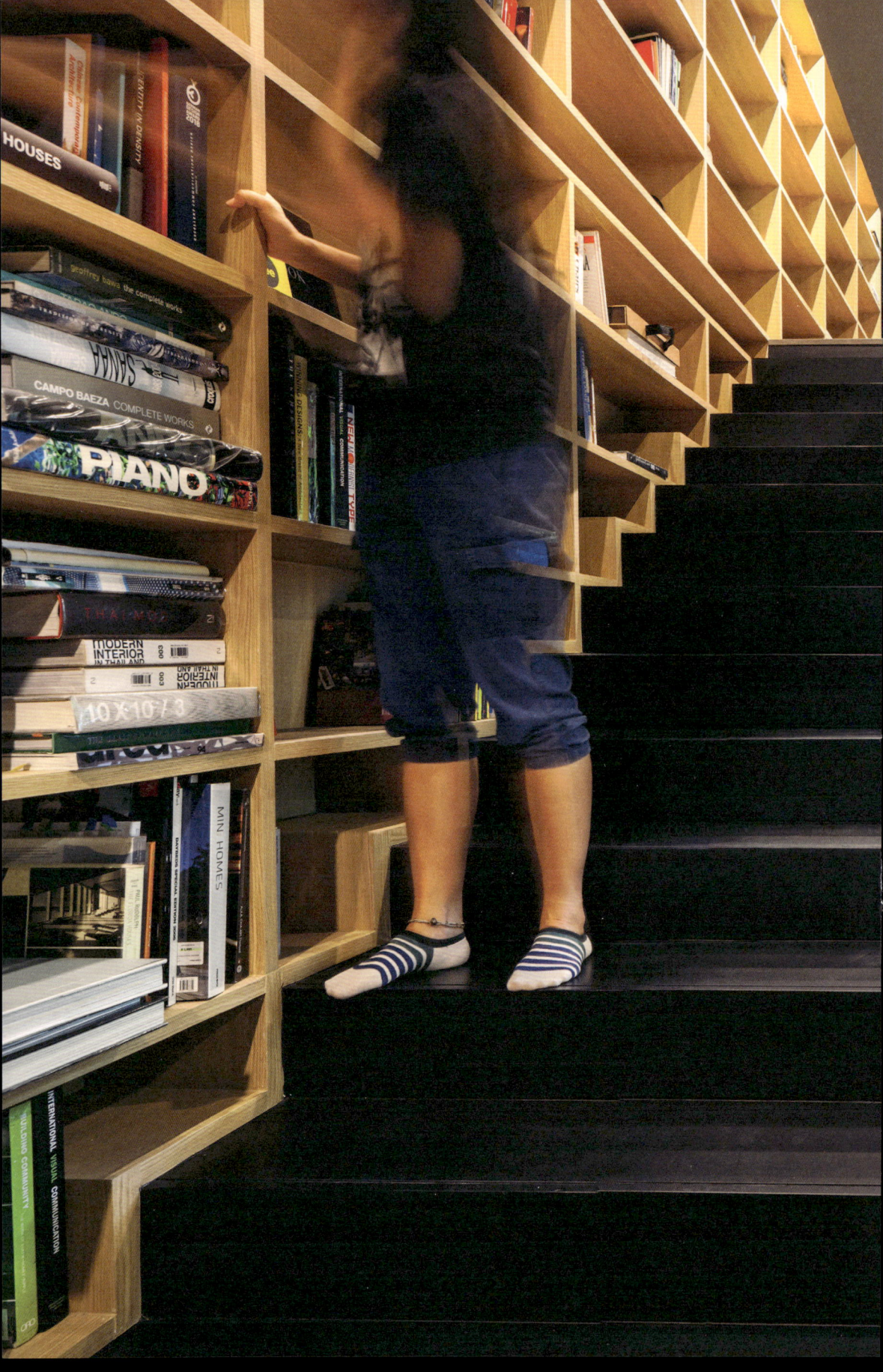

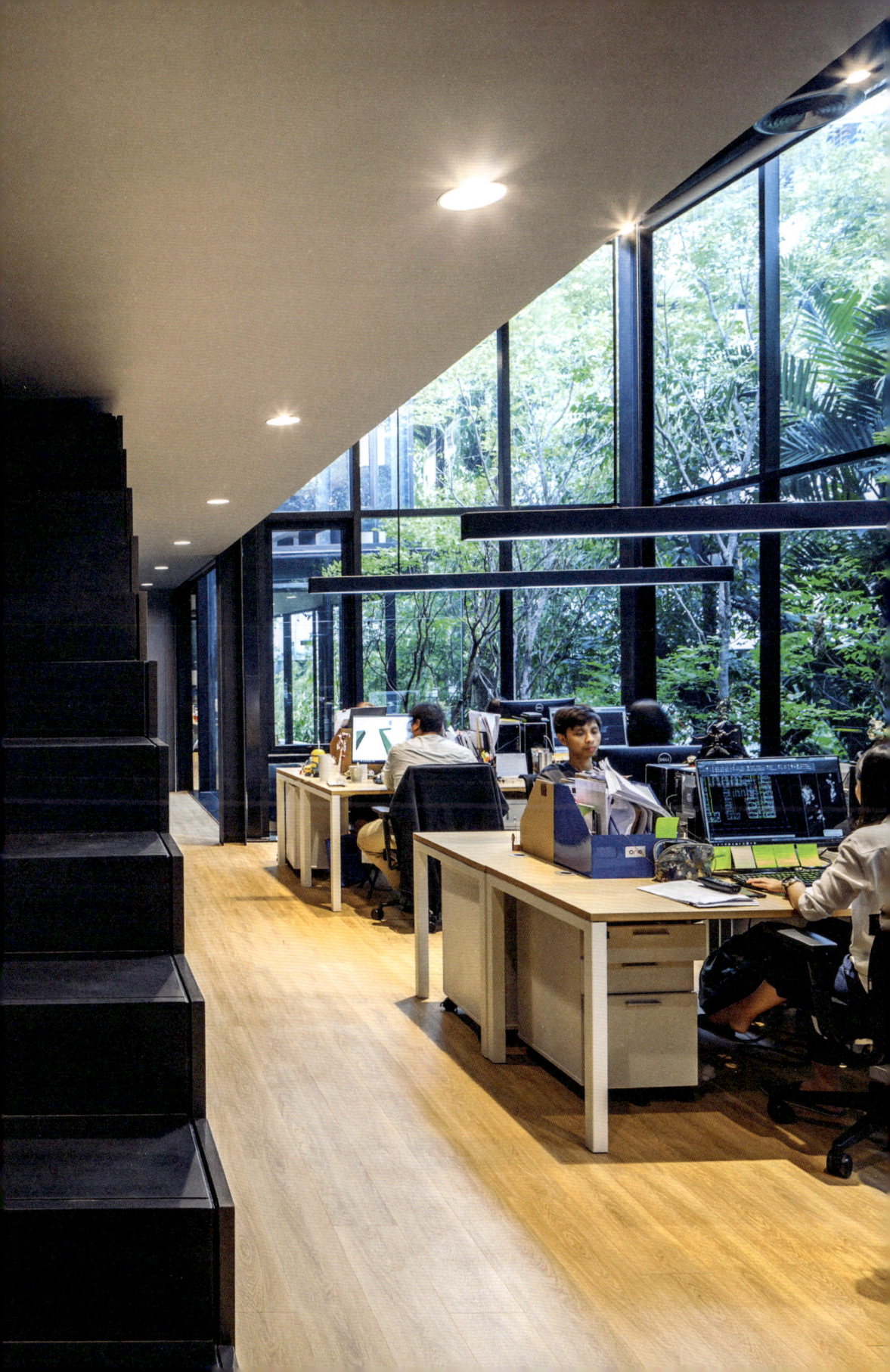

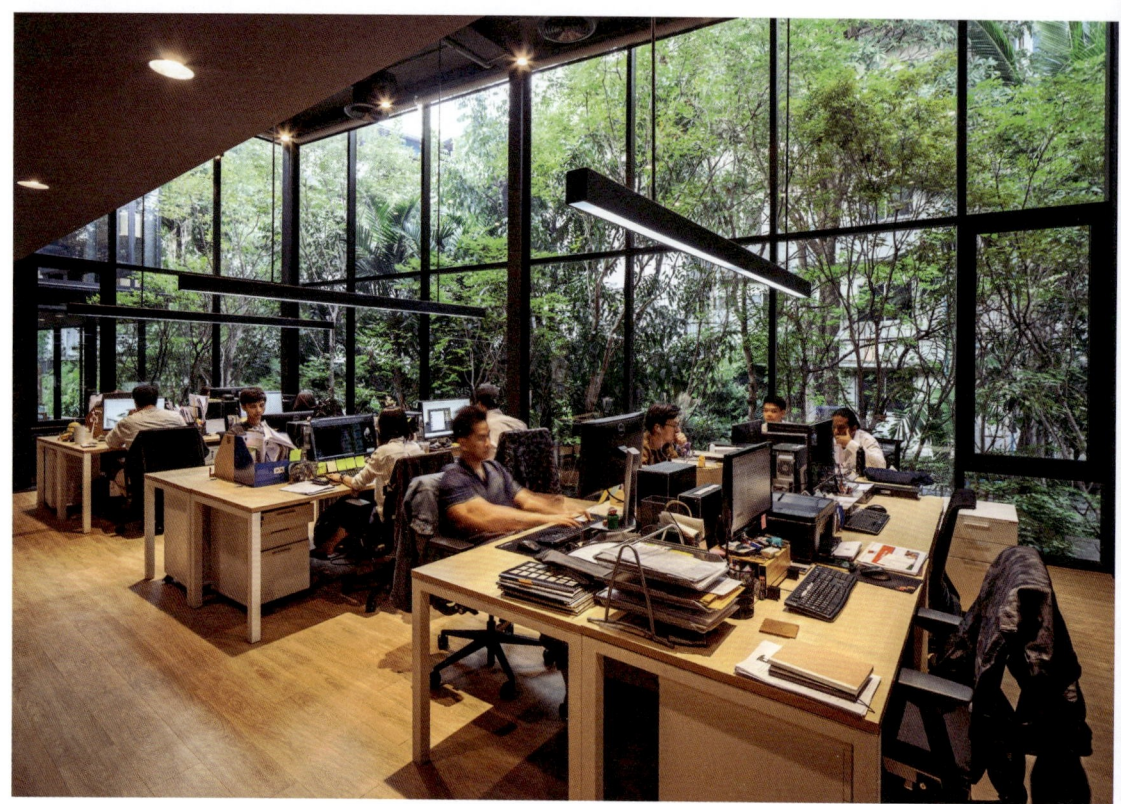

The architects' work area in the semi-public zone faces north and is enclosed with a Low-E glass wall to create a workspace haven that enjoys the calming, refreshing view of the greenery, and generous natural light. This zone for creative work is the heart of the building, and it is tailored to be a space with a relaxed atmosphere, quality lighting, and a comfortable temperature. Most of the west side of the building is composed of a solid wall to keep out the heat, which can sometimes be harsh and unforgiving, especially in Thailand's tropical climate. The staircase dedicated for the main circulation is aligned along the south to prevent heat transfer, which can cause erratic temperature fluctuations within the building. The staircase void is specifically designed to guide natural light in to create a comfortable level of lighting for people working in the building. As staff go about their tasks, swaying tree canopies and scattered sunlight instigate a cheeky game of hide-and-seek shadows in the work area, enlivening the environment.

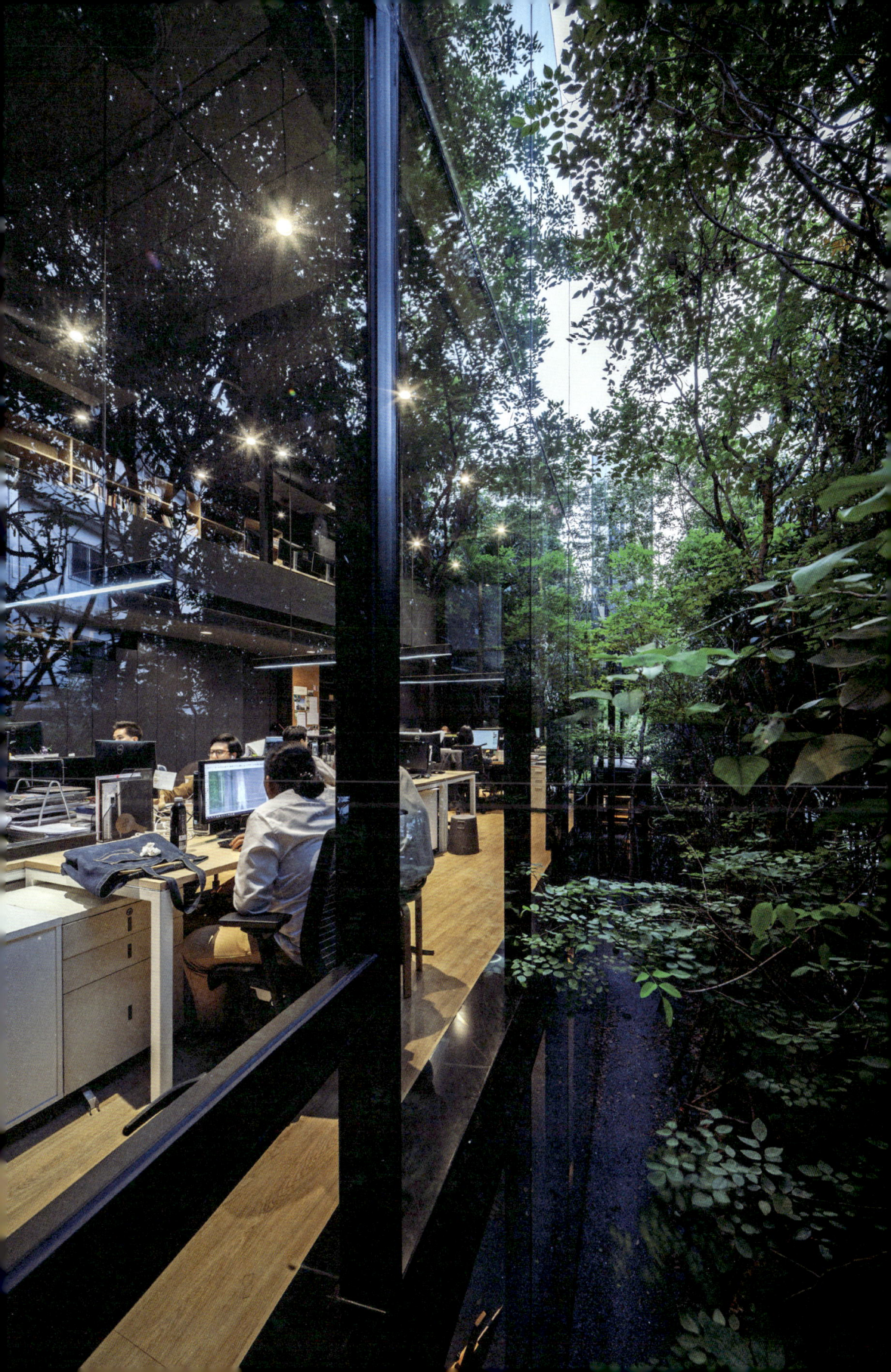

Mae Chan, Chiang Rai, Thailand, 2015

CHOUI FONG TEA CAFÉ

Nestled among the rolling, terraced hills of Choui Fong tea plantation in the north of Thailand, the Choui Fong Tea Café seems to pop out of the undulating landscape. Inspired by the captivating surroundings, the café is set into the hillside at the highest point of the plantation, instead of *on* the hilltop, to capture the mesmerizing views of the glorious tea fields.

The main building is composed of three interconnecting wings that extend radially in the direction of the plantation, each overlooking a different view. The construction appears to float on the landscape—a design intention to complement the serenity and splendor of the scenery. Achieving the floating effect was a structural challenge that was overcome with skill and creativity. Looking up from the foothills, it appears a single pile bears the entire building. A rooftop deck allows visitors to enjoy a scenic 360-degree view of the surrounding fields and observe farmers weaving through emerald pleats of tea bushes picking leaves. The retaining wall at the back is set at a distance from the building to create extra space for the green courtyard, as well as to provide shade in the area. Functional sections include a dining zone, café, tea shop, and restroom. Various combinations of scale and proportion play throughout the project, tuned to each area's practical use.

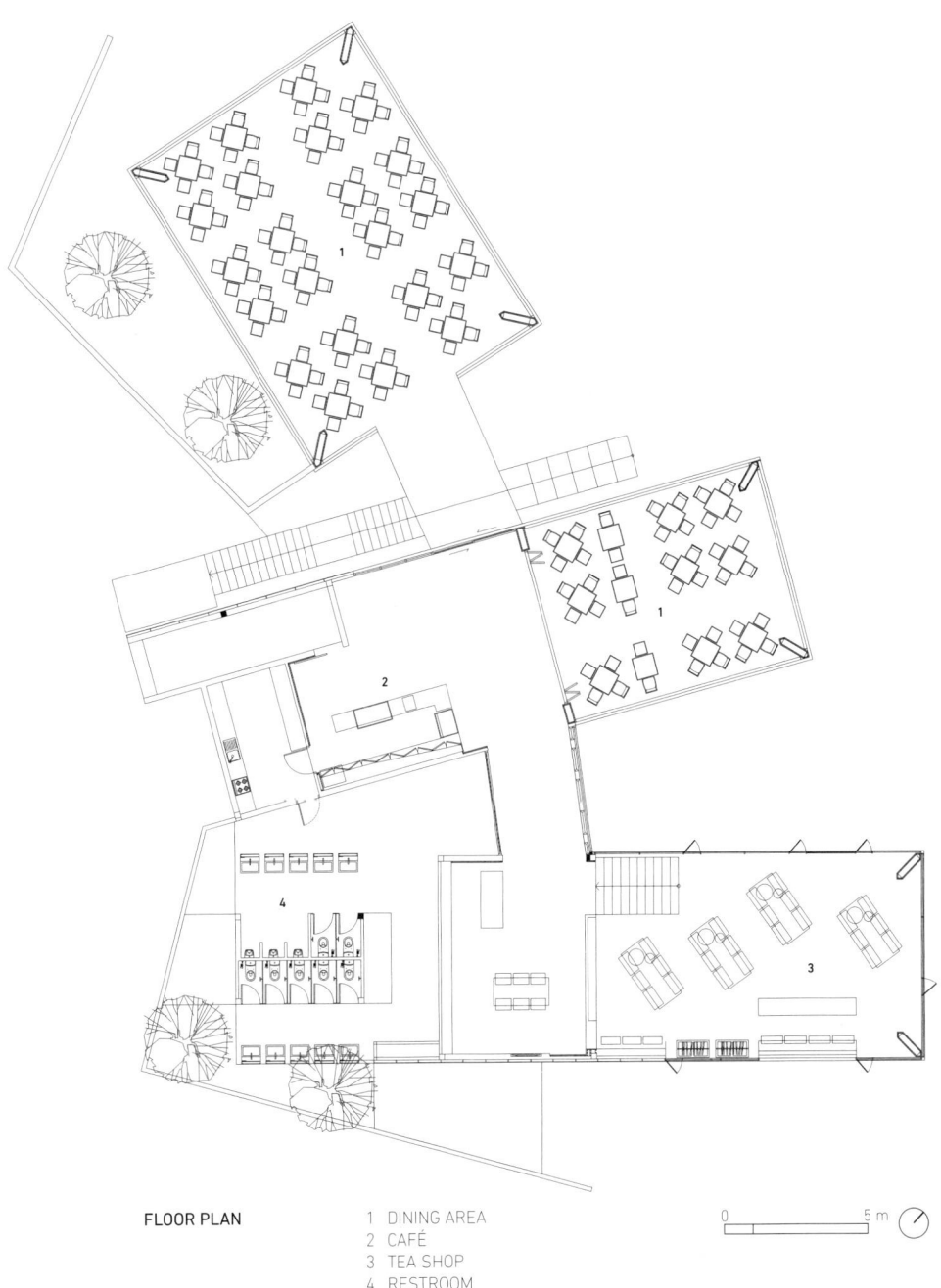

FLOOR PLAN

1. DINING AREA
2. CAFÉ
3. TEA SHOP
4. RESTROOM

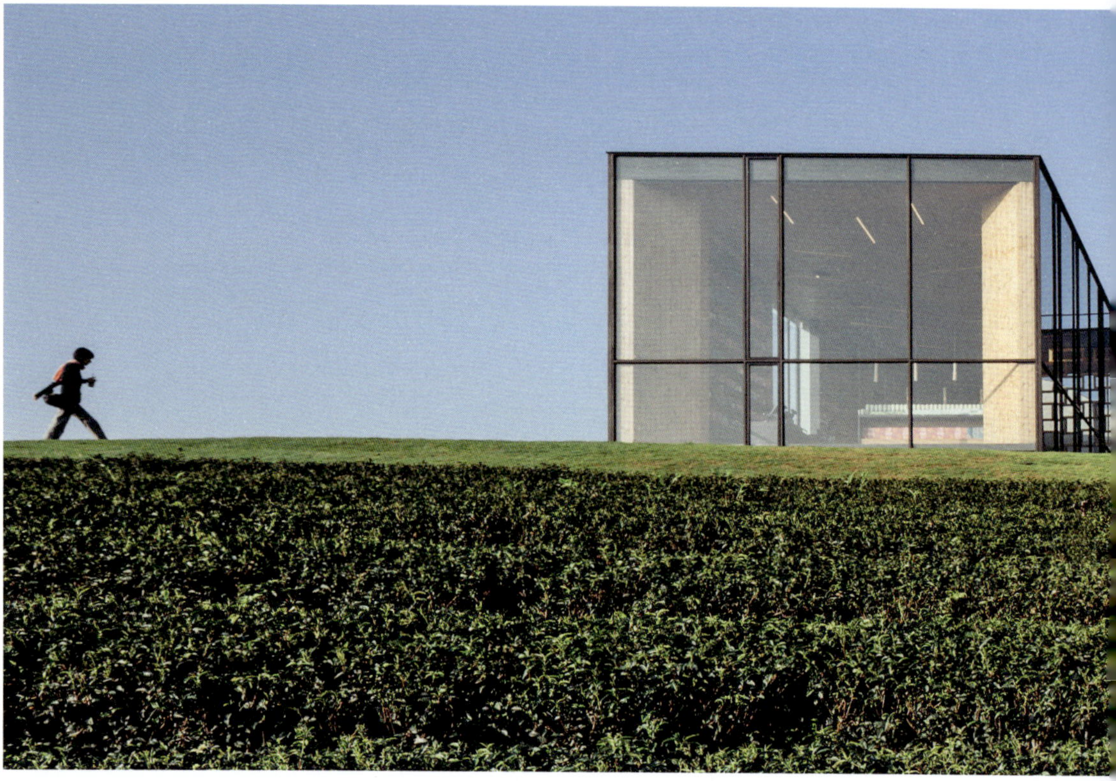

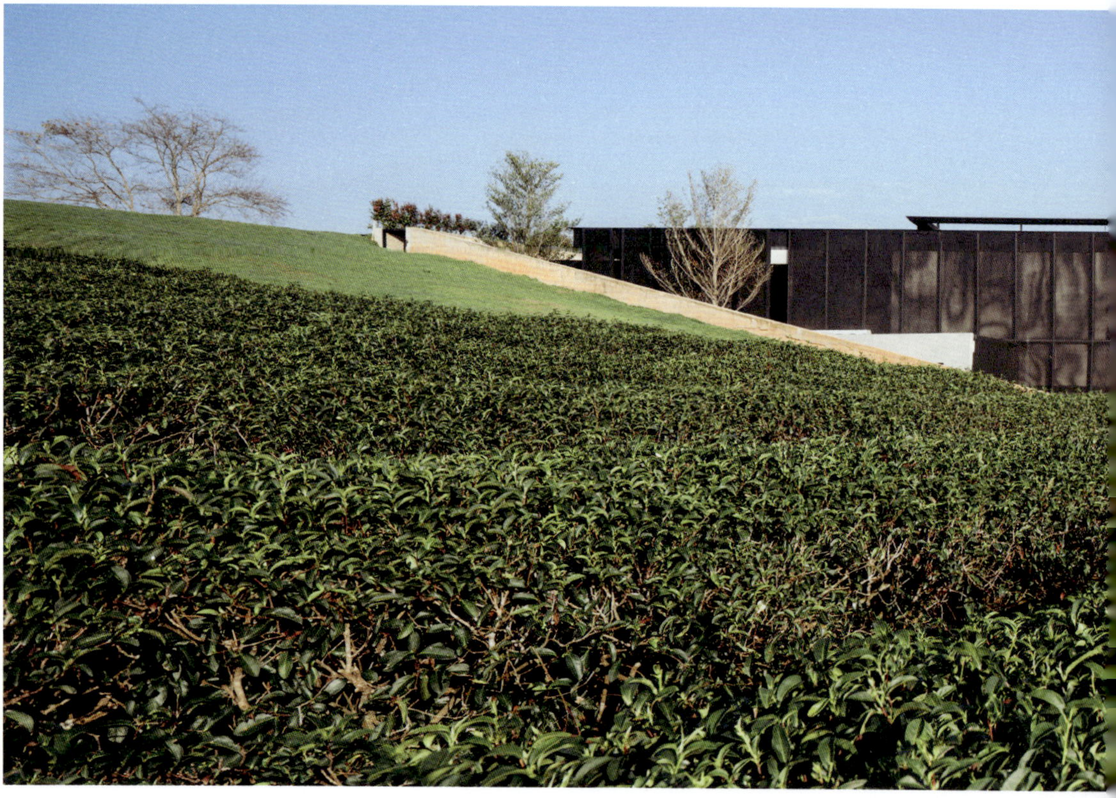

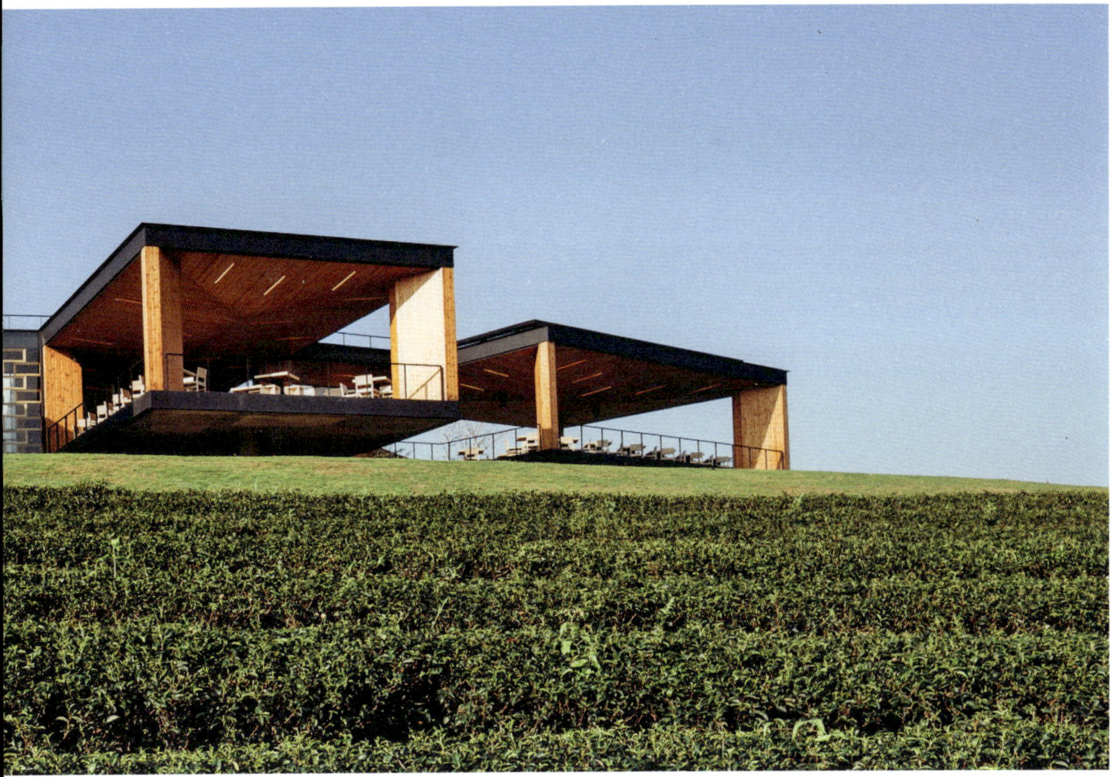

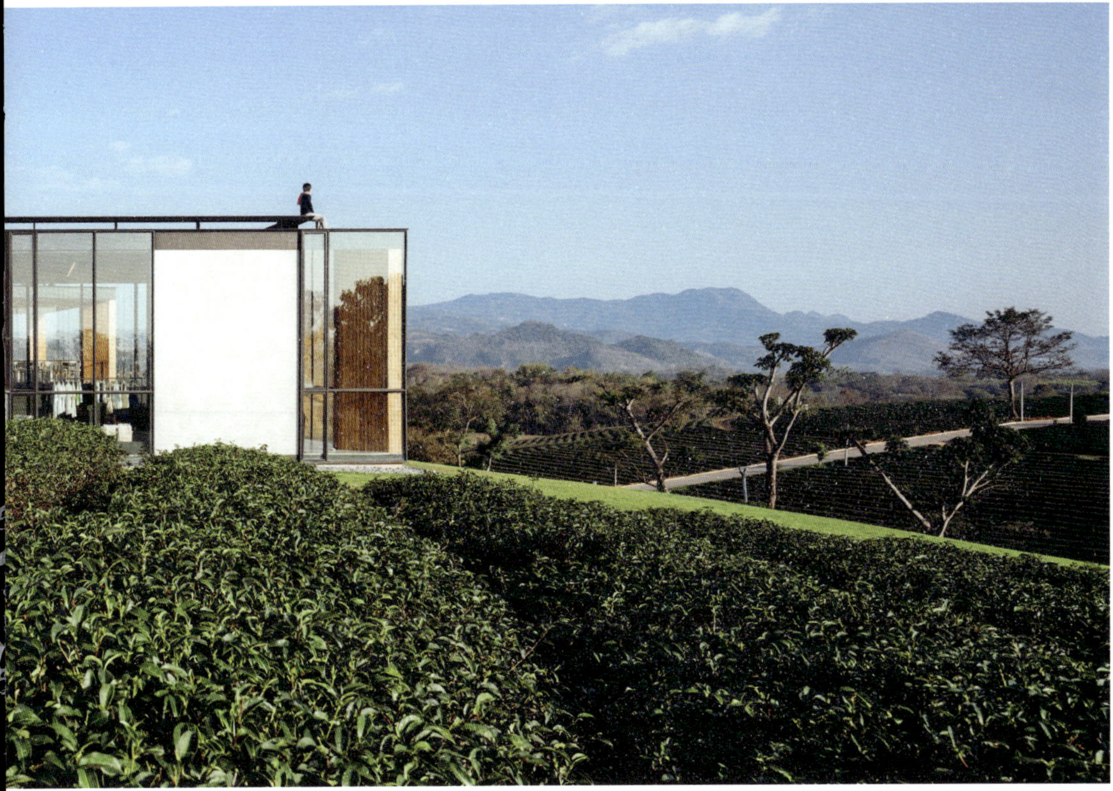

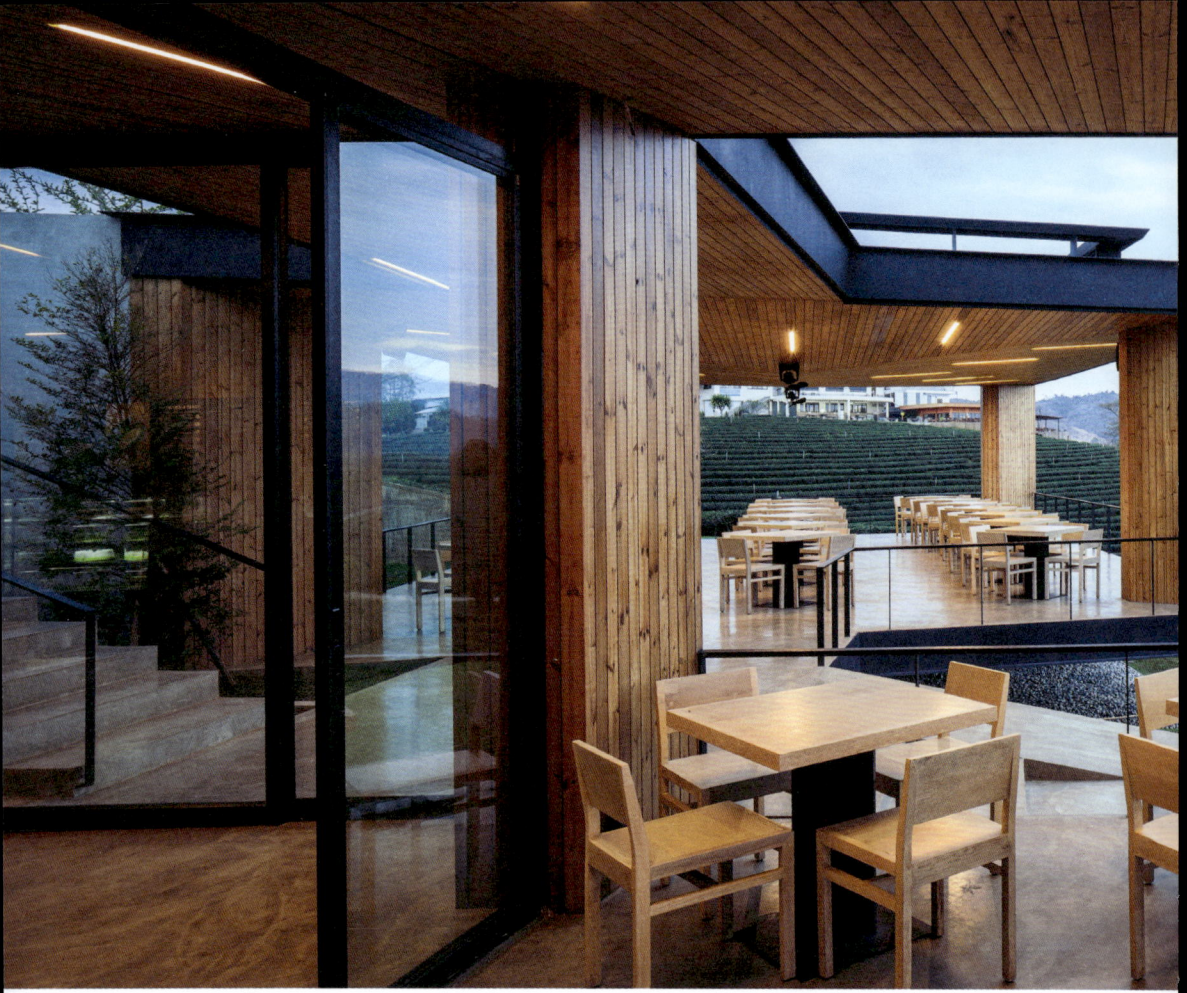

The café's interior design is tailored to realize the following objectives: "to create a natural feel, to feature elements of raw materials, and importantly, to be in harmony with the exterior design." An extremely conscientious material selection creates the atmosphere and sensory experiences that are intended. A contrast effect is impressed across the materiality so that visitors perceive the materials to be more expressive. Pinewood and steel as the main material profile are straightforward and unpretentious, and collaborate well to paint an image of chic simplicity; their natural origins also uphold Choui Fong's ideal of an organic plantation.

Pine imparts warmth to the ambiance, while steel takes on the heavy lifting to convey strength and rawness. Together, the symbiotic contrast works to play off each material's plus points to construct an elegant and inviting architecture that stands out without overshadowing its remarkable surroundings.

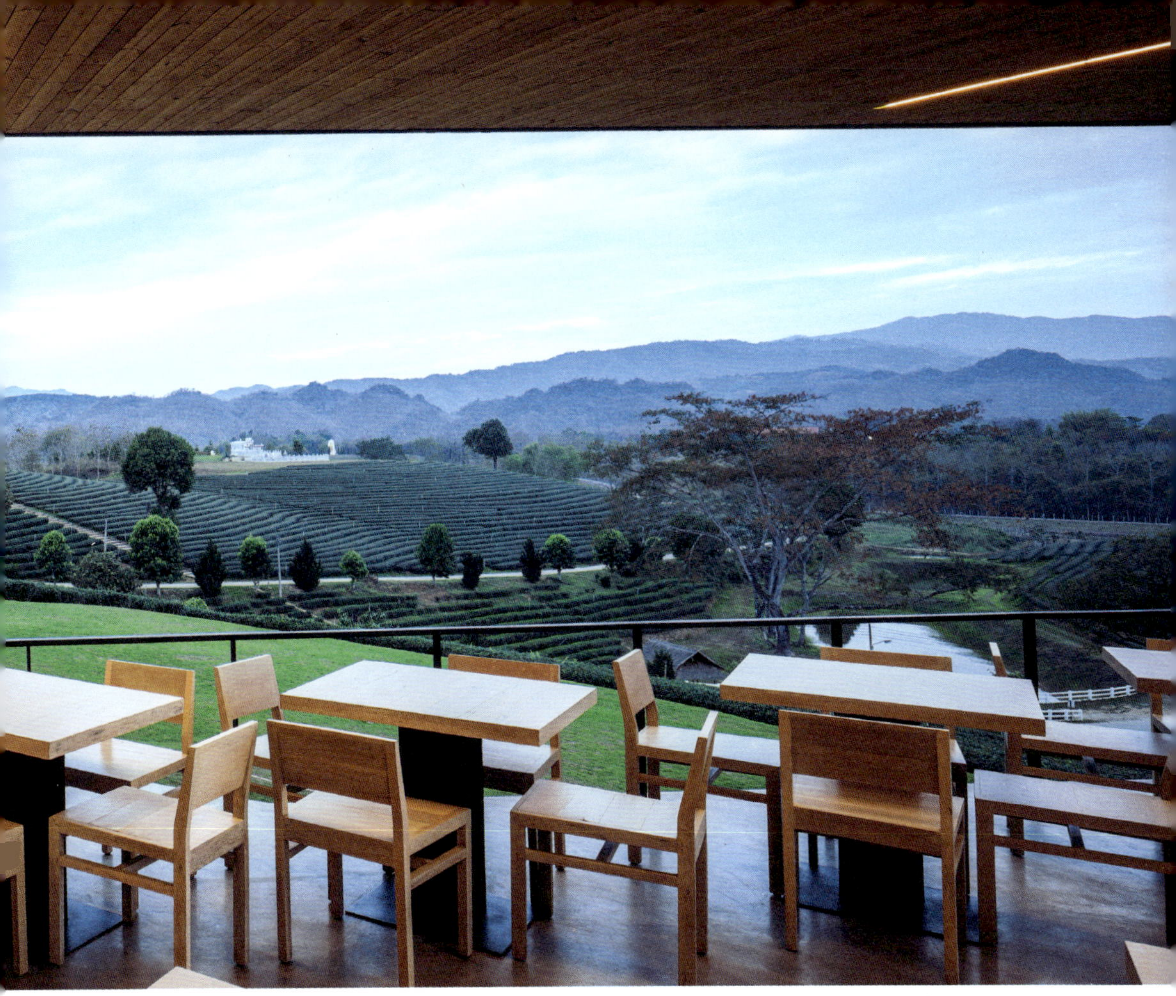

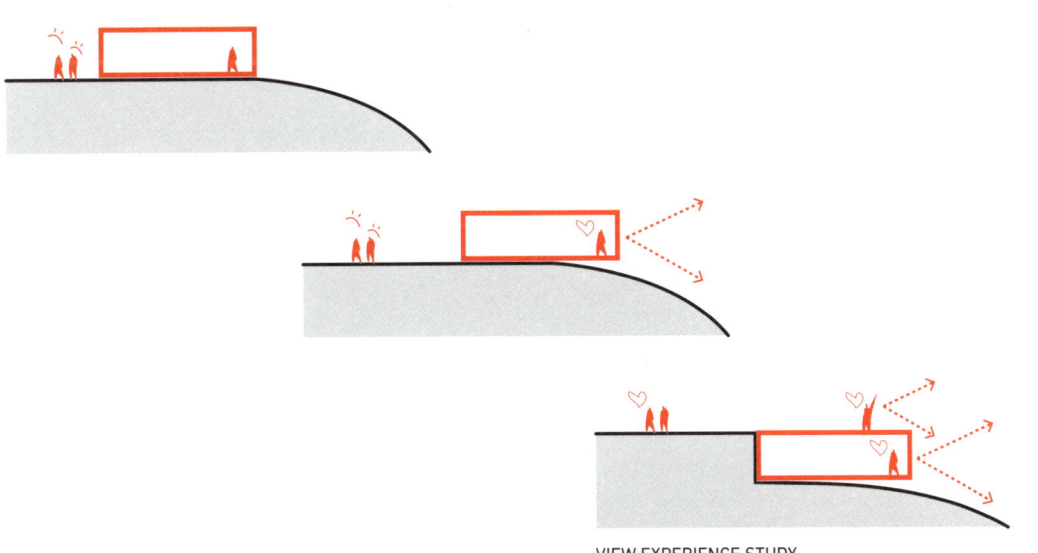

VIEW EXPERIENCE STUDY

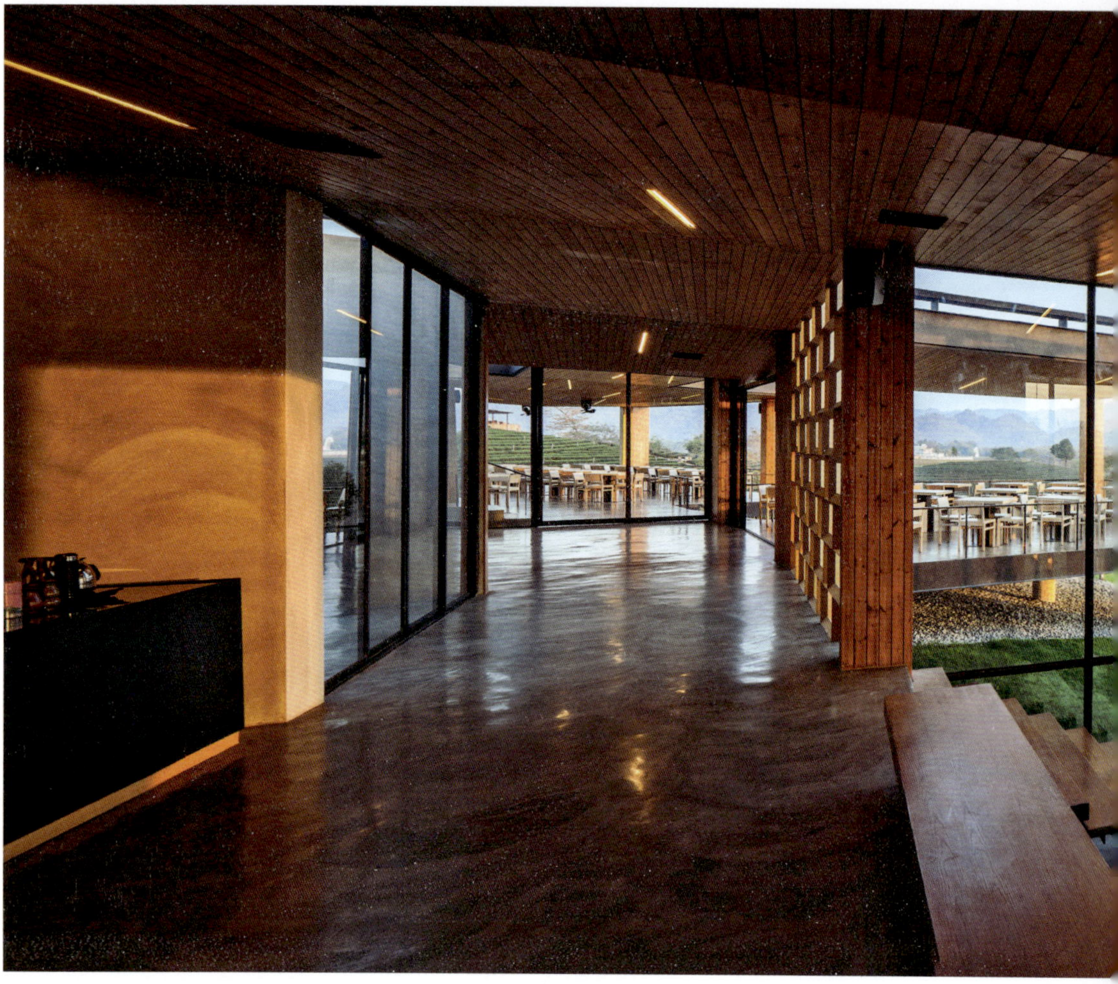

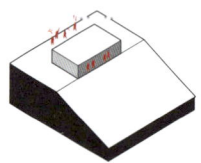
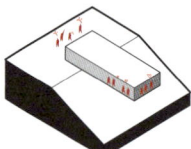
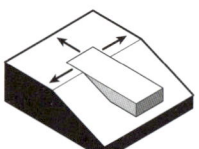
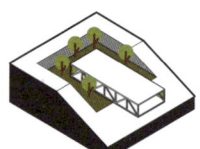
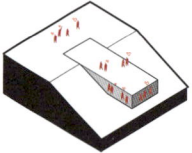
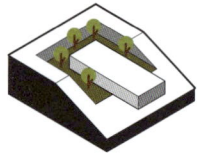
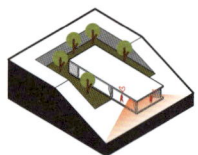

APPROACH STUDY POCKET COURTYARD STRUCTURE STUDY

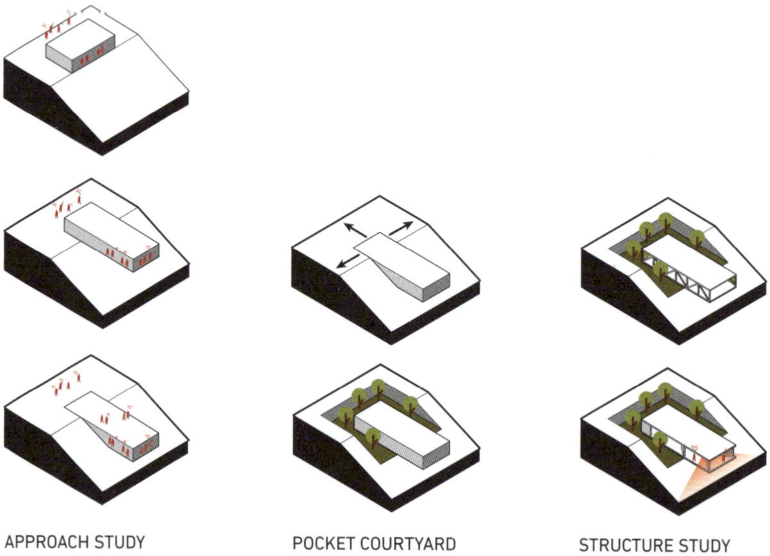

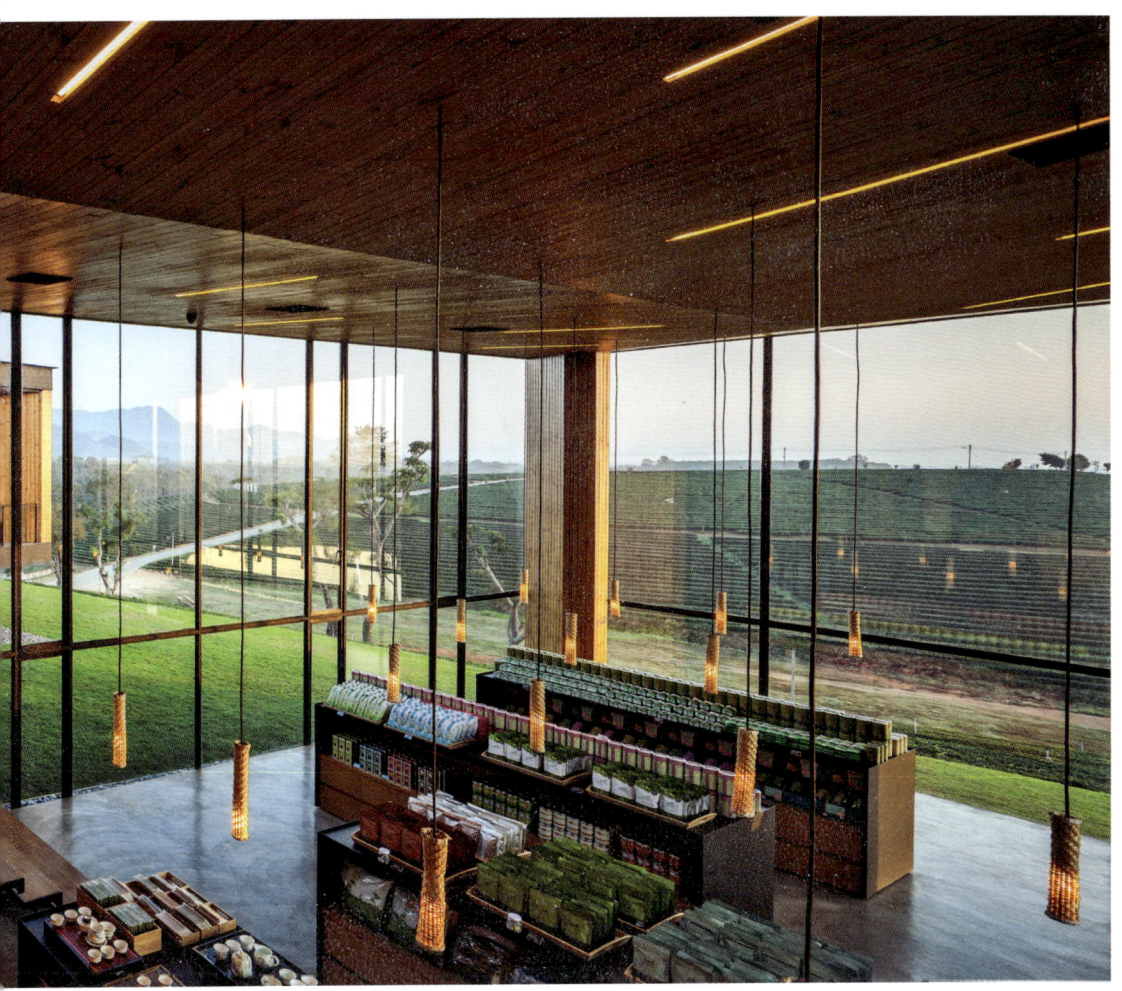

The unity between interior and exterior design is fundamental to a strong design framework. The diagonal wood pattern that marks the exterior is echoed in the interior to create a consistent design flow. In the souvenir/tea shop, the patterned cladding is applied to the display shelves for promotional items, helping to emphasize a material focal point around the products; the main material combination of steel and wood continues throughout the cabinetry. Design accents in black strengthen and anchor the overall design, adhering to the notion of contrast, while adding depth and dimension. These include the black pantry counters and perforated, black, steel décor in the restroom, which add shade in the daytime and create attractive lighting effects at night. The clever use of the dynamic contrast of materials in the café blends both interior and exterior spaces into a harmonious whole.

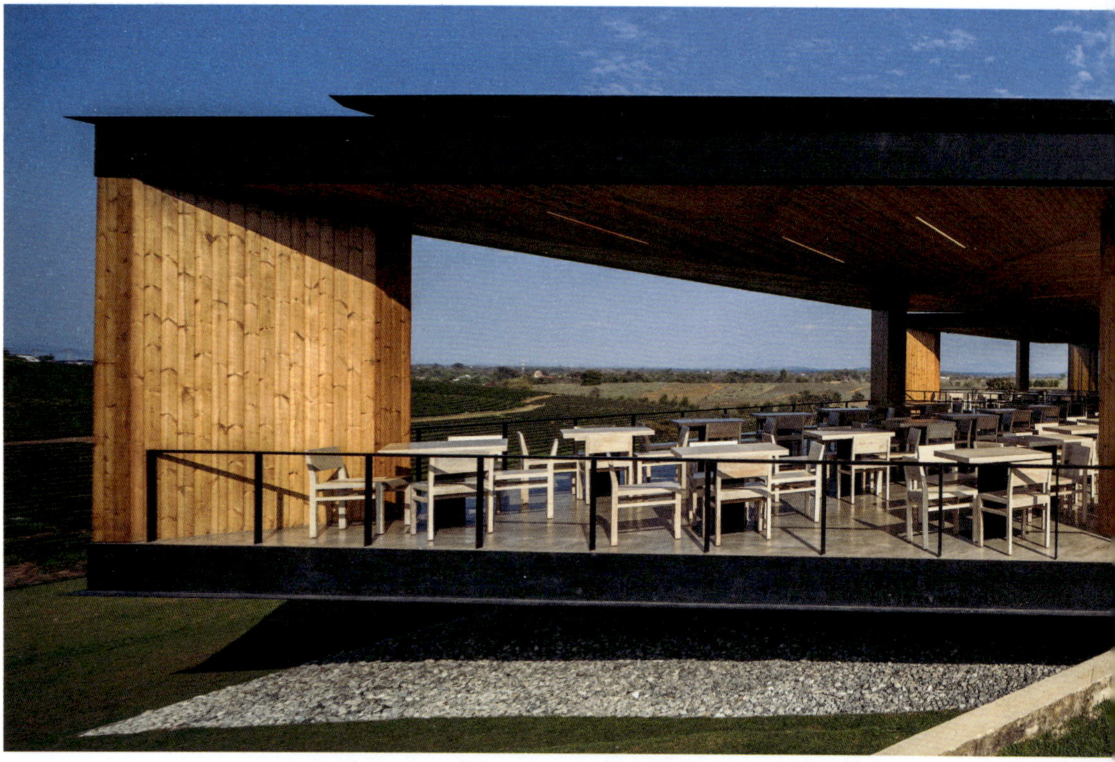

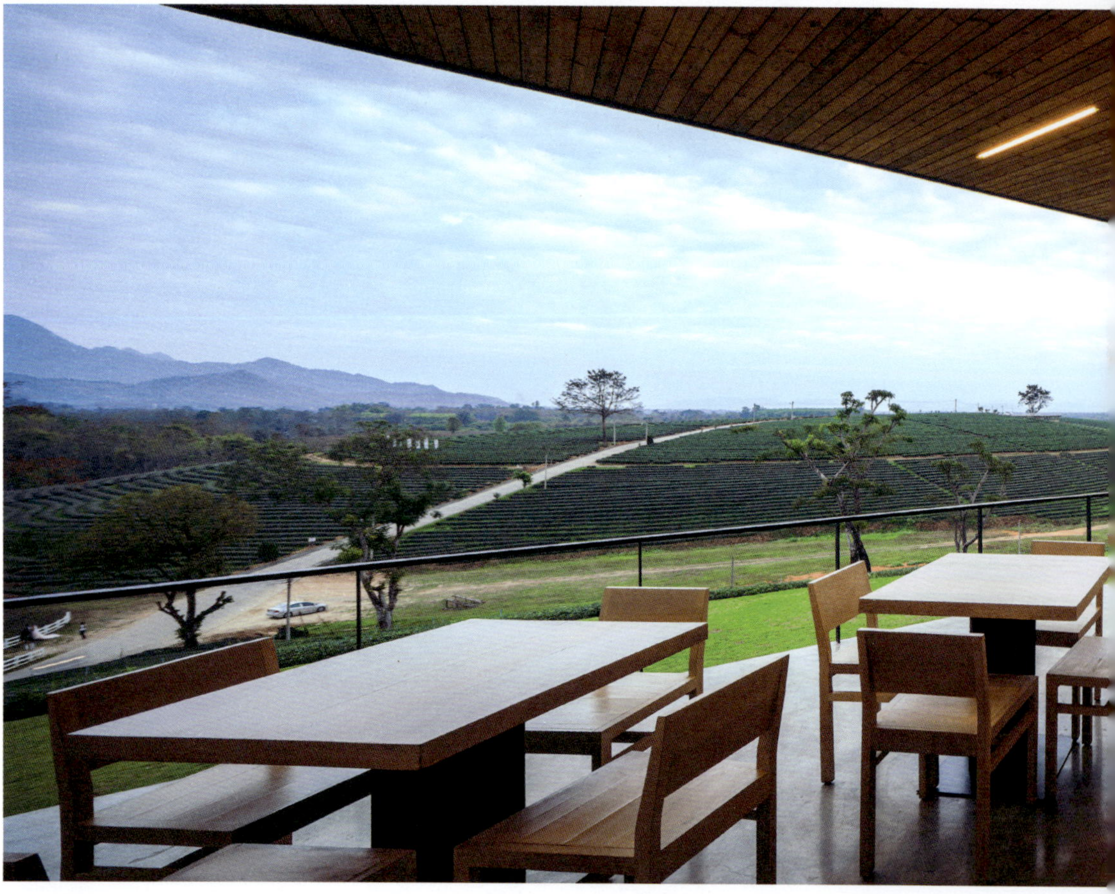

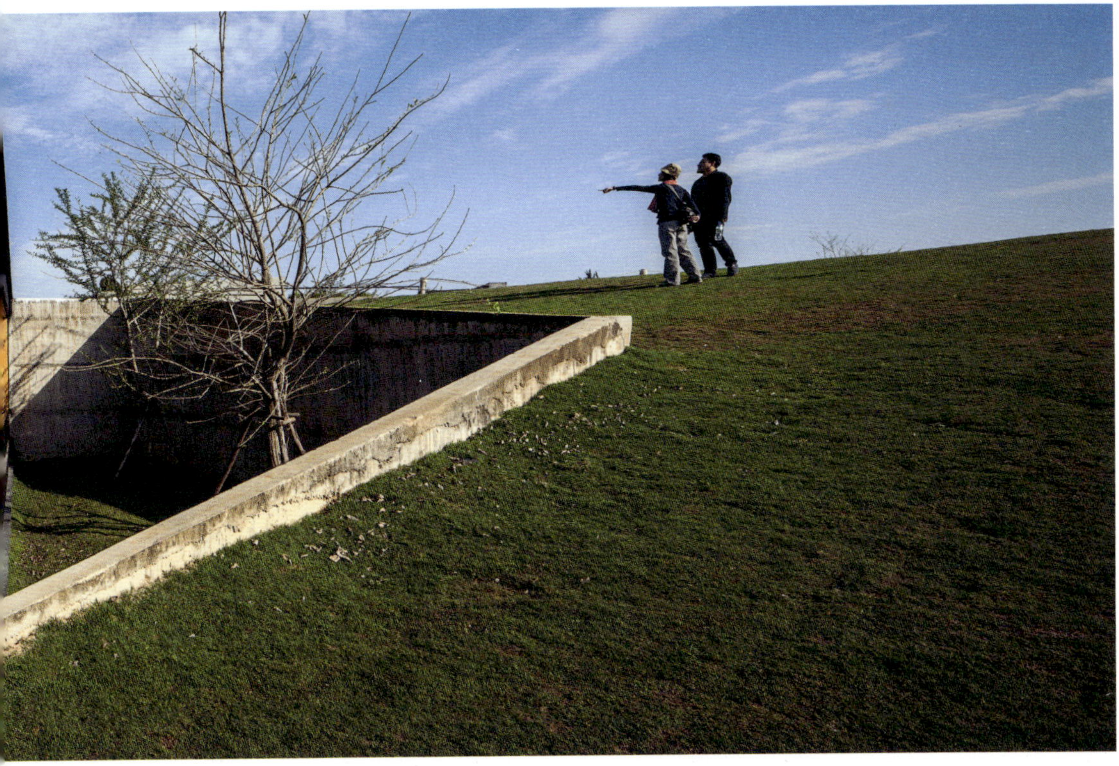

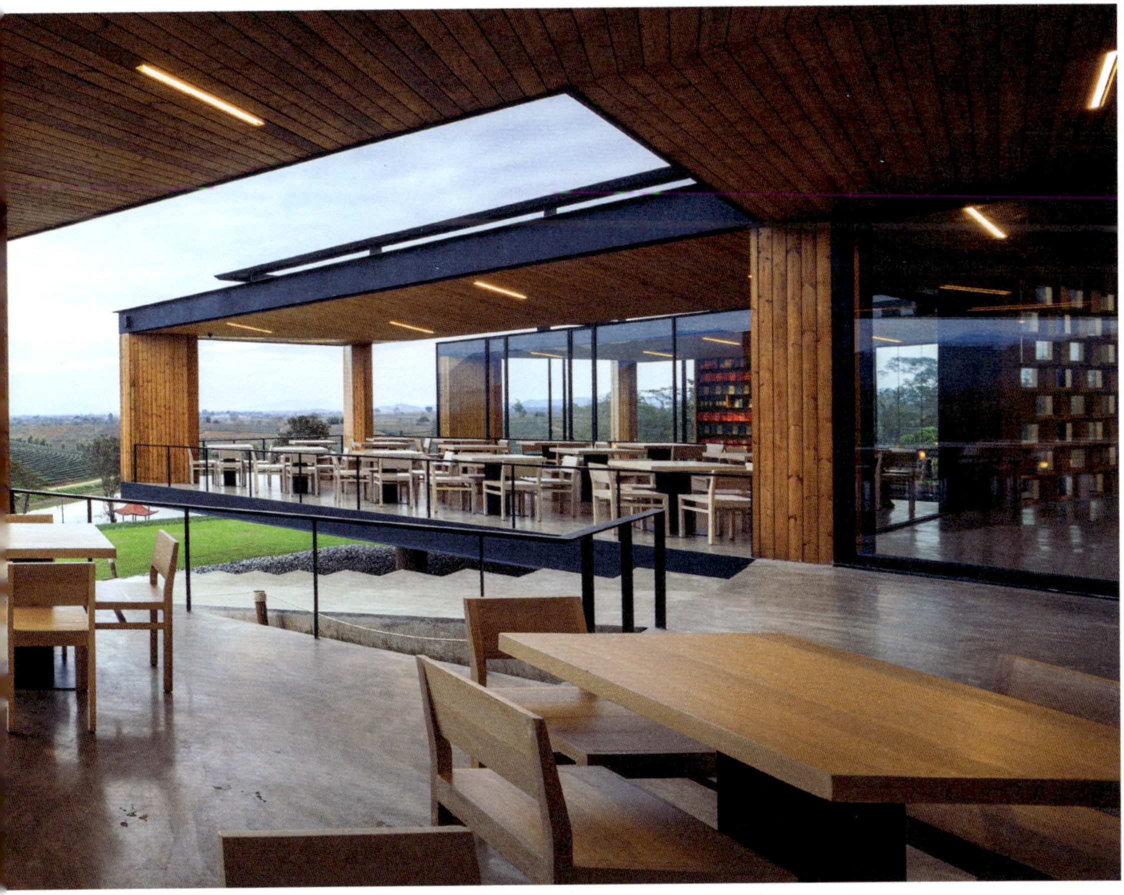

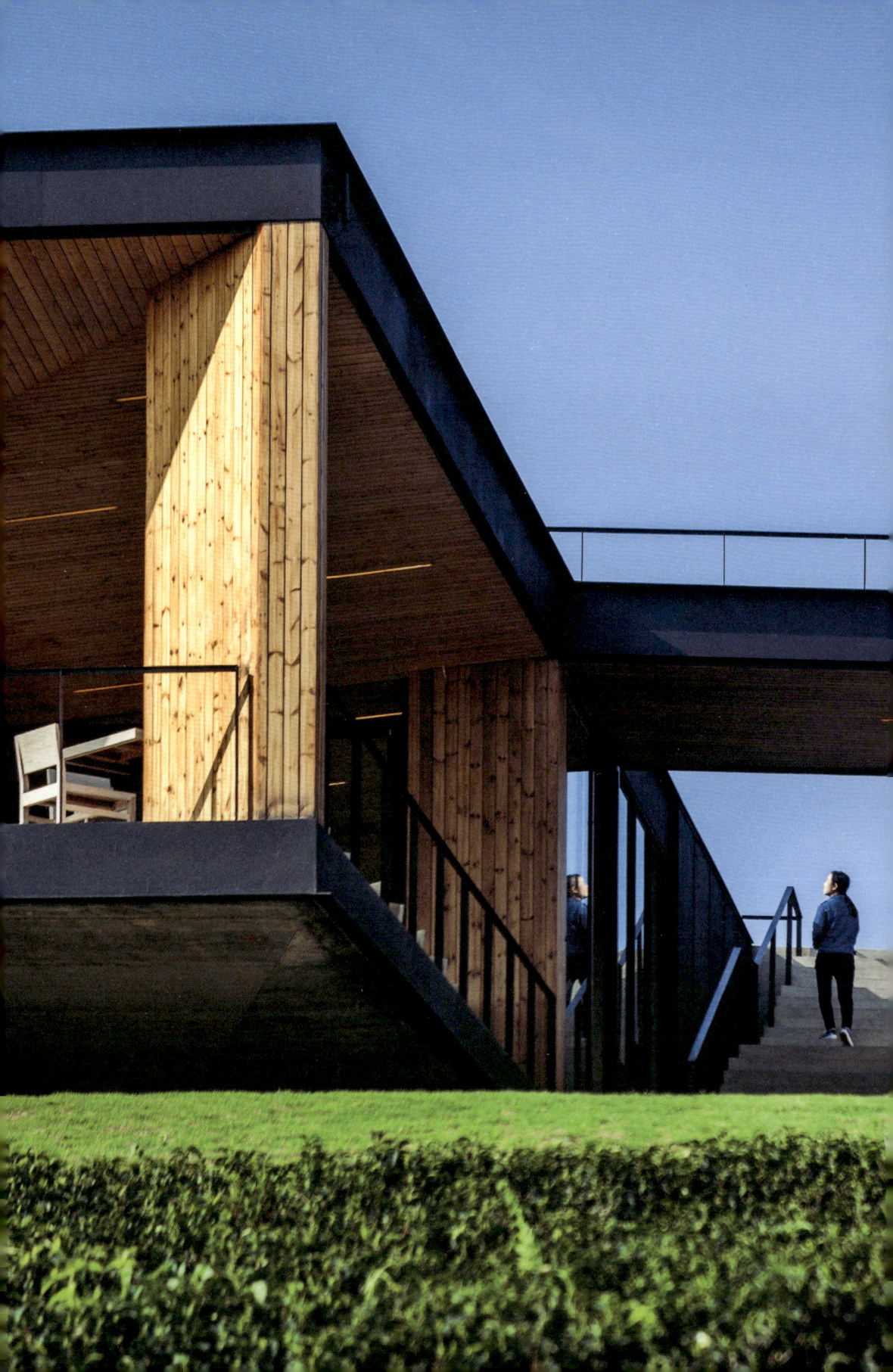

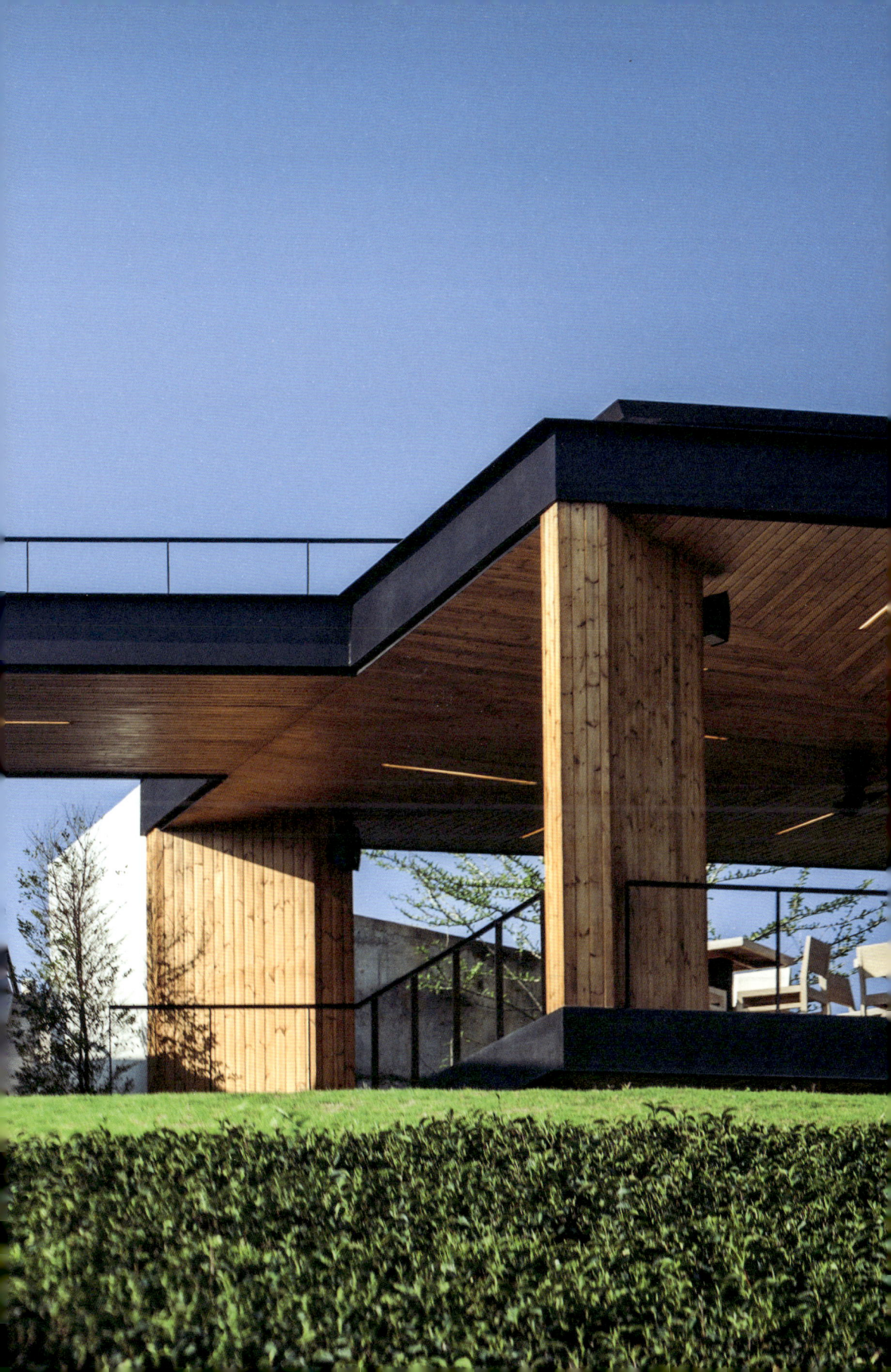

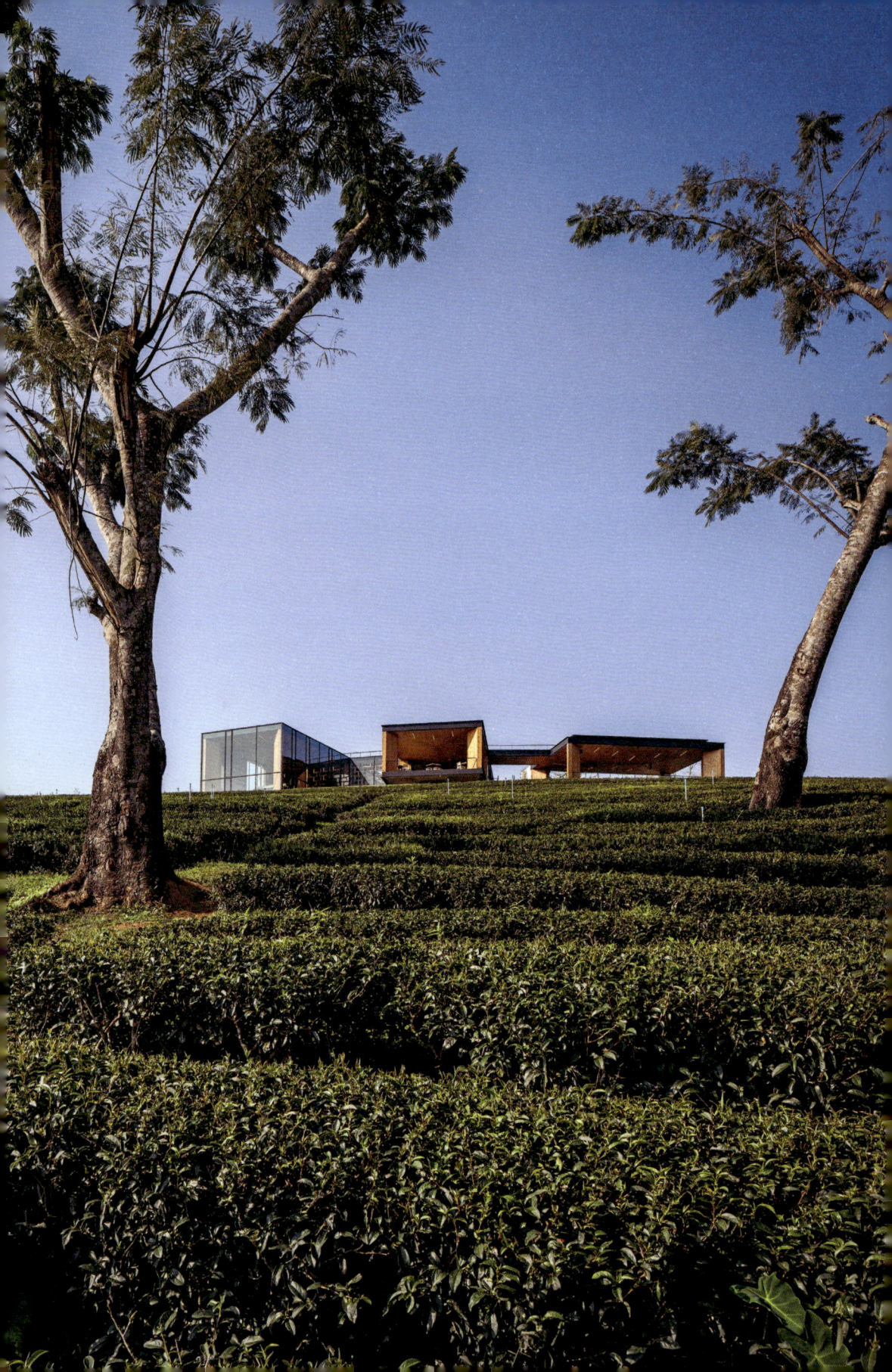

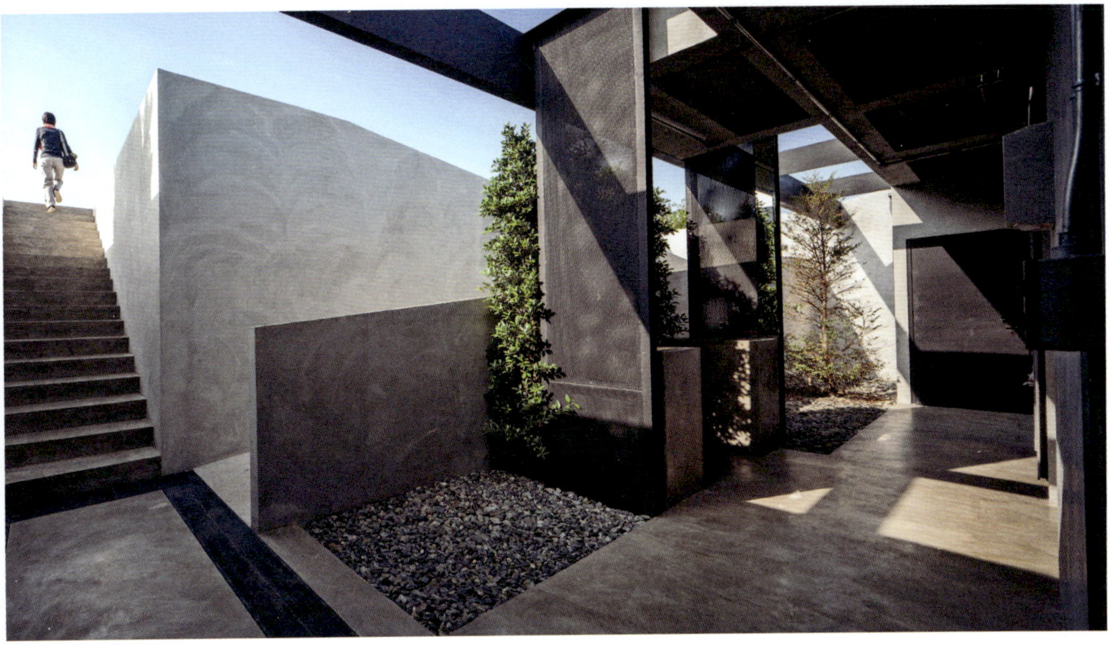

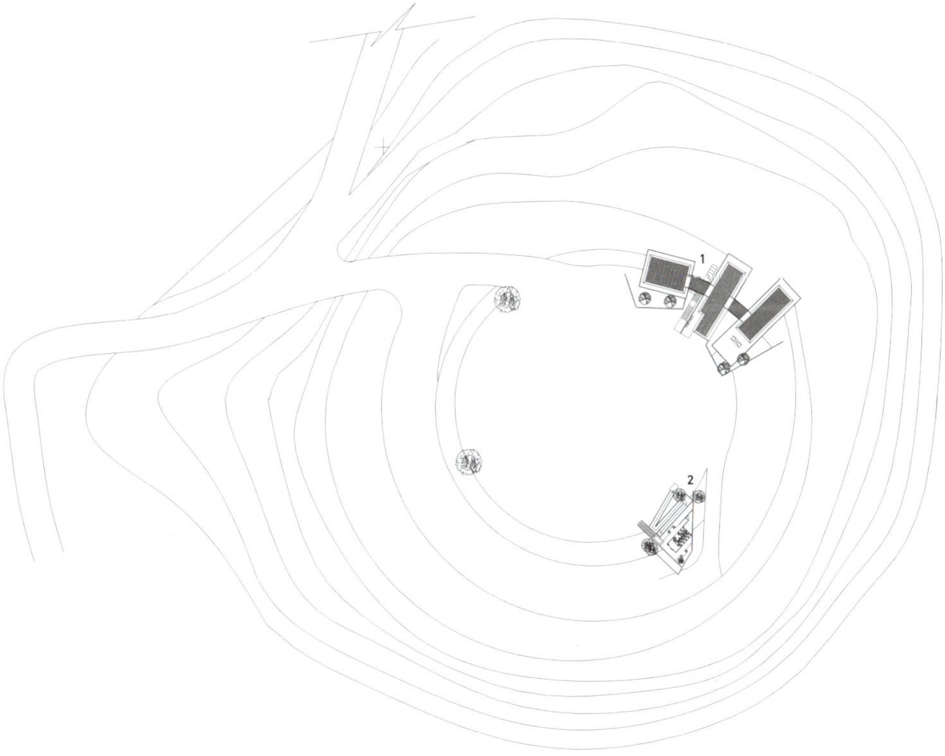

SITE PLAN 1 CHOUI FONG TEA CAFÉ
2 RESTROOM

CHOUI FONG TEA CAFÉ   43

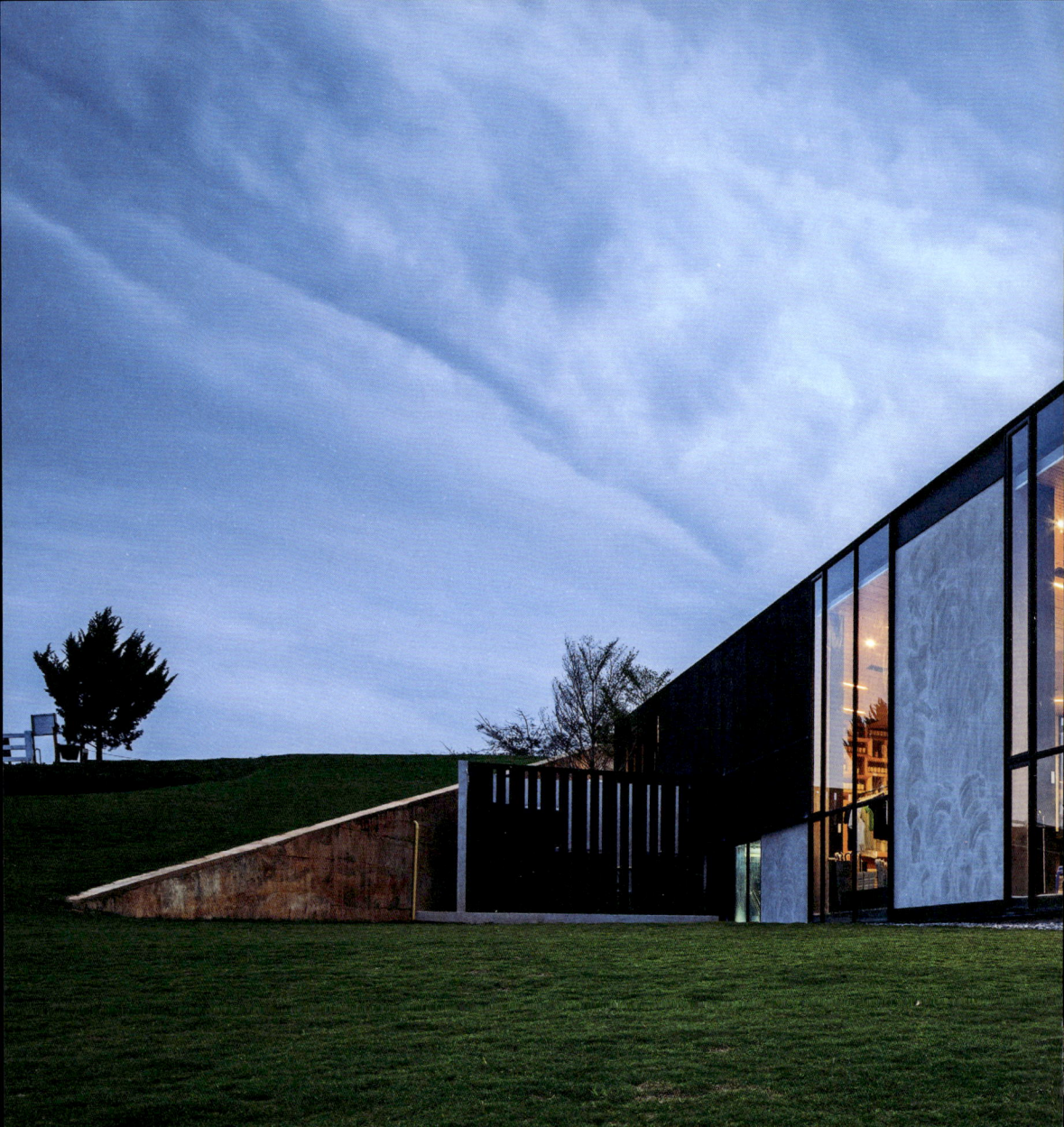

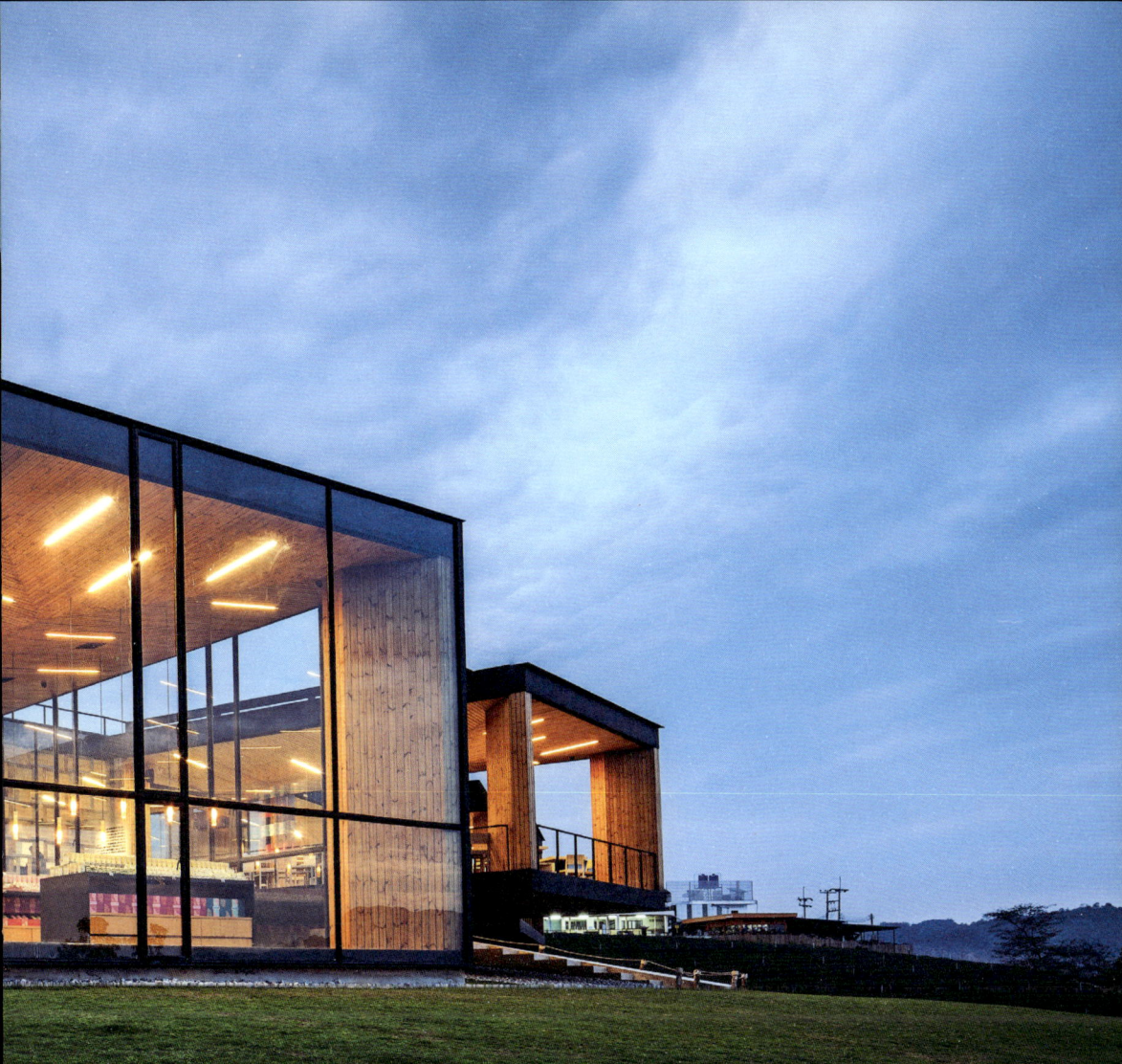

Mae Chan, Chiang Rai, Thailand, 2019

CHOUI FONG TEA CAFÉ 2

Since the first Choui Fong Tea Café opened in 2015, the Choui Fong tea plantation has gained plenty of tourist attention and become one of the most famous tourist attractions in Chiang Rai. Its growing popularity and overflow of tourists brought about the establishment of a second café on a plantation hill not far from the first café. Choui Fong Tea Café 2 is set next to the Choui Fong tea factory and, like the first, enjoys a gorgeous view of the plantation. It houses a dining area with a seating capacity of 250, a large souvenir shop, and an exhibition area where staff demonstrate the craft of brewing tea. The history of the Choui Fong plantation is also displayed to share the story of the plantation's beginnings with visitors.

Establishing a Universal Design was key in this project. The first café had identified family groups with elders as one of the main categories of visitors, and that became the focus in designing the second one. To that extent, the design flow is accessible and convenient, without causing difficulty to seniors or visitors with mobility issues.

Unlike the first café, which is set in the hillside, the second café stands *on* the hill as it requires a massive usable area and needed to also be level with the neighboring factory. The floor is rectangular, ensuring that seats within can fully view the surrounding landscape. The design lavishes visitors with a panoramic view of the plantation and lets them enjoy the natural surroundings during the dining experience.

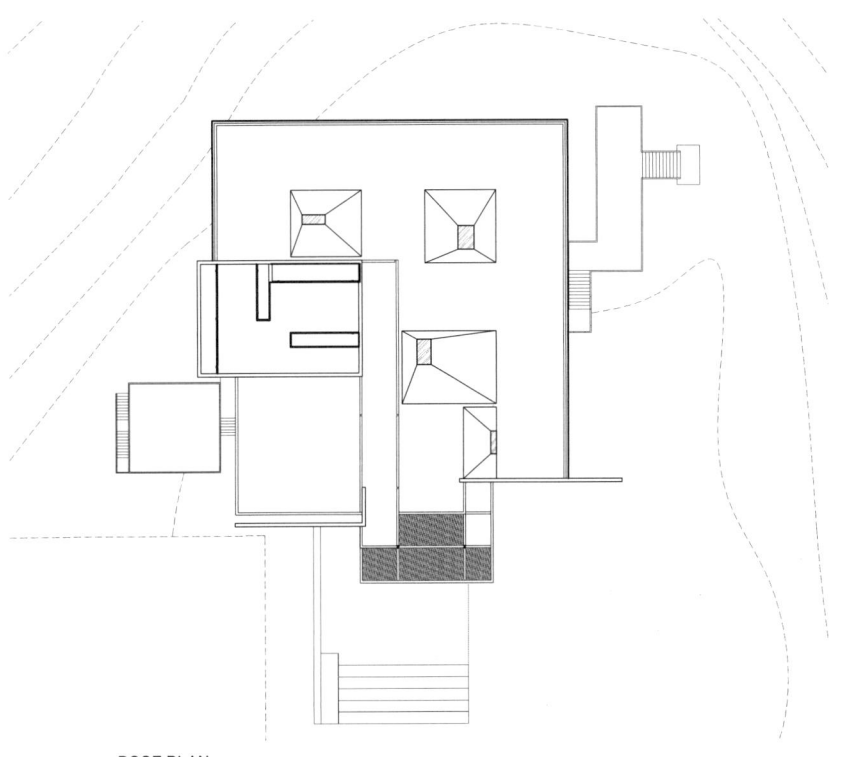

ROOF PLAN

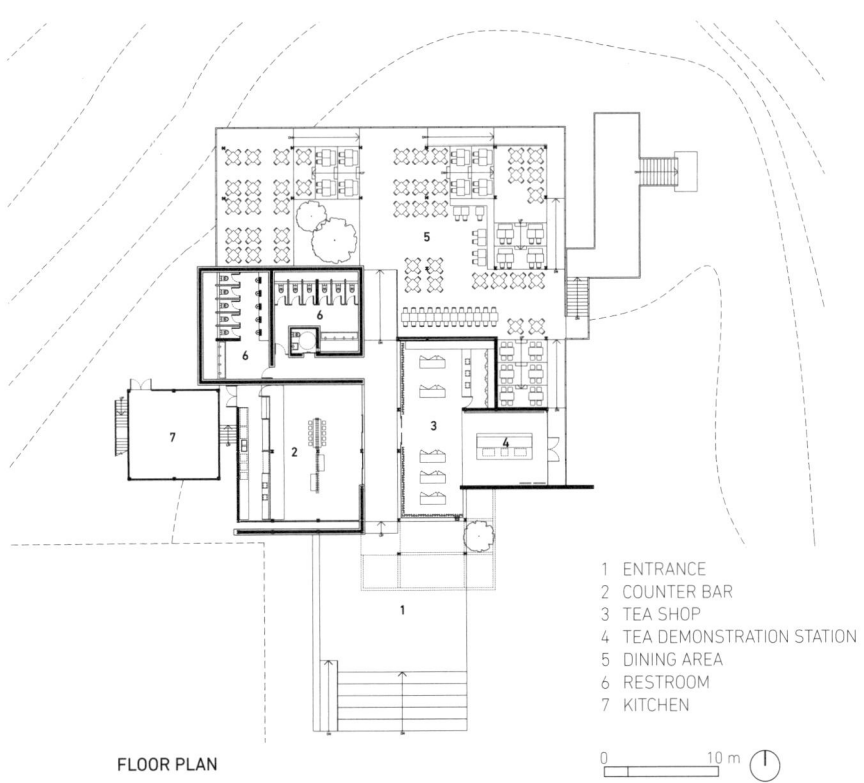

1 ENTRANCE
2 COUNTER BAR
3 TEA SHOP
4 TEA DEMONSTRATION STATION
5 DINING AREA
6 RESTROOM
7 KITCHEN

FLOOR PLAN

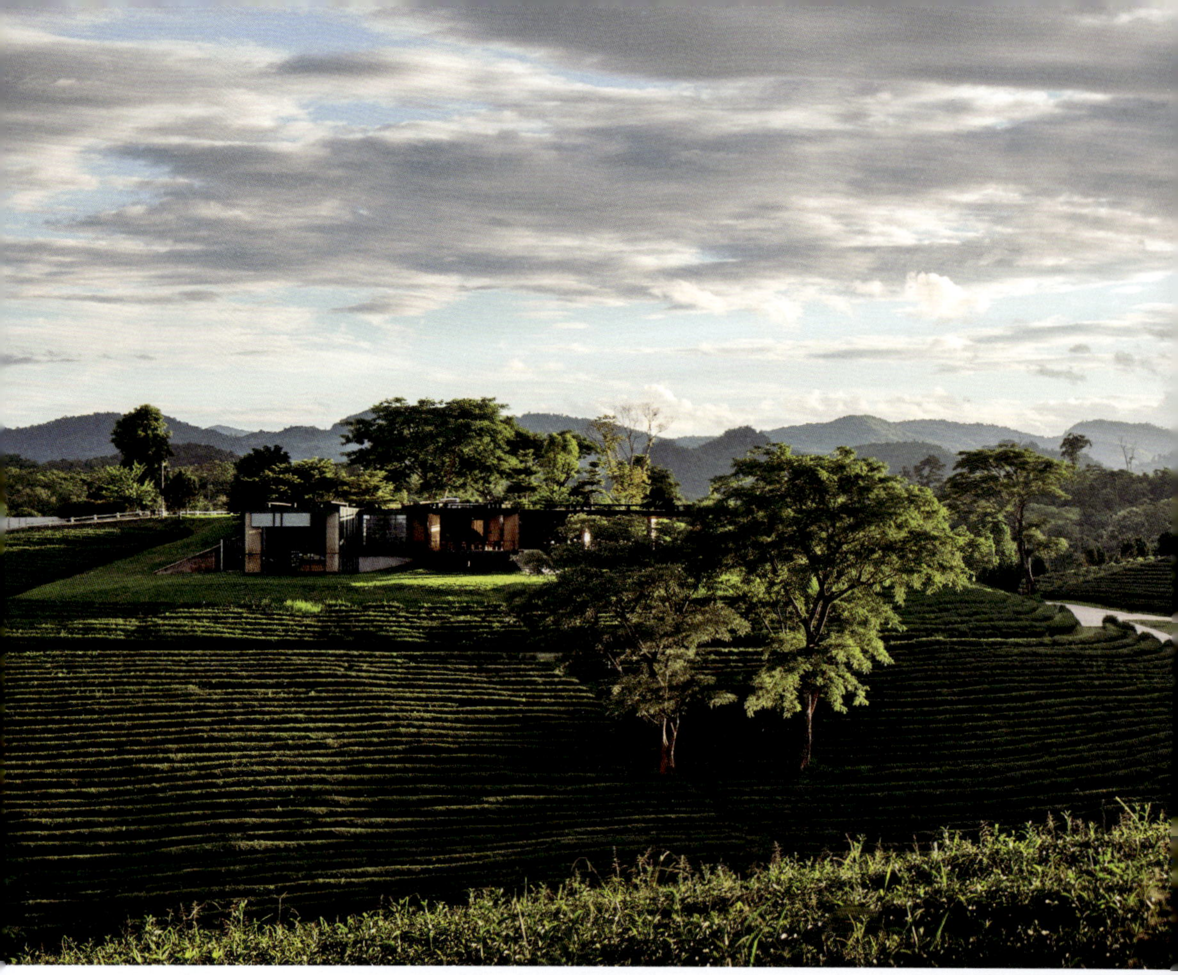

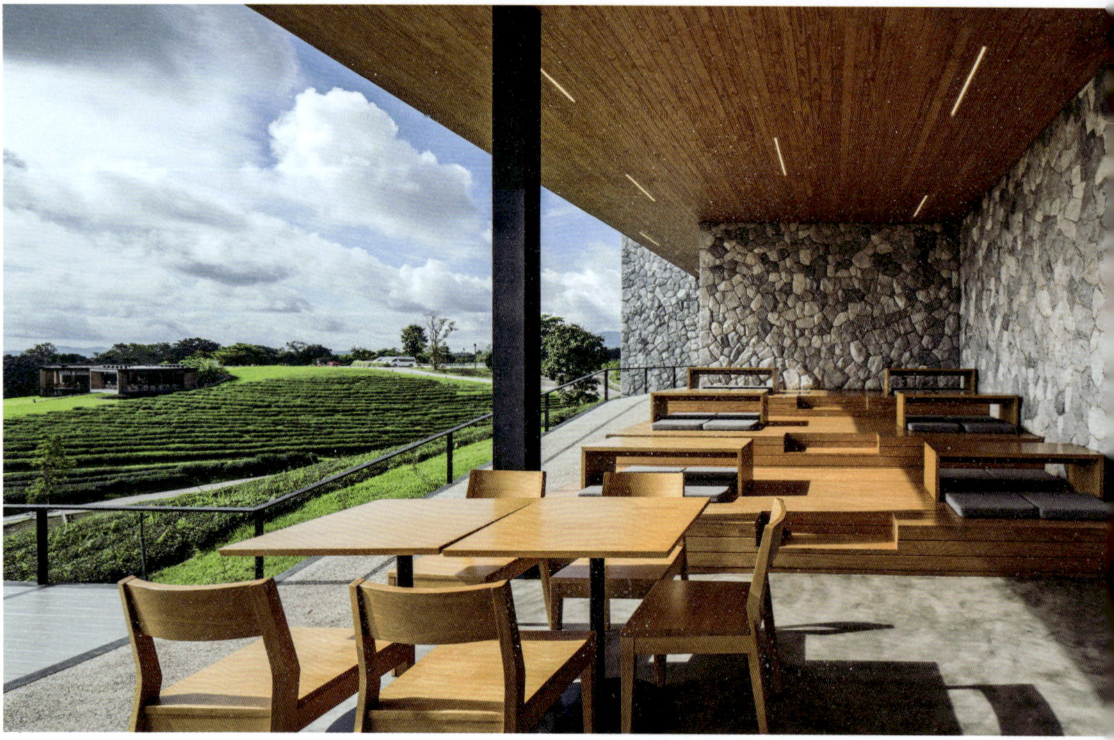

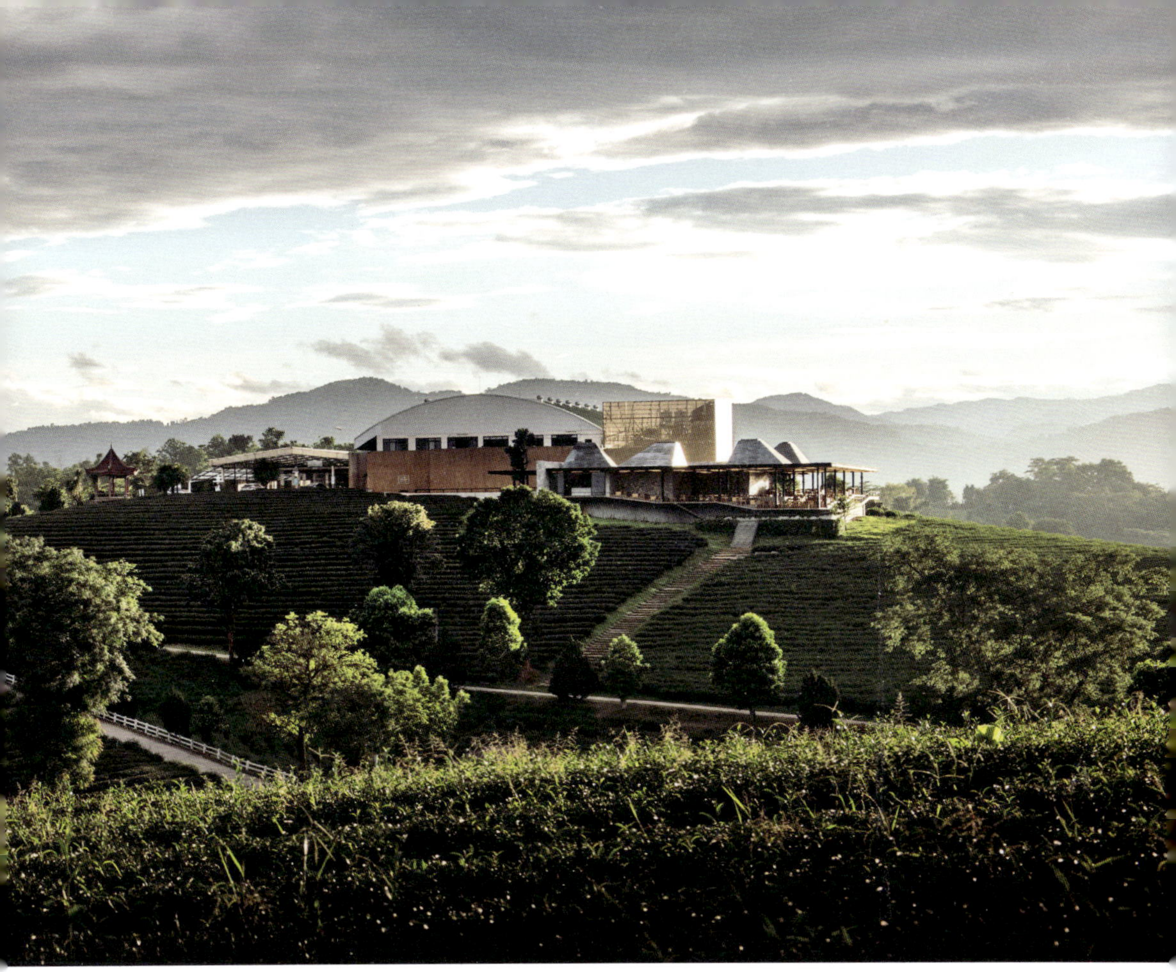

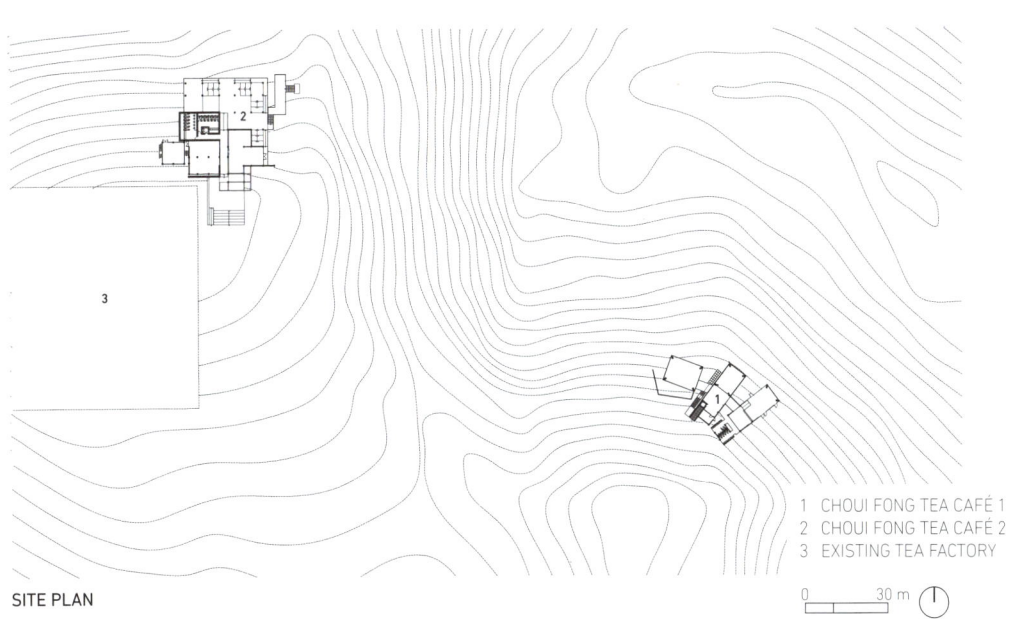

SITE PLAN

1 CHOUI FONG TEA CAFÉ 1
2 CHOUI FONG TEA CAFÉ 2
3 EXISTING TEA FACTORY

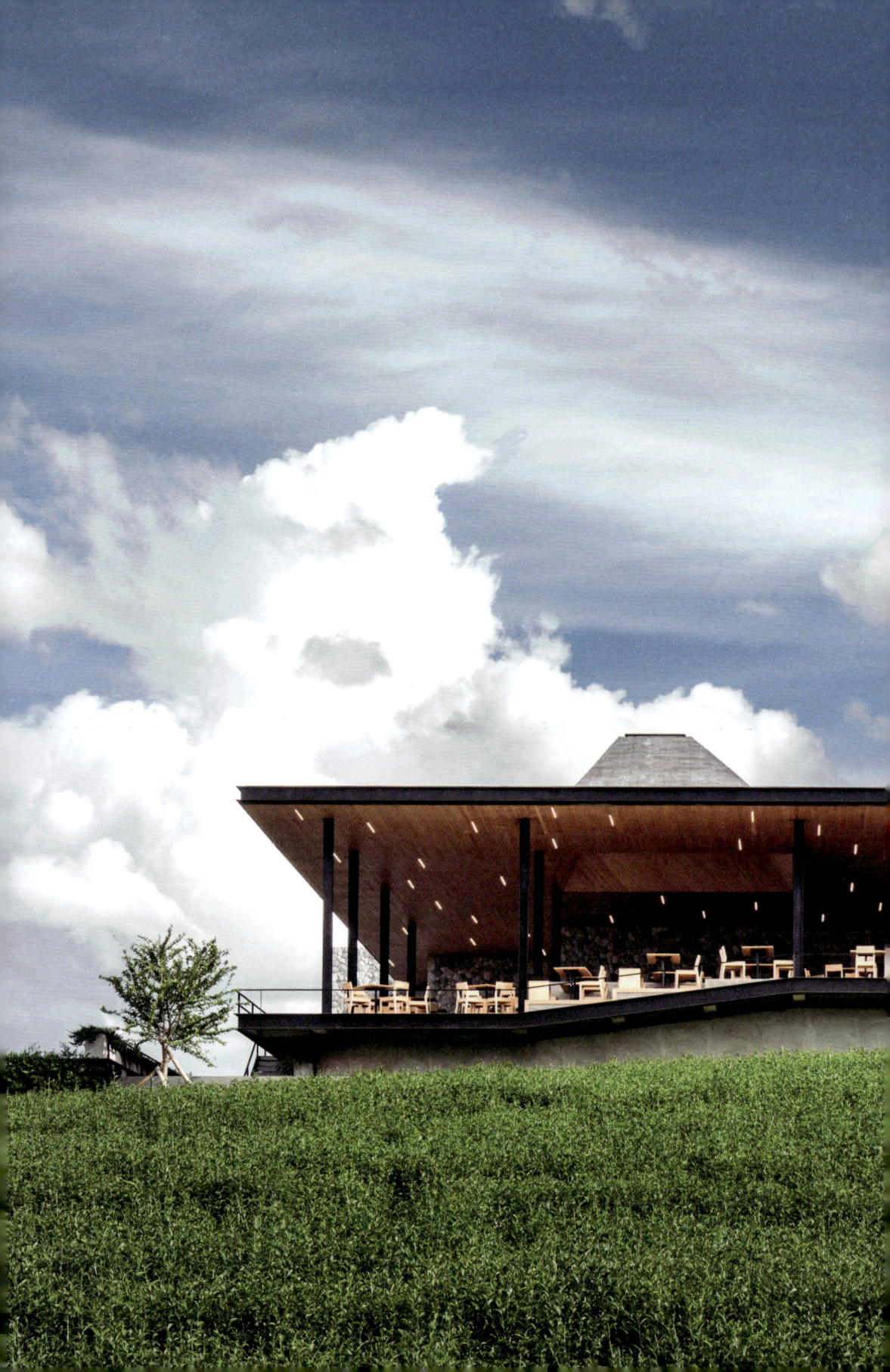

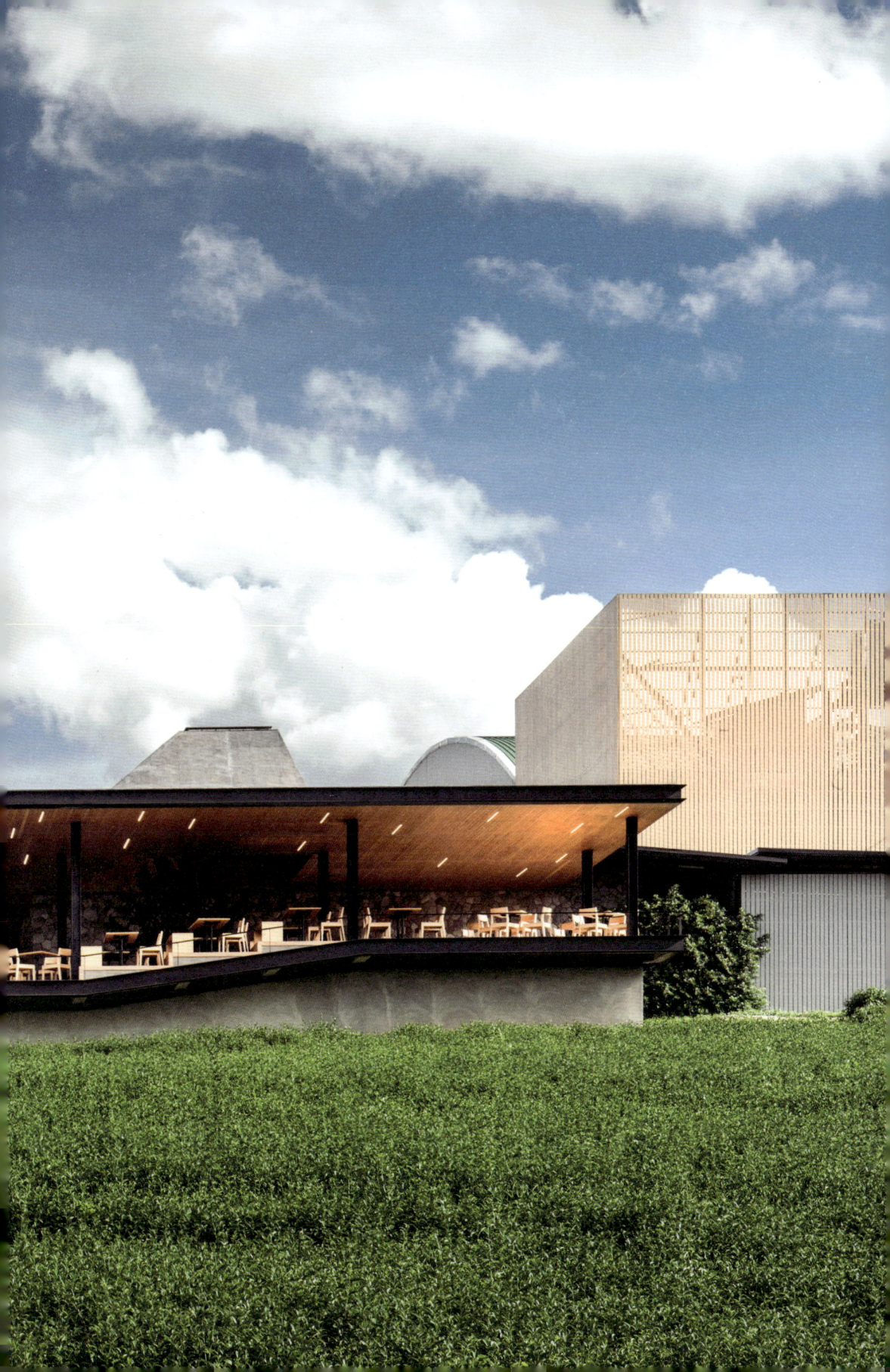

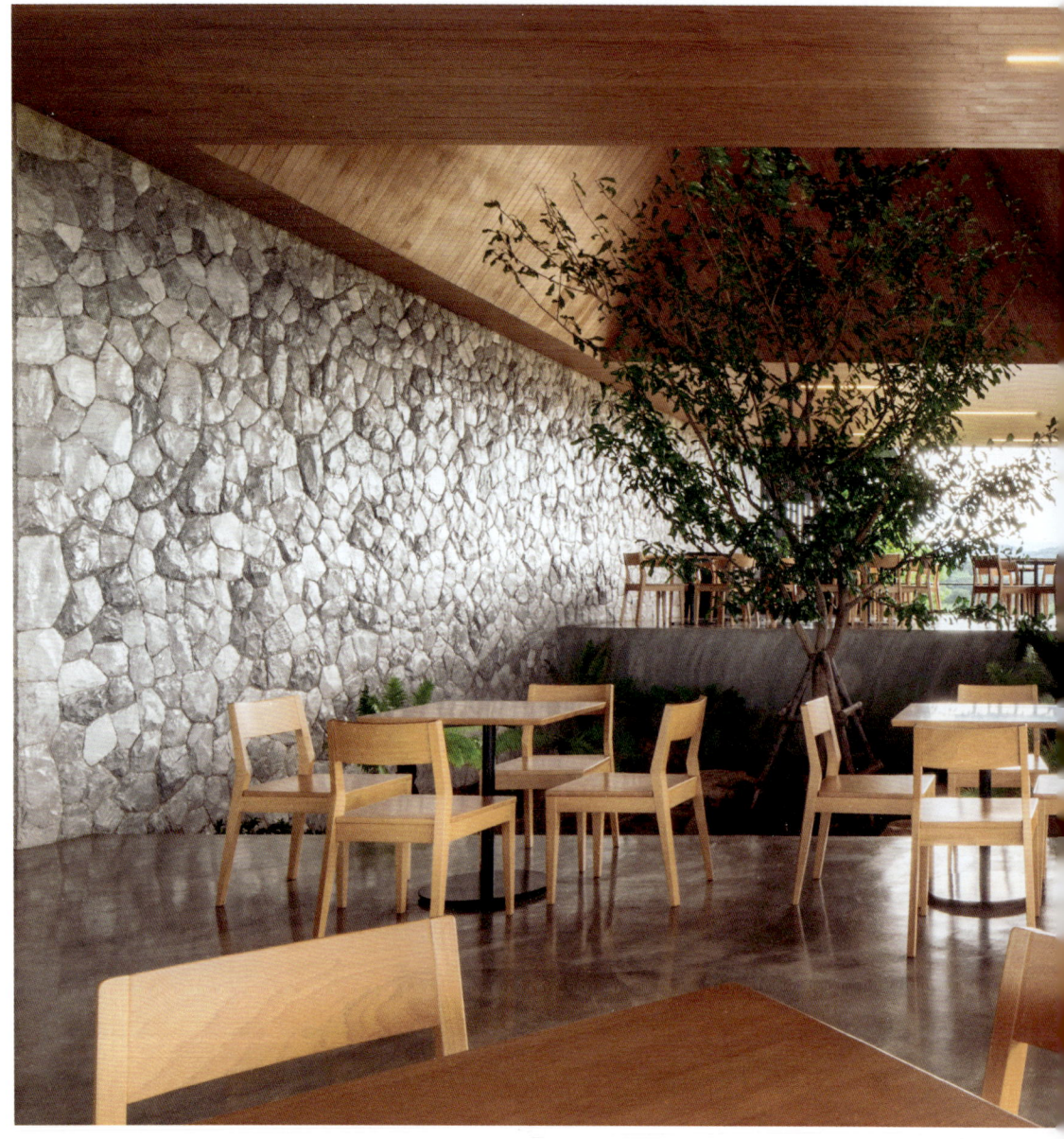

The dining area is tiered to mimic the land's sloping contour. This allows variations in eye level, which presents a different frame of scenery to each tier. Ramps surround the entries for patrons in wheelchairs to access all portions of the dining area. Customers seated on every tier can drink in an unobstructed view, but more importantly, this glorious scenery comes without inconvenience, especially for the elderly or those in a wheelchair. Above the ramps, extended eaves cover the dining area and protect against heavy rains.

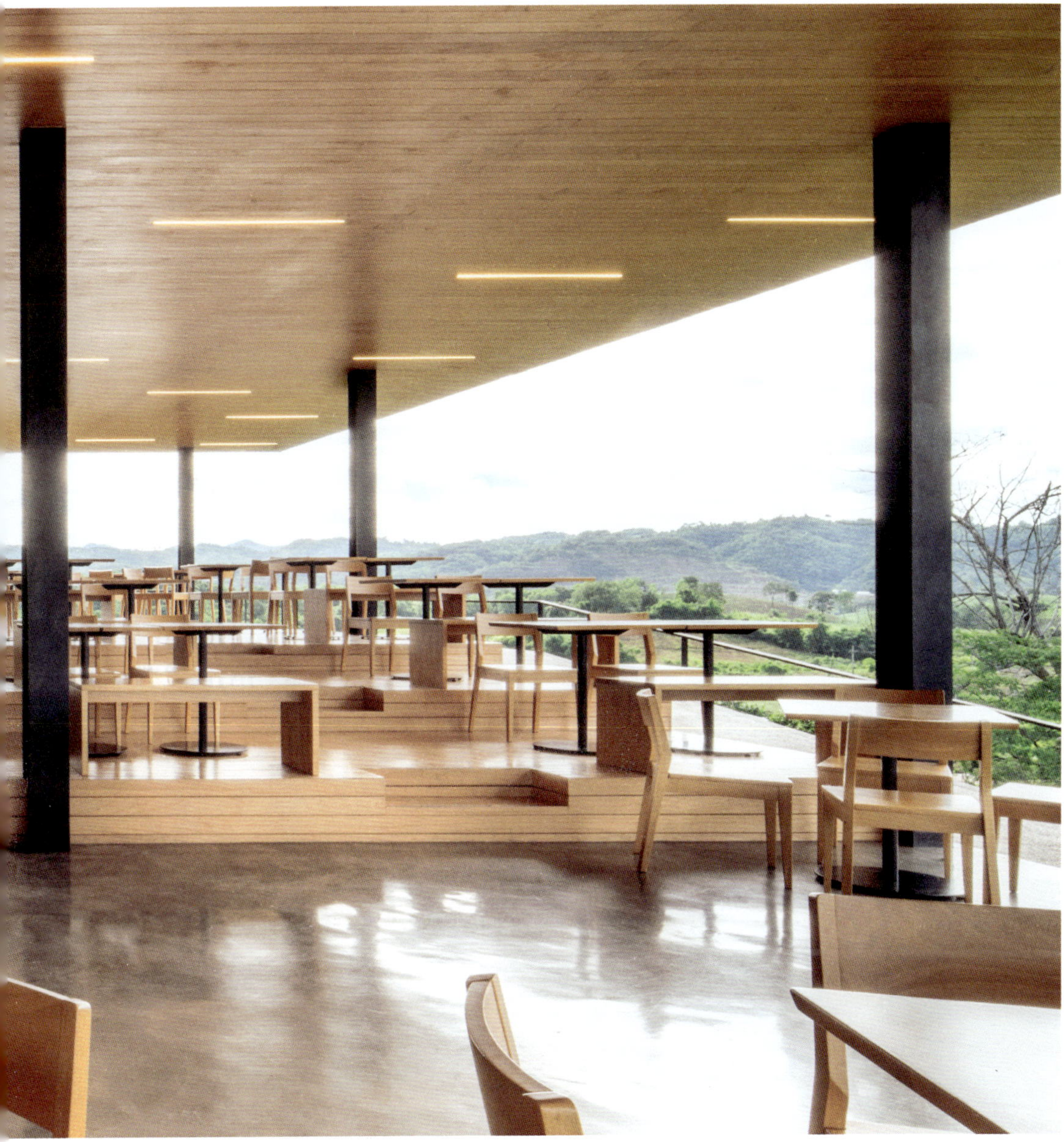

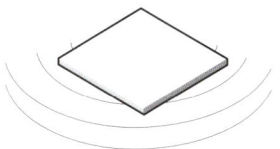

MAXIMUM AREA REQUIRED
IN A ONE-STORY BUILDING

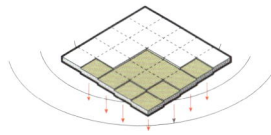

FLOOR PLANES ARE PUSHED DOWN
TO ENGAGE WITH THE CONTOUR

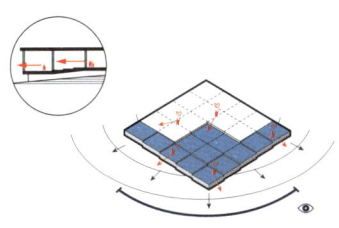

THE DINING AREA IS DESIGNED IN TIERS
TO BROADEN VIEWS OF THE PLANTATION

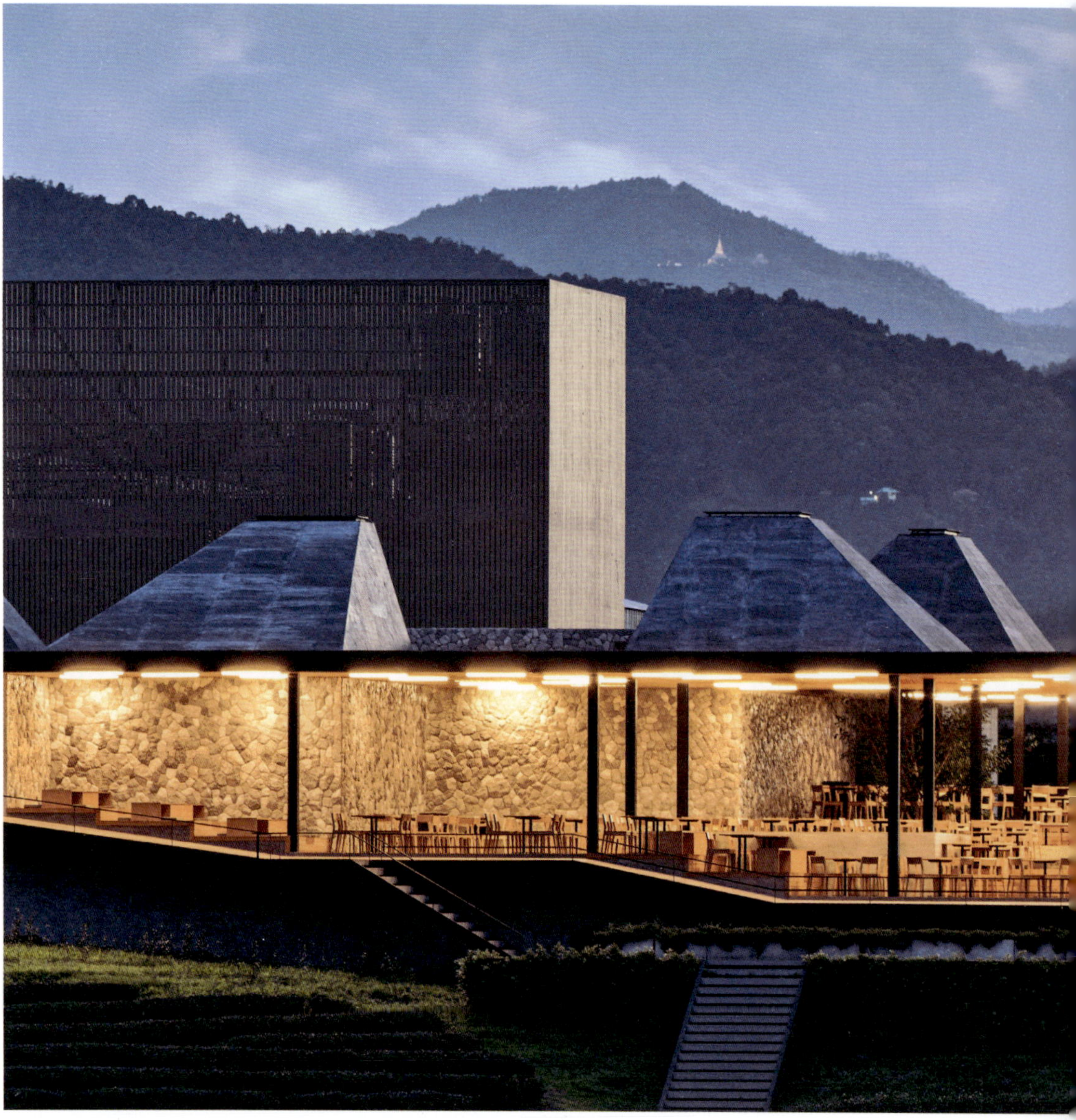

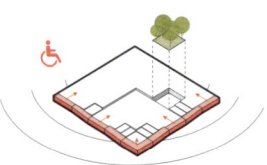

UNIVERSAL CIRCULATION
AND GREEN POCKET

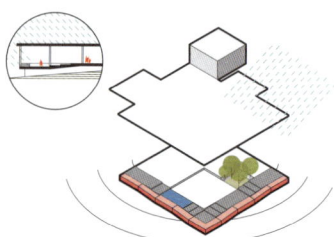

THE CIRCULATION ACTS AS A
RELIEVER THAT PROTECTS THE
DINING AREA FROM HEAVY RAINS

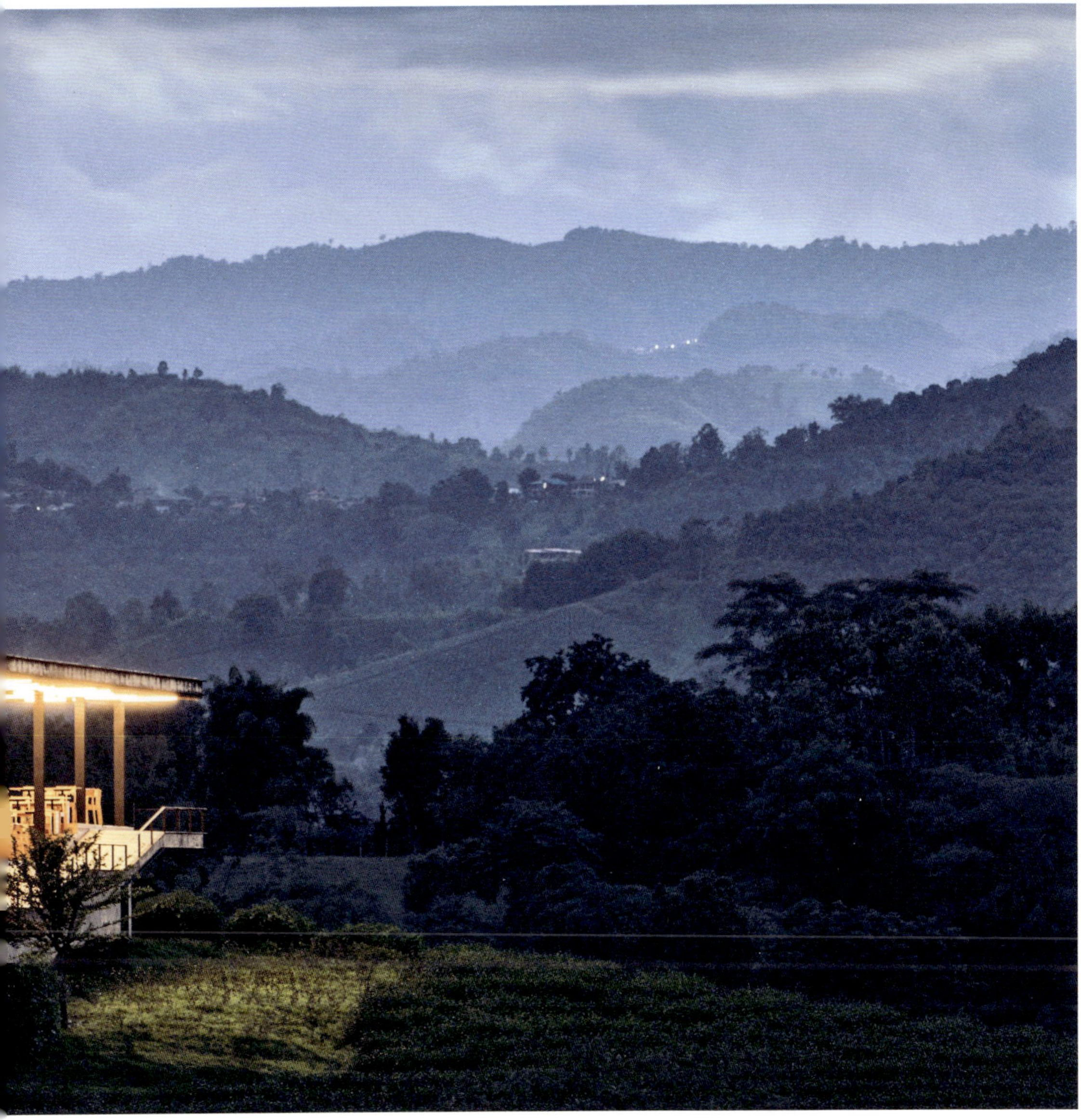

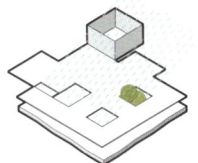

OPENINGS ADDED TO RESOLVE
THE LACK OF DAYLIGHT

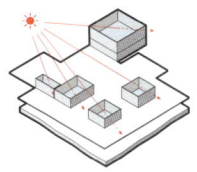

OPENINGS ARE COVERED WITH
GLASS TO CREATE SKYLIGHTS
AND PROTECT AGAINST RAIN

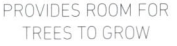

PROVIDES ROOM FOR
TREES TO GROW

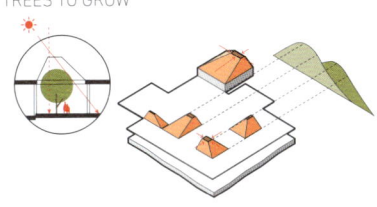

EXTRUDING CONE-SHAPED SKYLIGHTS
DIFFUSE LIGHT AND BLEND IN WITH THE
SURROUNDING MOUTAINSCAPE

CHOUI FONG TEA CAFÉ 2

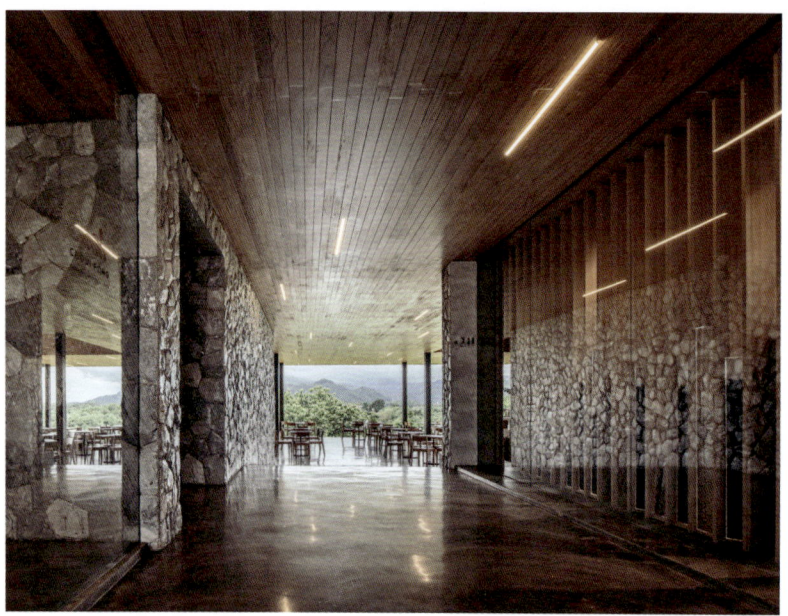

A visitor's unique experience at the Choui Fong Tea Café 2 begins at the entrance hallway. Built like a wind tunnel, it ushers in the breeze to welcome visitors and greet them with a rush of refreshing, cool, mountain air. The lighting is dim and gentle, and brightens gradually along the way leading to the dining area.

The floor plan is more than generous to meet the requirement for a large usable area within a one-story building. Skylights flood the café with natural light and resolve the lighting challenge in the interior, typical of such considerable floor area. They are small and distributed in various positions rather than installed as a large, single construction to prevent jarring and exposed joint structures that usually accompany the use of enormous glass panes. Their extruded cone-shape design effectively diffuses natural light into the required zones, while keeping their size small. The elevated shape also provides room for the trees in the café's courtyard to grow. Beyond practical functions, the cone-shaped extrusions also contribute to exterior aesthetics. Irregular in form with a stone finish, they reflect the mountainous landscape around, playing off the natural beauty of the setting, ensuring a sensorially rich merging of IDIN's philosophy for an aesthetic creation that results in better living.

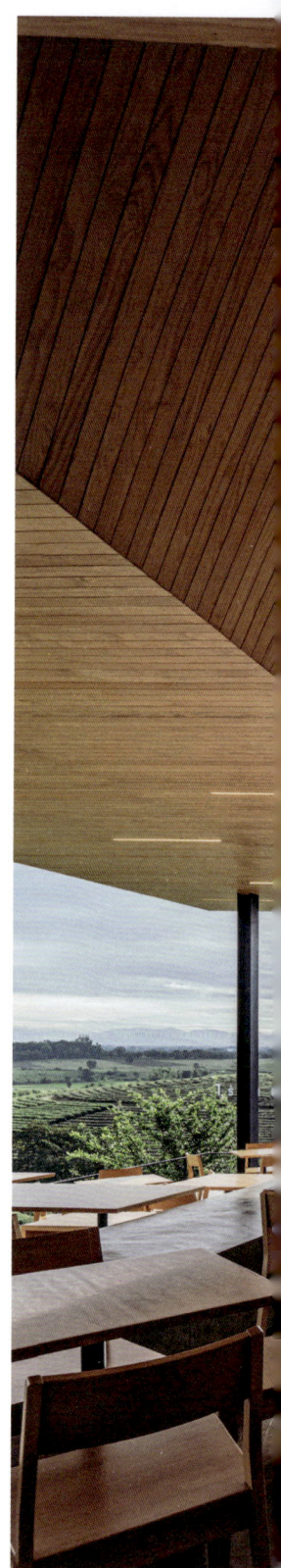

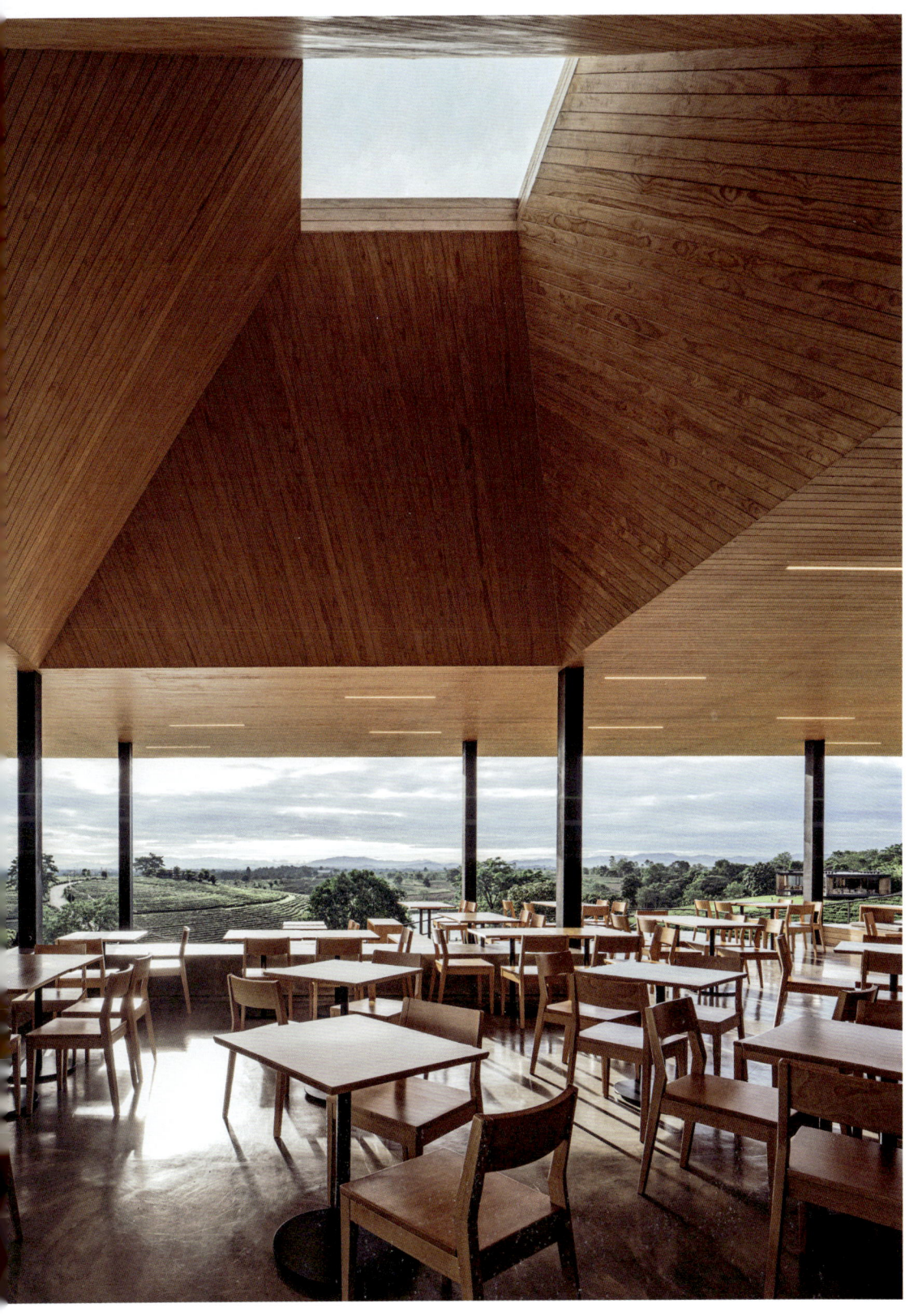

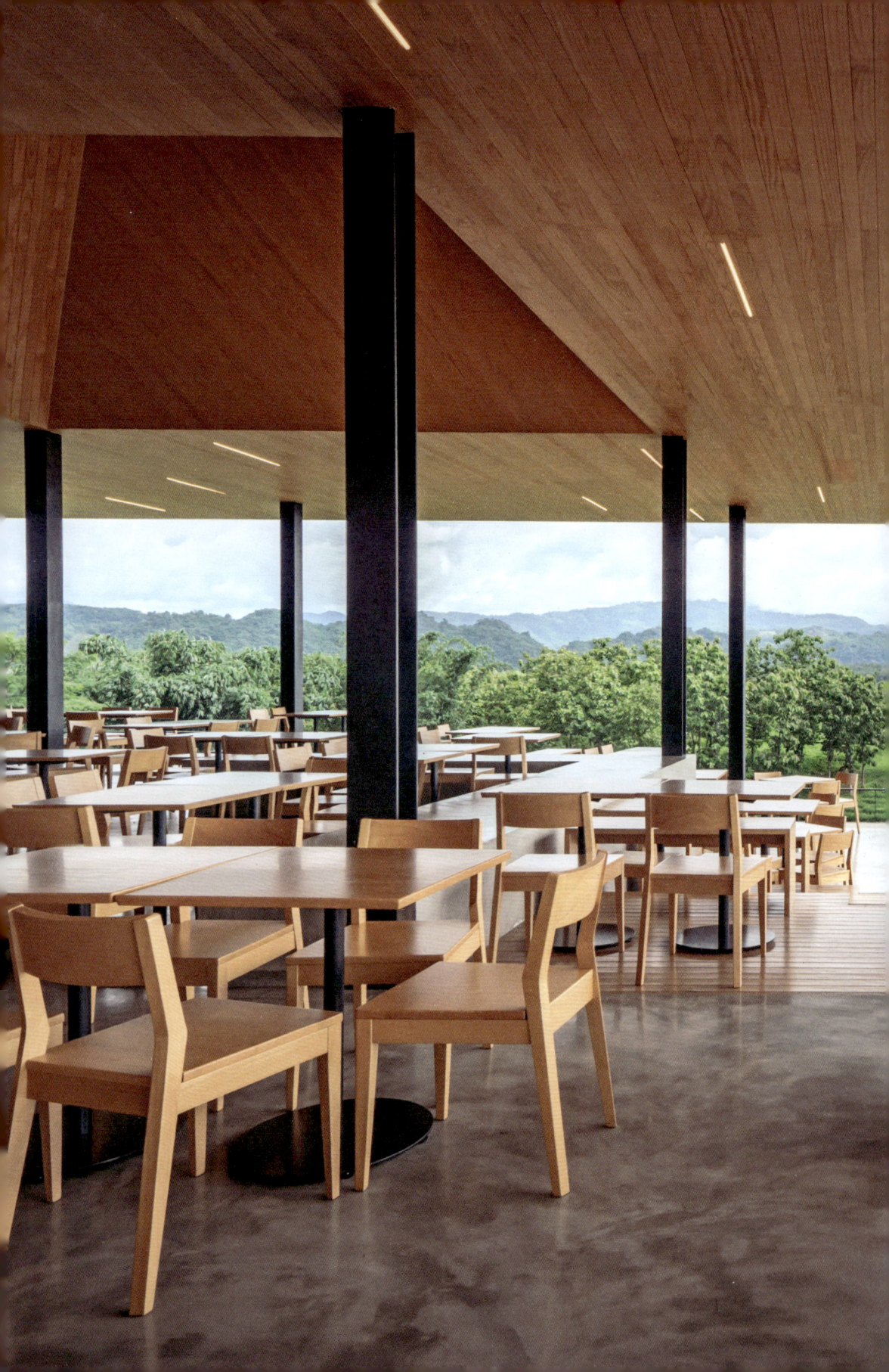

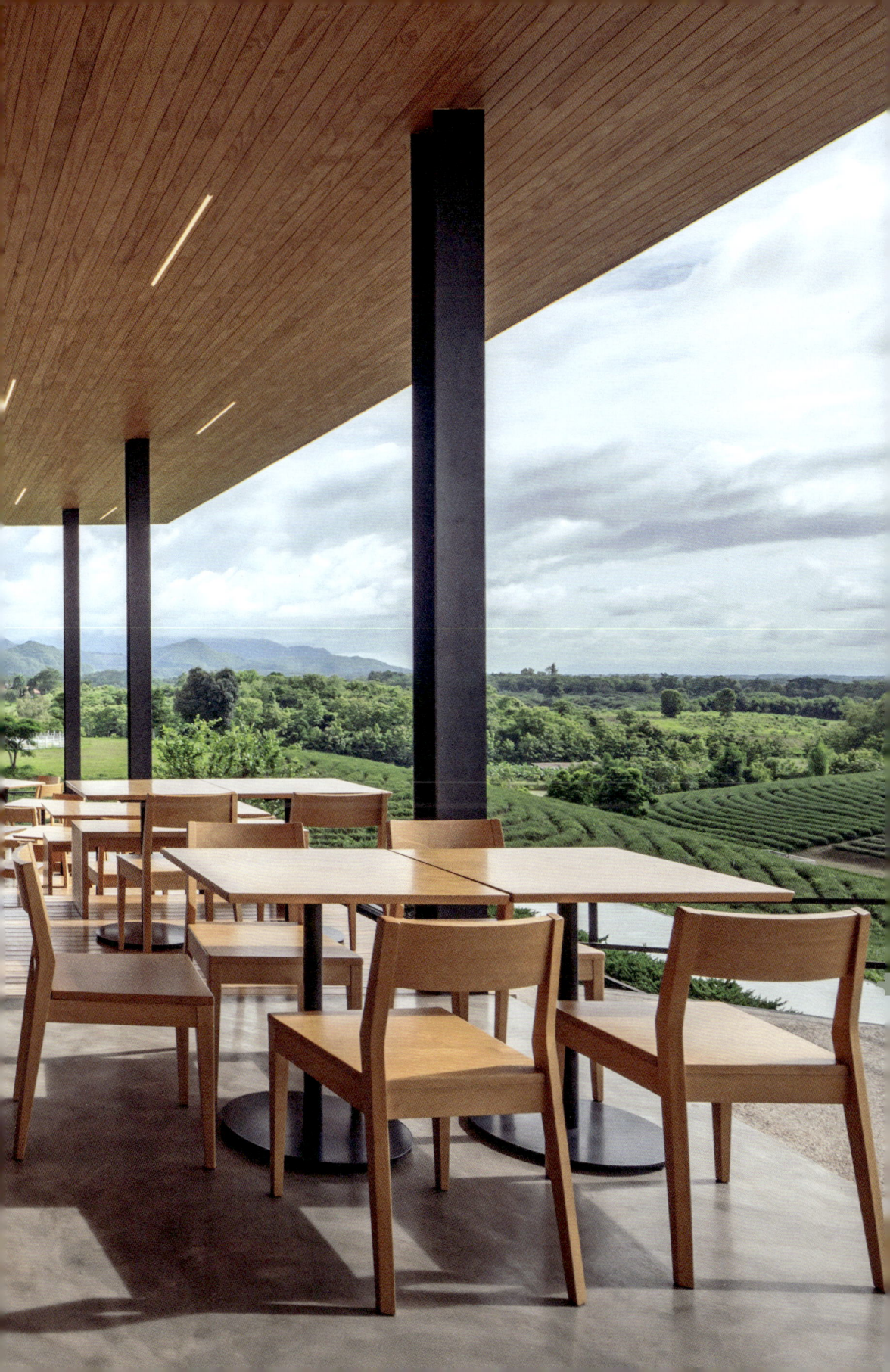

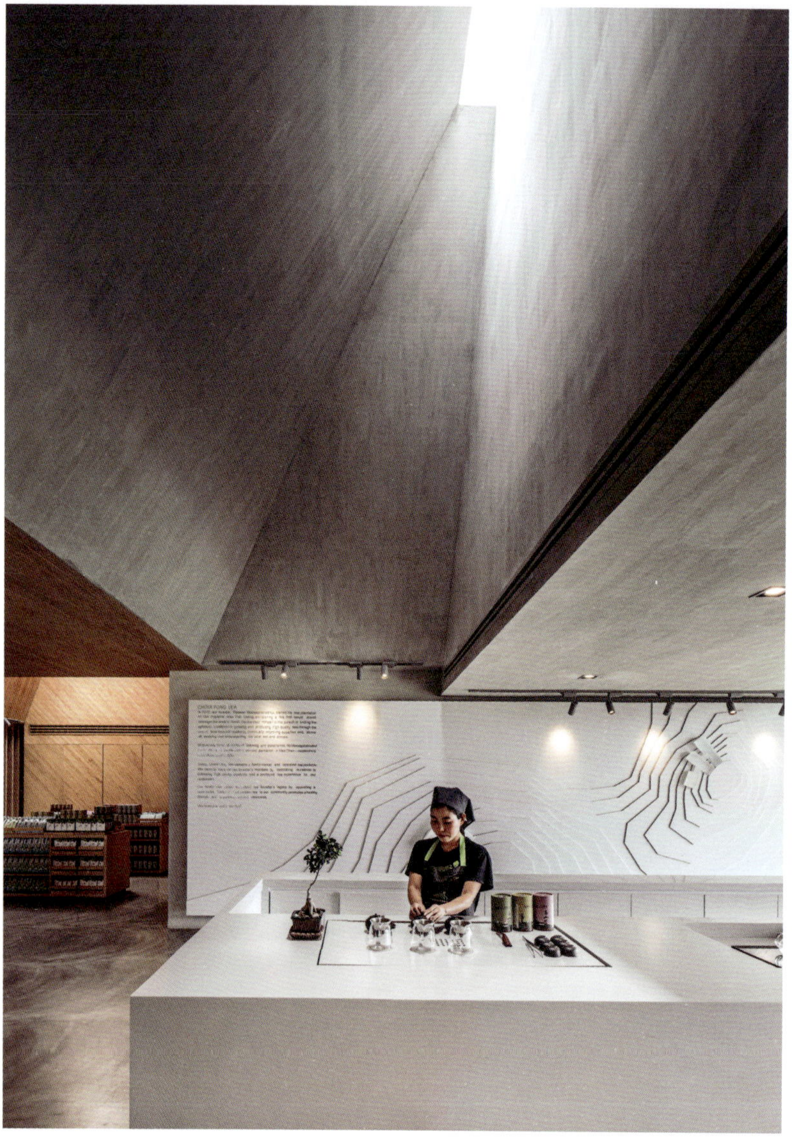

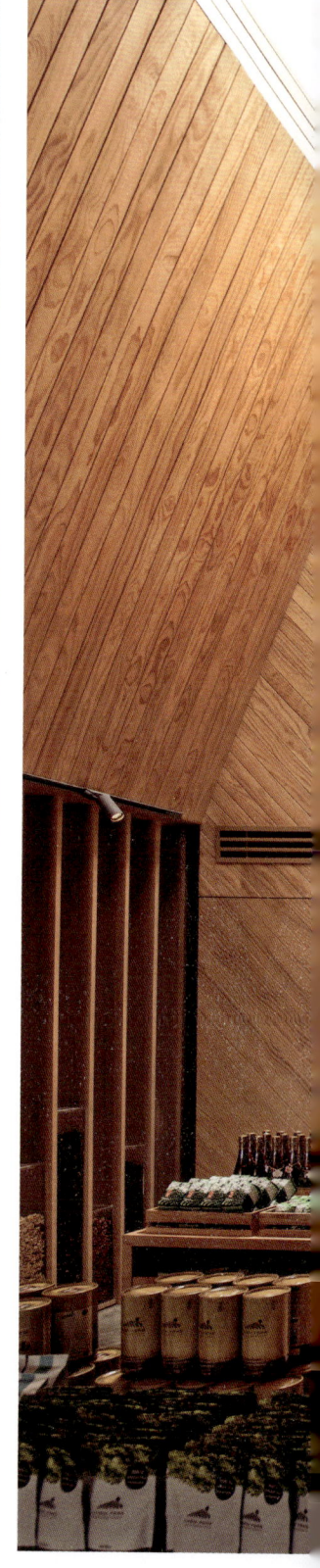

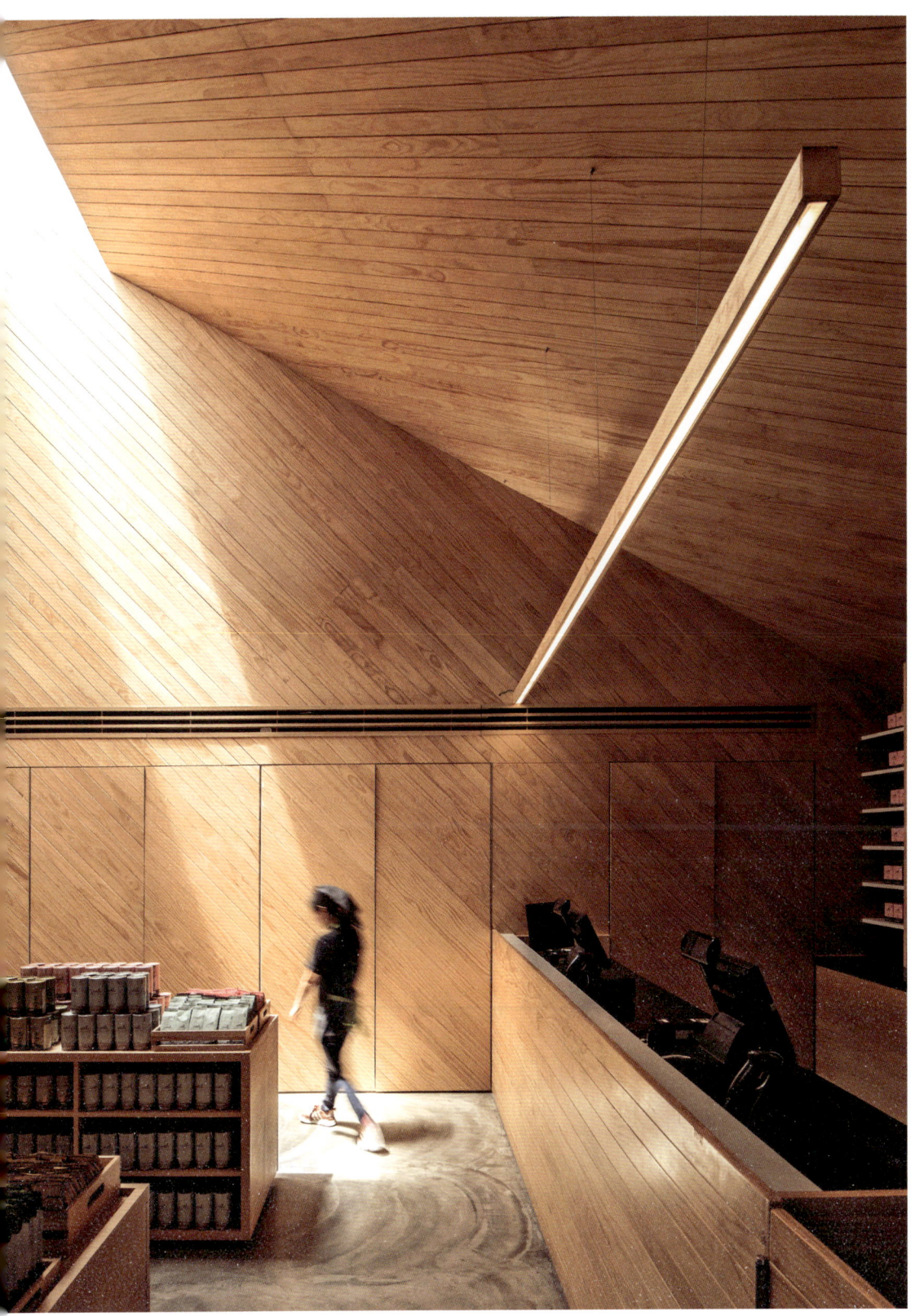

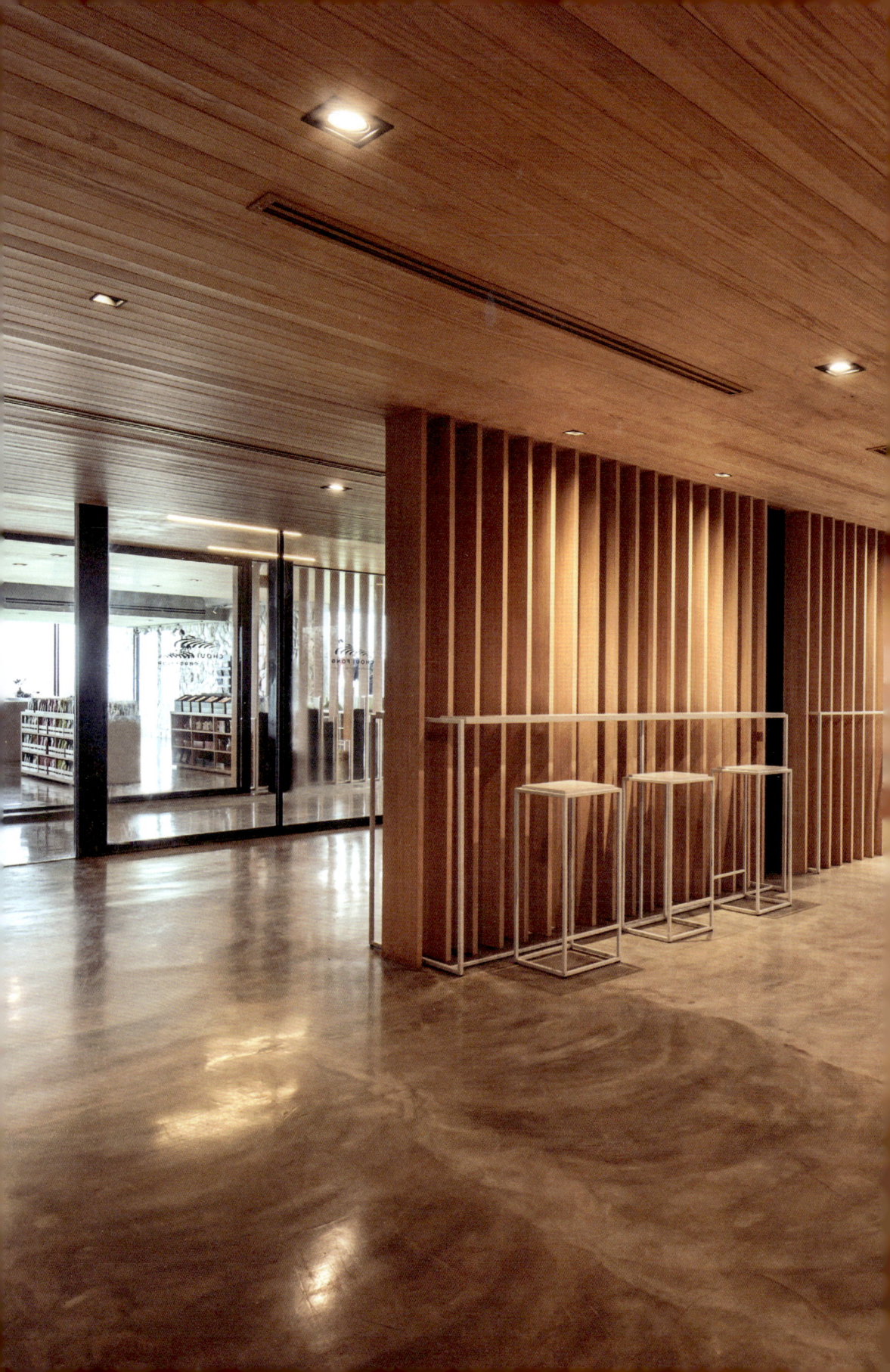

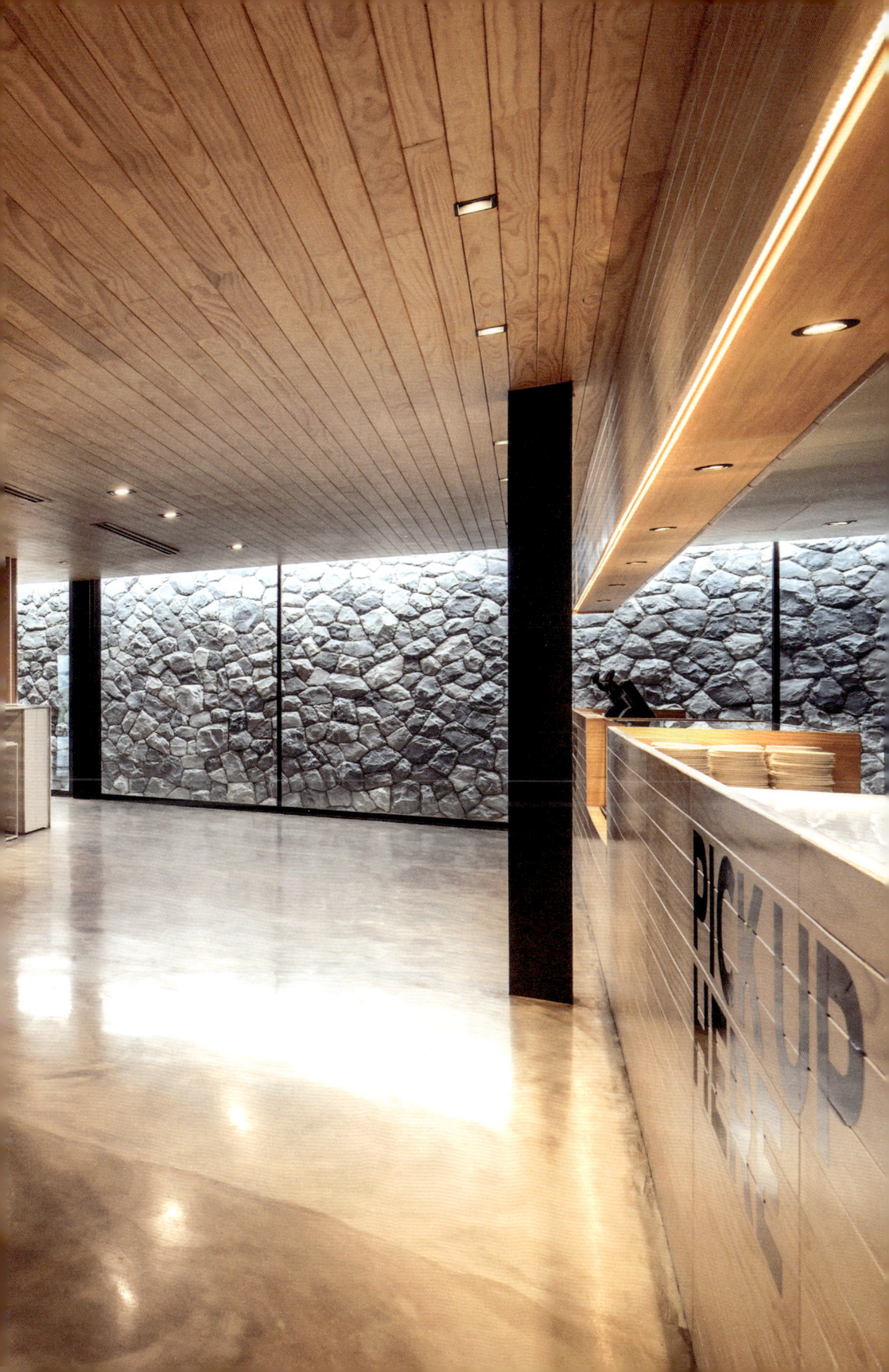

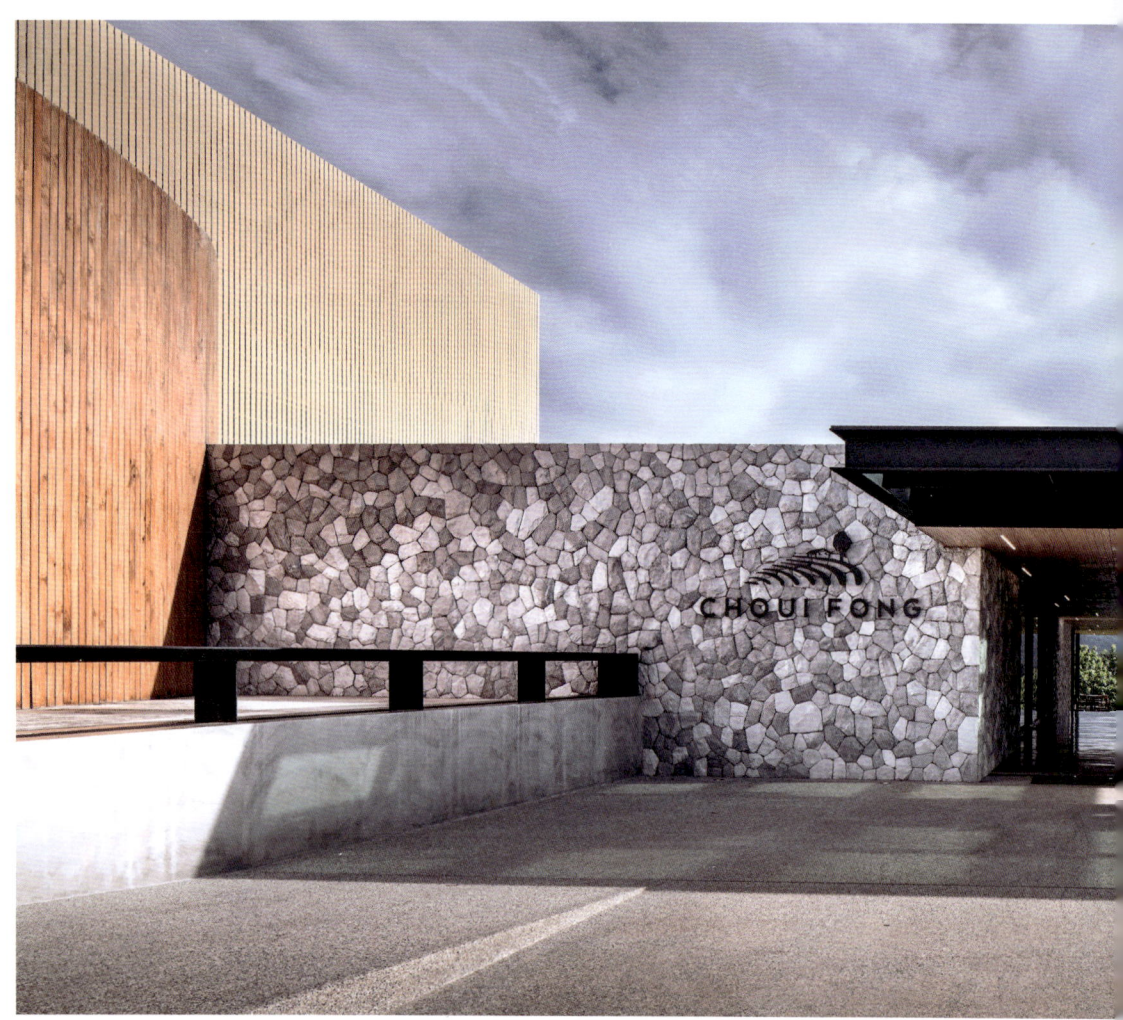

The material profile in the second café is aligned with that of the first; a modest ensemble of pinewood, steel, and glass, with the addition of mountain stone, mold into an honest character that is unique, warm, and hospitable, while also reflecting Choui Fong's philosophy of an organic plantation.

On the design front, the interior is detailed according to user-patterns derived from the first café; layout functions are interpreted and incorporated into the program such that while the "feel" is similar, the aesthetic resemblances embrace an altogether different and distinctive personality.

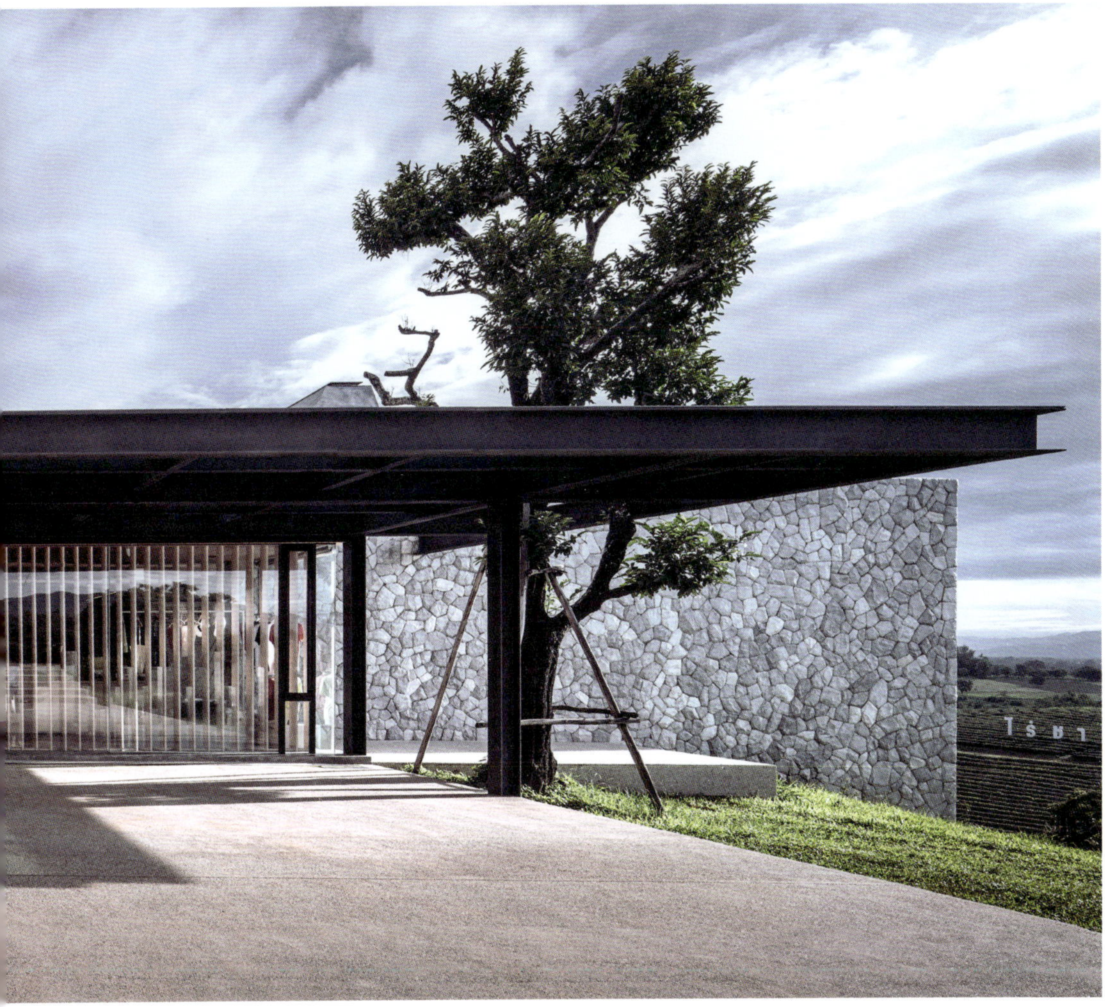

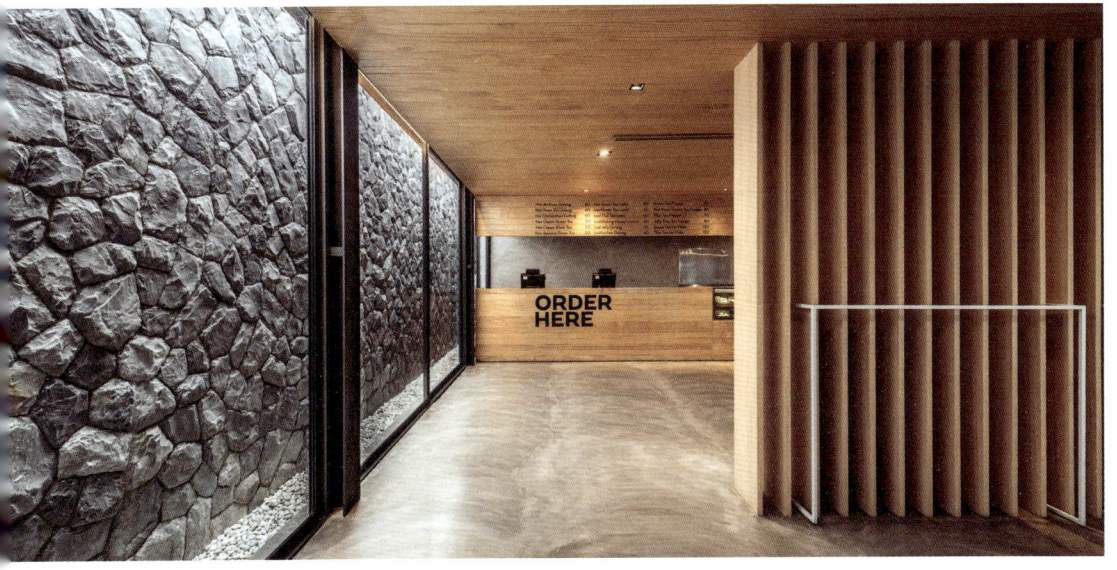

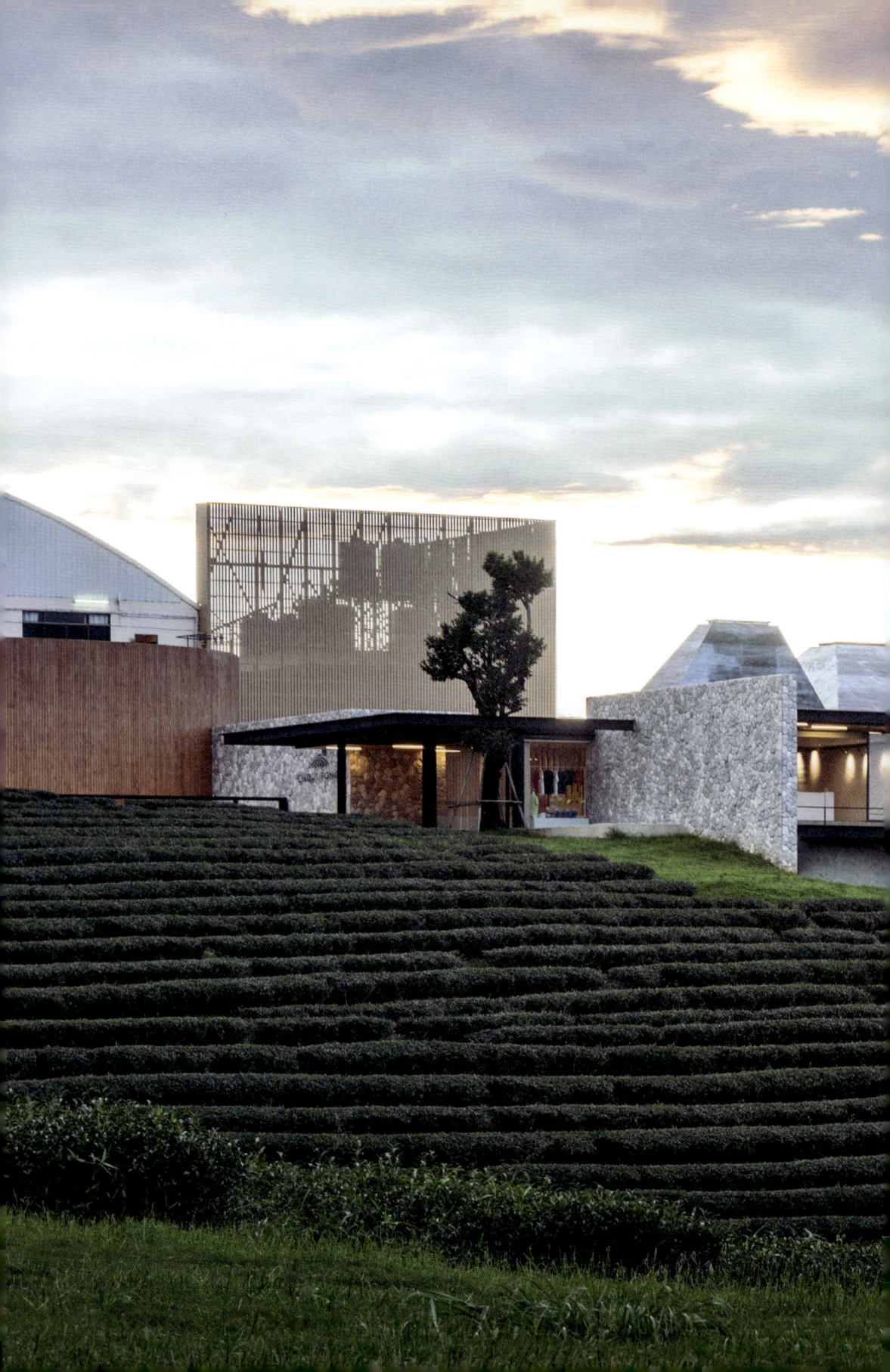

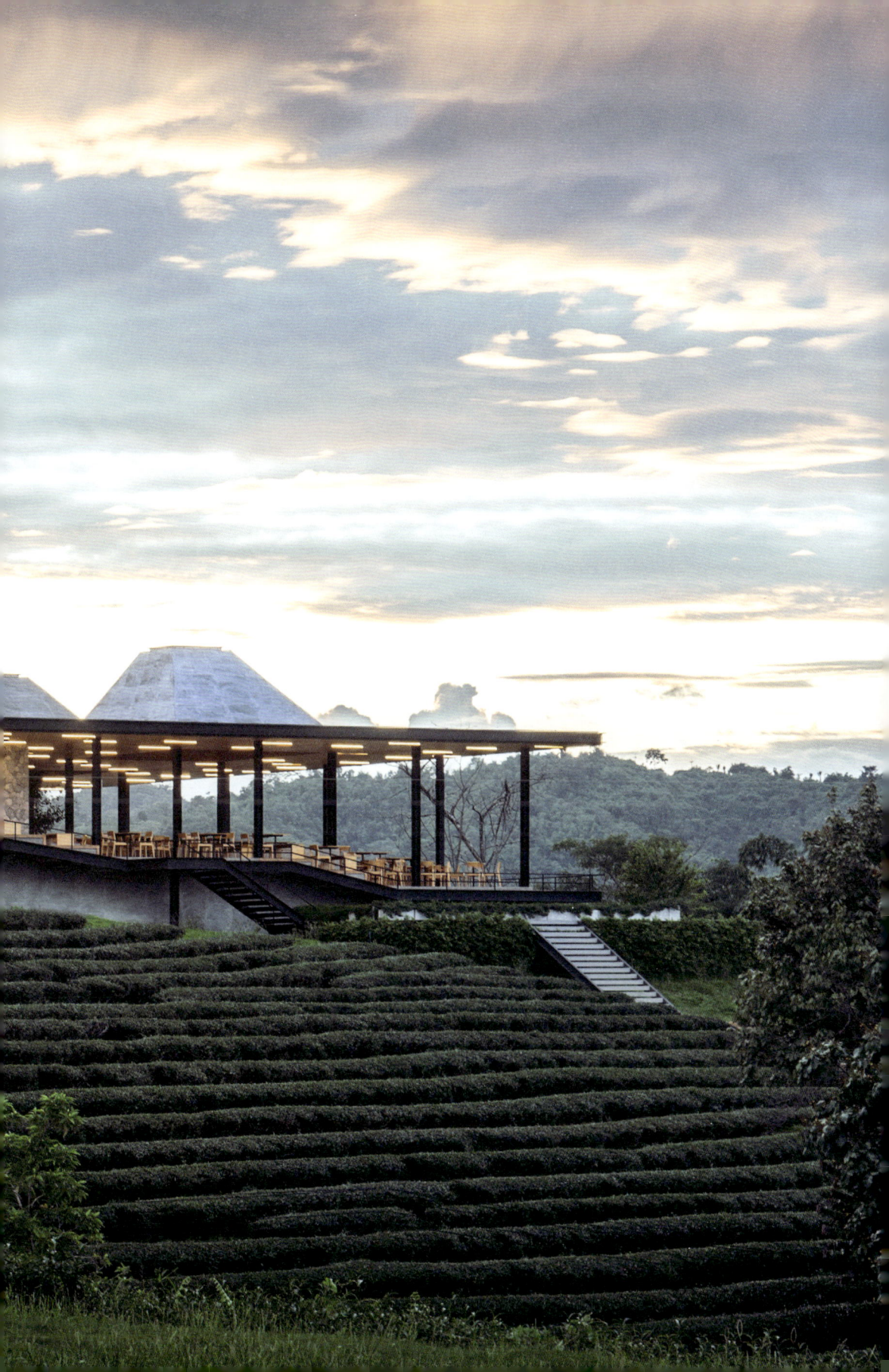

Nakhon Chai Si, Nakhon Pathom, Thailand, 2017

JB HOUSE

Celebrating an architecture that not only supports the needs of everyday life, JB House also goes a step further to enhance the users' relationships with each other. By creating new possibilities for varied spaces, programs, and activities, the owners' experiences of the space are elevated, creating a greater appreciation of their home and in turn, their time within together.

The design of the house has been conceptualized around a couple with no extended family or children, so each individual enjoys the privileged sanctuary of their own little world that accommodates their lifestyle. He loves photography and baking, while she is a book lover with a passion for drawing. His main activity revolves around the kitchen island; her work in publishing requires a large work table for reading and writing. IDIN Architects finds its place in gathering all these requirements and reformulating them into a lively design concept. A common space at the heart of the house allows the couple to "run into" each other during the day and enjoy some interaction together although they each have a different daily routine.

Two main activity areas are split over two floors. She reigns on the upper level, while he commands the lower. A clear-glass work table in her upper-floor station overlooks the kitchen island, an area he frequently occupies, providing them a visual connection with each other. This also creates a sense of proximity though they are on different levels engaged with their own tasks. The stacking of these primary spaces creates an interlocking element that ties the whole house together.

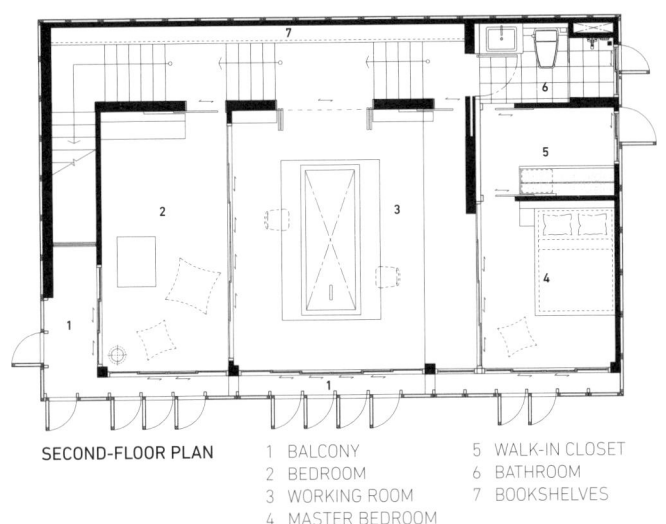

SECOND-FLOOR PLAN
1 BALCONY
2 BEDROOM
3 WORKING ROOM
4 MASTER BEDROOM
5 WALK-IN CLOSET
6 BATHROOM
7 BOOKSHELVES

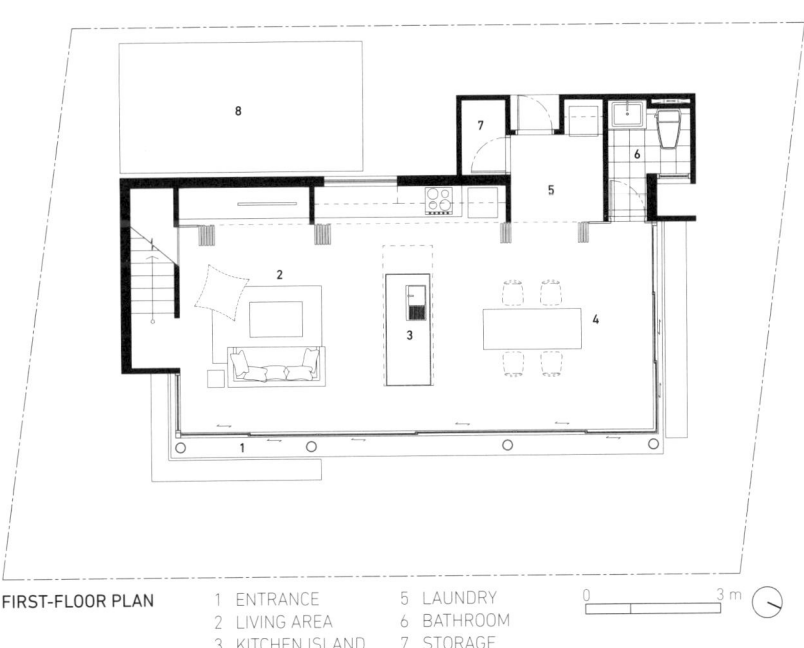

FIRST-FLOOR PLAN
1 ENTRANCE
2 LIVING AREA
3 KITCHEN ISLAND
4 DINING AREA
5 LAUNDRY
6 BATHROOM
7 STORAGE
8 PARKING

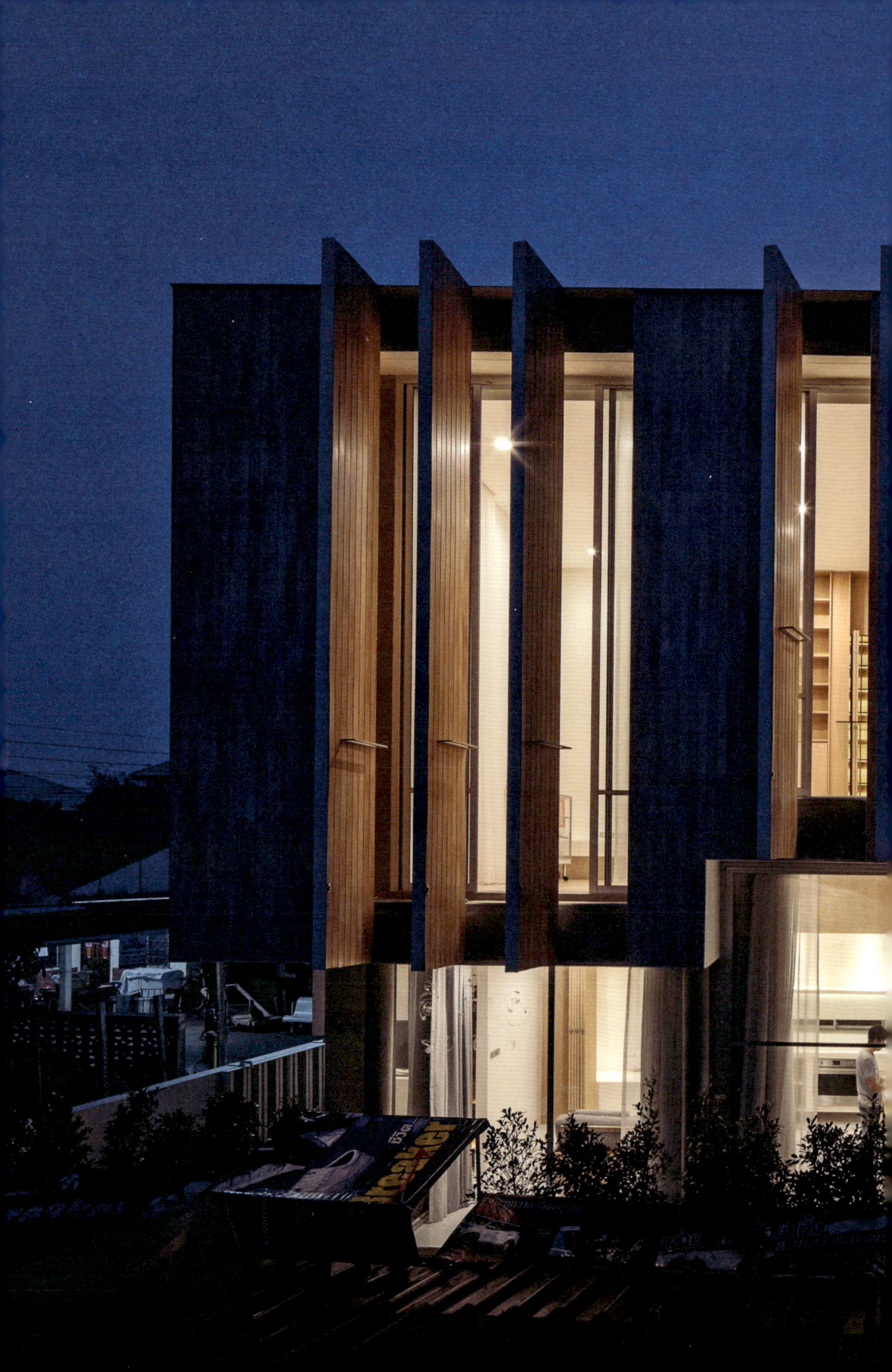

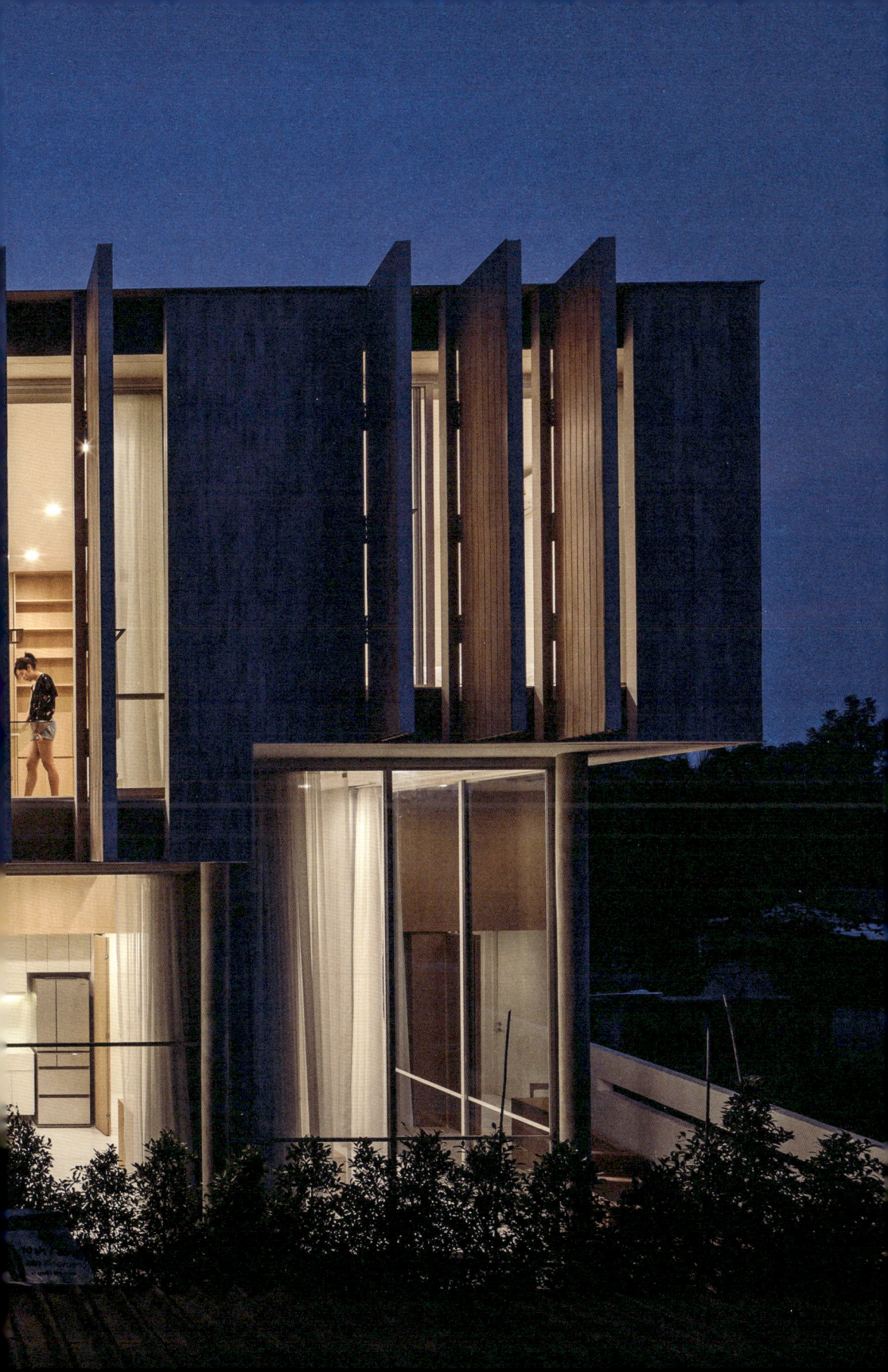

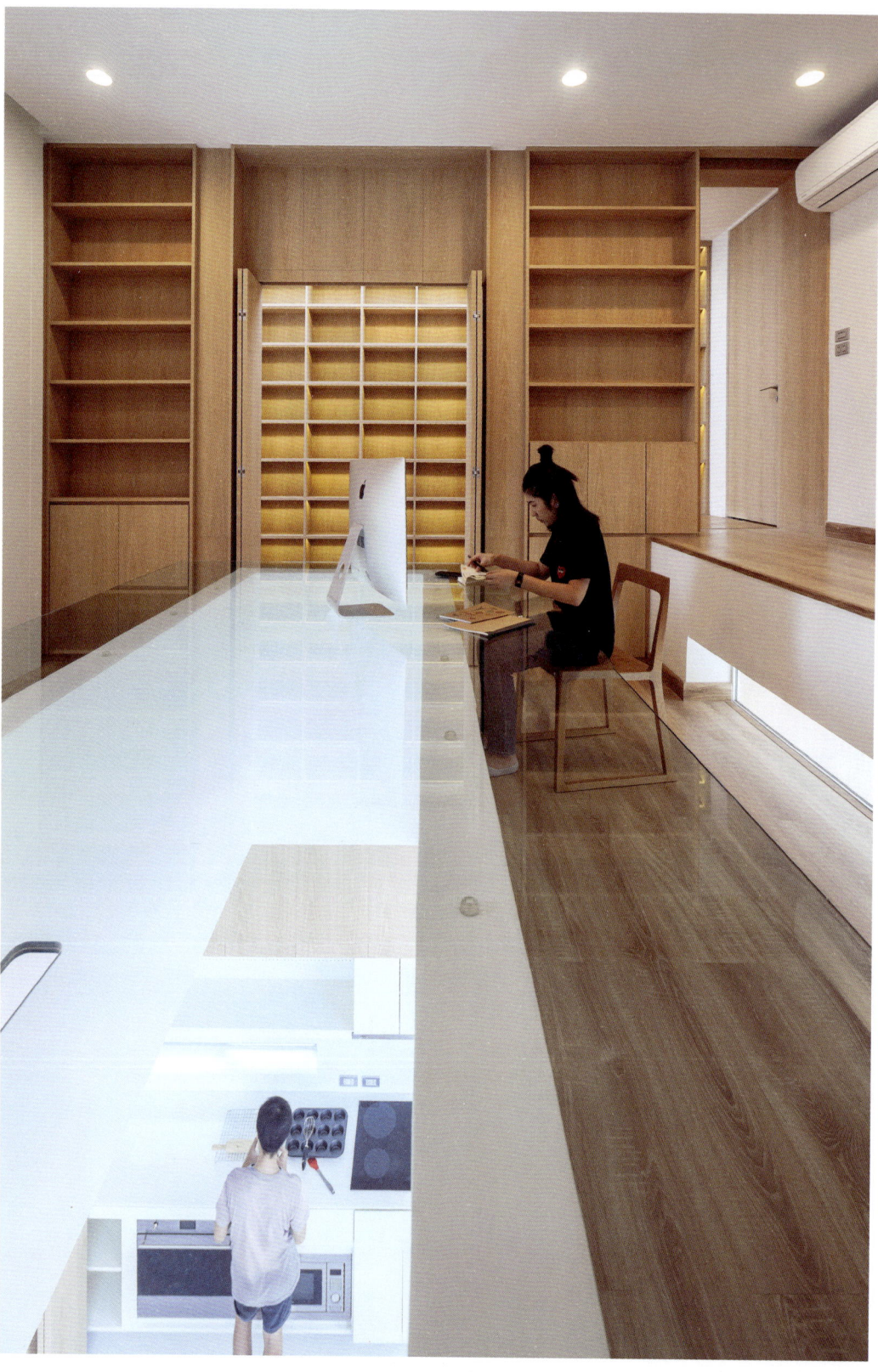

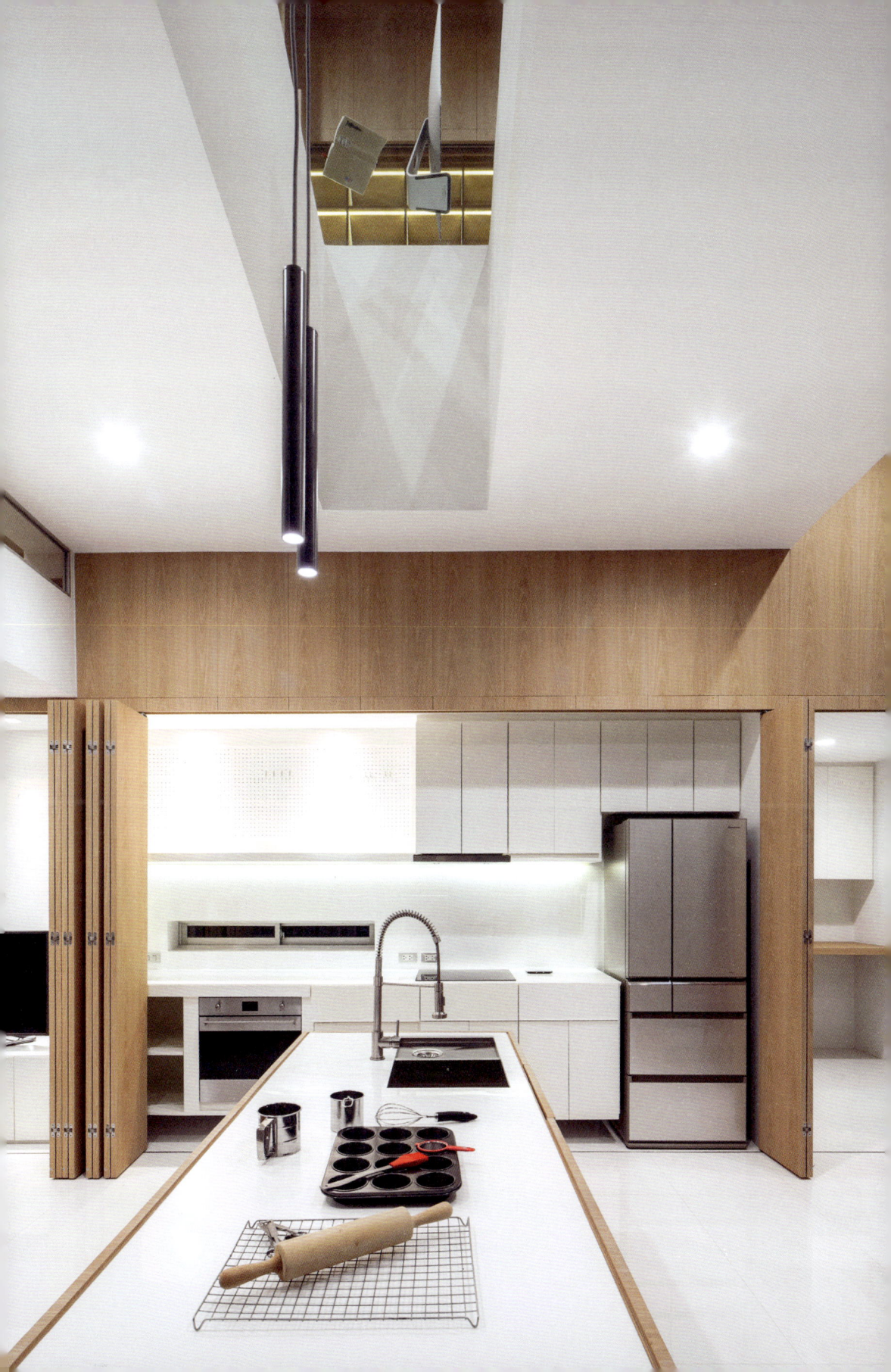

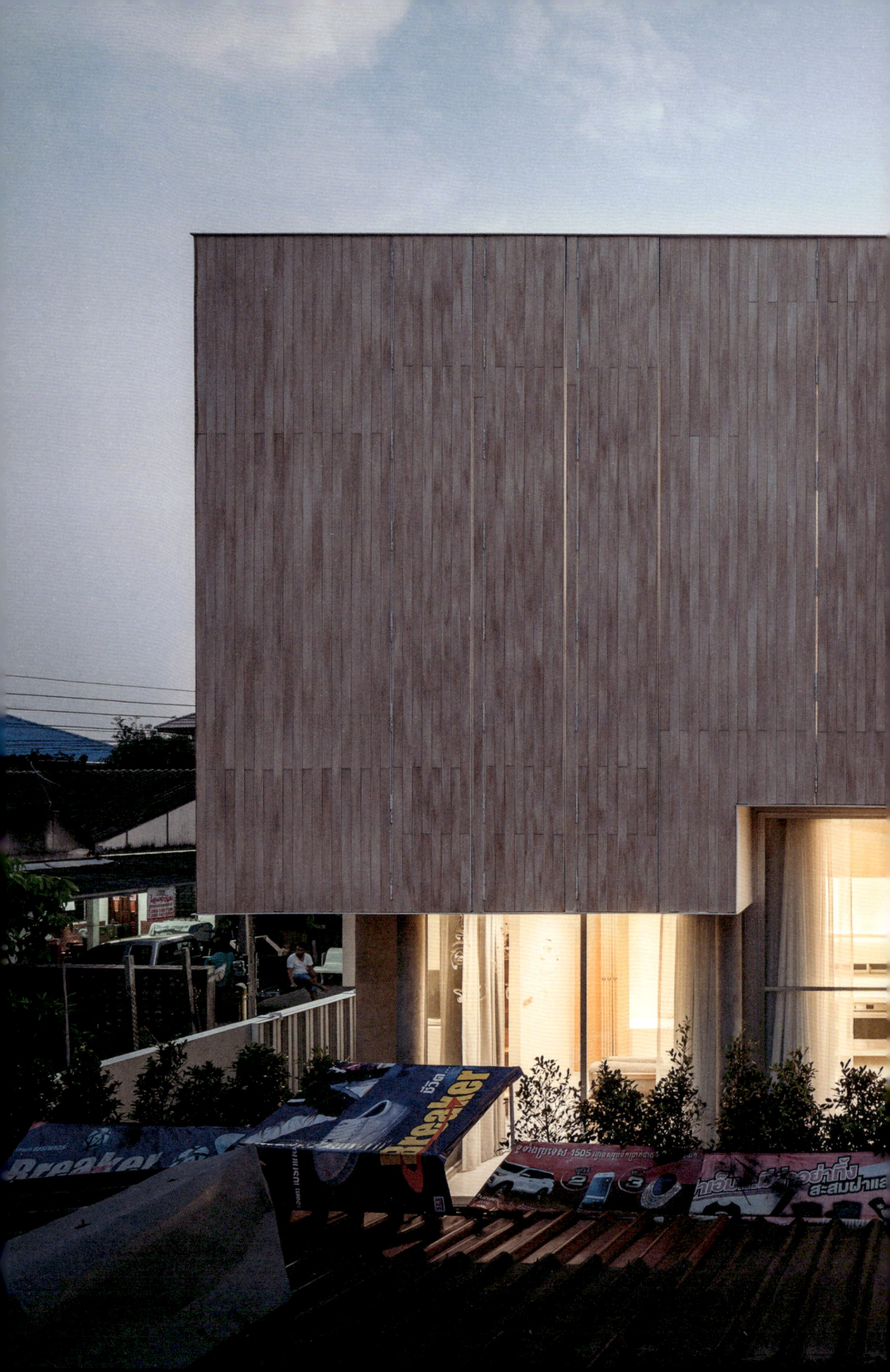

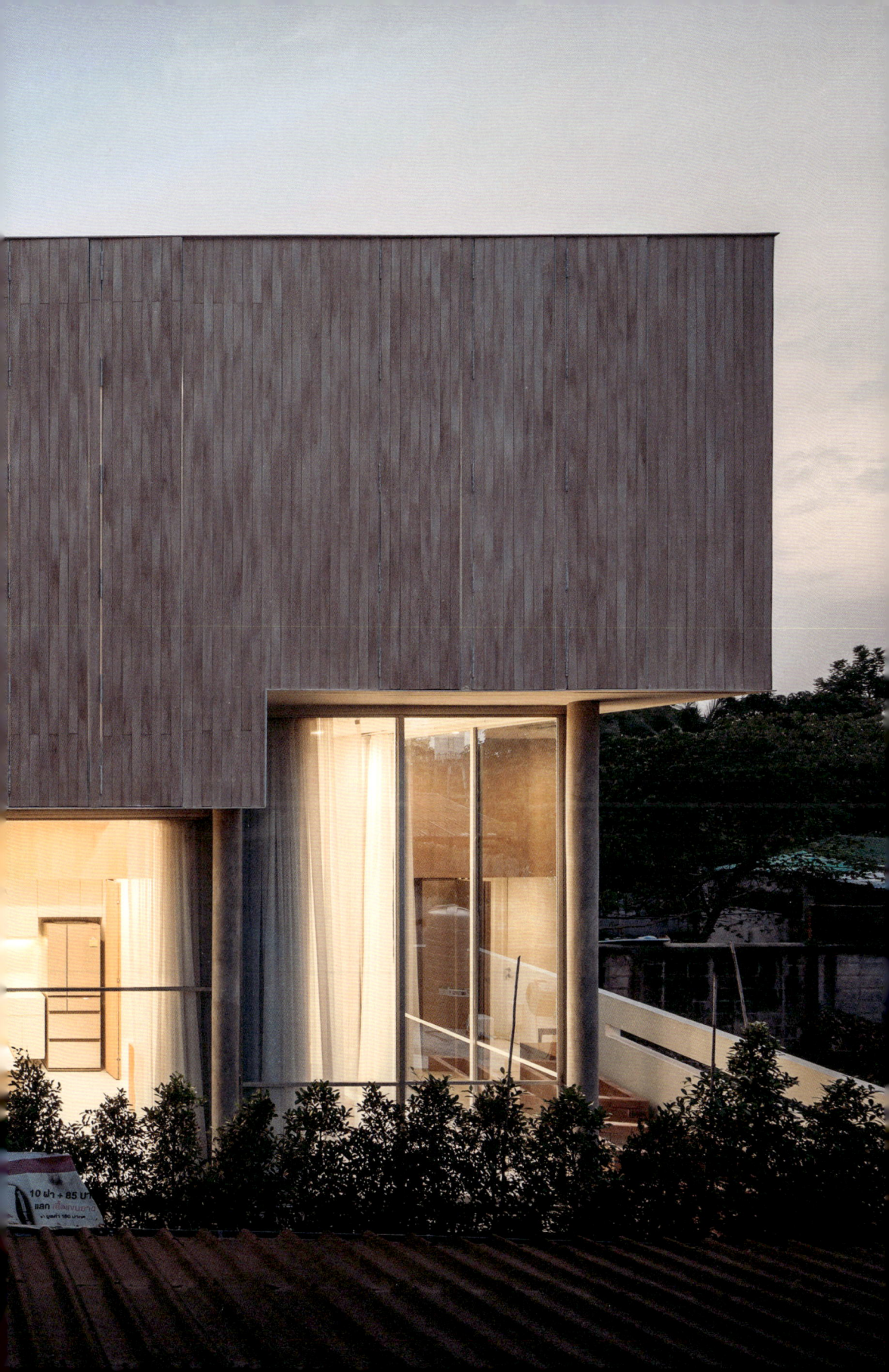

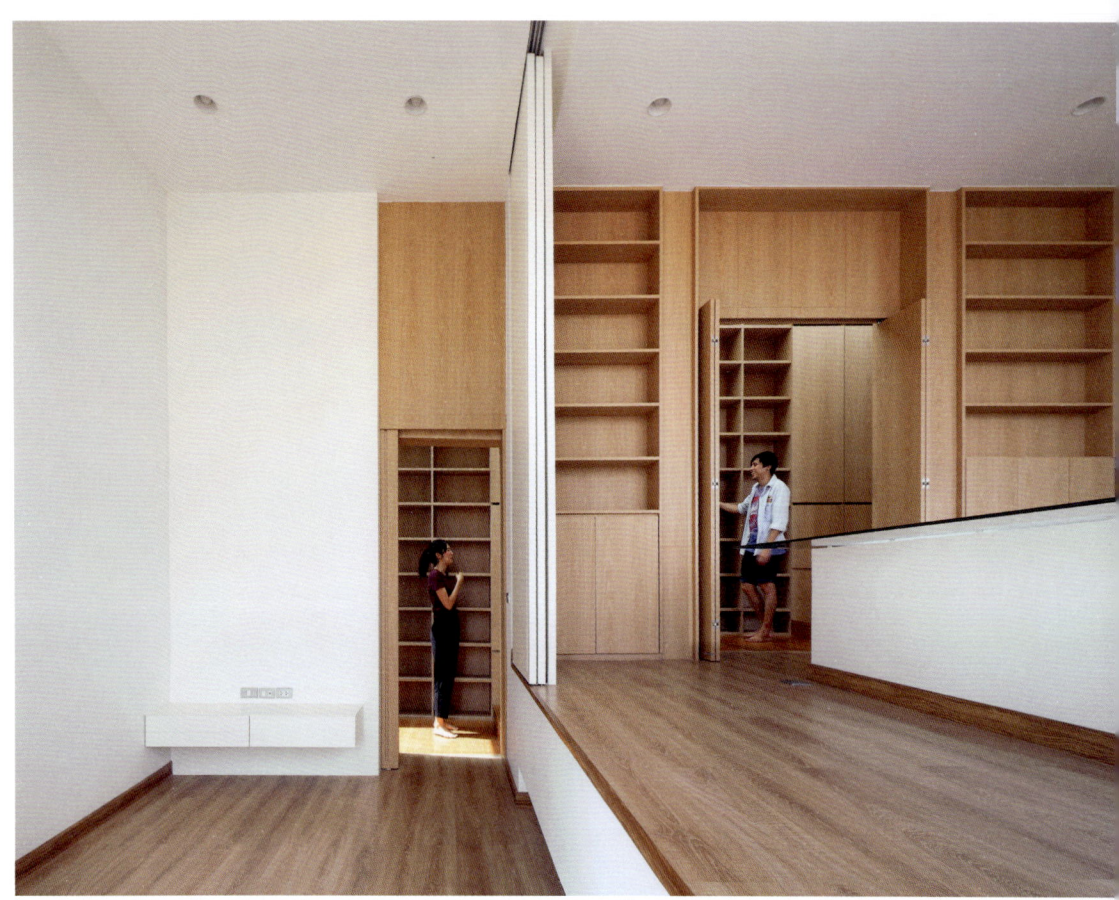

The upper level is accessed by three connecting flights of steps, designed in this manner to ensure privacy and keep the upper level out of view when guests are present. The walls lining these steps and the aisle beyond are specially constructed, integrating tall, extending rows of bookshelves to indulge the book lover in her. A strip of skylight above the bookshelves brightens the otherwise enclosed area and creates a pleasant browsing experience. All areas on the upper floor are fitted with double wood screens, which may be opened or closed to provide privacy, as well as protection from heat filtering in from the outside.

The design of JB House expresses the belief that architecture affects the inhabitants' behaviors, and can also contribute to strengthening their relationship and connection with each other. The facilities and spaces in this project are conceived to construct a place where the couple can be *one* together, while still being their own individual.

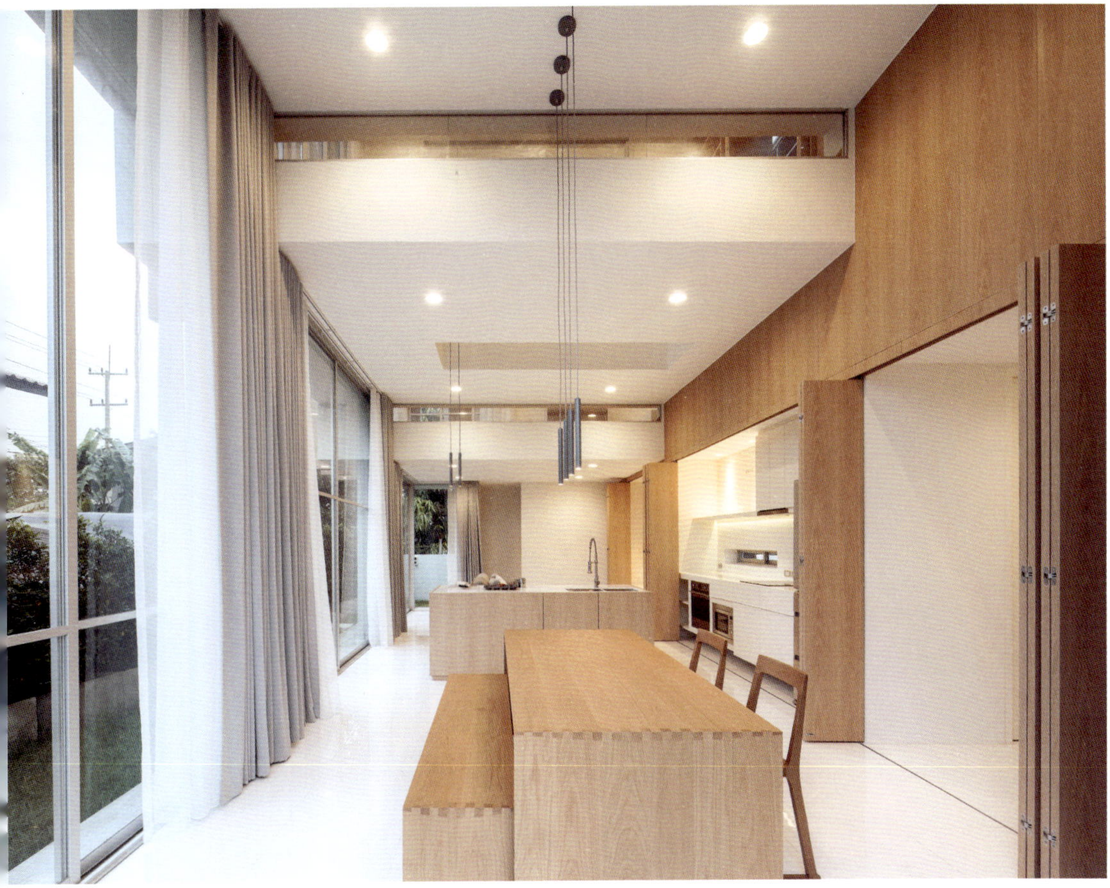

COUPLE'S INDIVIDUAL LIFESTYLES

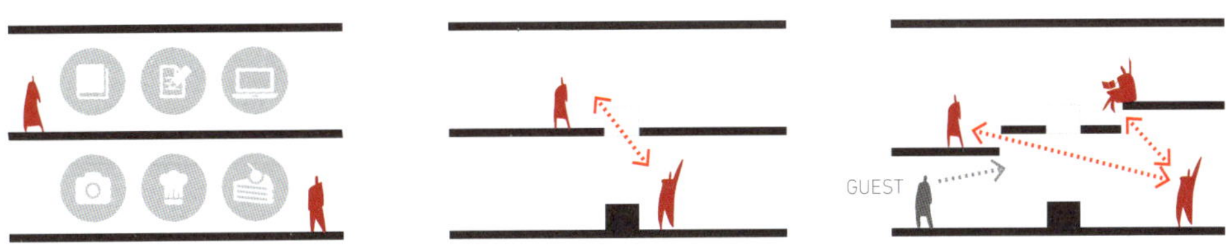

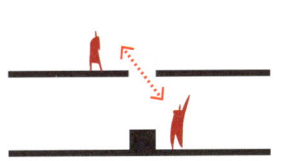
ENABLES VISUAL CONNECTION

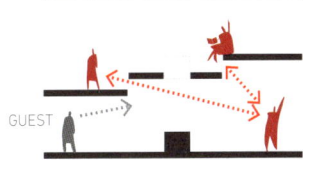
ENABLES VISUAL CONNECTION, YET PROVIDES PRIVACY

JB HOUSE

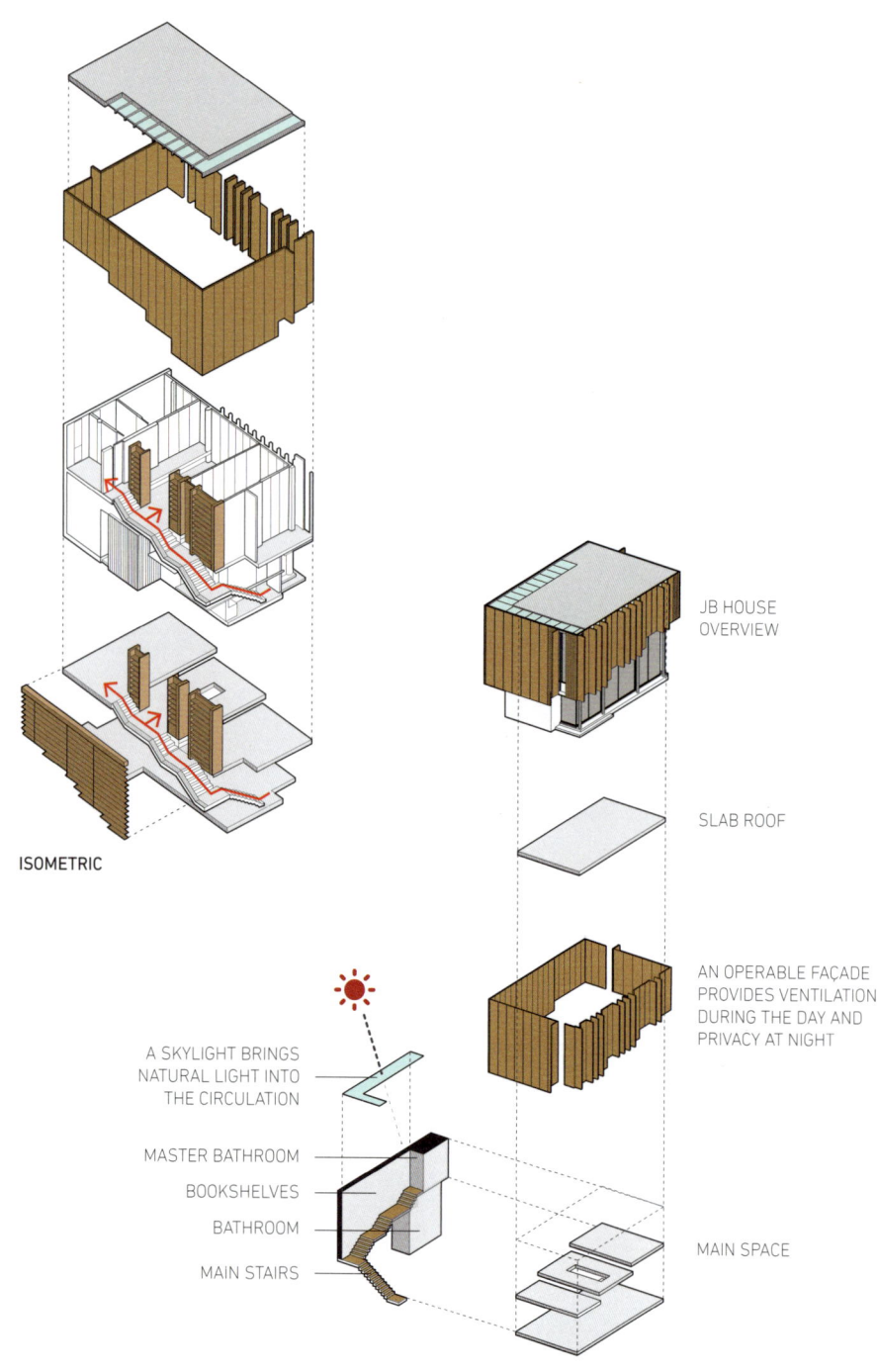

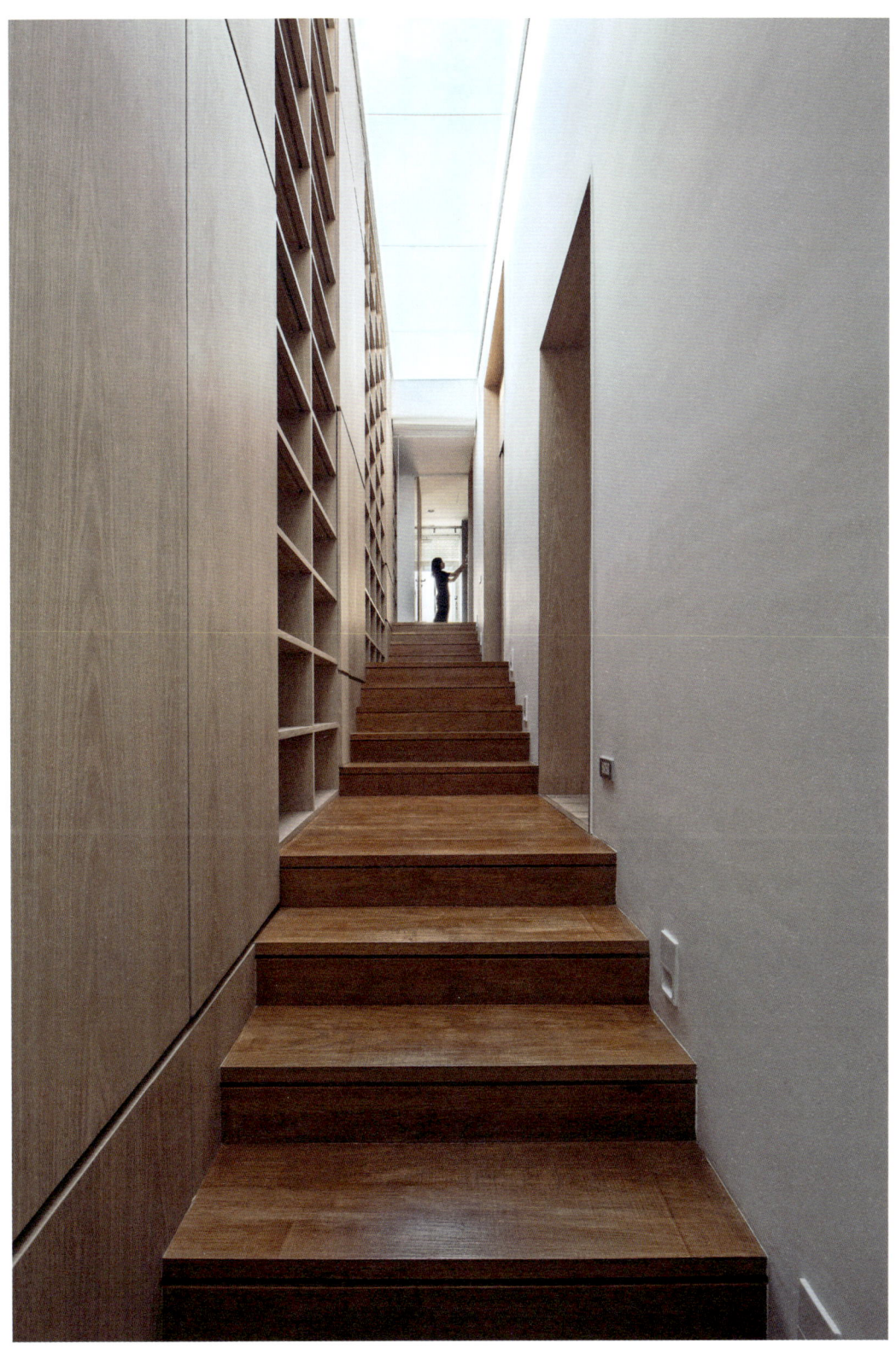

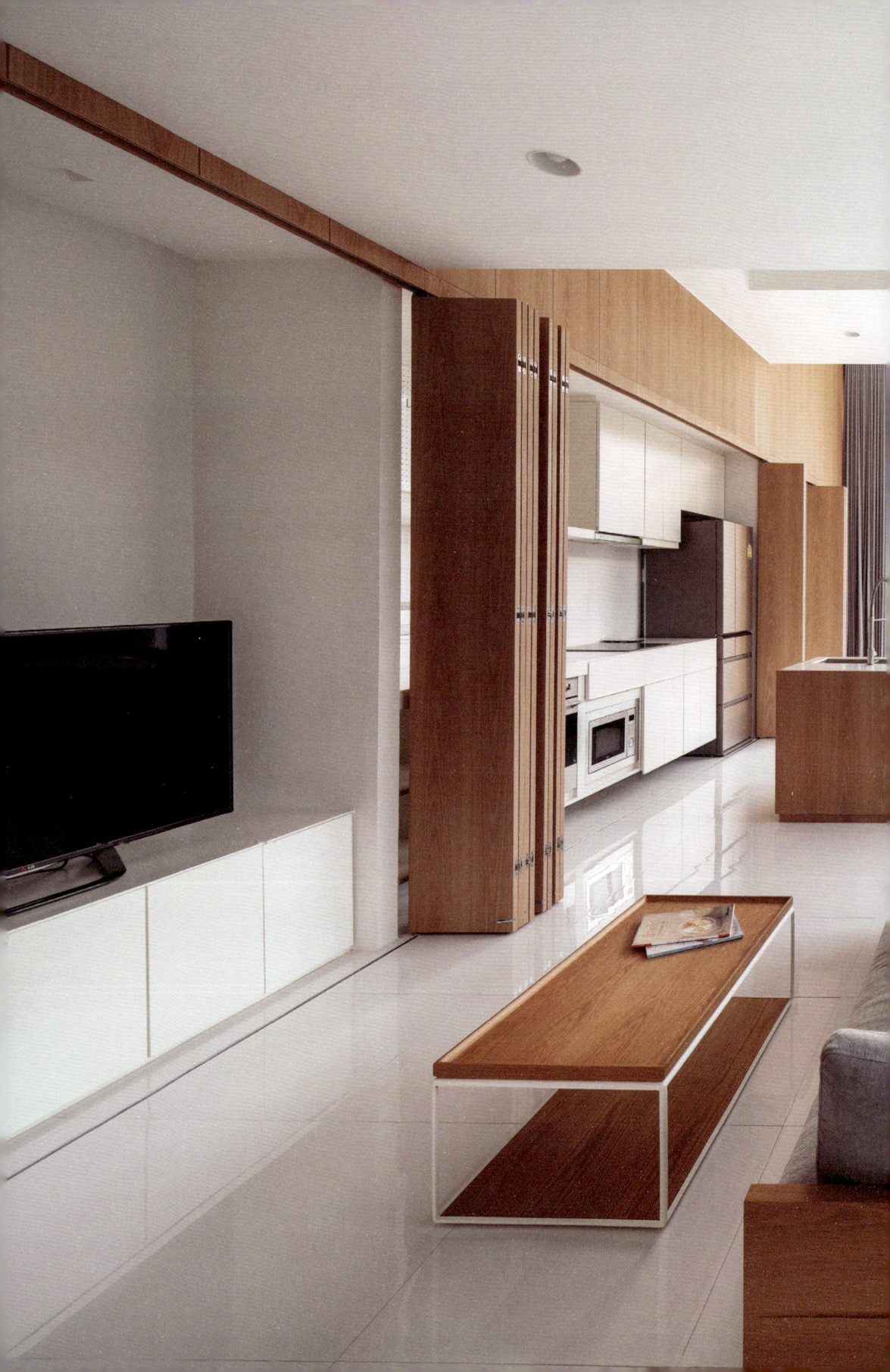

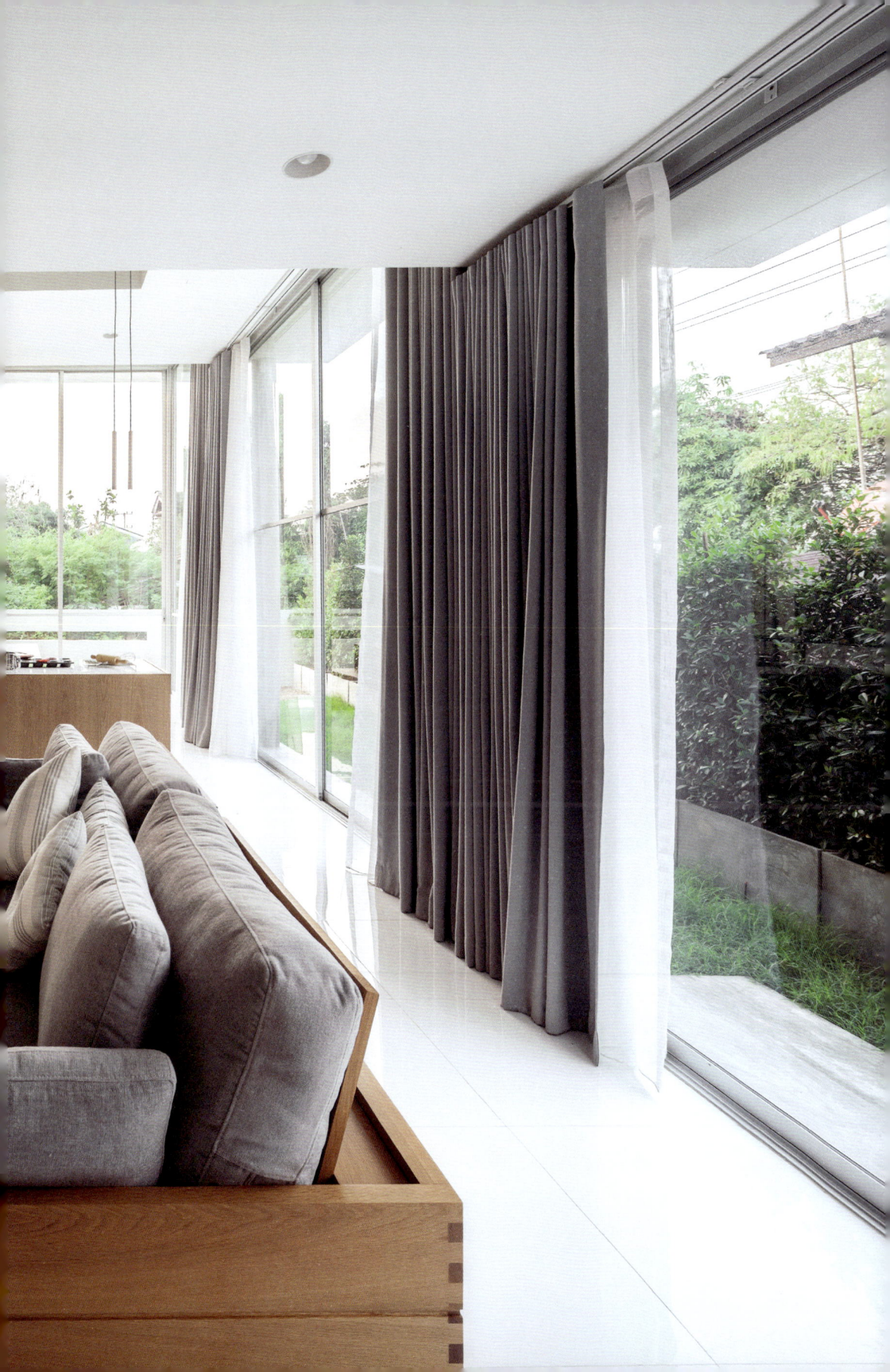

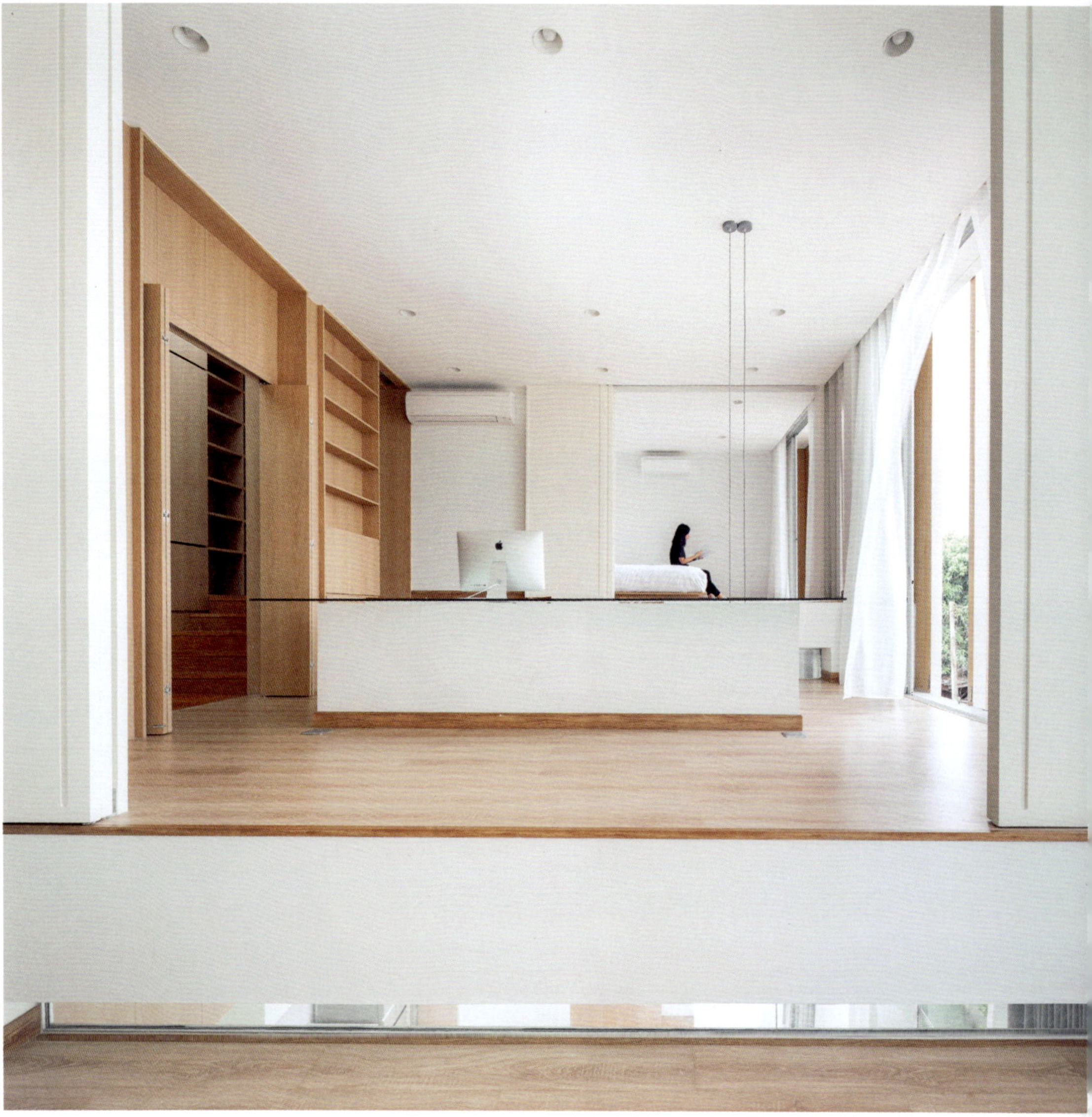

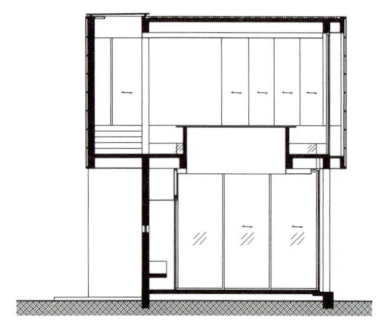
CROSS SECTION

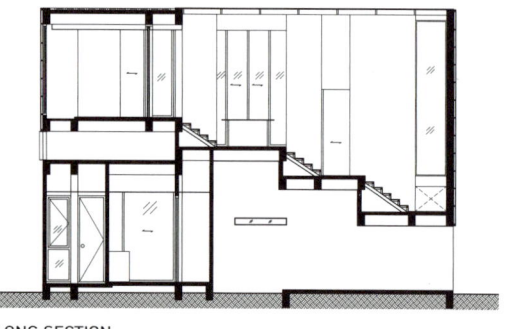
LONG SECTION

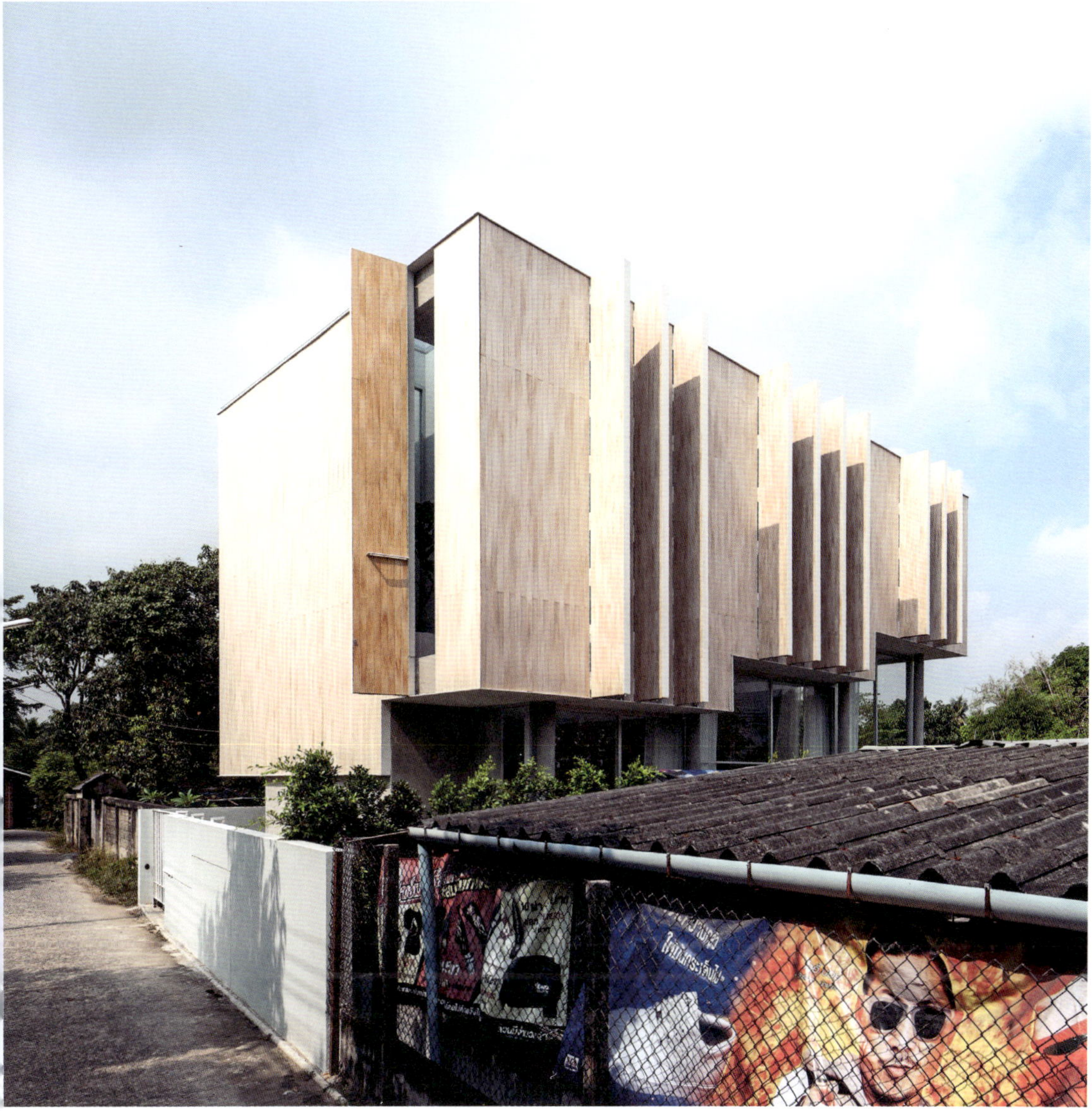

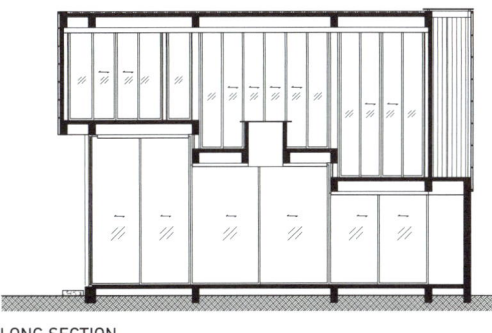
LONG SECTION

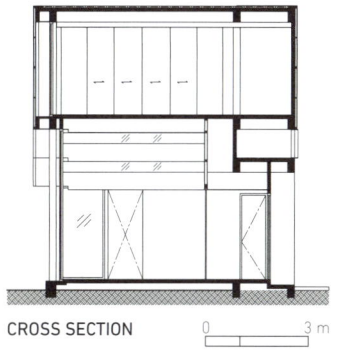
CROSS SECTION 0 3 m

JB HOUSE

Suriyawong, Bangkok, Thailand, 2015

SIRI HOUSE

SIRI House is a renovation project that transforms a commercial building into a viable accommodation that serves a family of four siblings and their future extended families. The existing commercial building is over 40 years old and it has a trapezoid-like plan that narrows sharply toward the back of the building. The main challenge was in maximizing the available space effectively to provide each sibling with a compact, private unit comprising a rest area, a pantry, bedrooms, as well as a living room; more importantly, the units needed to have a generous flow of natural light.

Building upon the owners' requests to convert each floor into an individual unit, two-story units with different space articulations are designed for each member based on the concept of the well-known puzzle game *Tetris*. In the game, when a piece does not fit in the allocated space of the puzzle, an empty space is created as the piece attaches itself to build the puzzle. Sparked by that arrangement, the units are constructed around a central void, allowing the inhabitants visual interaction with each other as they move about their space through the day. The central void also serves as one of two inner courtyards, and doubles as a lightwell channeling natural light into the units. The other courtyard is at the rear of the building; developing the design in this way effectively eliminates the challenge of insufficient natural light—a common problem faced in commercial buildings of similar design.

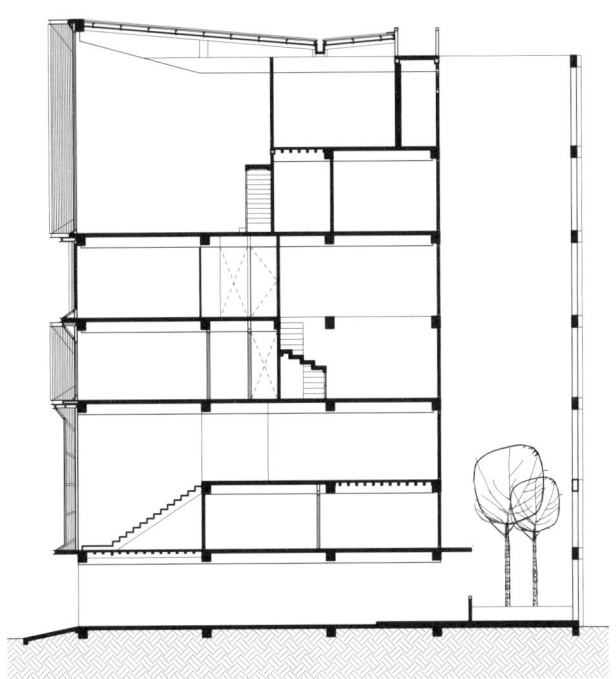

LONG SECTION

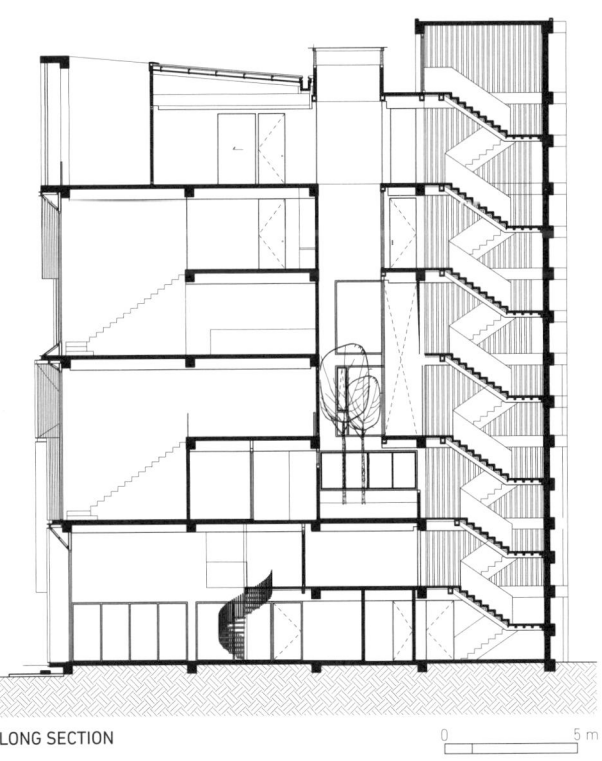

LONG SECTION

0 5 m

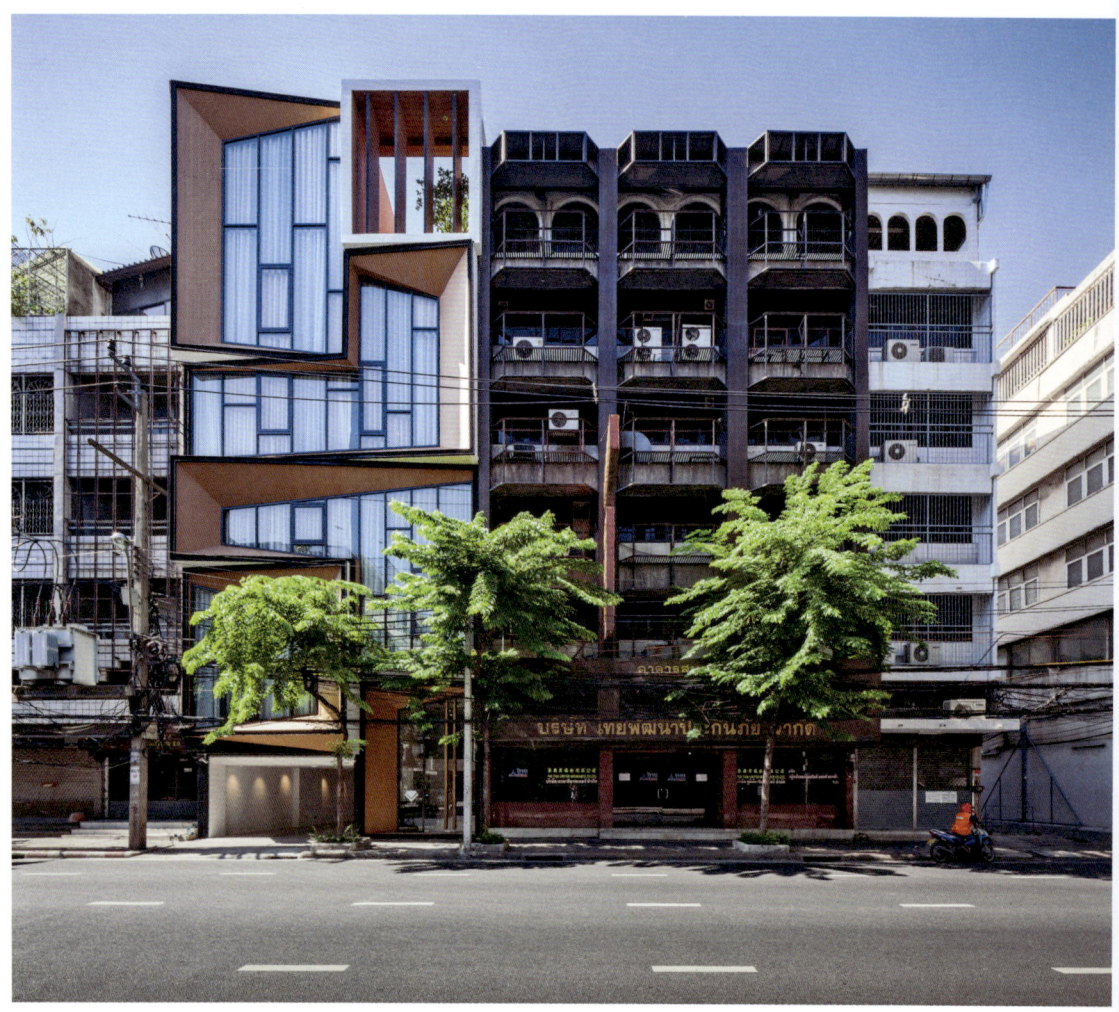

The main entrance to the units is at the rear of the building, grouped with the elevator and stairs. The common area and family dining room sit on the top floor, designed as a dual-storied space, while the other stories house the living units.

To achieve the *Tetris*-like overlapping structure, and to accommodate the addition of bathrooms and a lightwell, part of the floor area was removed. This required the inclusion of a new steel frame to strengthen the structure of the aged, weathered building. The façade shows off the composition of the units in an eye-catching *Tetris*-like formation, and presents the family's jewelry business in a two-storied boutique on the first floor.

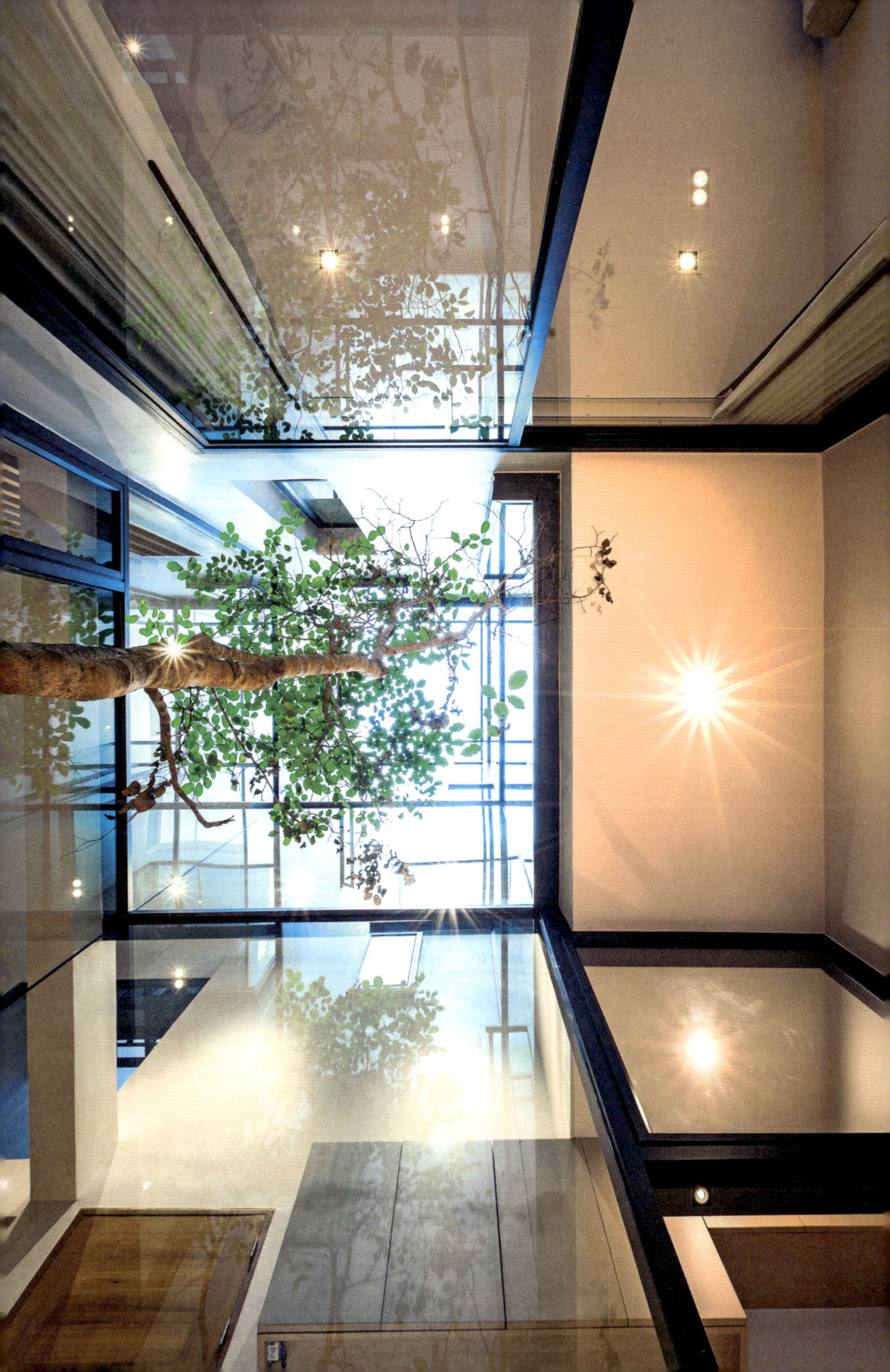

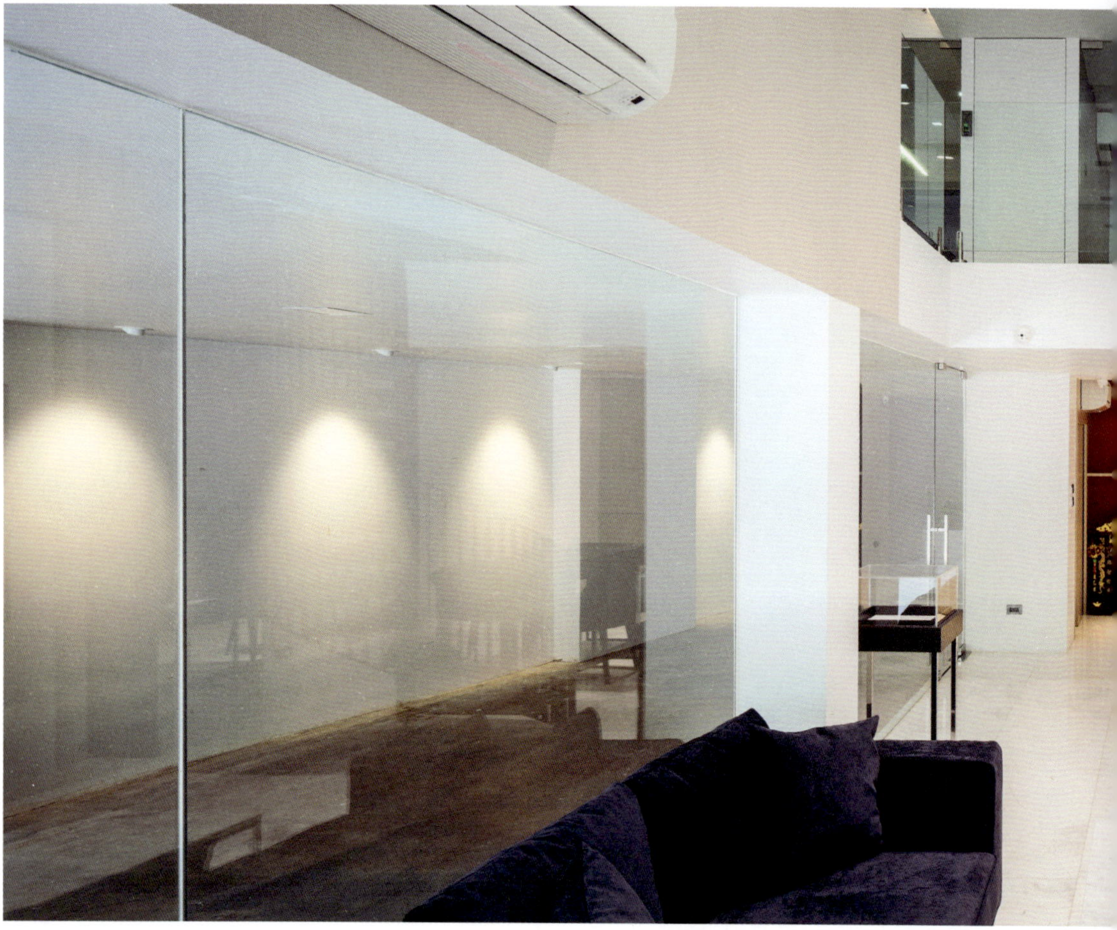

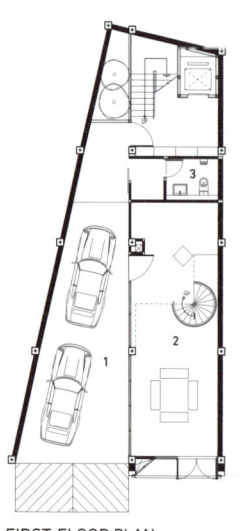
FIRST-FLOOR PLAN

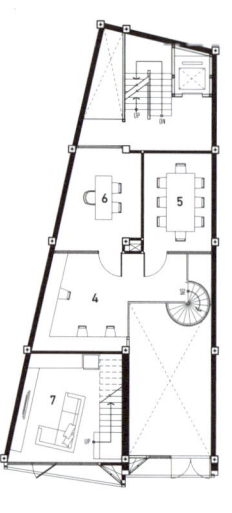
SECOND-FLOOR PLAN

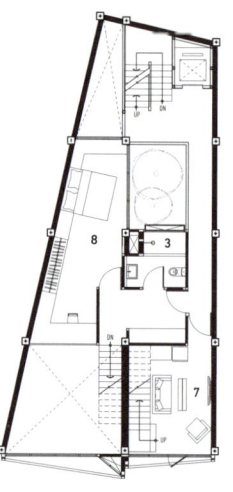
THIRD-FLOOR PLAN

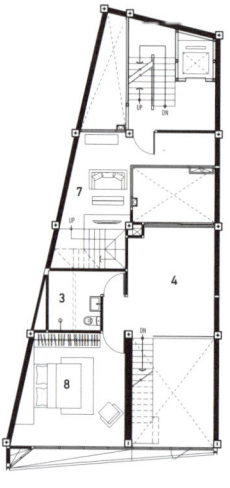
FOURTH-FLOOR PLAN

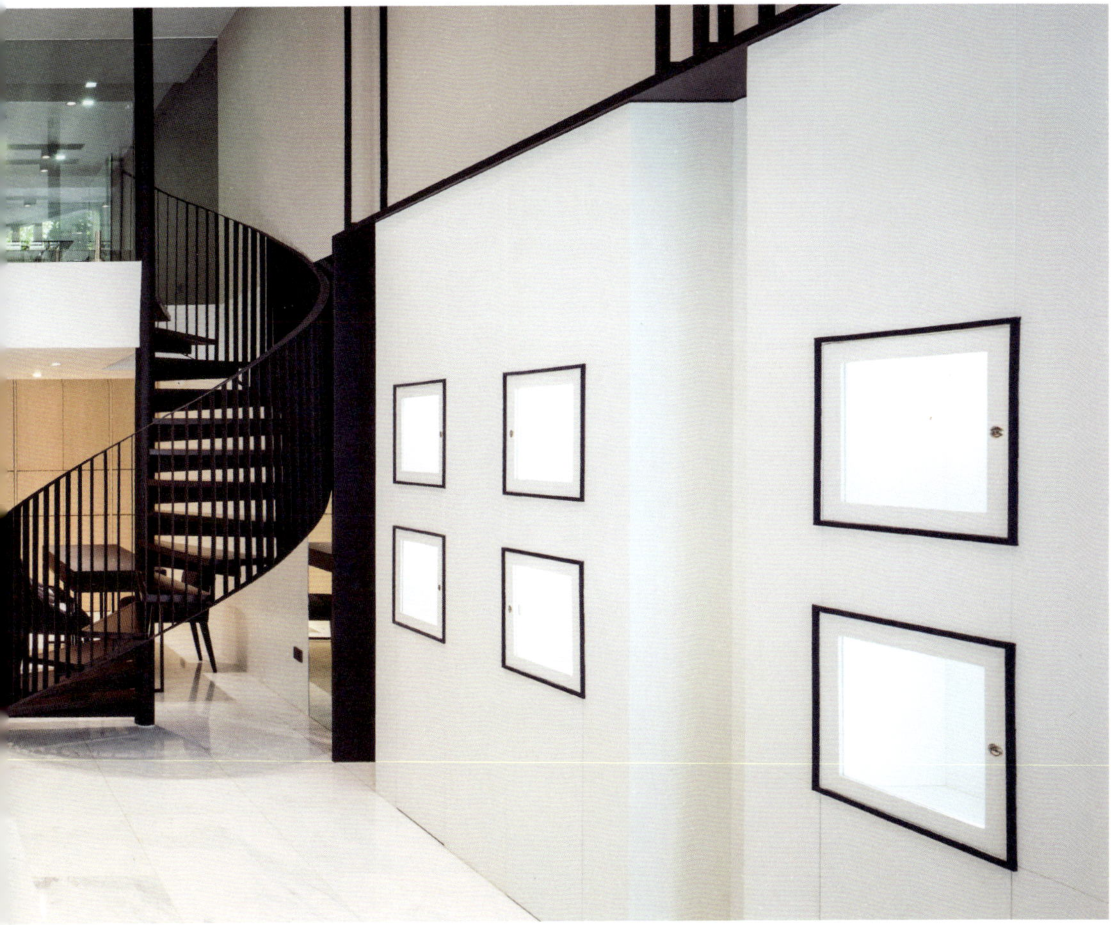

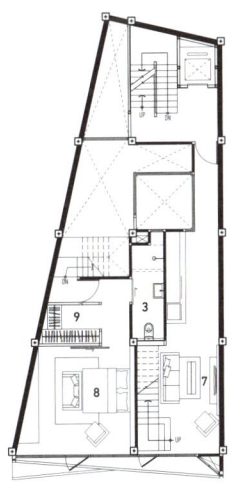

FIFTH-FLOOR PLAN

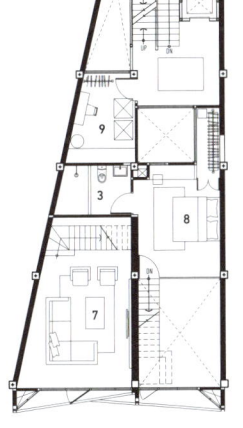

SIXTH-FLOOR PLAN

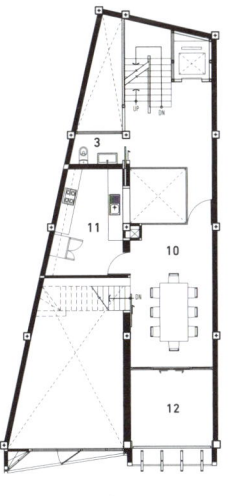

SEVENTH-FLOOR PLAN

1 PARKING
2 JEWELRY SHOP
3 BATHROOM
4 WORKING AREA
5 MEETING ROOM
6 WORKING ROOM
7 LIVING ROOM
8 BEDROOM
9 WALK-IN CLOSET
10 COMMON ROOM/DINING AREA
11 KITCHEN
12 BALCONY

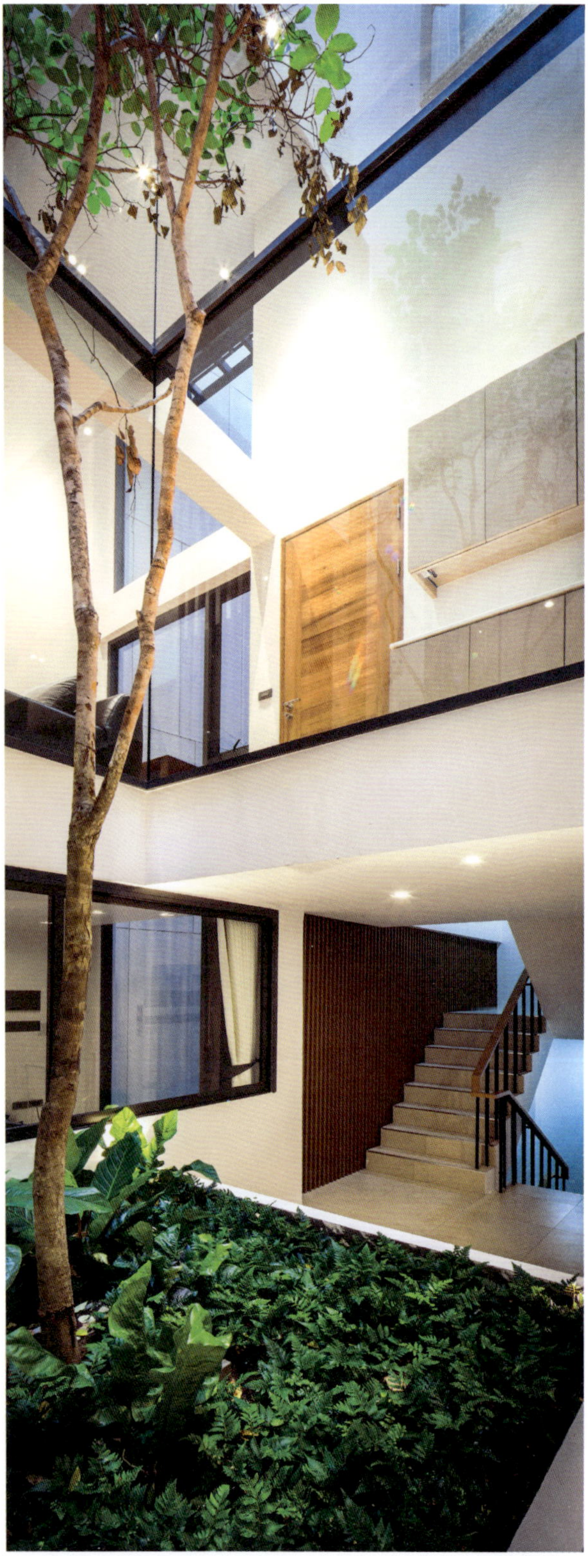

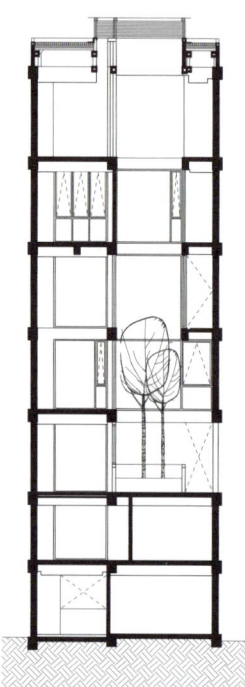

CROSS SECTION

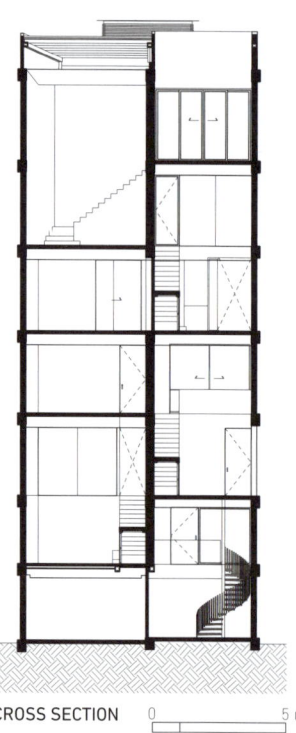

CROSS SECTION 0 5 m

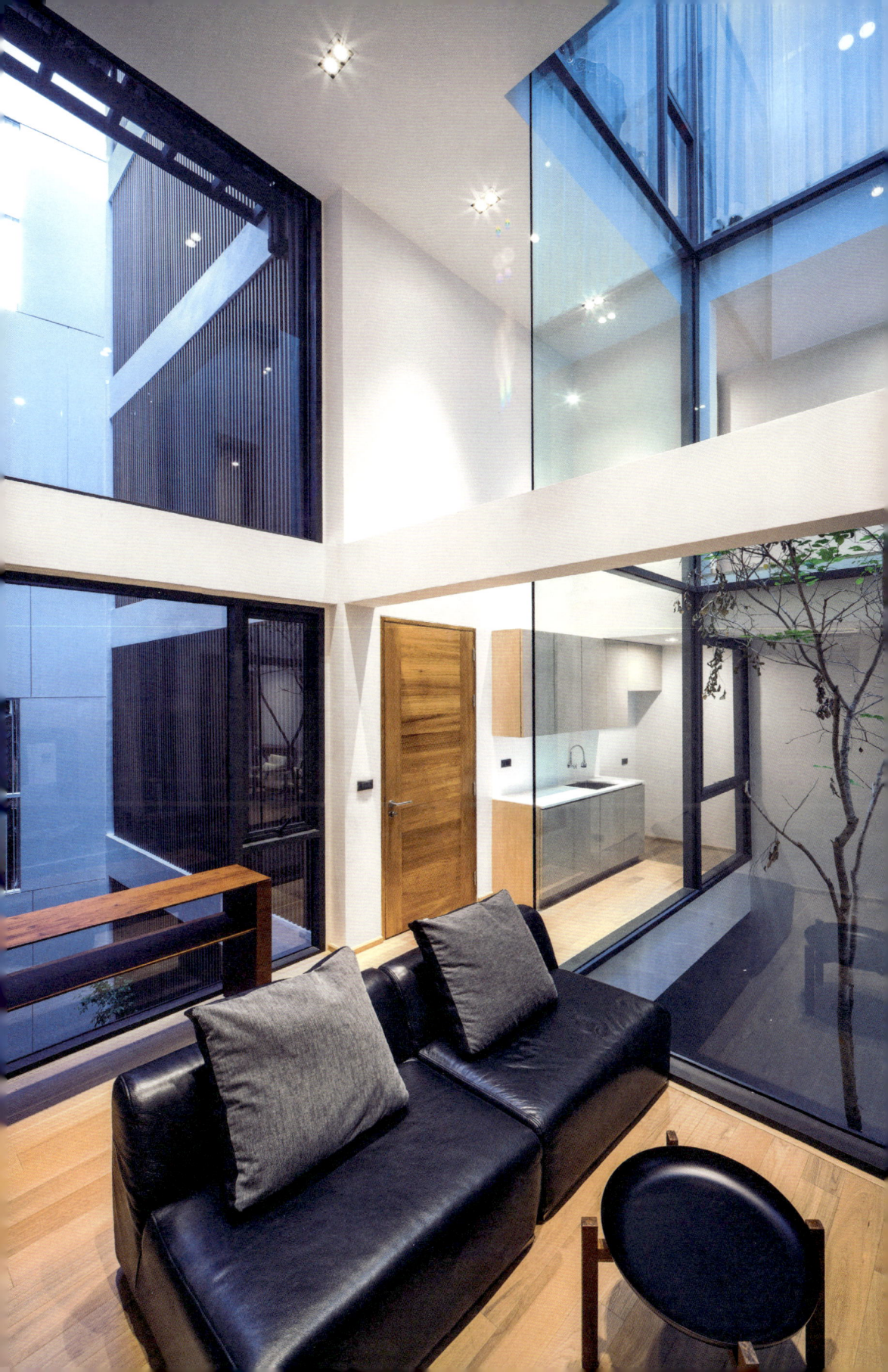

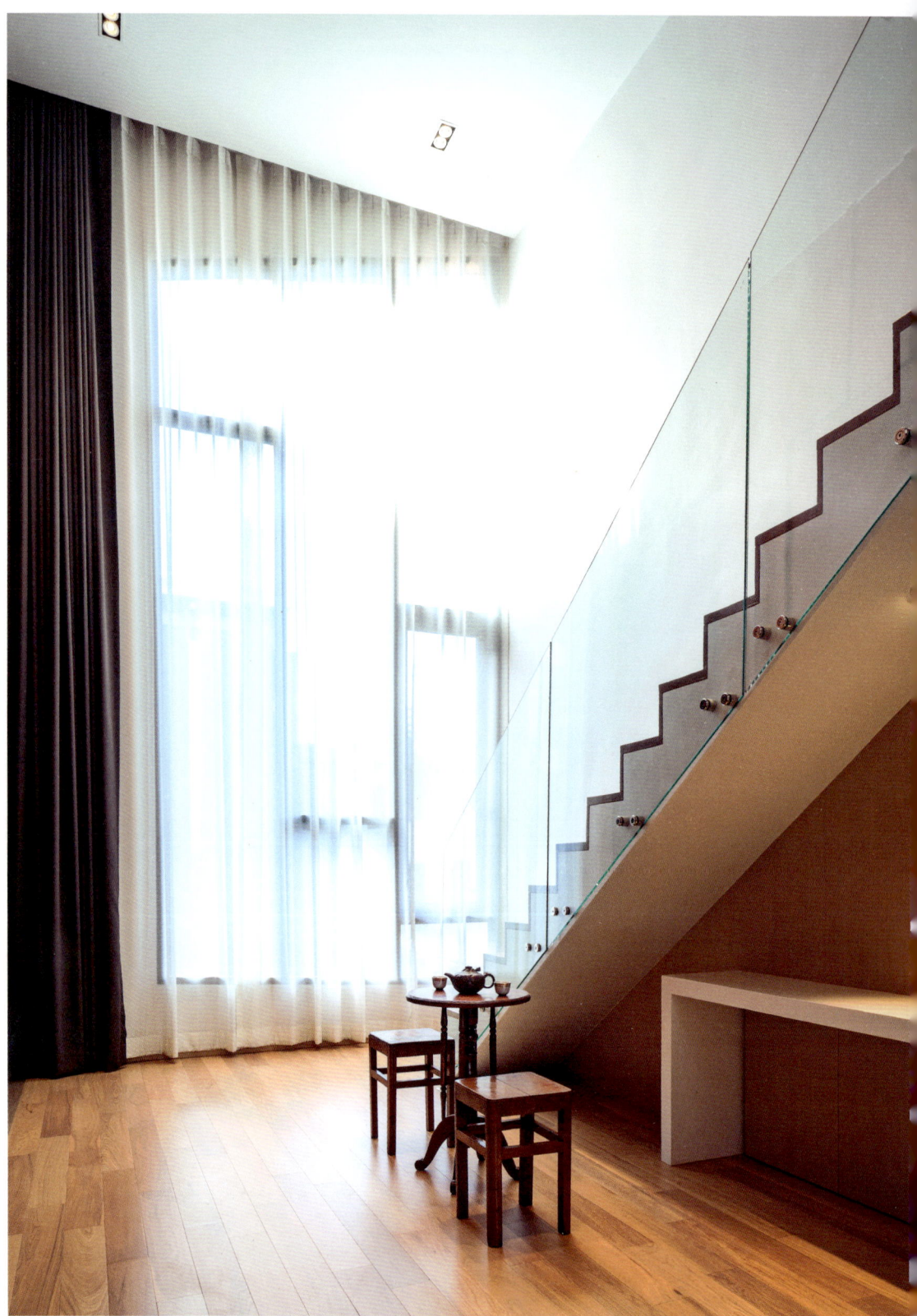

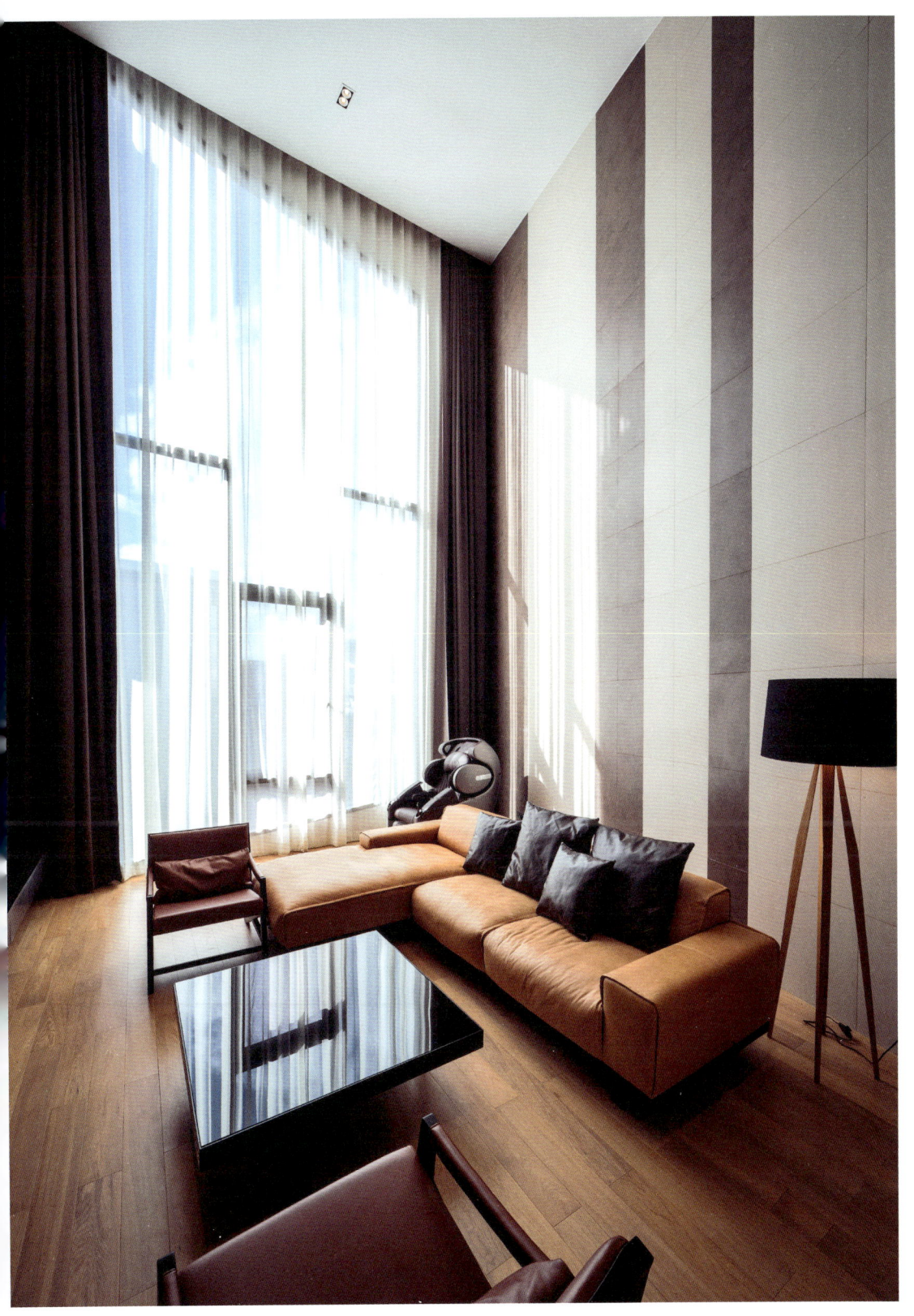

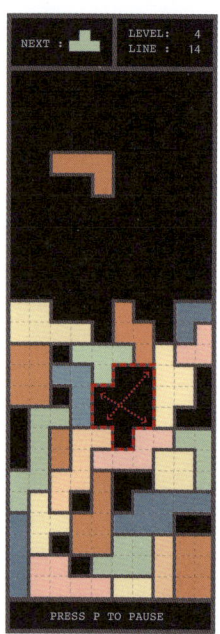

TETRIS-LIKE CONCEPT

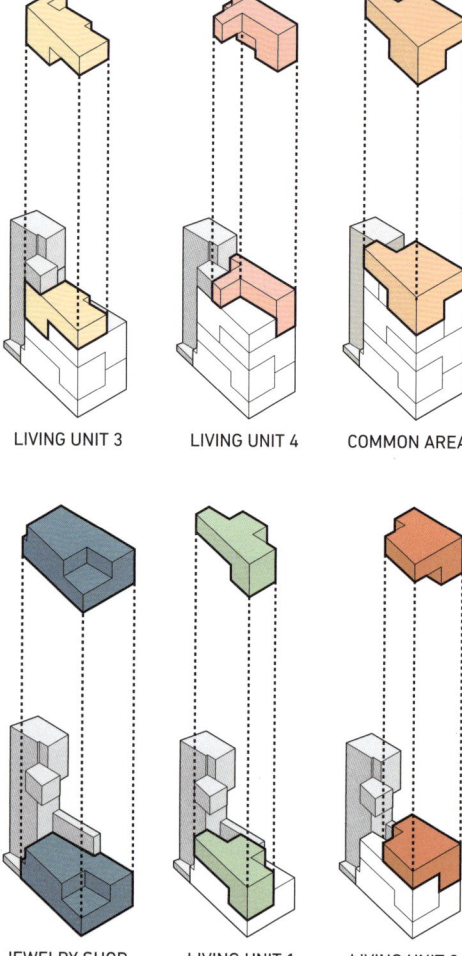

LIVING UNIT 3   LIVING UNIT 4   COMMON AREA

JEWELRY SHOP   LIVING UNIT 1   LIVING UNIT 2

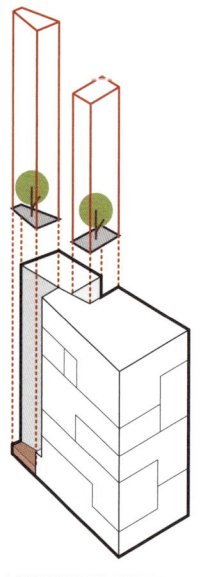

COURTYARDS INSERTED

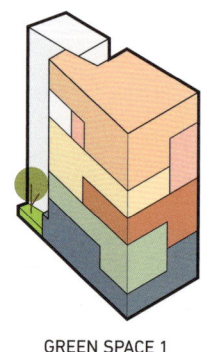

GREEN SPACE 1

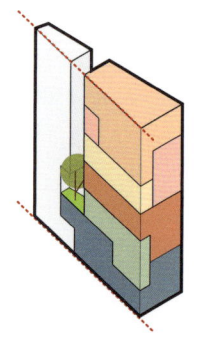

GREEN SPACE 2

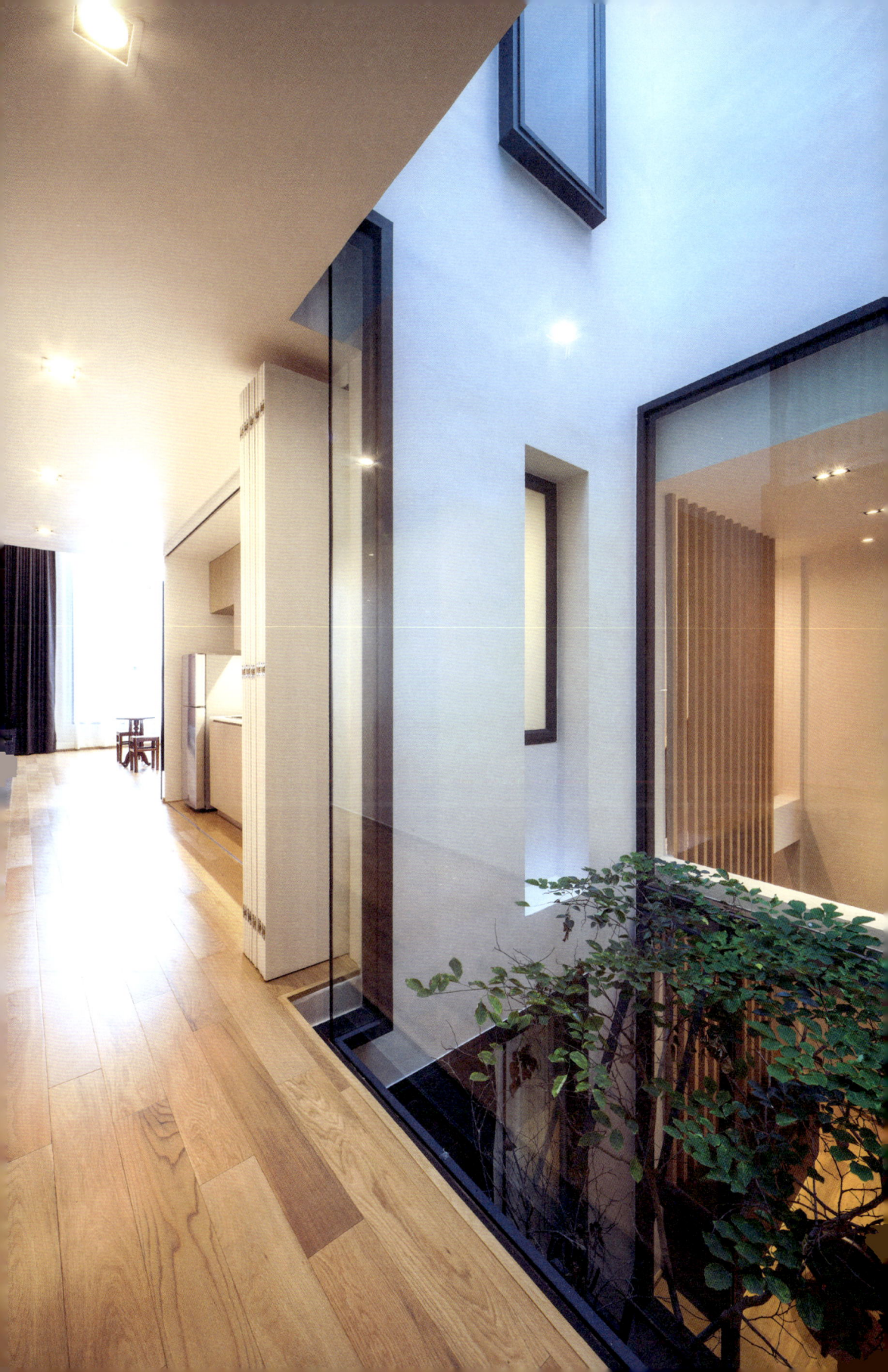

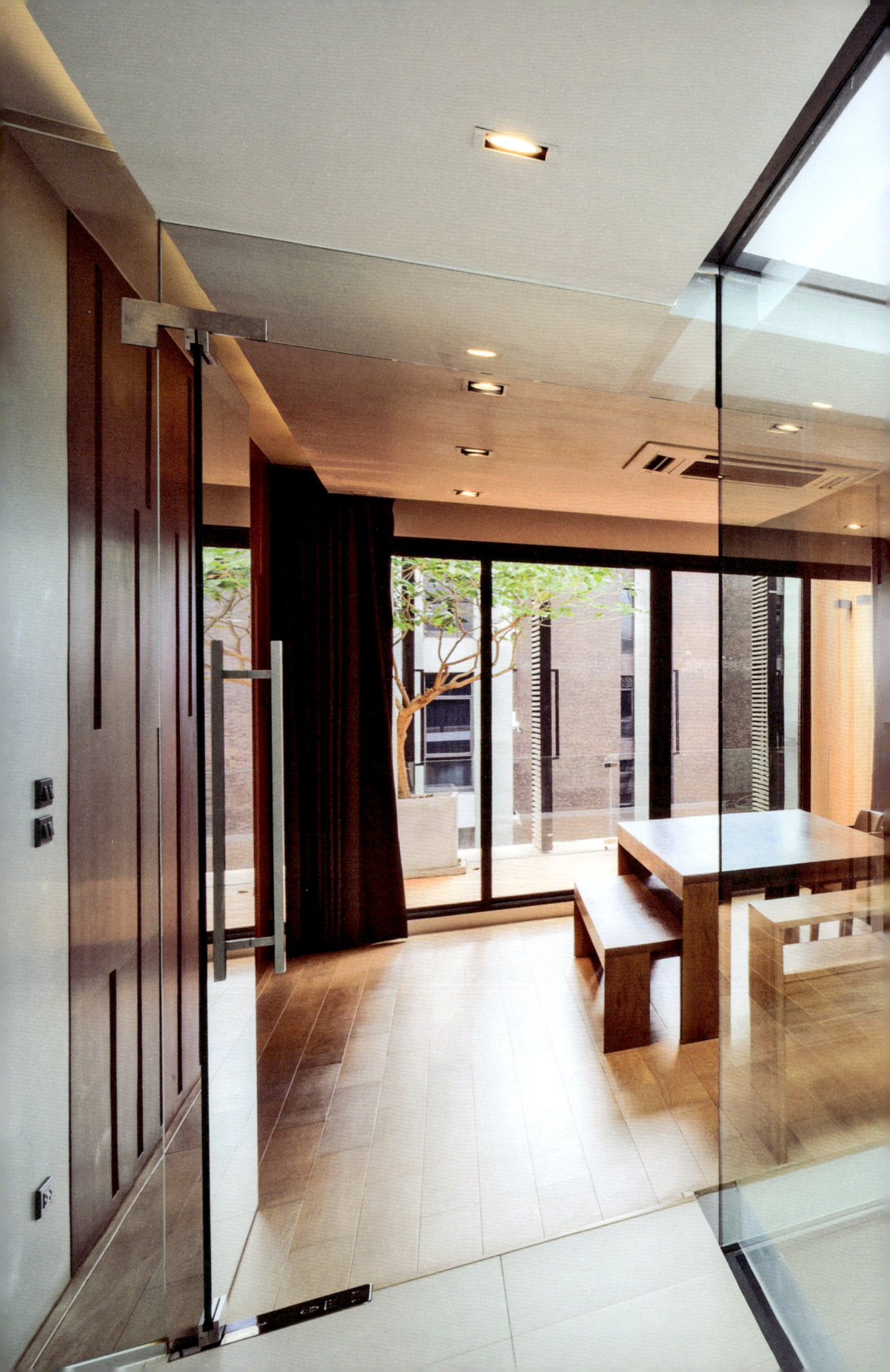

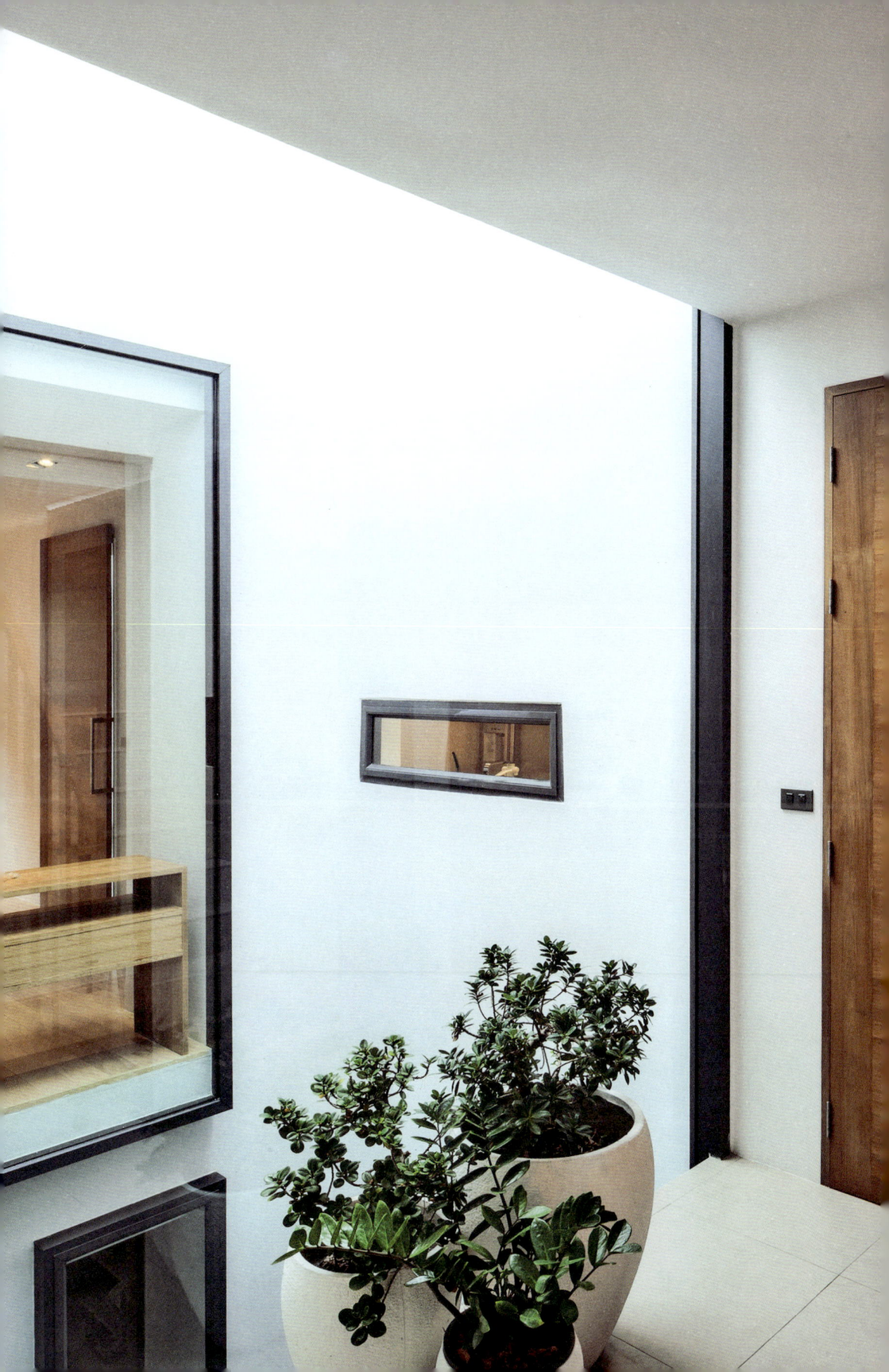

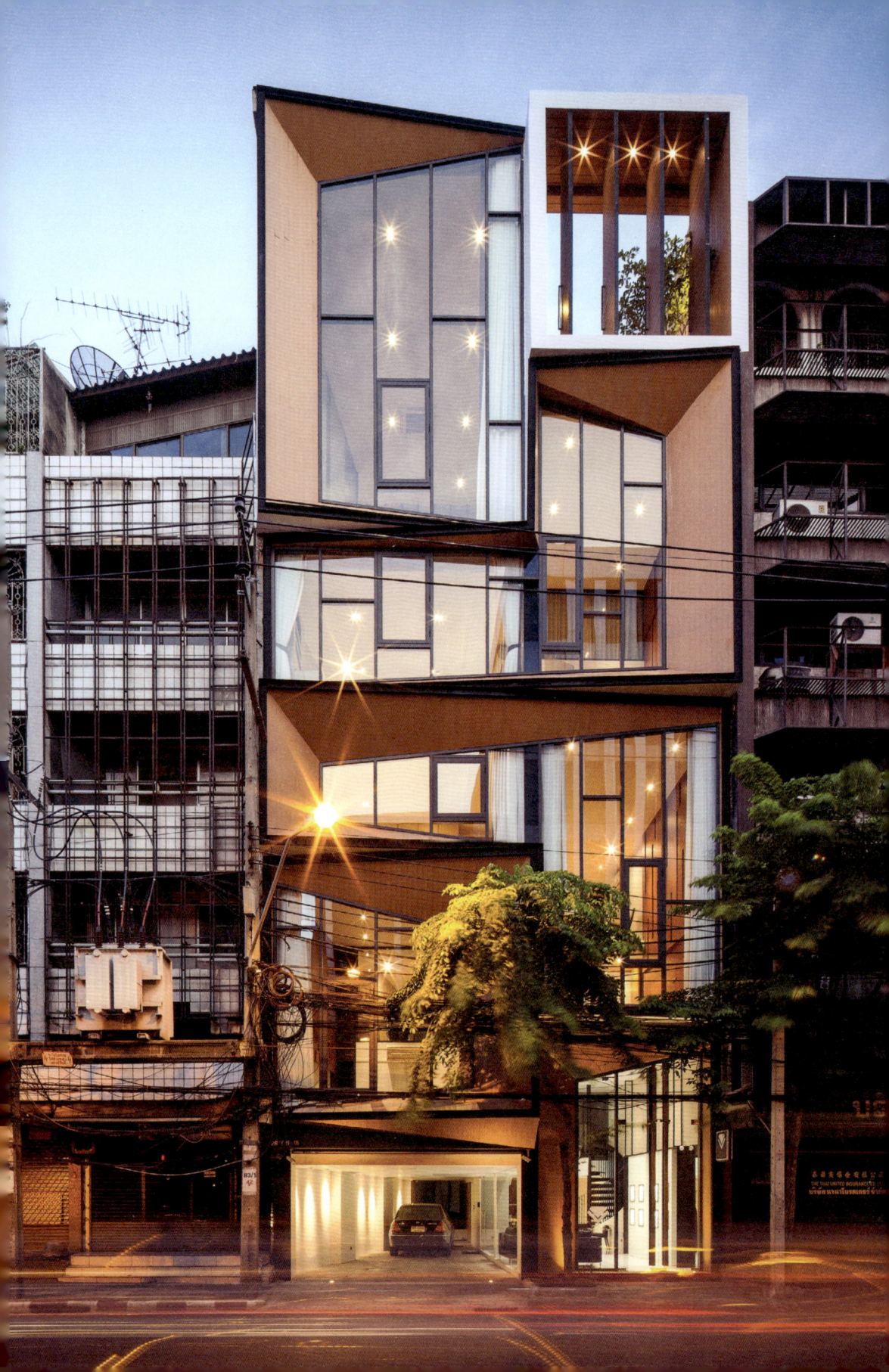

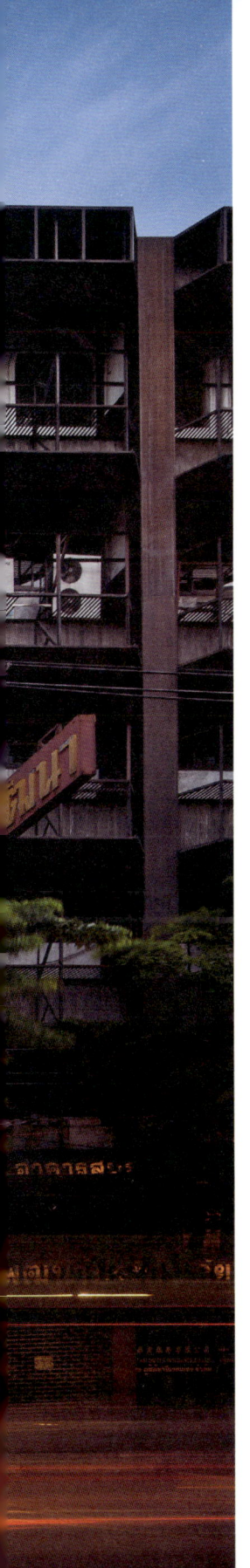
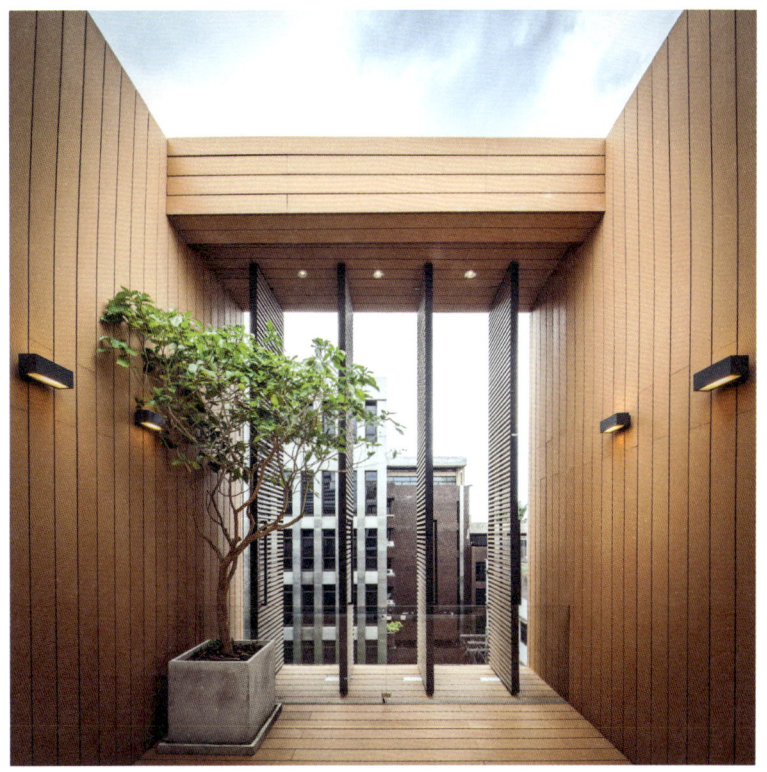
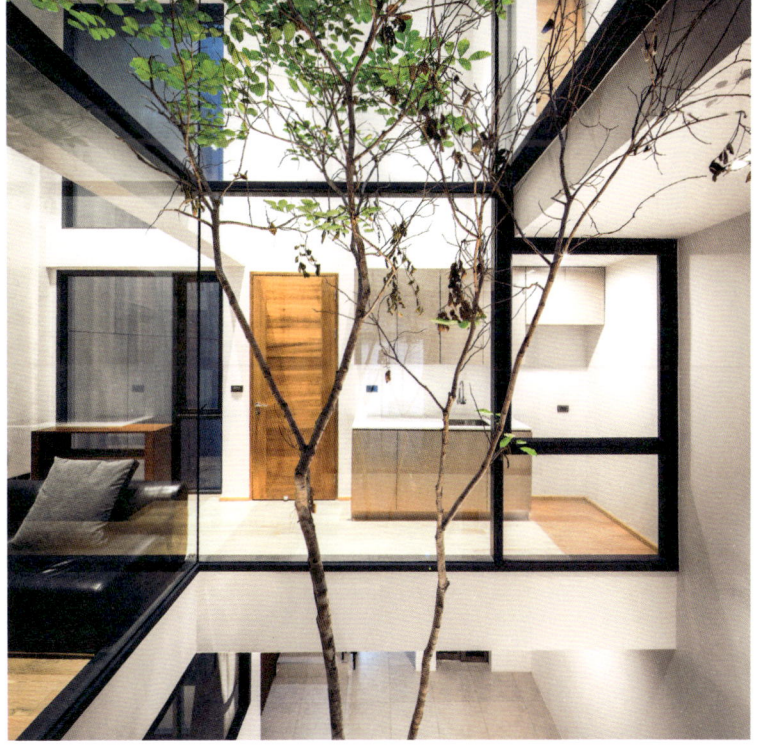

Pak Chong, Nakhon Ratchasima, Thailand, 2015

KA HOUSE

This vacation villa is designed for a couple who enjoys relaxing outdoors. A grand yard, a wide deck, and a pool make great spots for relaxation and time with family. One can lay down with a book and a refreshing cocktail, run about in a game of tag with family, or simply catch a tan while enjoying the calming view toward the nearby lake. The design of KA House began with a simple question: While we acknowledge that a 'home' refers to a space for family members to spend time together, is it necessary for that space to always be enclosed? Could an open space not be as good a home for a family who loves outdoor activities?

Leading with this unconventional approach, the main entrance is set in the perimeter wall. A rustic fence trails the access road to the main entrance and guides the vista from a rural scenery to the urban outline of the house. Upon entering, the sequence of the space gradually shifts and reveals the building, the interior, and the grand yard beyond enclosed within the compound. Inside, the design plays with perspective and presents the interior yard, which faces the lake, more like the front of the house, and the front access more like the rear. Emphasizing this altered perspective is a second entrance access from the yard. The parking space is set a half-level underground to take advantage of the site's slope. Doing so enables the continuity of the vista, as well as hides the house from the "disorder" of the outside world.

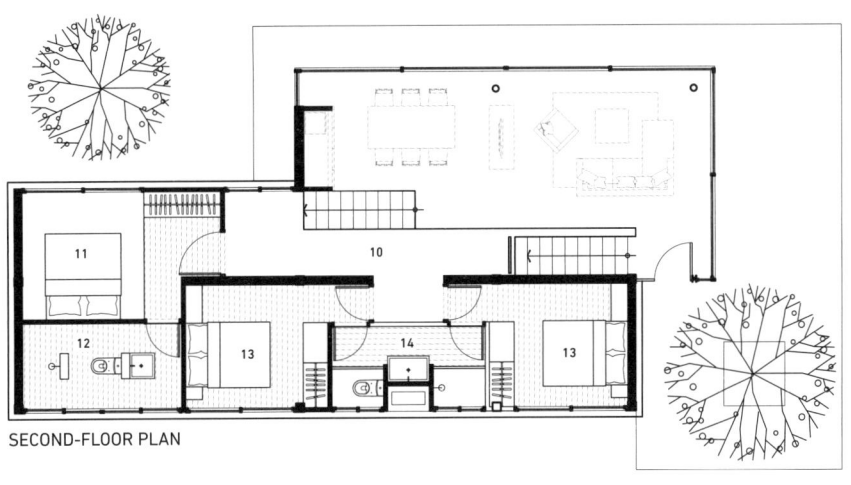

SECOND-FLOOR PLAN

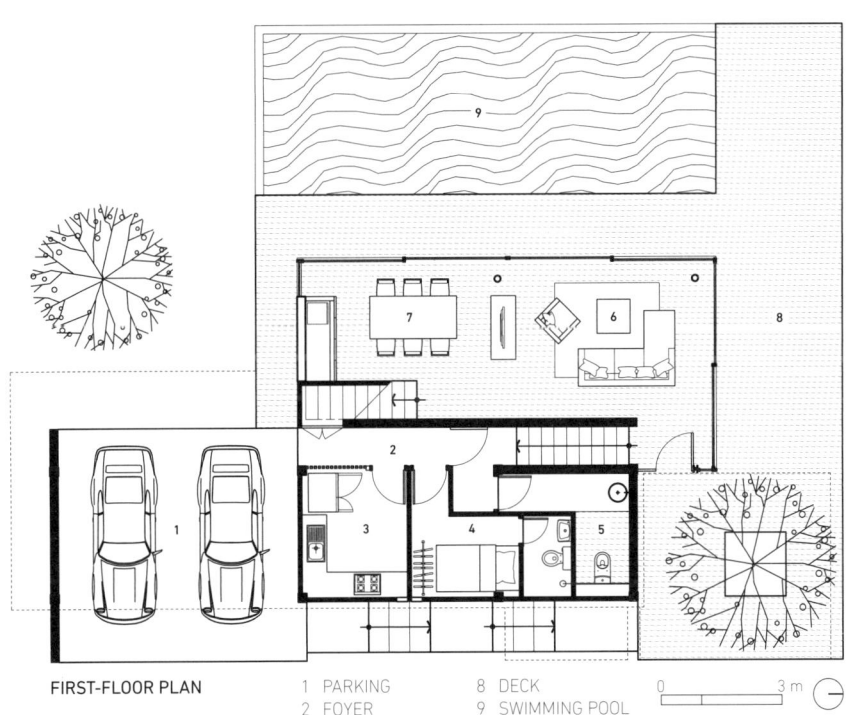

FIRST-FLOOR PLAN

1 PARKING
2 FOYER
3 KITCHEN
4 MAID'S ROOM
5 BATHROOM
6 LIVING ROOM
7 DINING ROOM
8 DECK
9 SWIMMING POOL
10 CORRIDOR
11 MASTER BEDROOM
12 MASTER BATHROOM
13 BEDROOM
14 BATHROOM

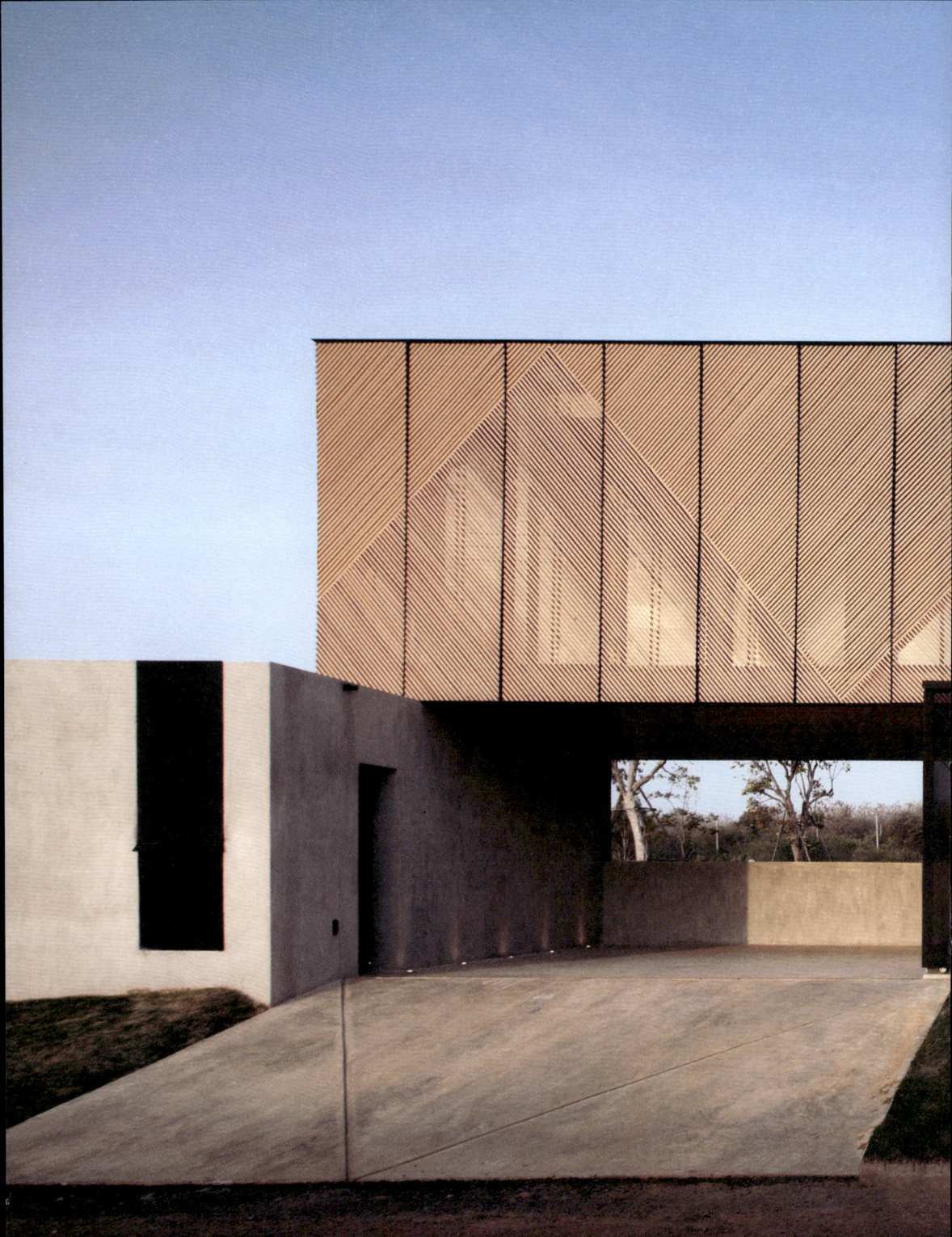

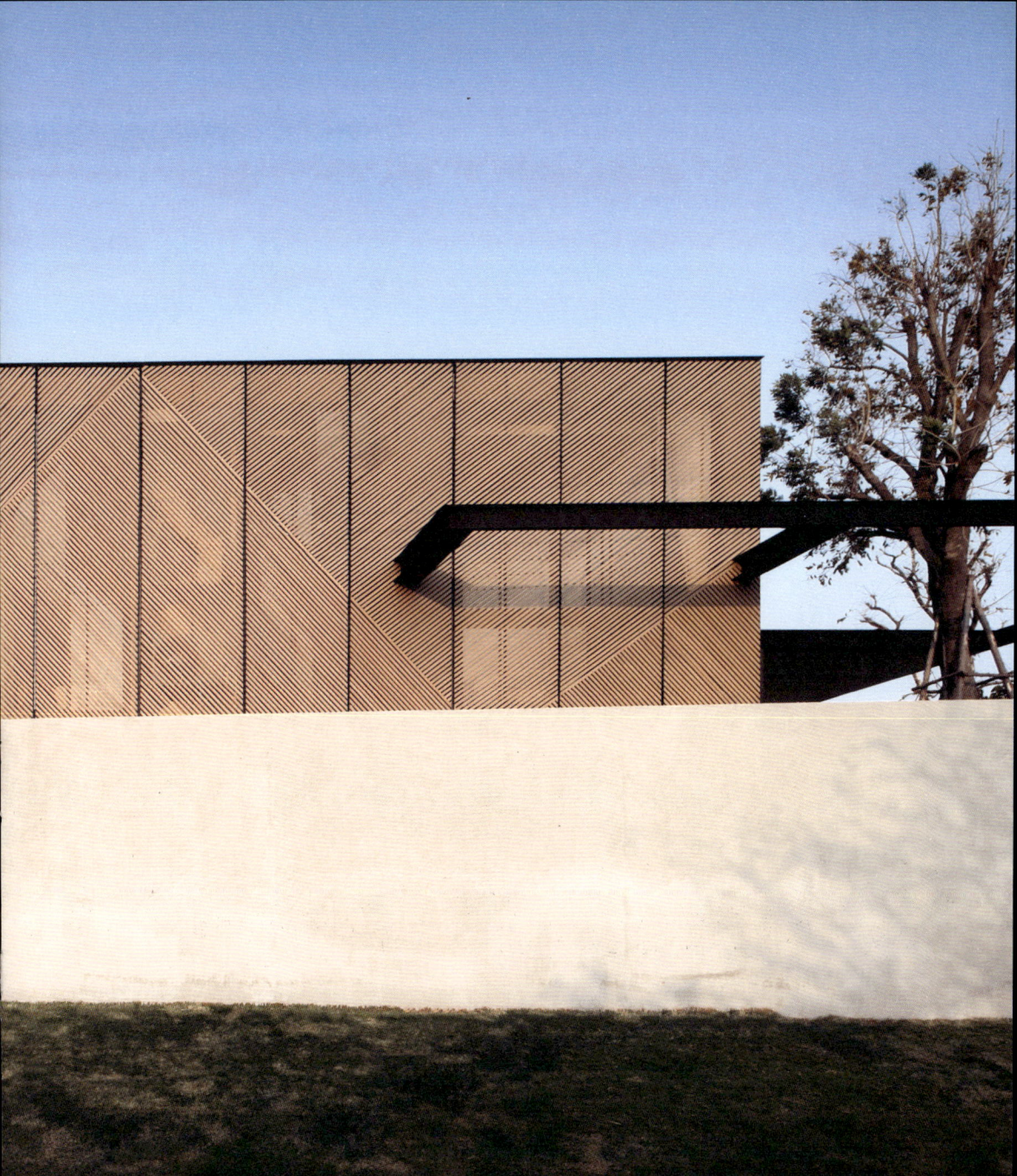

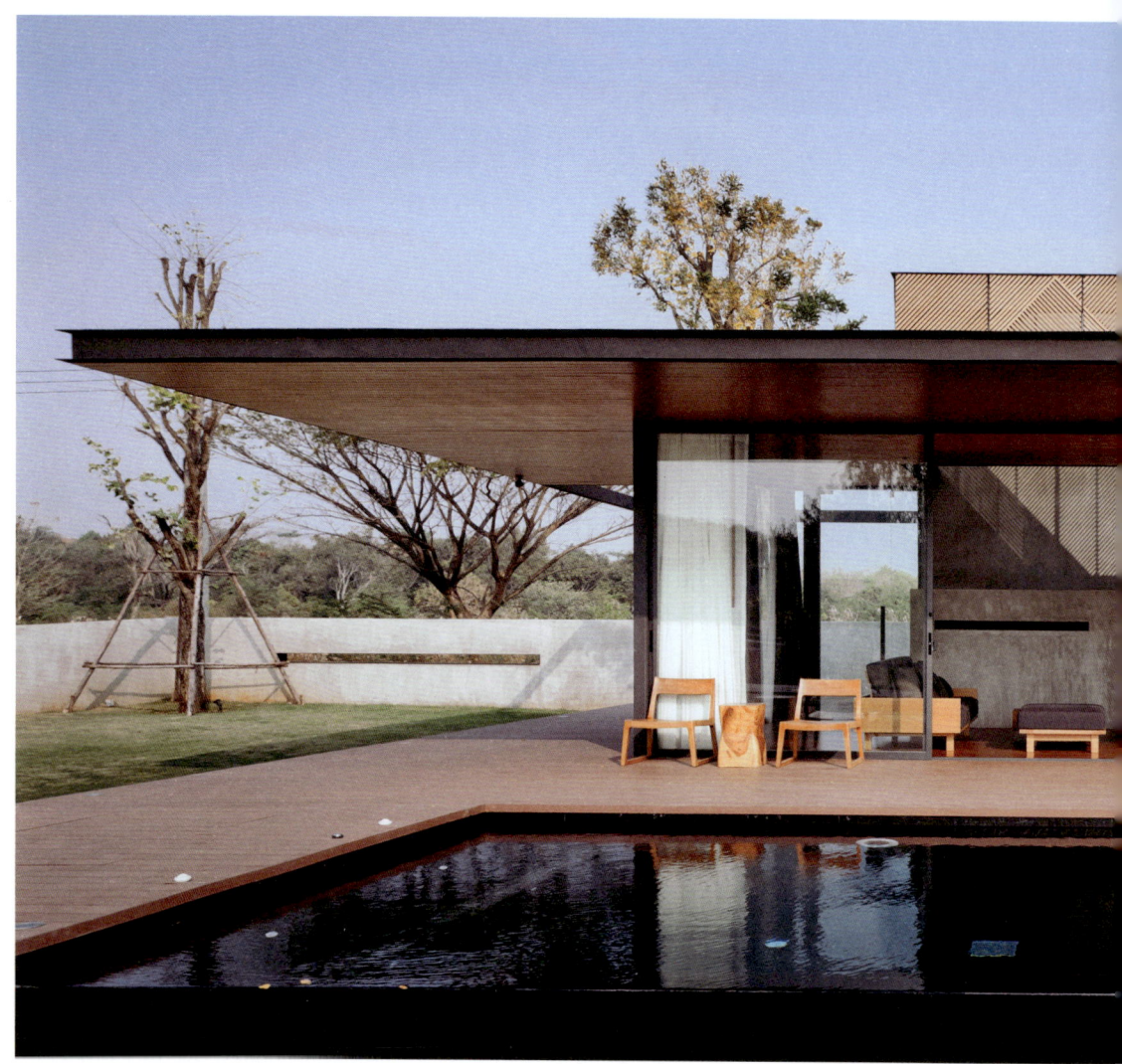

The main building is divided into two levels. The lower level contains the living and dining space, and extends out to the spacious deck; the mezzanine level houses the bedrooms. Activities around the house, from the mezzanine to the pool, can be easily observed, highlighting the home's openness, while also encouraging togetherness and involvement as everyone is on track with what is happening around them.

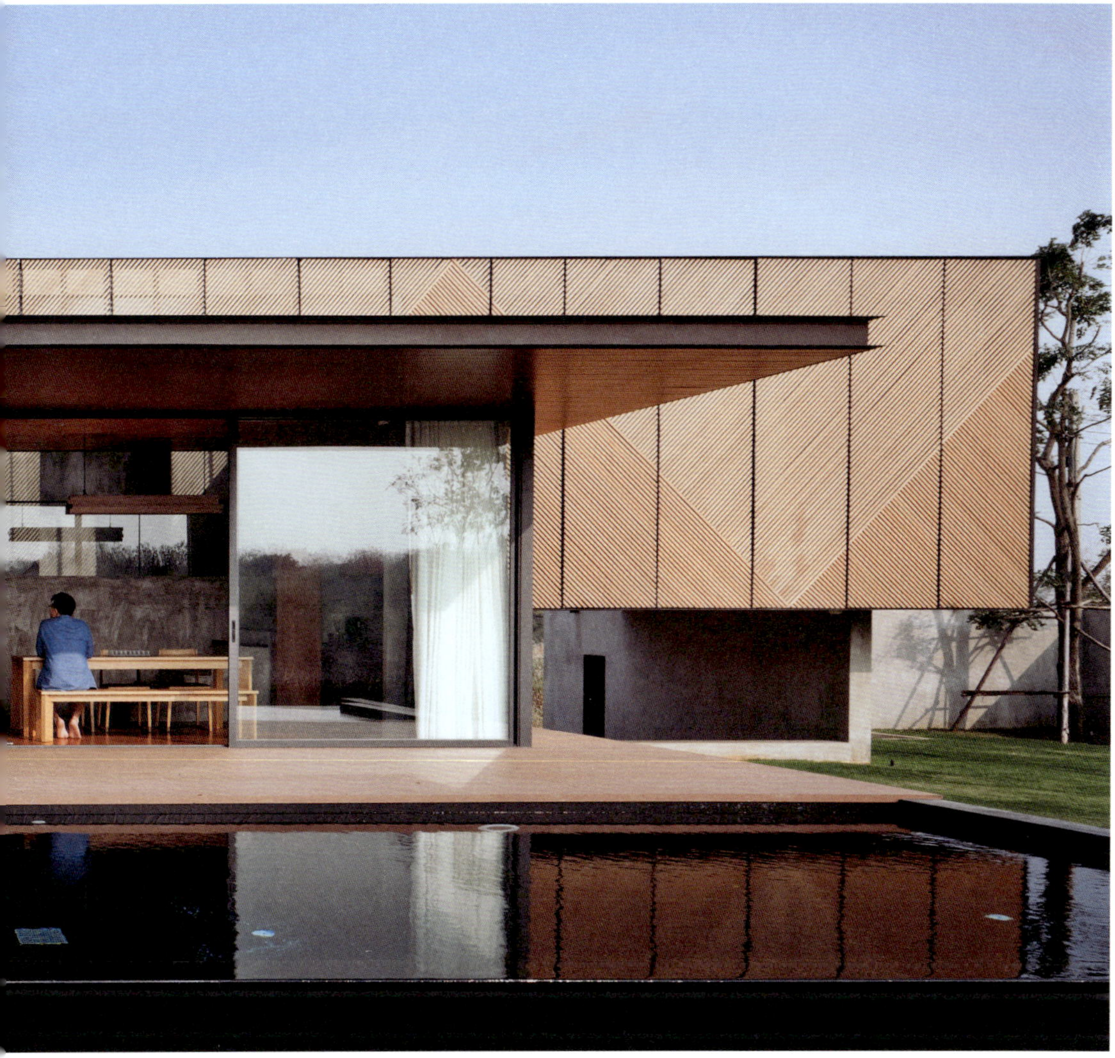

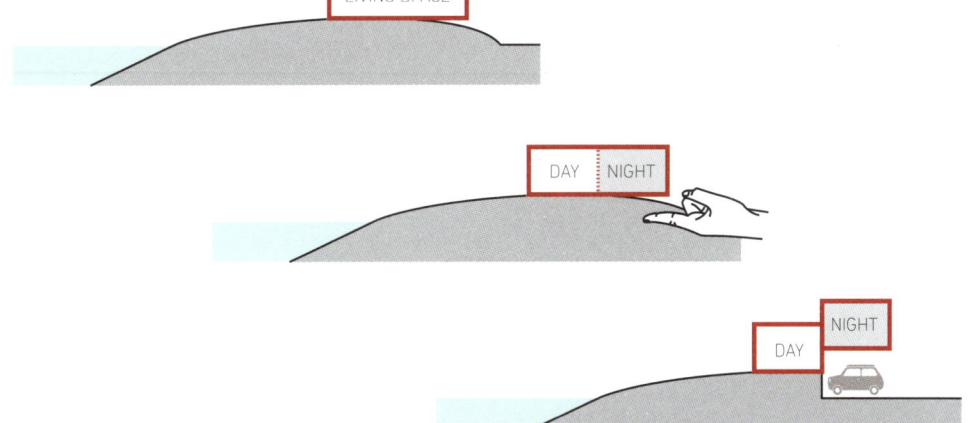

LIVING SPACE

DAY | NIGHT

DAY | NIGHT

KA HOUSE

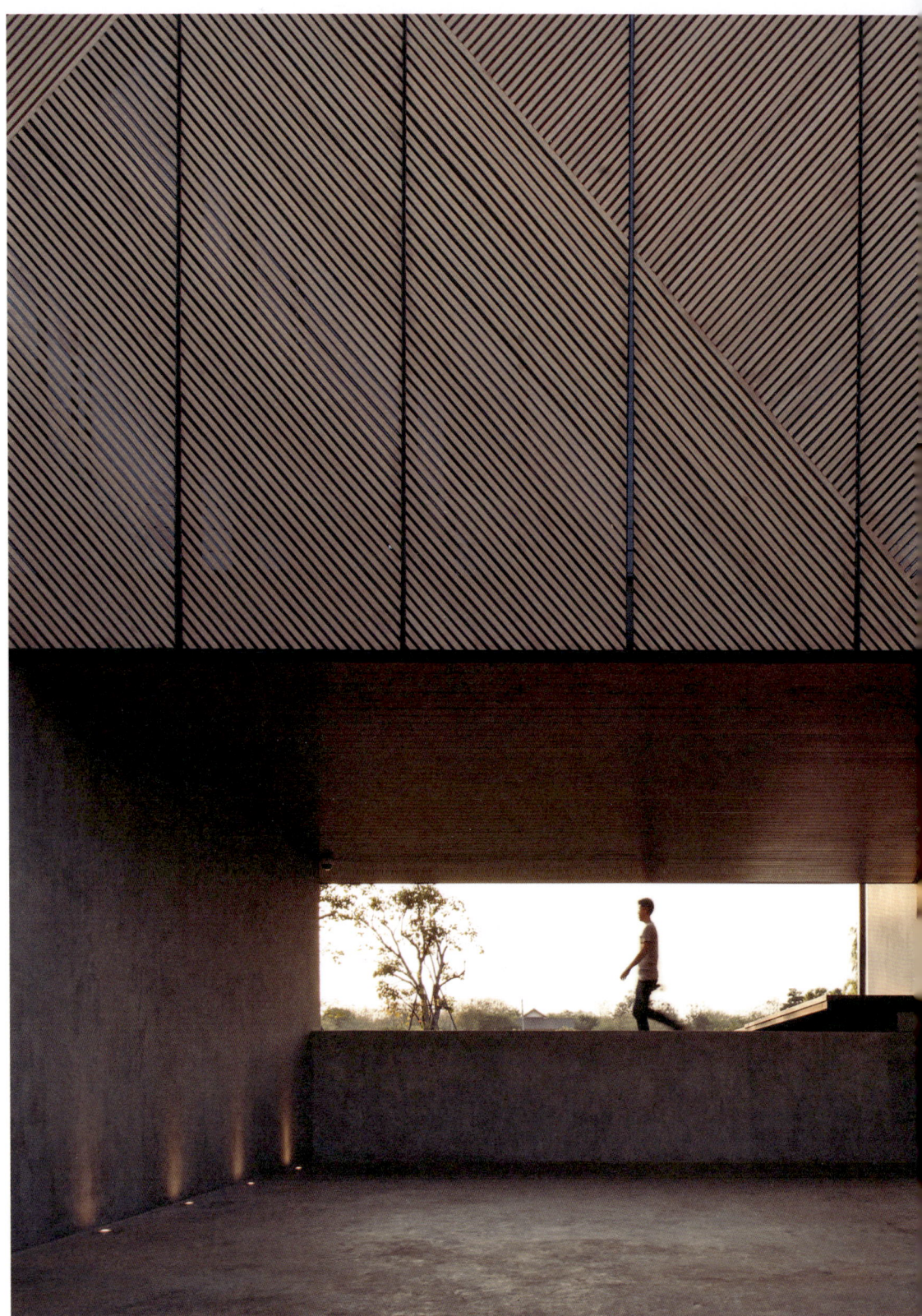

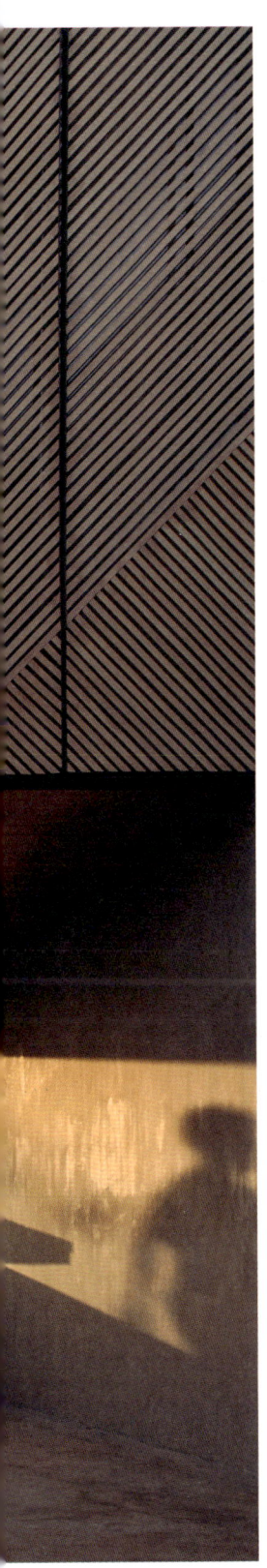
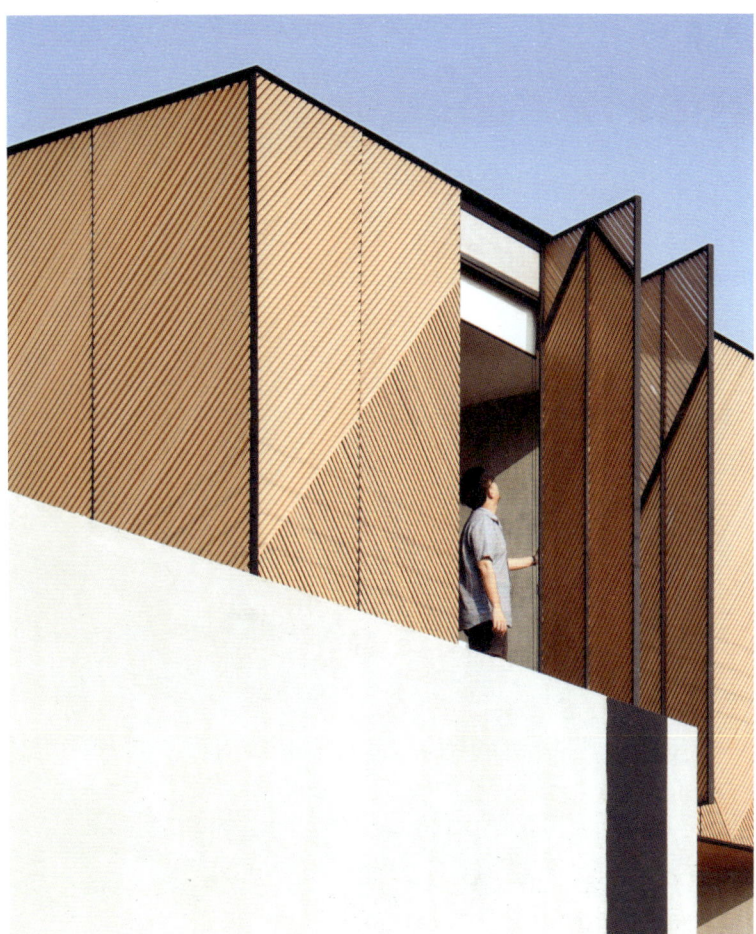

The house is wrapped in wooden laths angled to form triangular designs on the façades. This design element veils the interior in a creative patchwork of light and shadow through the day, creating variations of shade and radiance in many areas of the house. In the morning, soft light enters the bedrooms with an entourage of lanky shadows that play on the walls and the floors; in the afternoon, the traveling sun casts its rays into the living area and hallway, creating beautiful light murals on the walls. Beyond their display of shadows, the wooden laths also function as sunshade in the day and an added privacy shield at night.

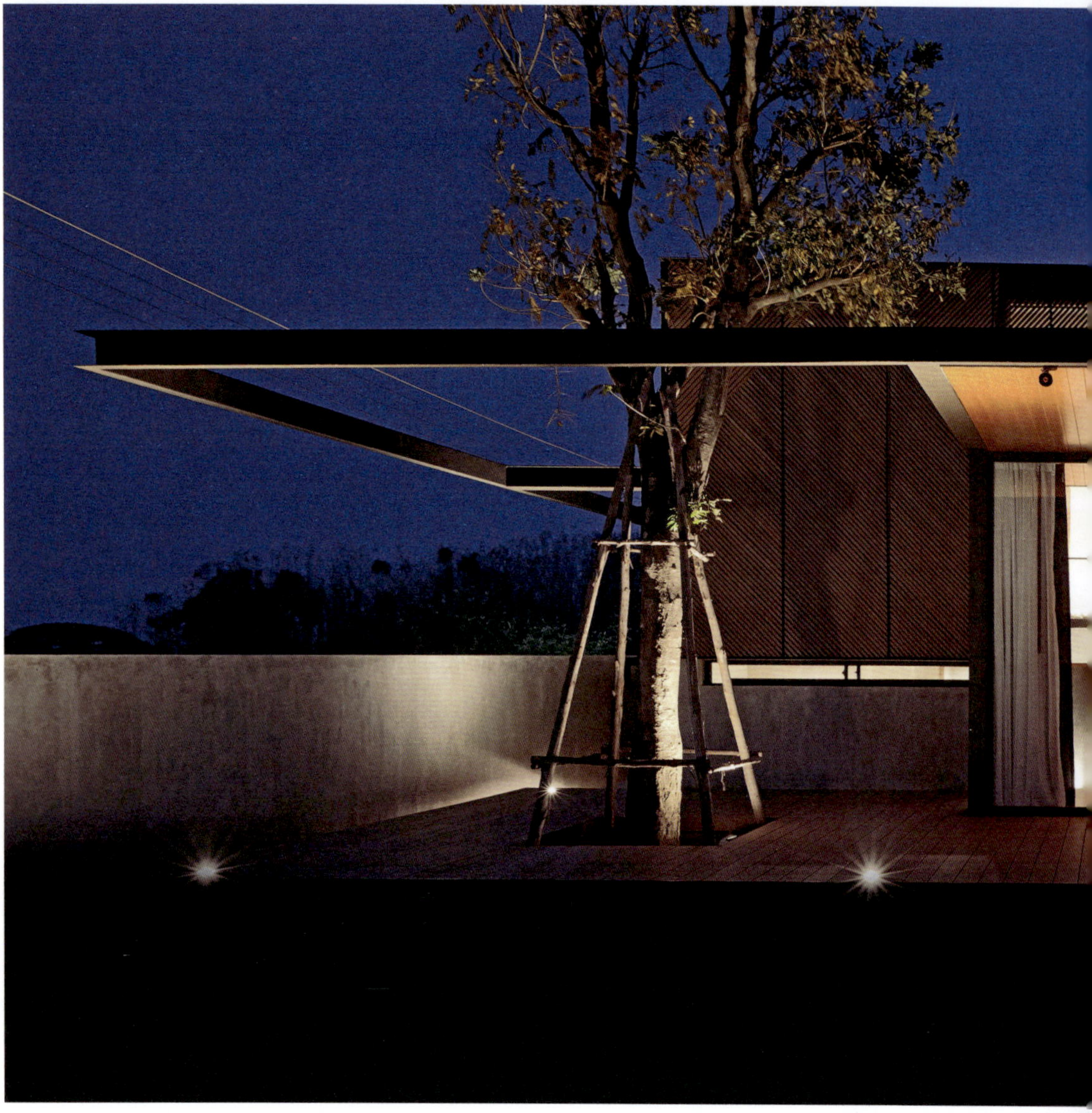

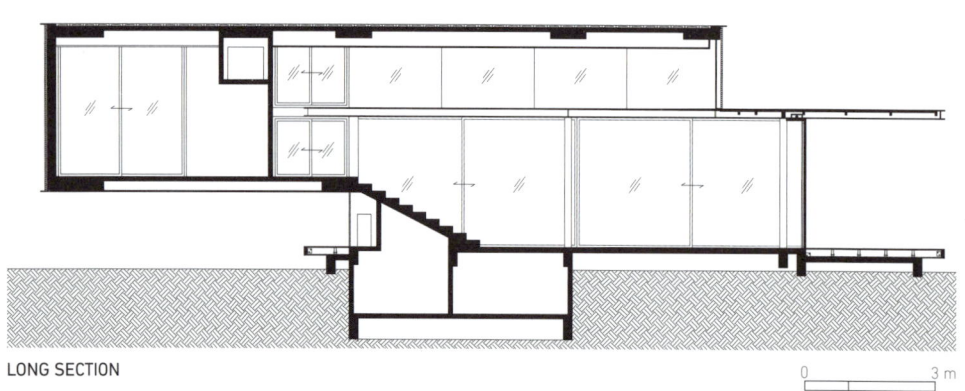

LONG SECTION

0   3 m

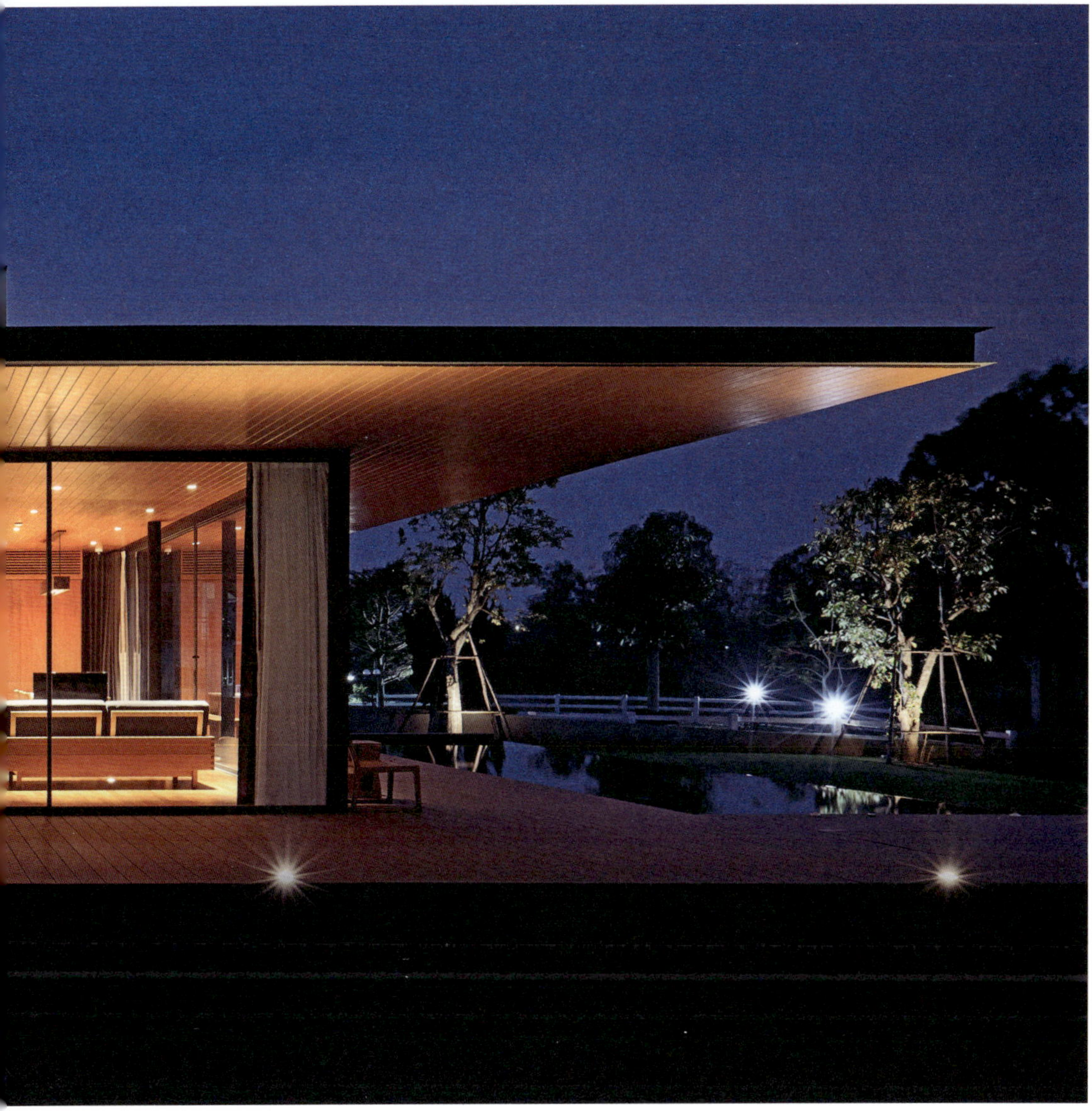

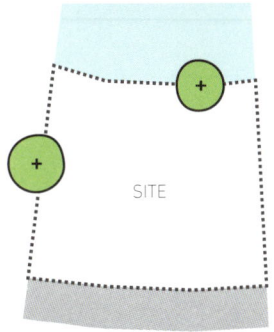
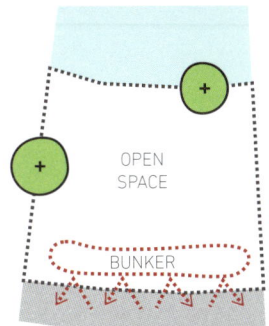
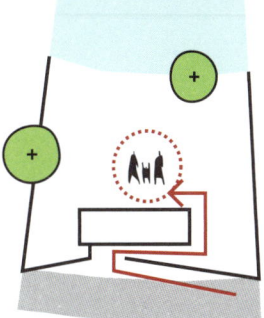

SITE STUDY

KA HOUSE

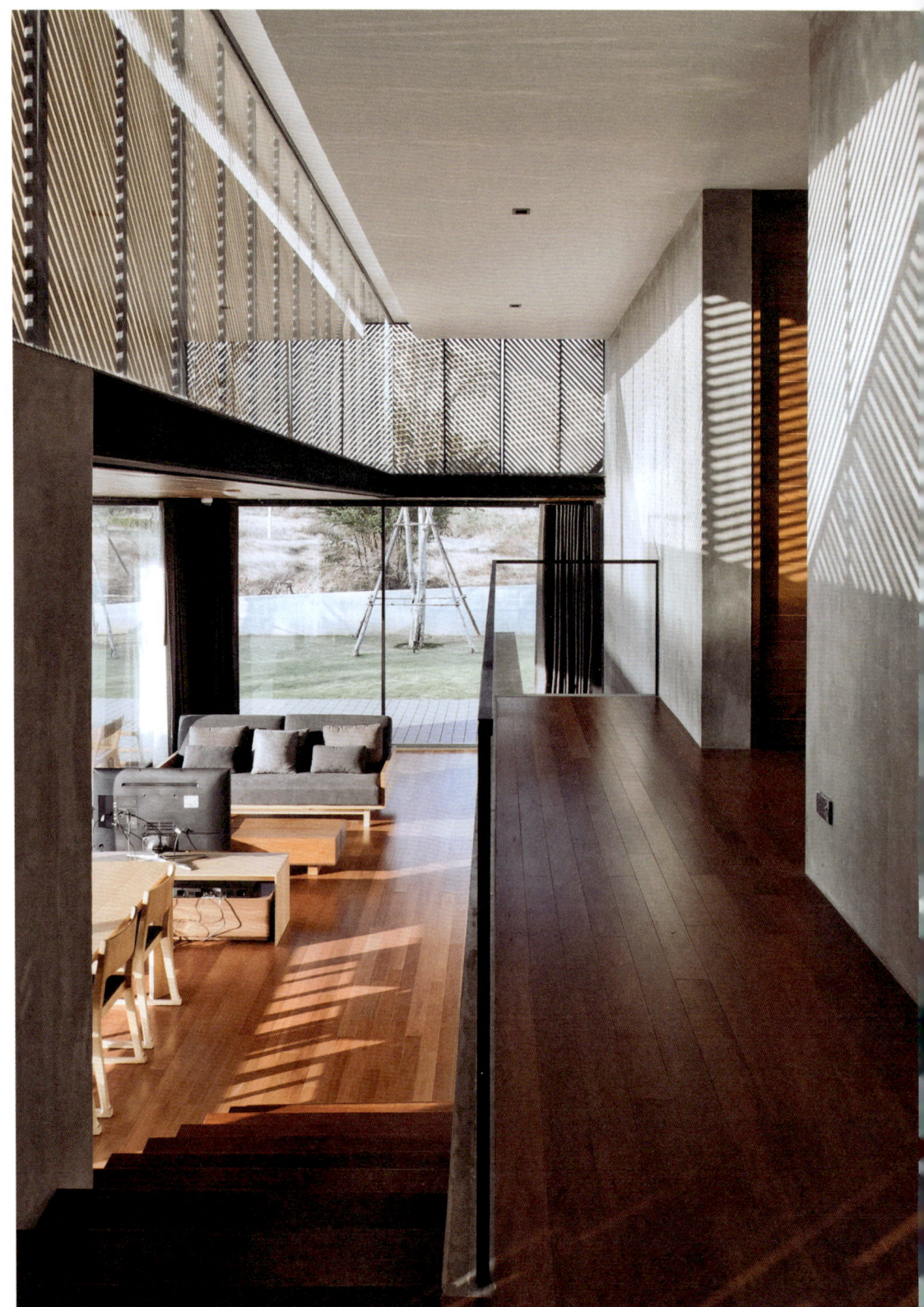

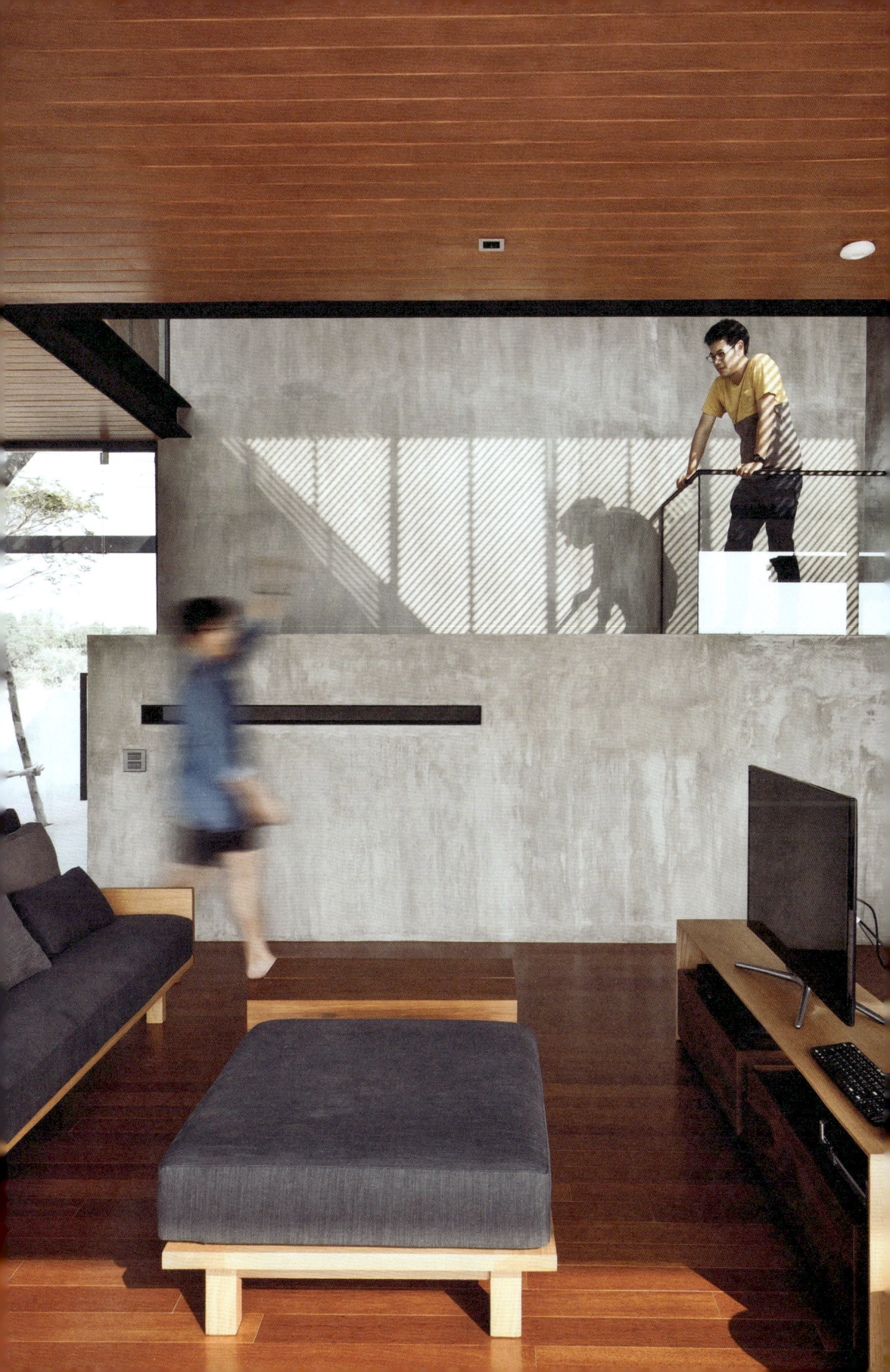

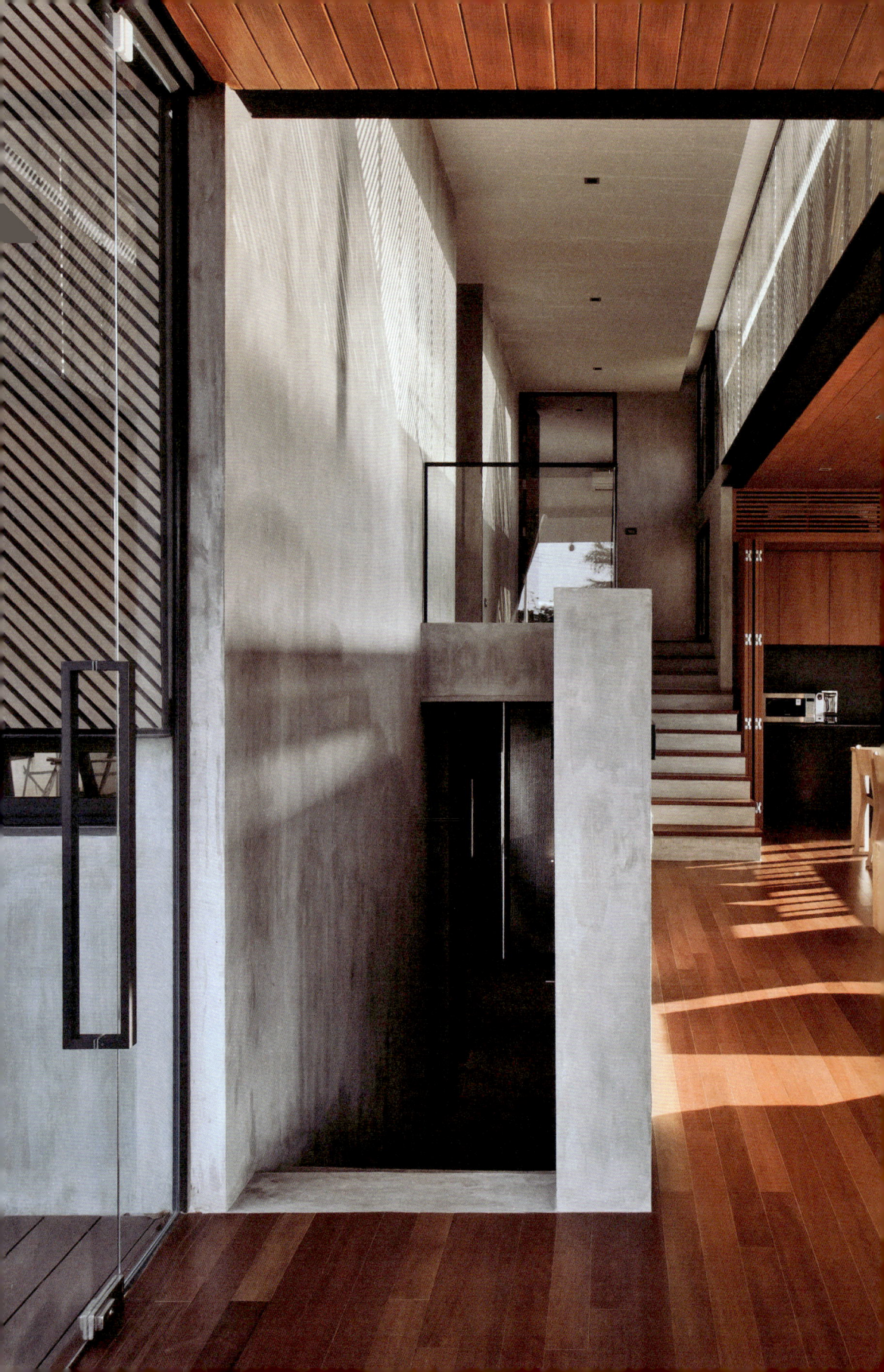

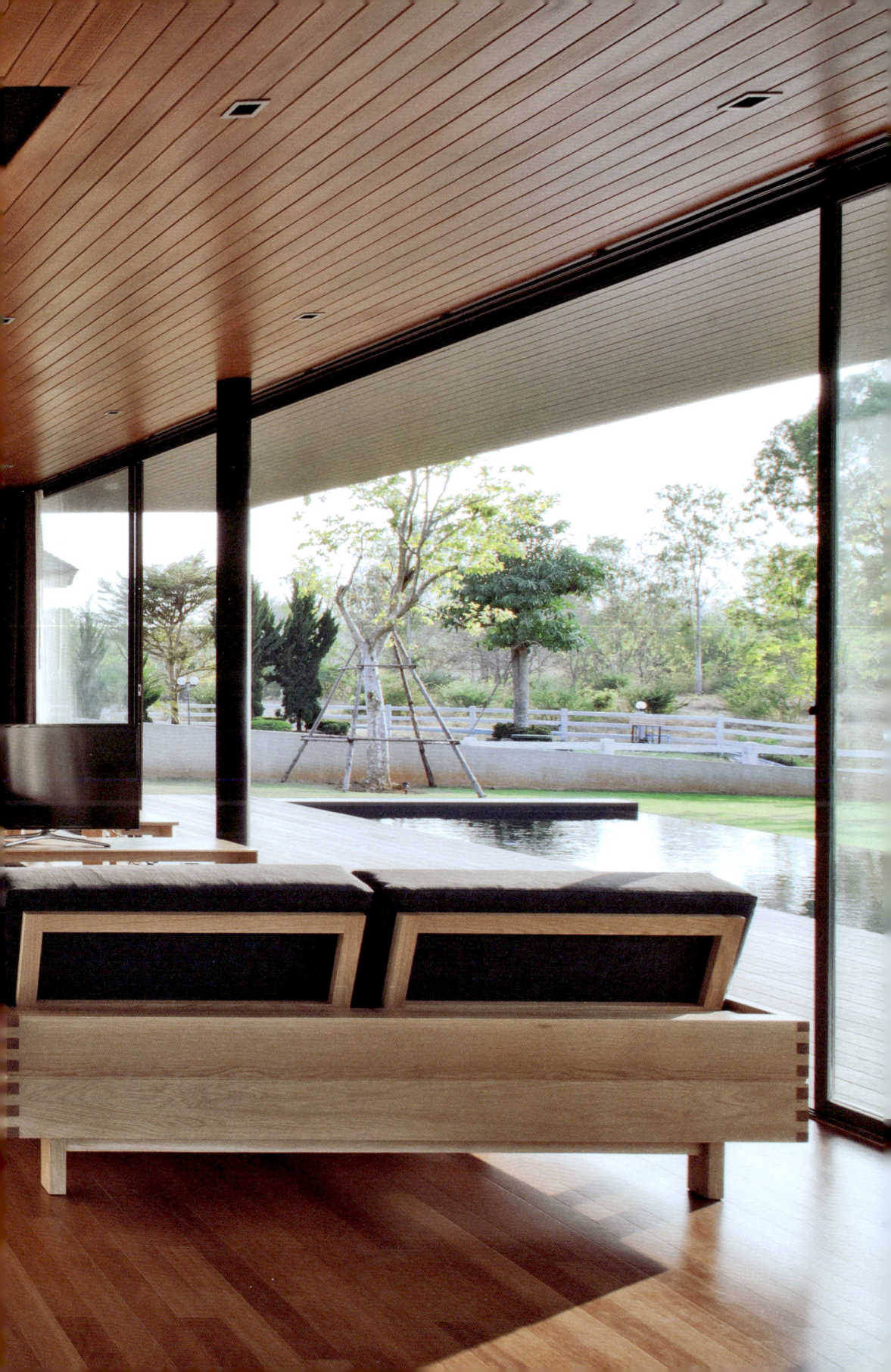

Phraeng Sanphasat, Bangkok, Thailand, 2018

PA PRANK

Pa Prank is a renovation project that transformed two shophouses into a hostel, and added a café on the first floor. Located in the district of Phraeng Sanphasat, a historical community in famous Old Town Bangkok (Rattanakosin), it is close to several popular tourist attractions, such as the Grand Palace and Wat Pho (home to Thailand's largest reclining Buddha).

Deviating from the conventional concept of a renovation, which typically maximizes the number of guestrooms while emphasizing a stylish décor, this project trades off a quarter of usable area in order to improve the quality of the place—by enhancing space, light, and ventilation. Buildings of the shophouse typology are commonly challenged by a lack of natural light and an unsatisfactory quality of interior space due to their long, linear design, which has adjacent units sharing a dividing wall. Light that enters through the front is usually minimal and insufficient to create a properly lit environment.

To combat this drawback, a seven-foot-wide (two-meter-wide) void, stretching along the side of the hostel, from front to back, is integrated as a comprehensive design solution. All walls and floors stacked atop this strip of void are removed to make way for natural light and ventilation. This redesign also makes room for a small courtyard on the first floor and creates two uniquely structured private guestrooms, as well as a common area, that seem to be hovering in the air. The roofs of the hovering units double as open terraces for the floor above them, showcasing a clever, multifunctional composition. In the guestrooms, tall windows open out to let in daylight and natural ventilation—features rarely enjoyed in similar hostels nearby.

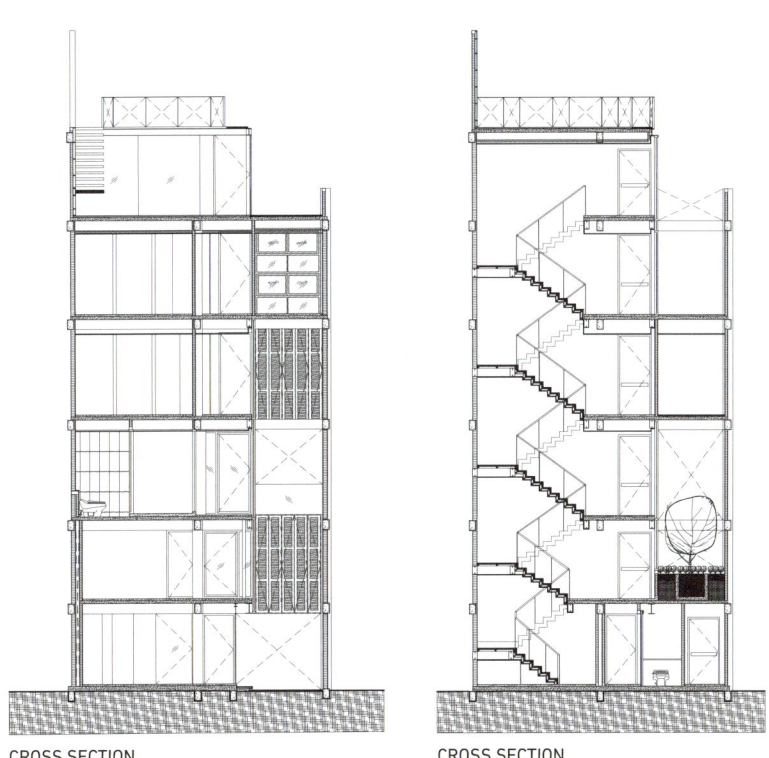

CROSS SECTION

CROSS SECTION

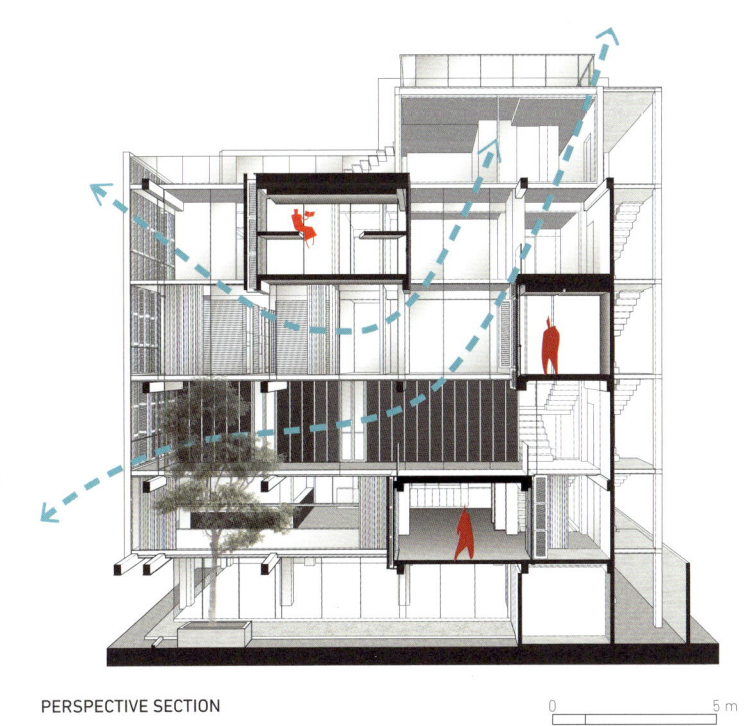

PERSPECTIVE SECTION

0 5 m

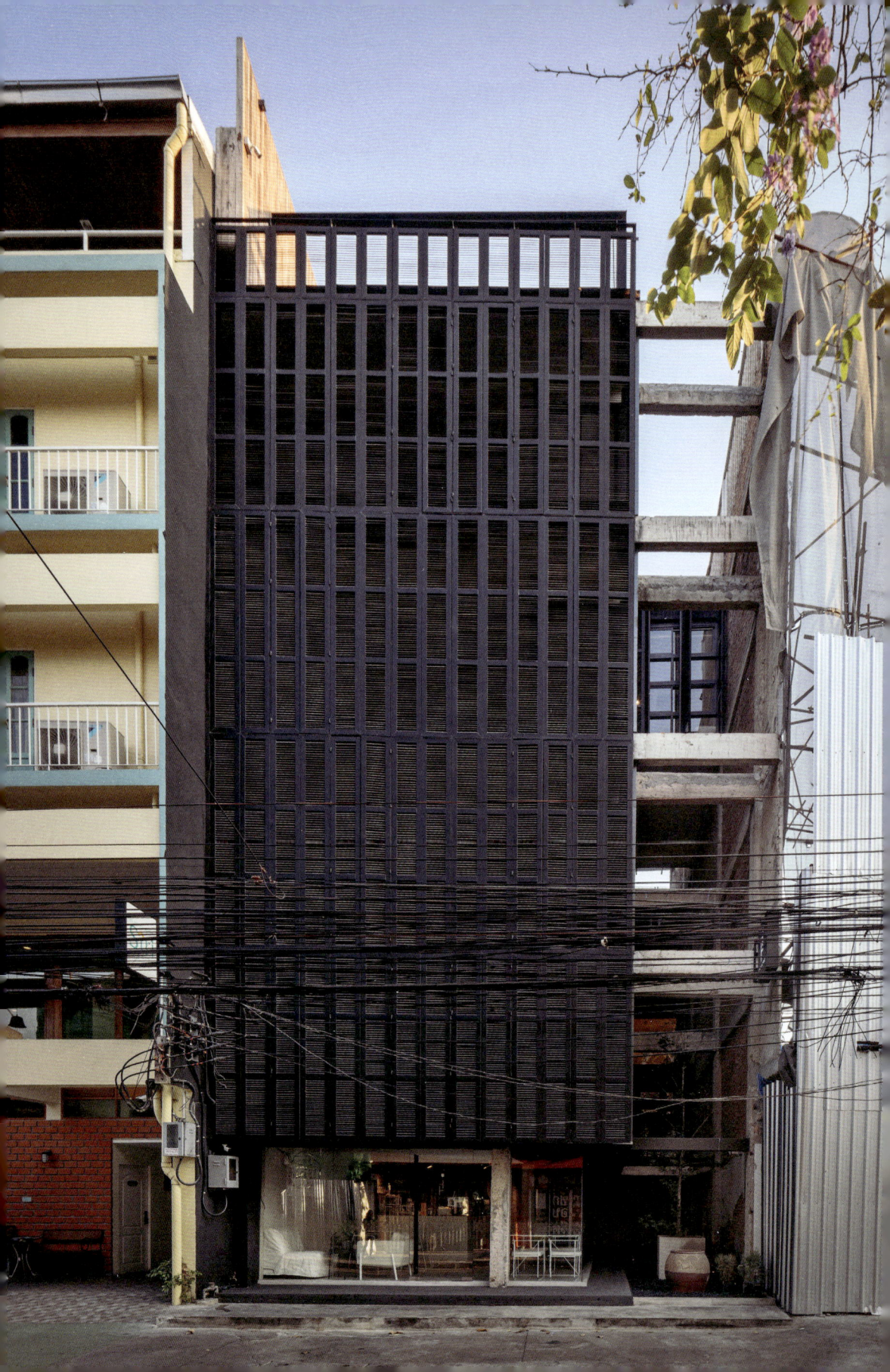

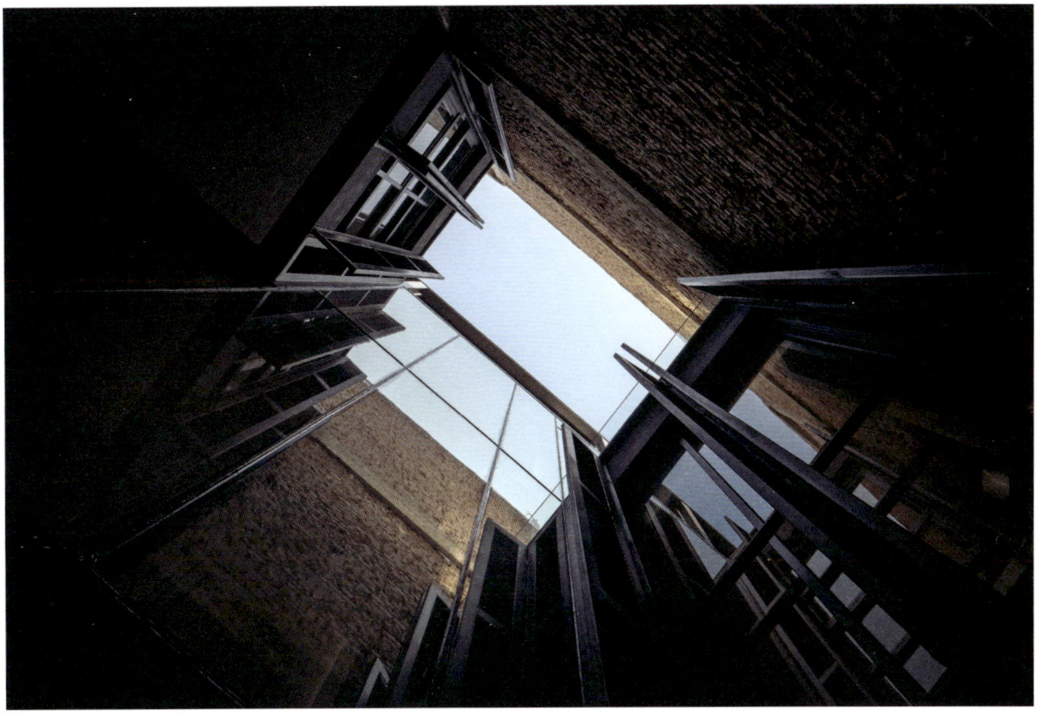

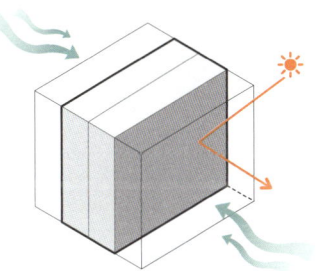

LIGHT AND VENTILATION WERE BLOCKED BY ADJACENT BUILDINGS

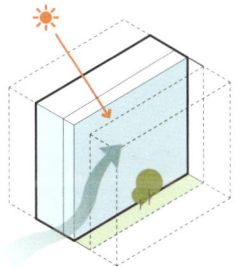

OFFSET AREA REPLACED WITH A COURTYARD

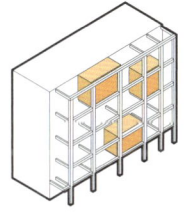

PRIVATE ROOMS AND COMMON AREA PLACED ON EXISTING STRUCTURE TO IMPROVE VENTILATION

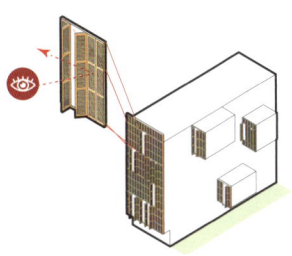

STREET-FACING EXTERIOR IS A STEEL FAÇADE INSPIRED BY TRADITIONAL THAI WINDOW FRAMES

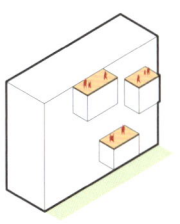

ROOFS OF EXTENDED ROOMS BECOME BALCONIES

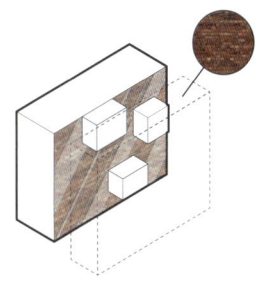

A CURTAIN WALL CREATES CONTRAST, REFLECTING THE PAST ON THE NEW GLASS SIDE FAÇADE

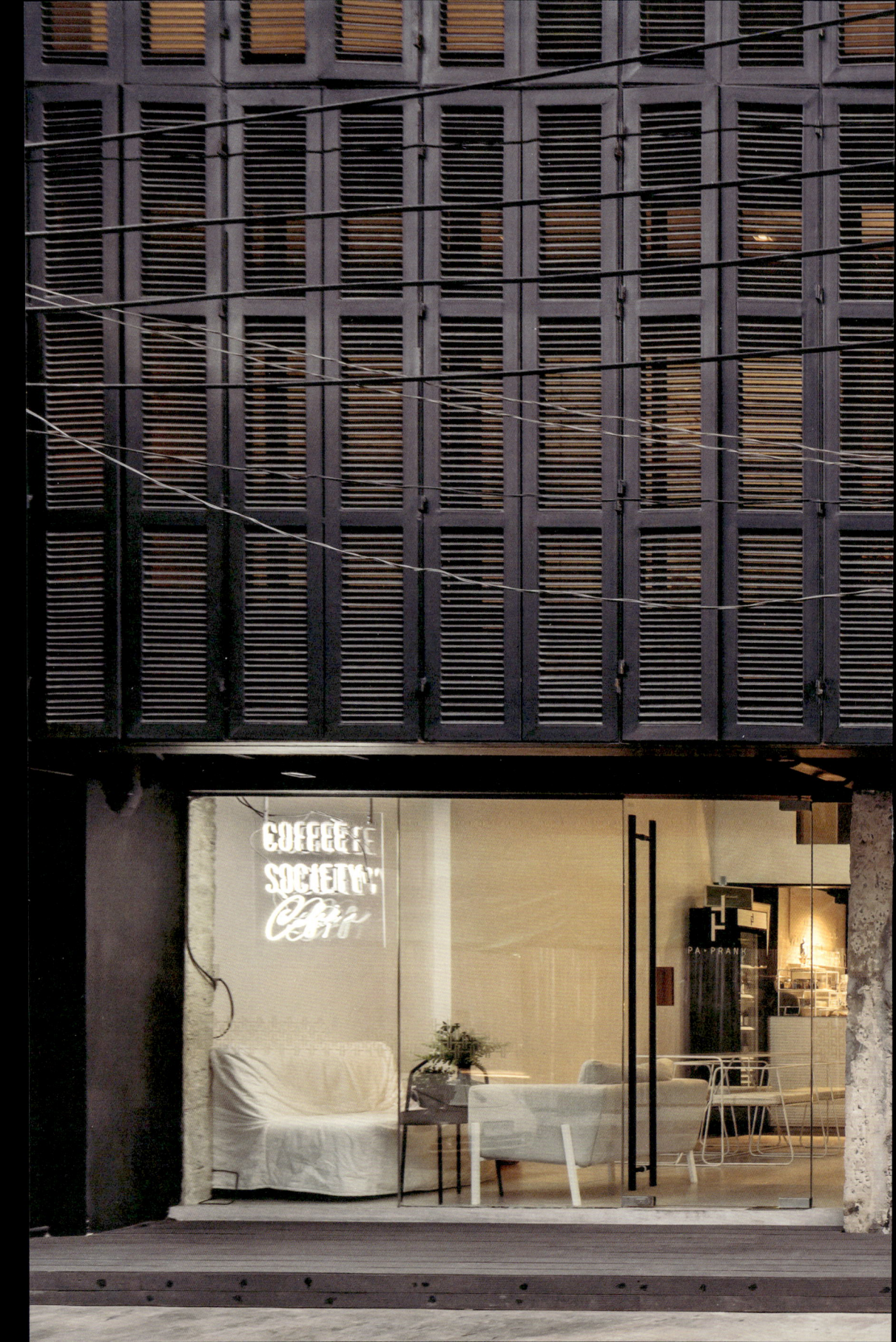

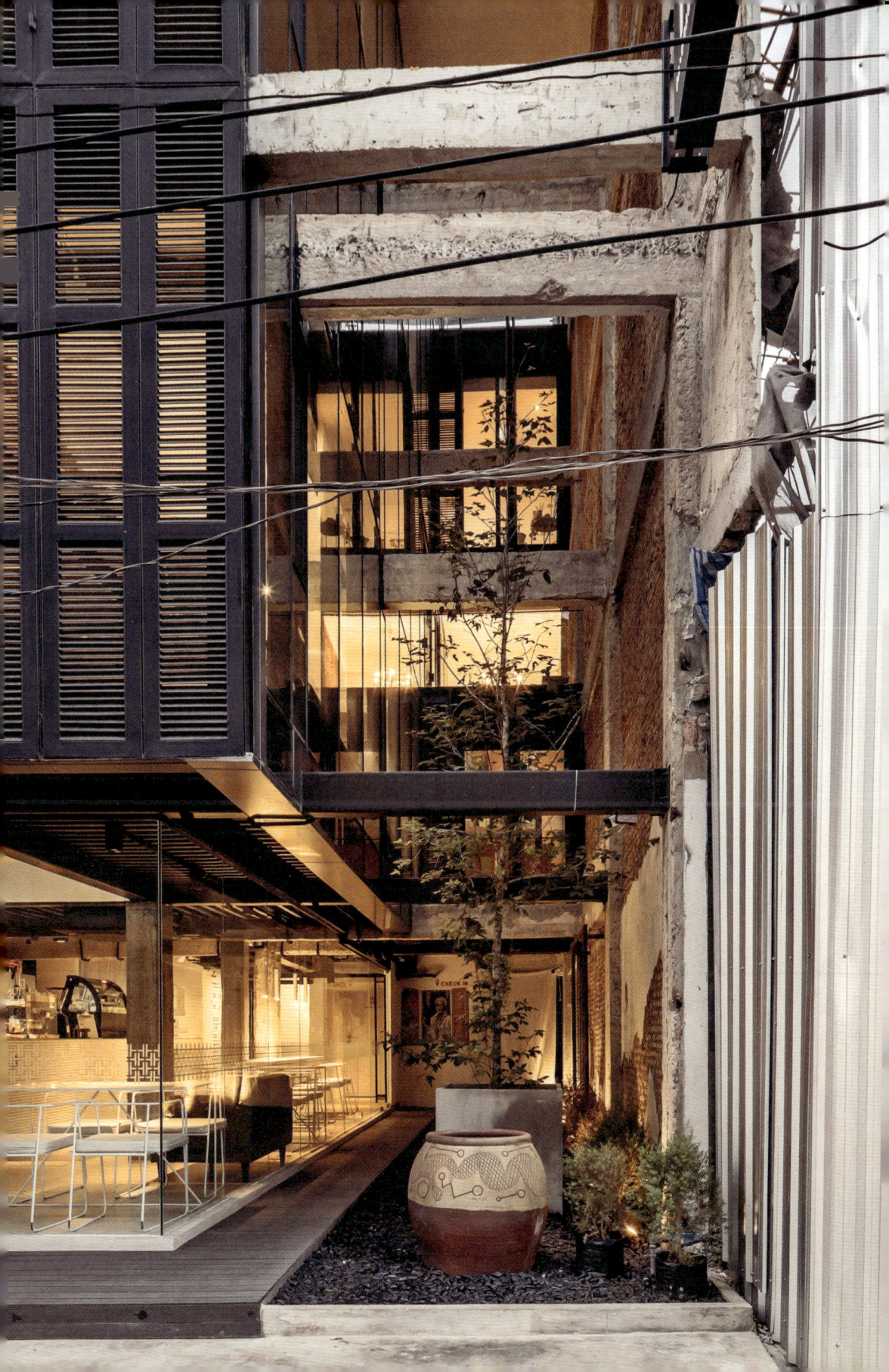

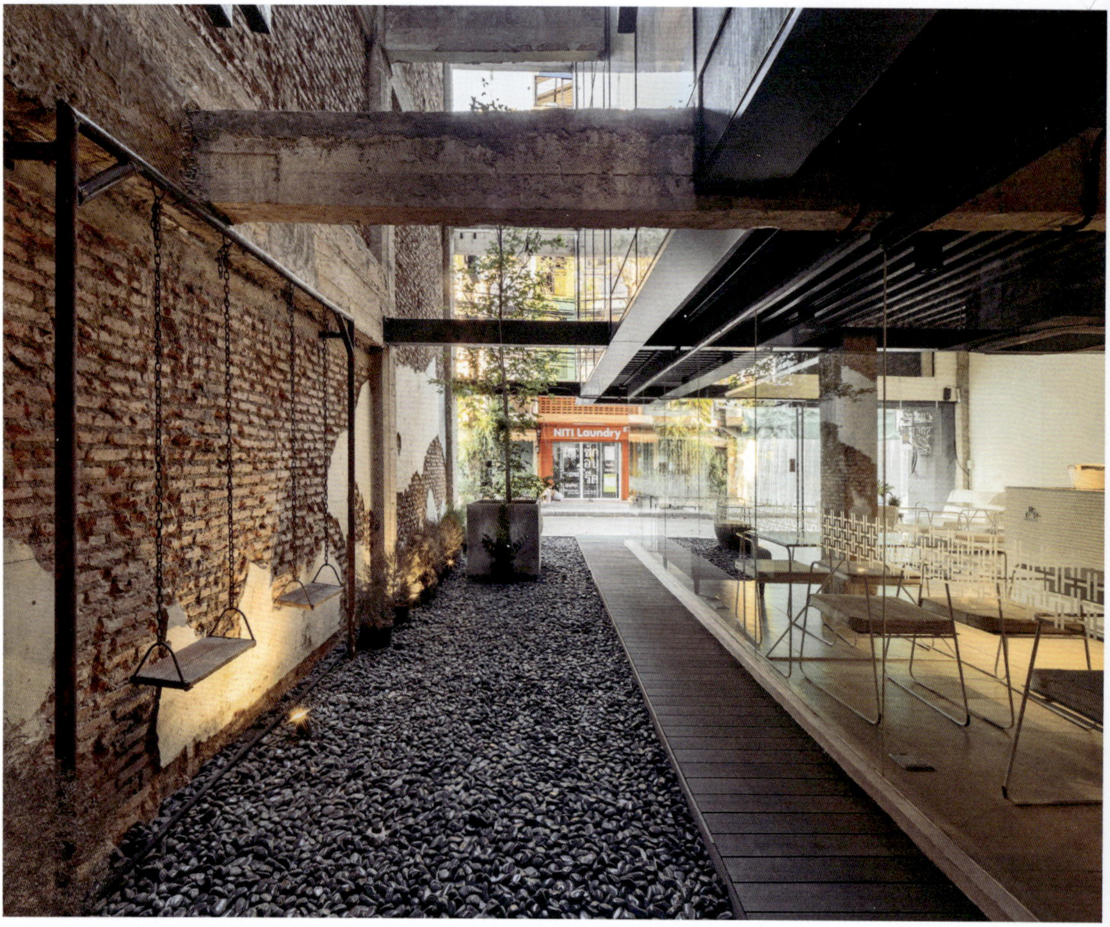

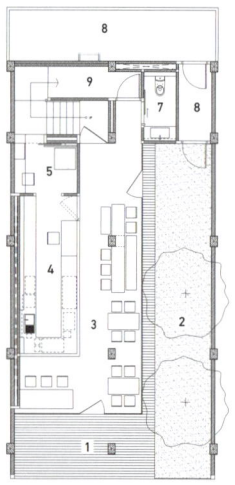

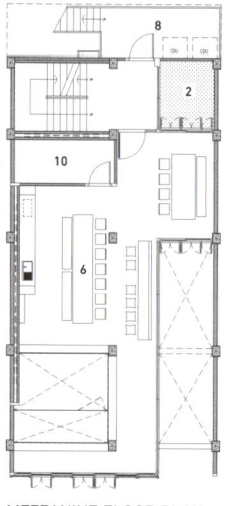

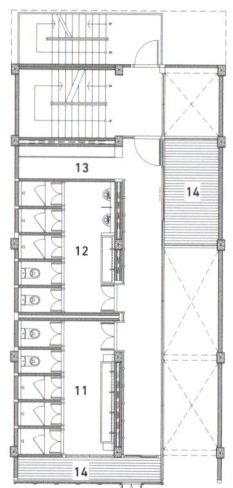

FIRST-FLOOR PLAN   MEZZANINE FLOOR PLAN   SECOND-FLOOR PLAN

1 ENTRANCE DECK
2 COURTYARD
3 CAFÉ
4 BAR AND RECEPTION
5 BACK OFFICE
6 COMMON AREA
7 RESTROOM
8 SERVICE AREA
9 STORAGE
10 EE ROOM
11 LADIES' RESTROOM
12 MEN'S RESTROOM
13 LOCKER ROOM/
   LAUNDRY ROOM
14 TERRACE

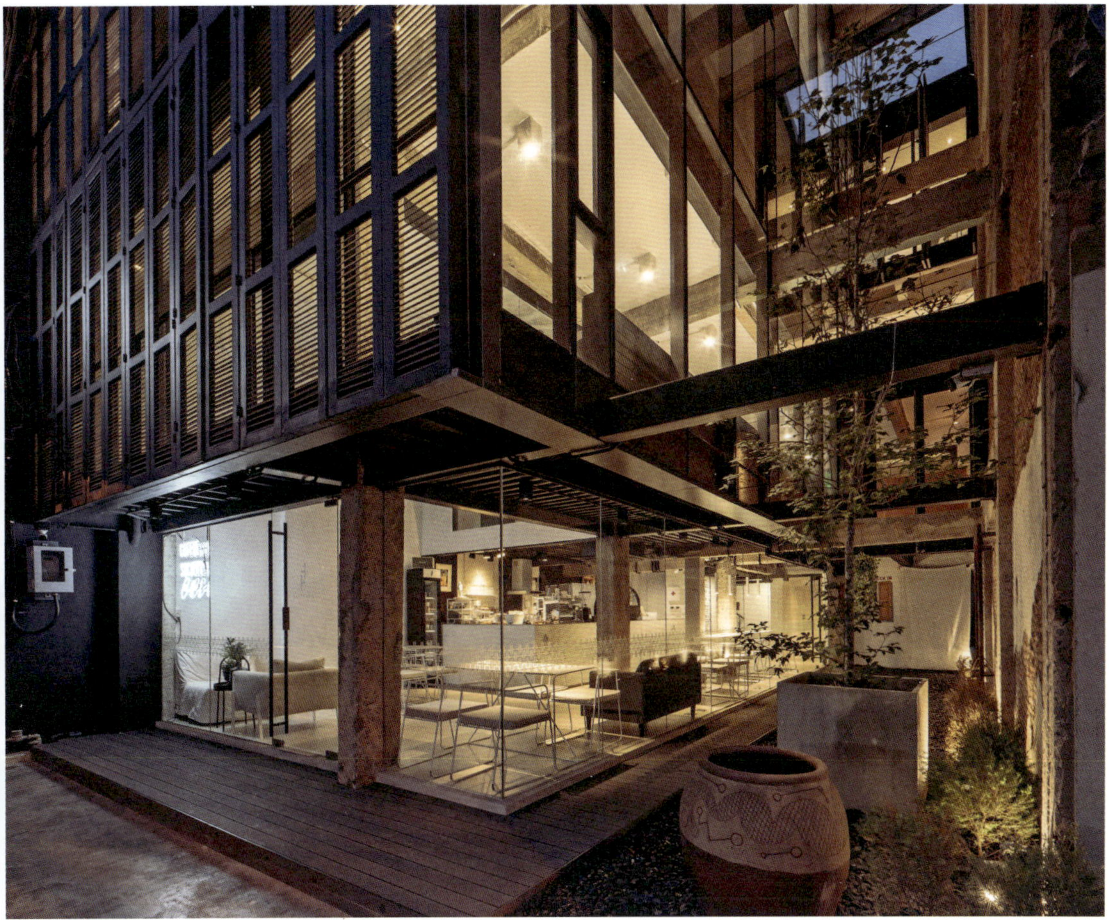

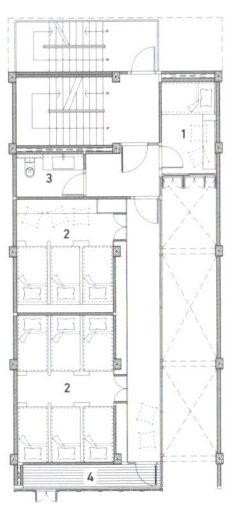

THIRD-FLOOR PLAN

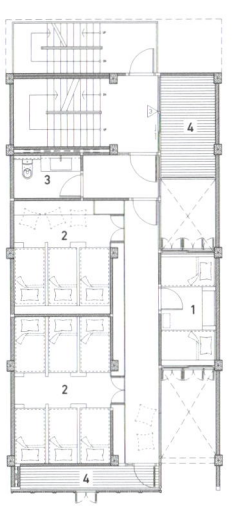

FOURTH-FLOOR PLAN

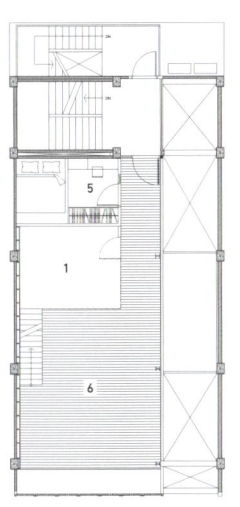

FIFTH-FLOOR PLAN

1 PRIVATE GUESTROOM
2 DORMITORY
3 RESTROOM
4 TERRACE
5 STAFF BEDROOM
6 BOXING TERRACE

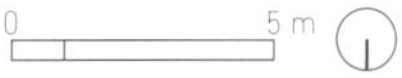

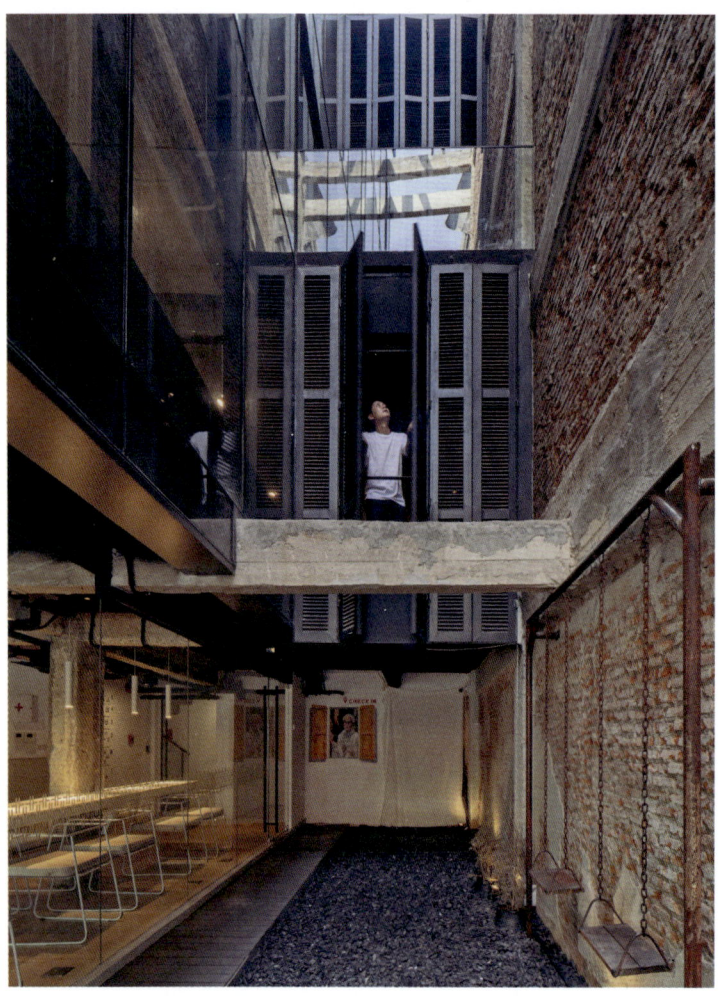
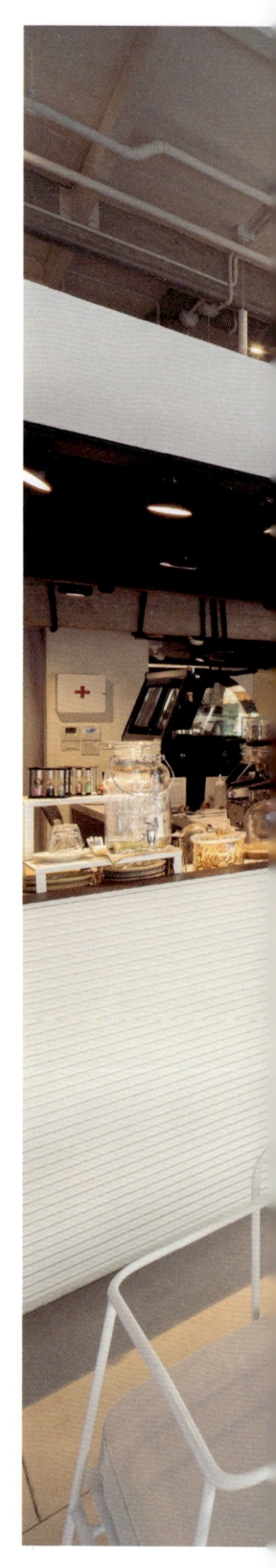

The play between new and old is artfully and deliberately expressed in the remodeling, especially in the courtyard. There is apparent contrast between the retrofit building parts and the existing old, chapped, brick wall, which is a heartening memento of the past that stands guard over the present in a faded red cloak. The juxtaposition of old and new extends beyond the building site into the neighborhood as the bold, dark façade, courtesy of tall, black window shutters is backdropped by more weathered building exteriors. Though inspired by traditional shophouse windows, the façade bears the mark of the contemporary in material and color: steel and the stark shade of black. In keeping with the traditional character of the window shutters, interior spaces are showcased in white, so as to be simple and unpretentious.

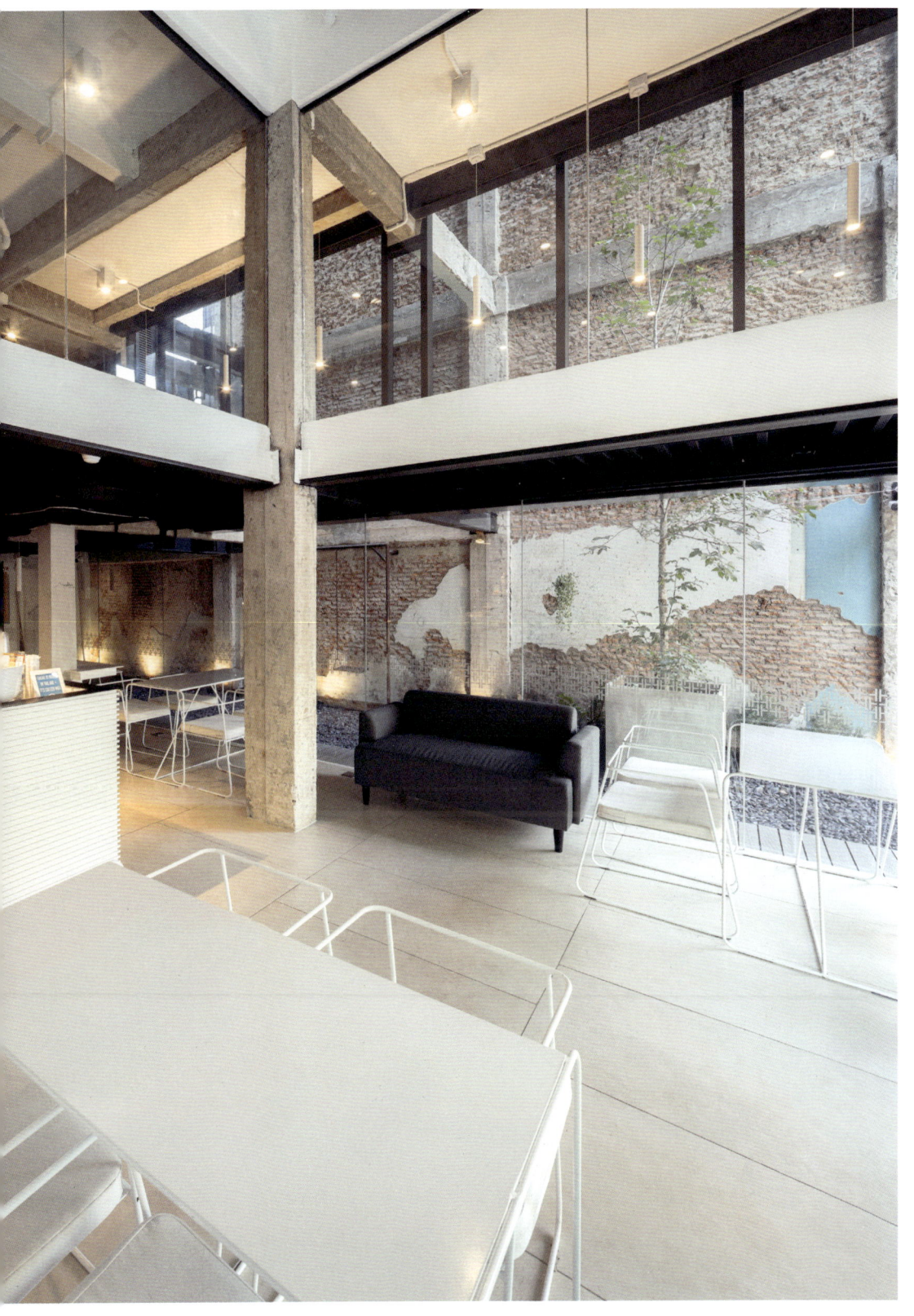

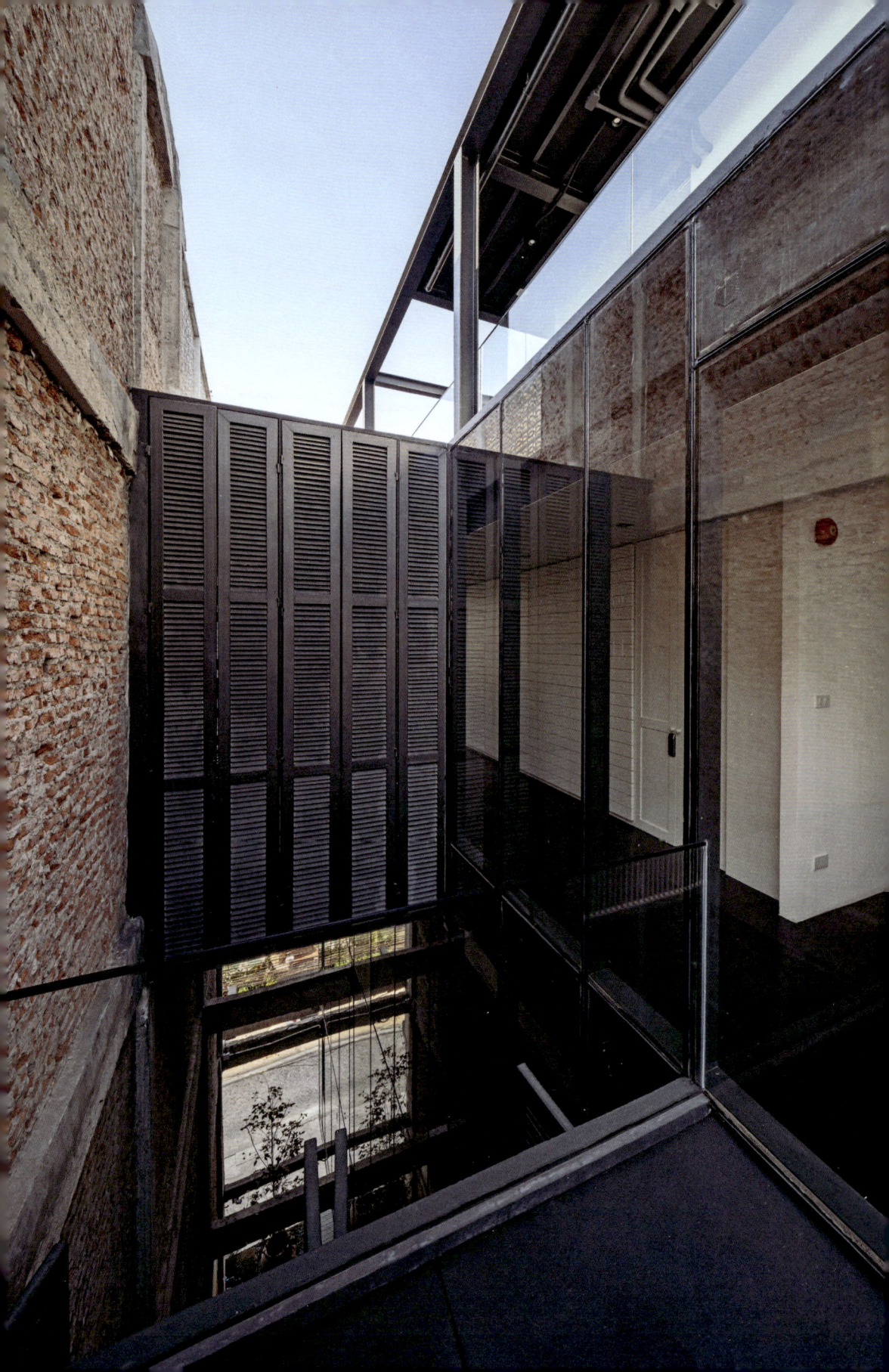

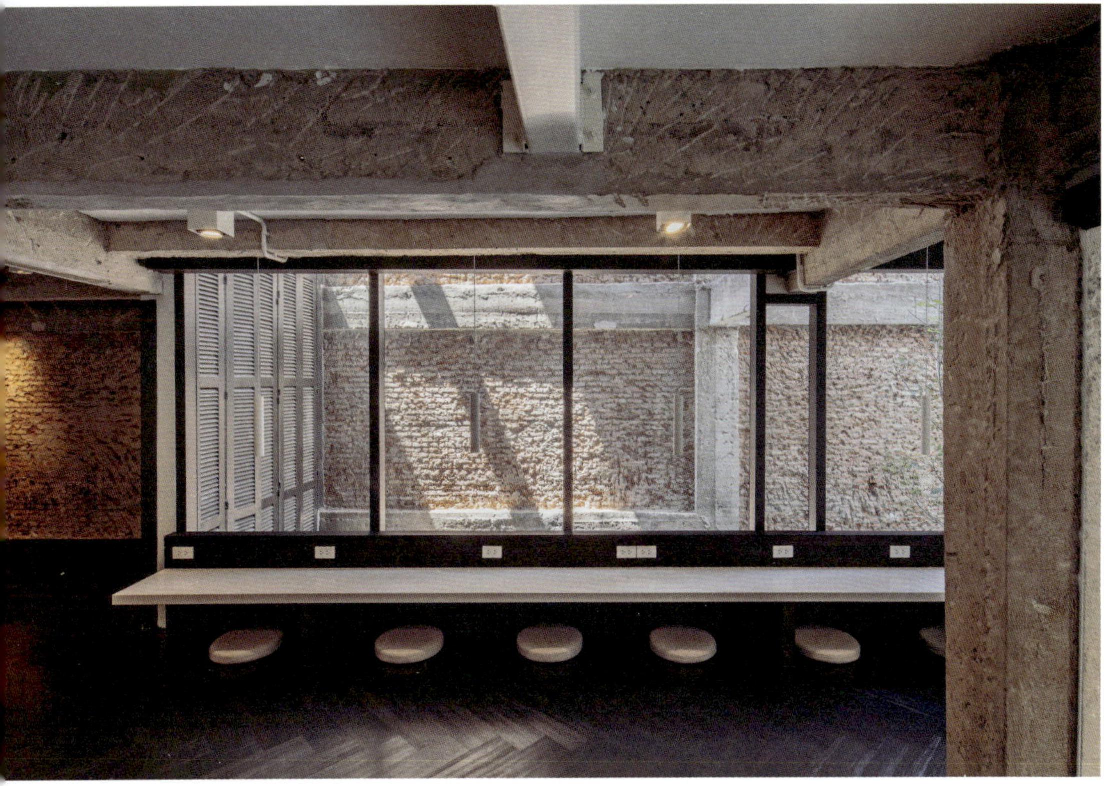

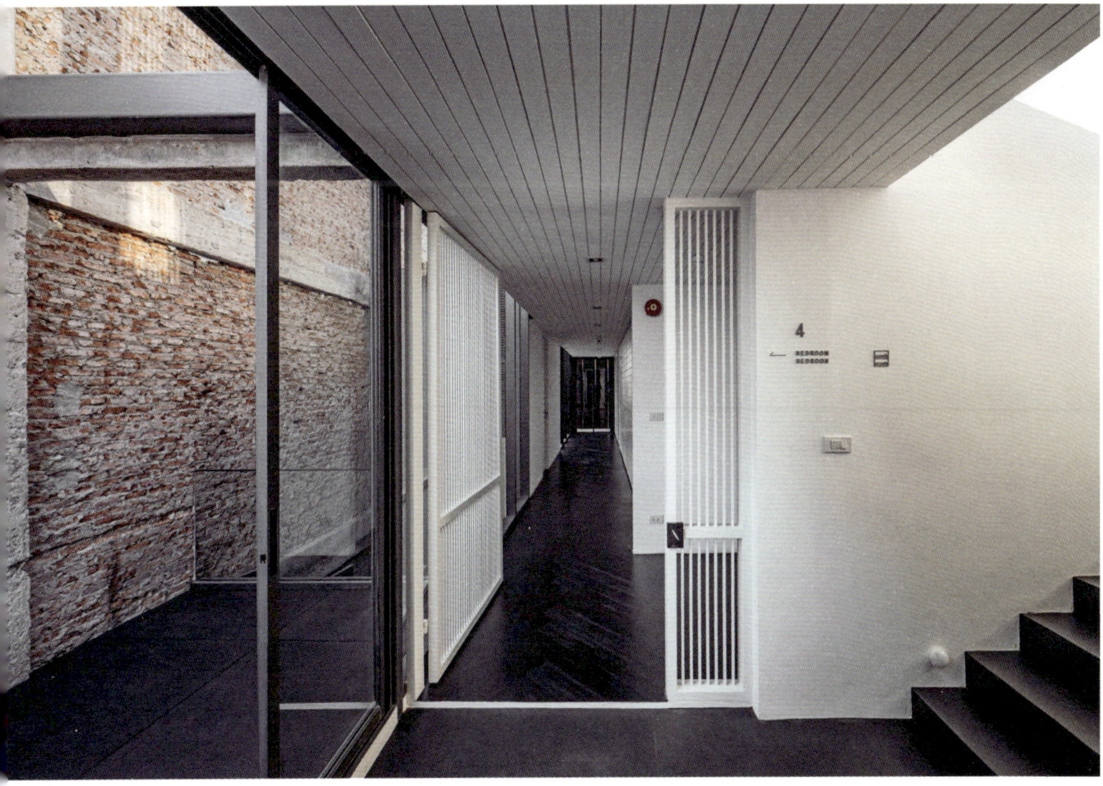

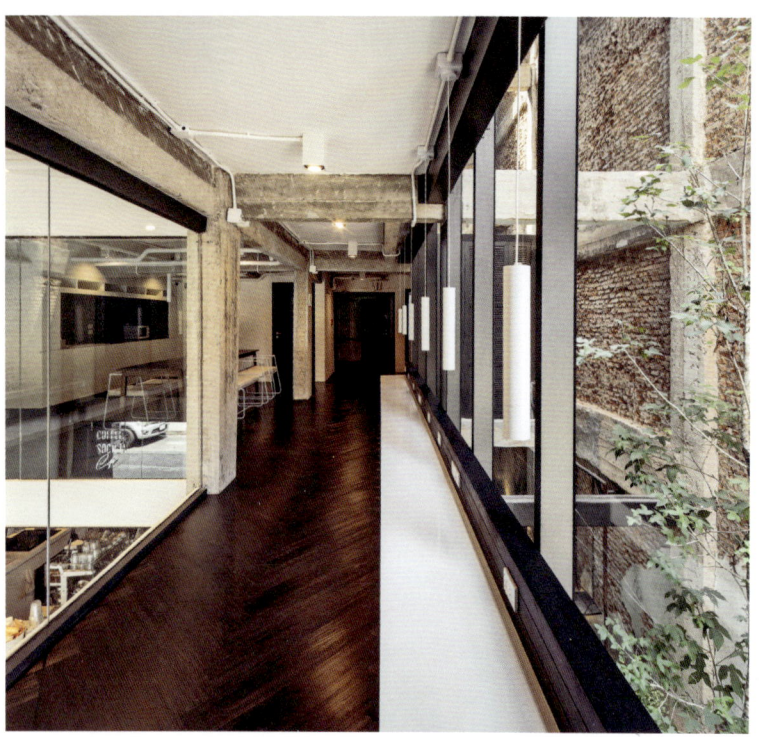

In designing the functional arrangement of Pa Prank, user convenience was a primary consideration. The common area on the mezzanine can be accessed from both the café and activity area on the first floor, and guestrooms on the upper floors. The bathroom, locker room, and laundry area occupy the second floor, leaving the third and fourth for guestrooms. The rooftop hosts the yoga and boxing class zones, presenting a colorful, historical backdrop of the surrounding city for these activities. Fusing the spirit of modernity with traditional elements, Pa Prank honors the past while reaching for the future through non-conventional solutions that still keep an eye on a rich heritage.

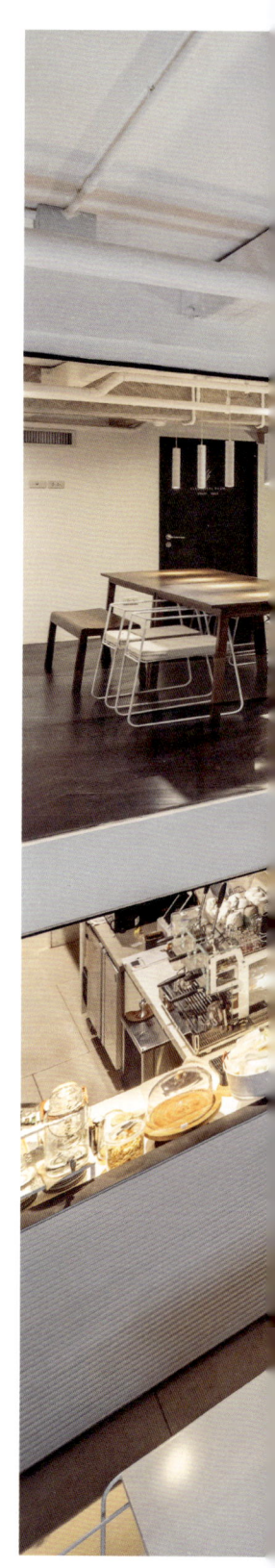

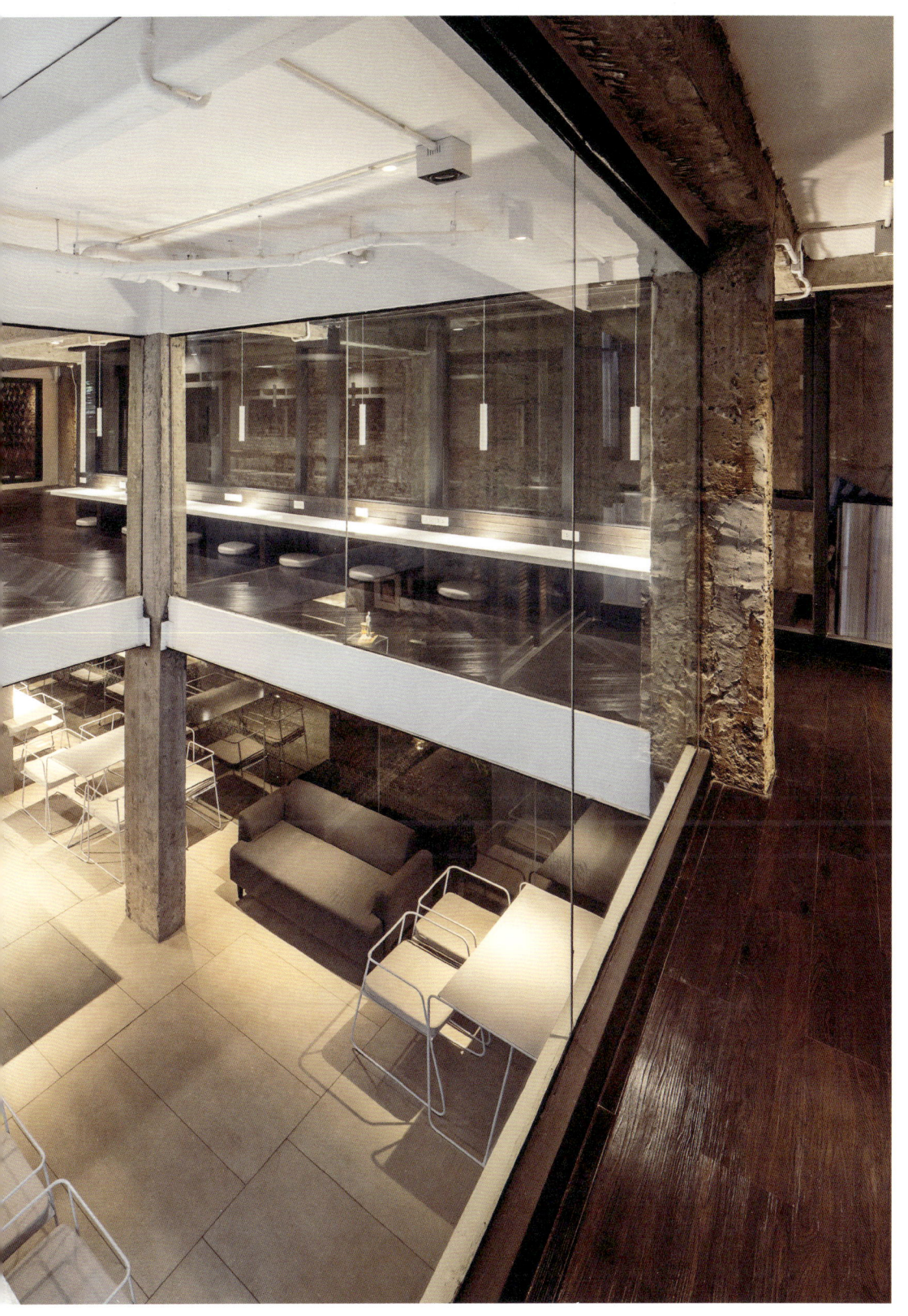

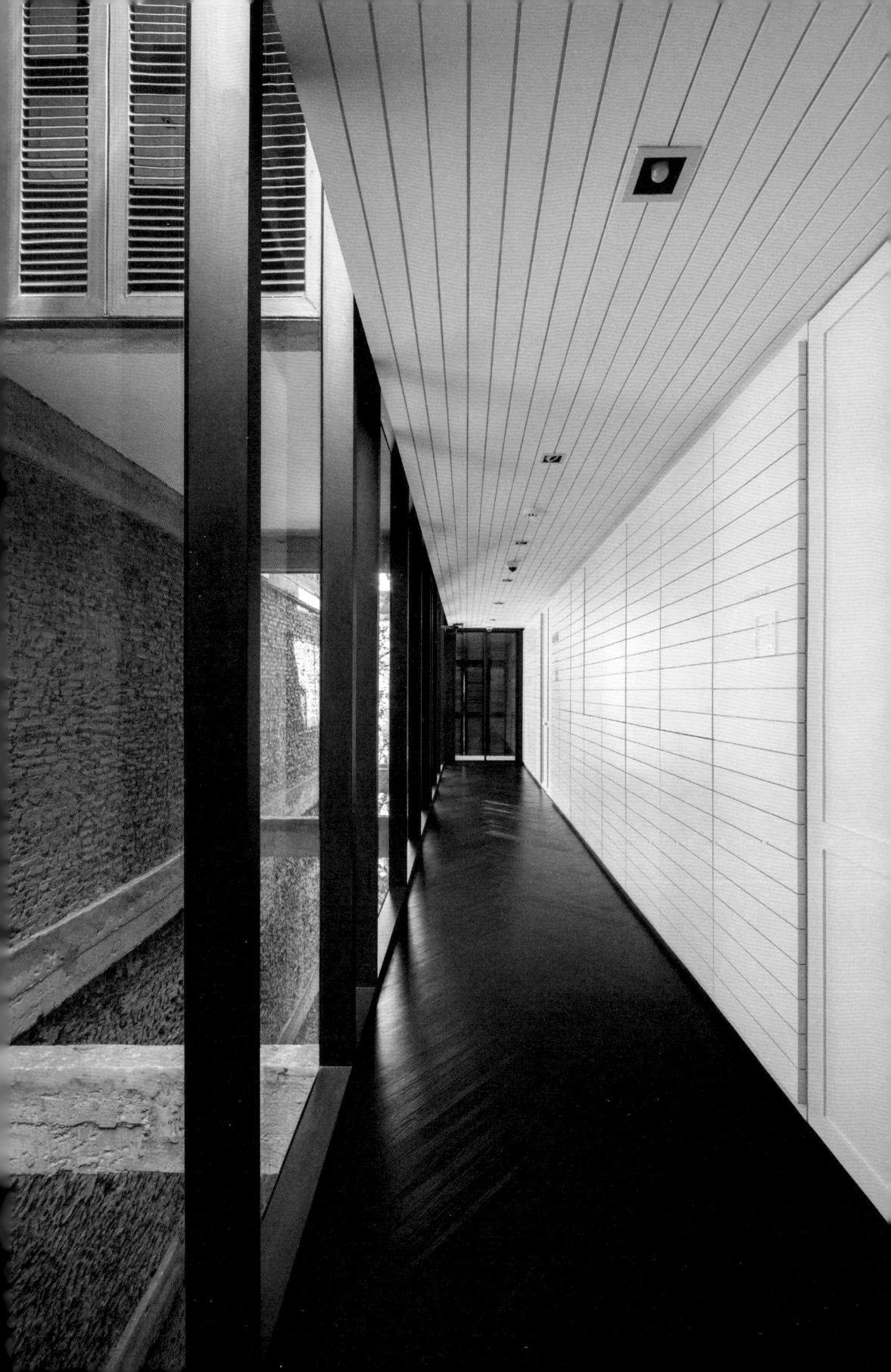

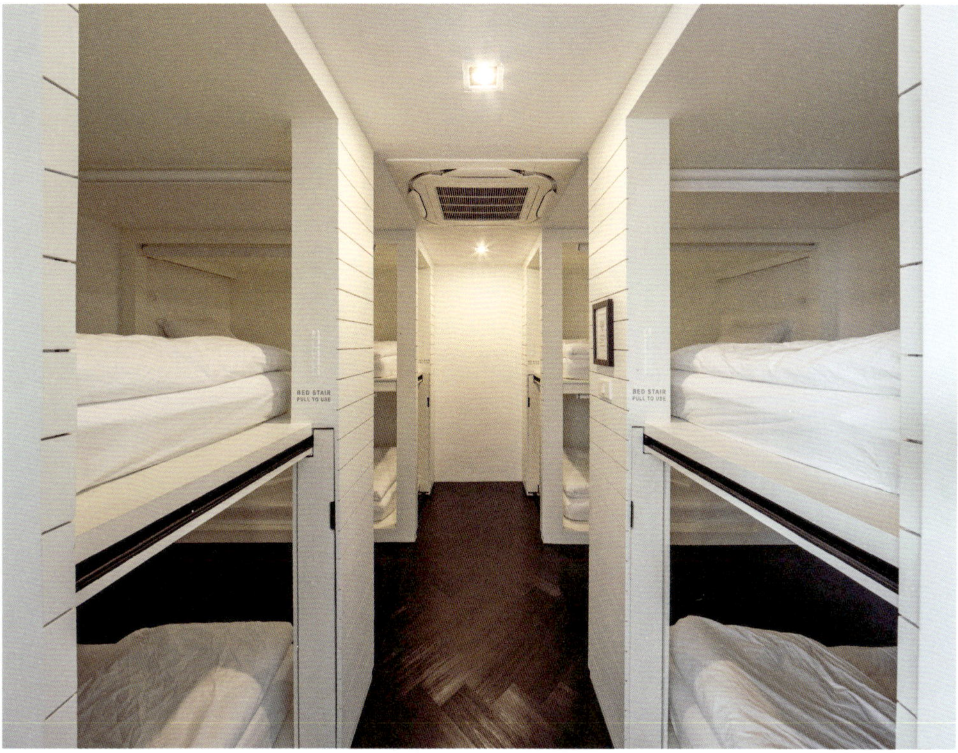

PA PRANK

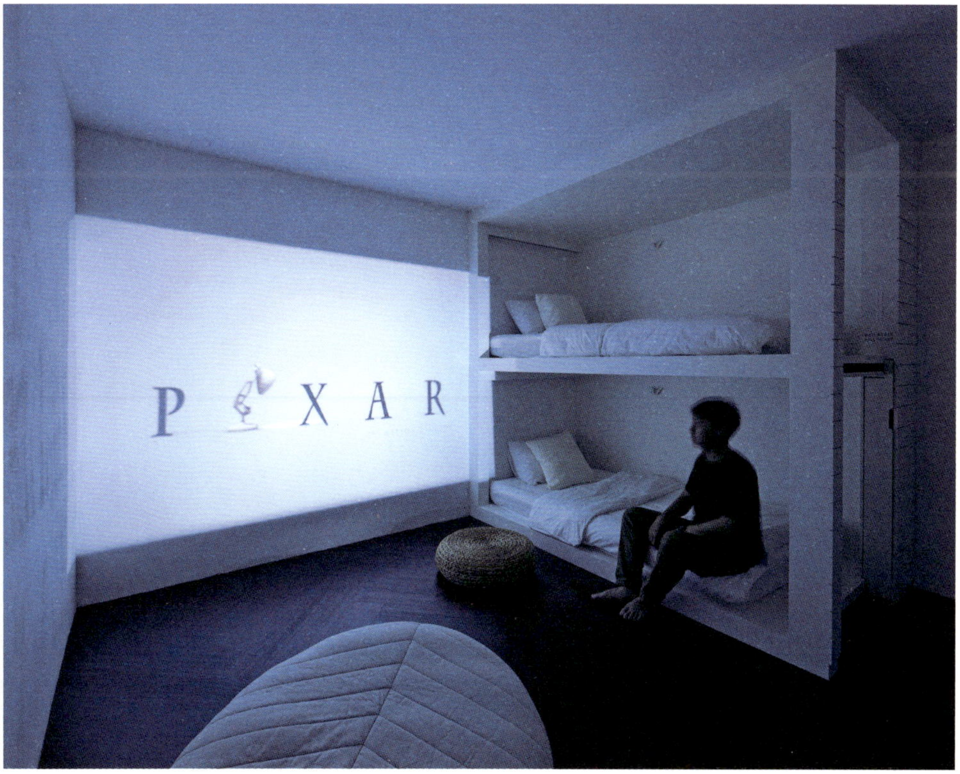

Koh Samet, Rayong, Thailand, 2015

LIMA DUVA

The latest offering of the Lima Resort Group, Lima Duva, is a modern iteration of adjacent older resort Lima Bella. They are both located on Koh Samet, an exotic island paradise that is popular among couples planning a romantic getaway and travelers seeking a tropical island adventure.

The design process began with a judicious delve into the history of the island, which reveals itself through two iconic sculptures: the ogress and the mermaid, which feature as characters from the epic story *Phra Aphai Mani*, written by revered Thai poet Sunthon Phu in the nineteenth century. They look upon the faces of tourists and spin the lore that envelopes Koh Samet.

In this olden tale, Koh Samet assumes the backdrop in a chapter of passion: the main character Phra Aphai Mani attemps to negotiate his release from his amorous captor, the ogress, on the grounds that a human and a non-human would never live happily ever after. He eventually manages an escape with the help of a mermaid, and when they arrive at Koh Samet, they fall in love and the mermaid soon gives birth to a baby boy. Though the mermaid was non-human, like the ogress, it is said that the island's spell of romance was so strong and irresistible that the union came to be.

Till this day, the island is regarded as a romantic destination and, therefore, the design of Lima Duva cleverly serves both couples and family-group guests. To that end, basic functional areas within each room are arranged in a loop layout rather than a linear configuration; the terrace is moved to the side instead of placed at the end of the room as this isolates each room and minimizes noise escaping to the adjacent room. In this layout, every unit becomes almost like a private villa, but with the units composed within a building format.

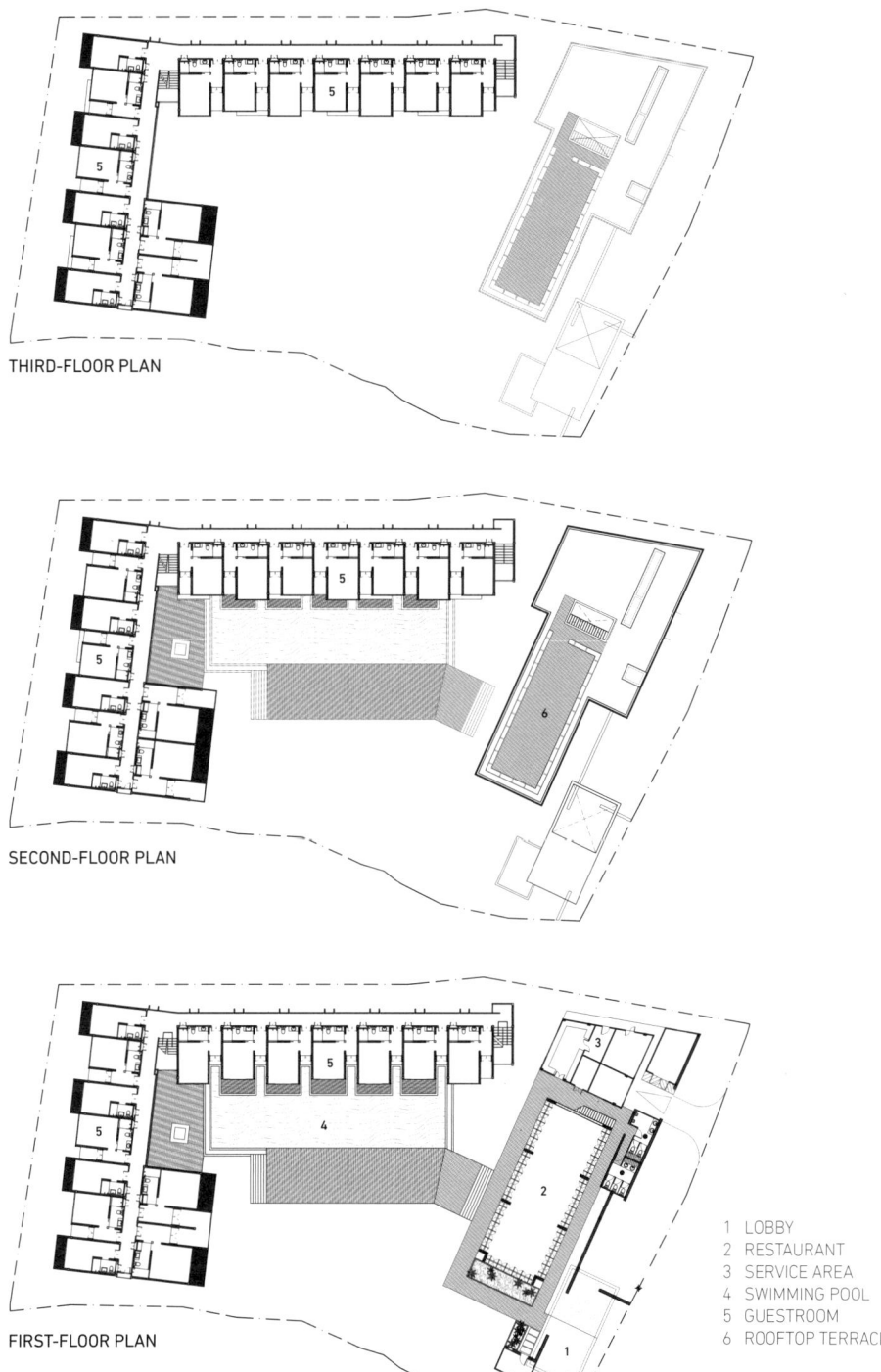

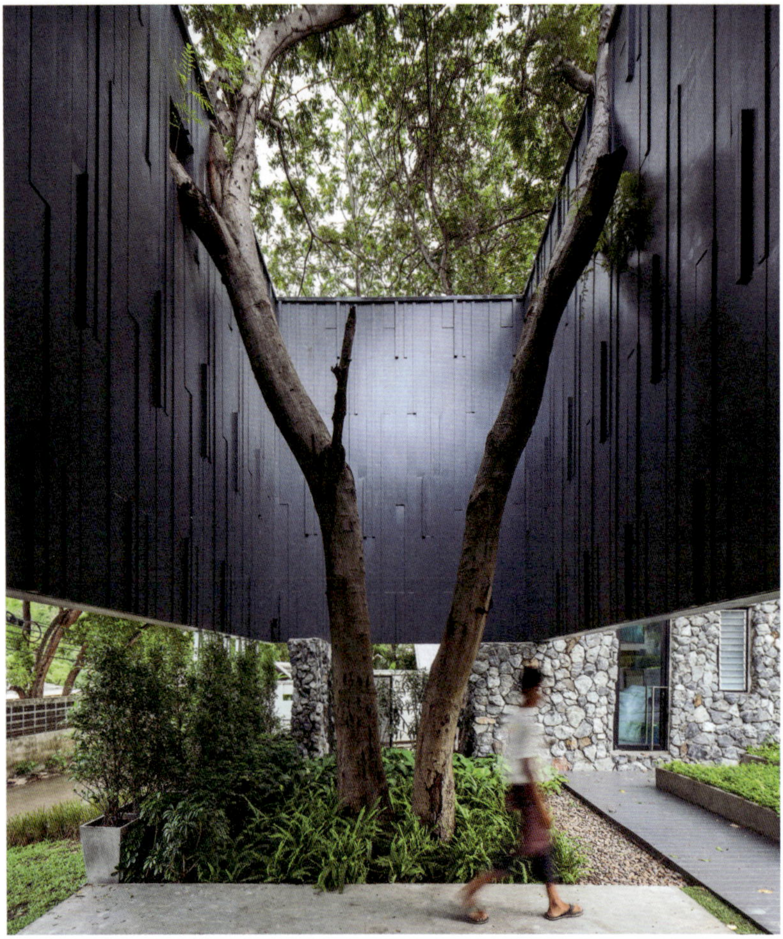

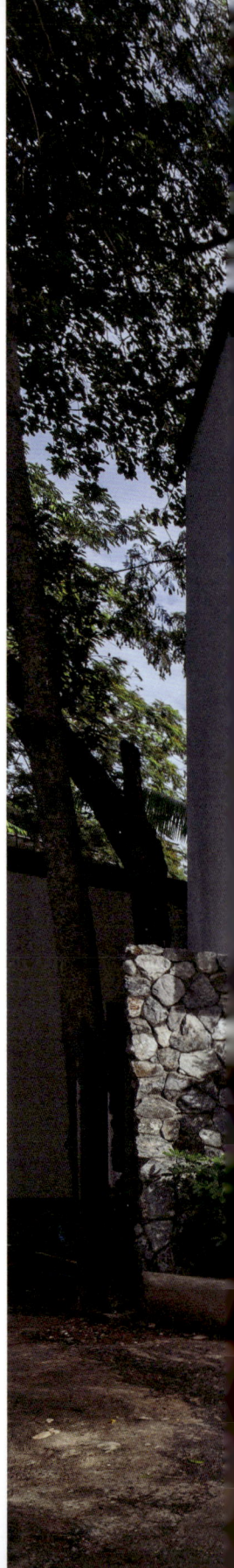

The design concept of Lima Duva is based on piquing the curiosity of passersby. Looking in from the outside, it's hard to perceive what the inside might be or what function the building serves. A combined main entrance and lobby are configured within a booth, with a shady, towering tree (originally on-site) as a booth mate. White on the exterior and black on the interior, the booth sits raised on exquisite, rustic stone walls, such that the void below forms the entrance. The "doorway" is set low so that guests bend to enter and exit—an uncommon gesture that amplifies the experience of the space, which is made even more unusual with a swaying canopy of leaves. Guests can enjoy more of the compound's natural ambiance during outdoor movie nights that are reminiscent of simpler, olden days as the courtyard is turned into an open-air theater with the booth's white exterior used as a projector screen.

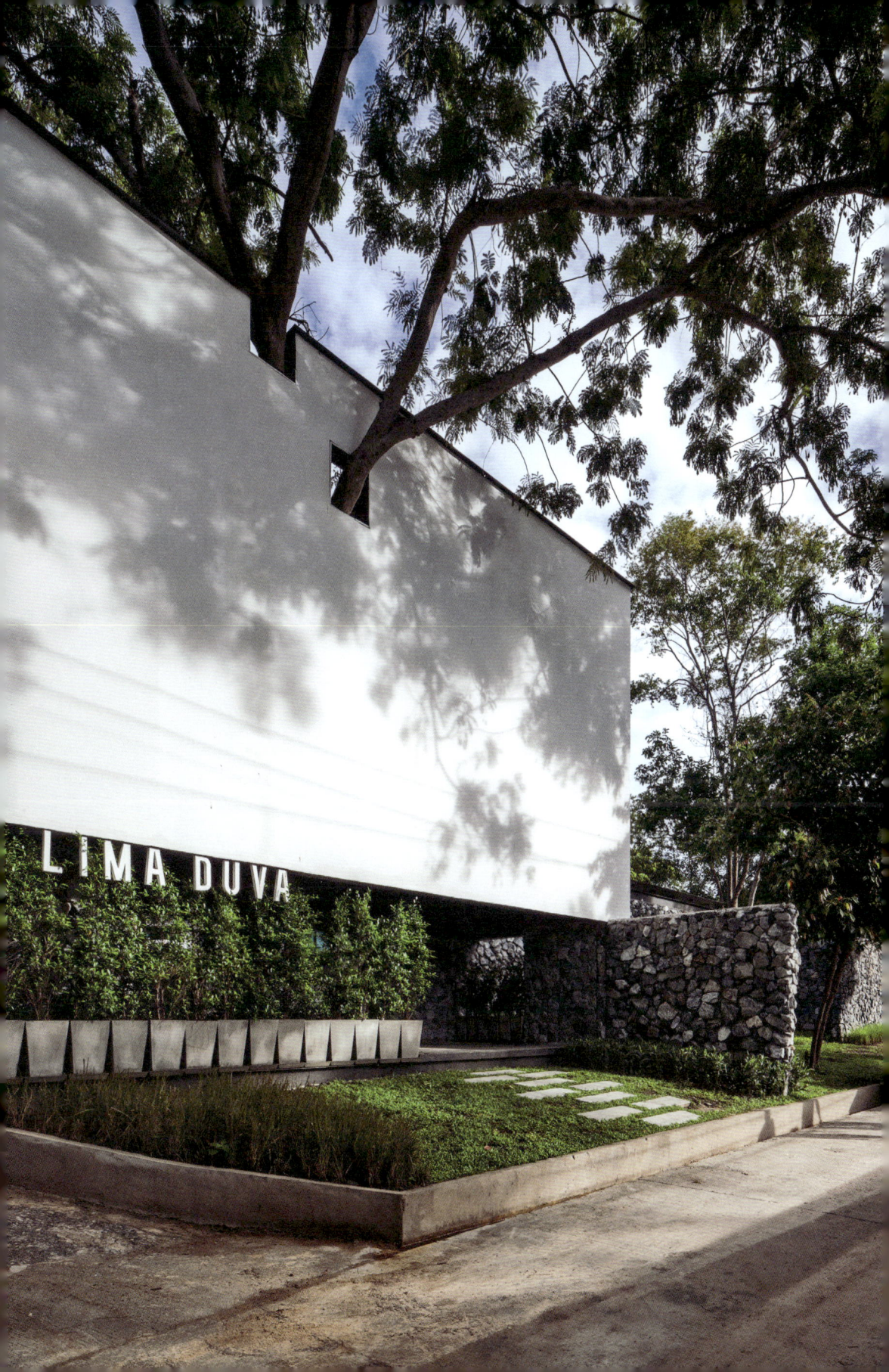

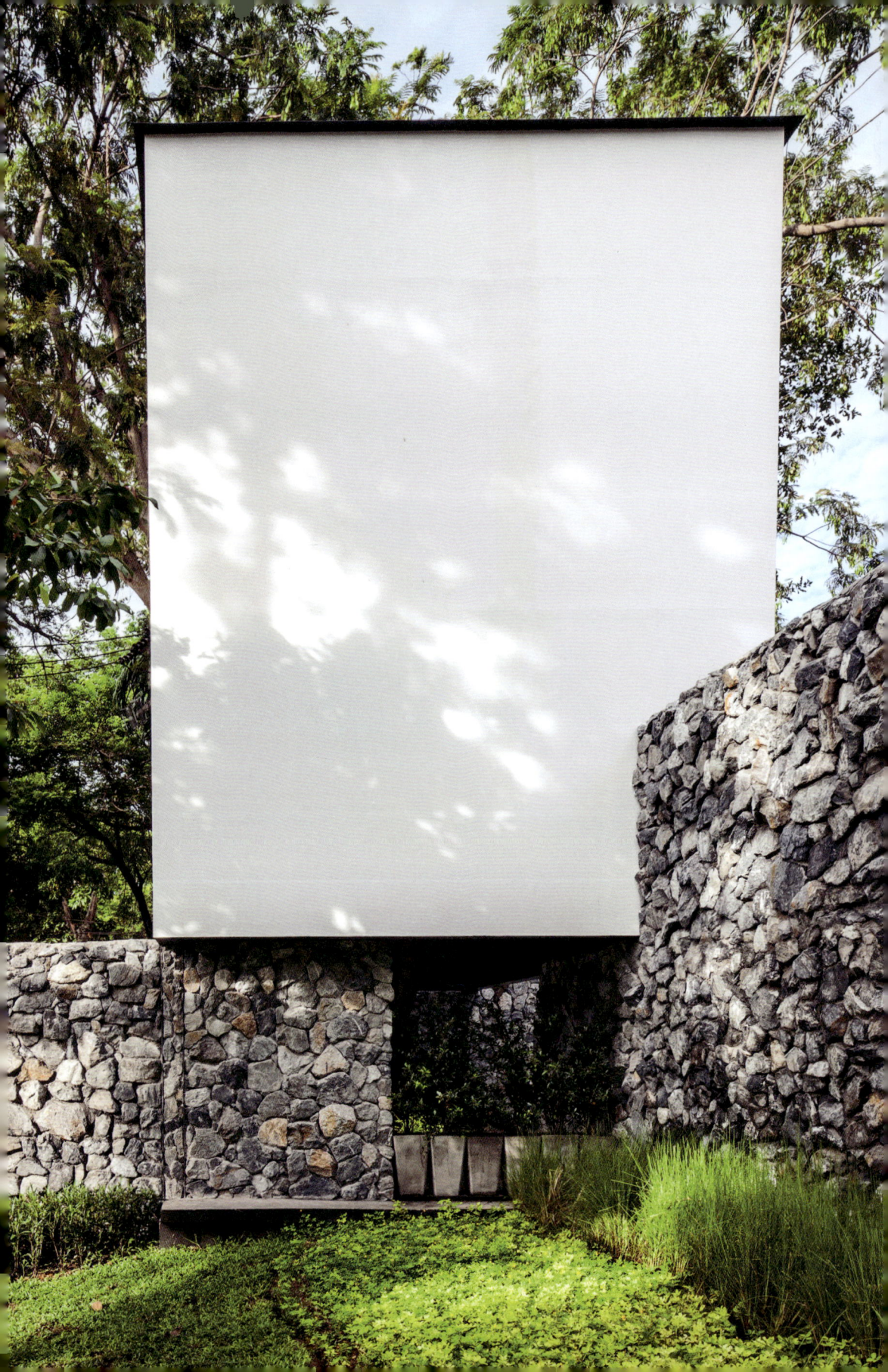

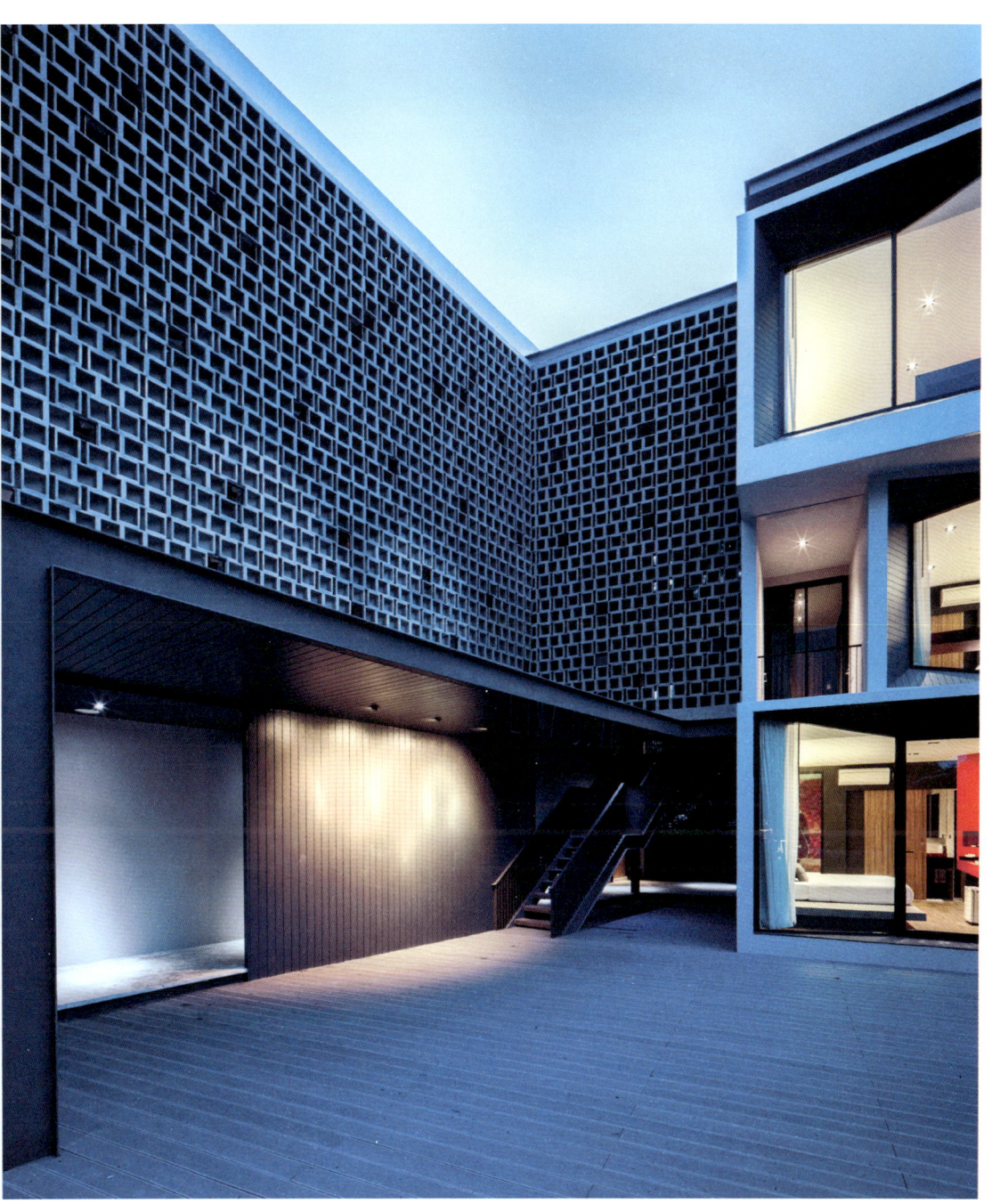

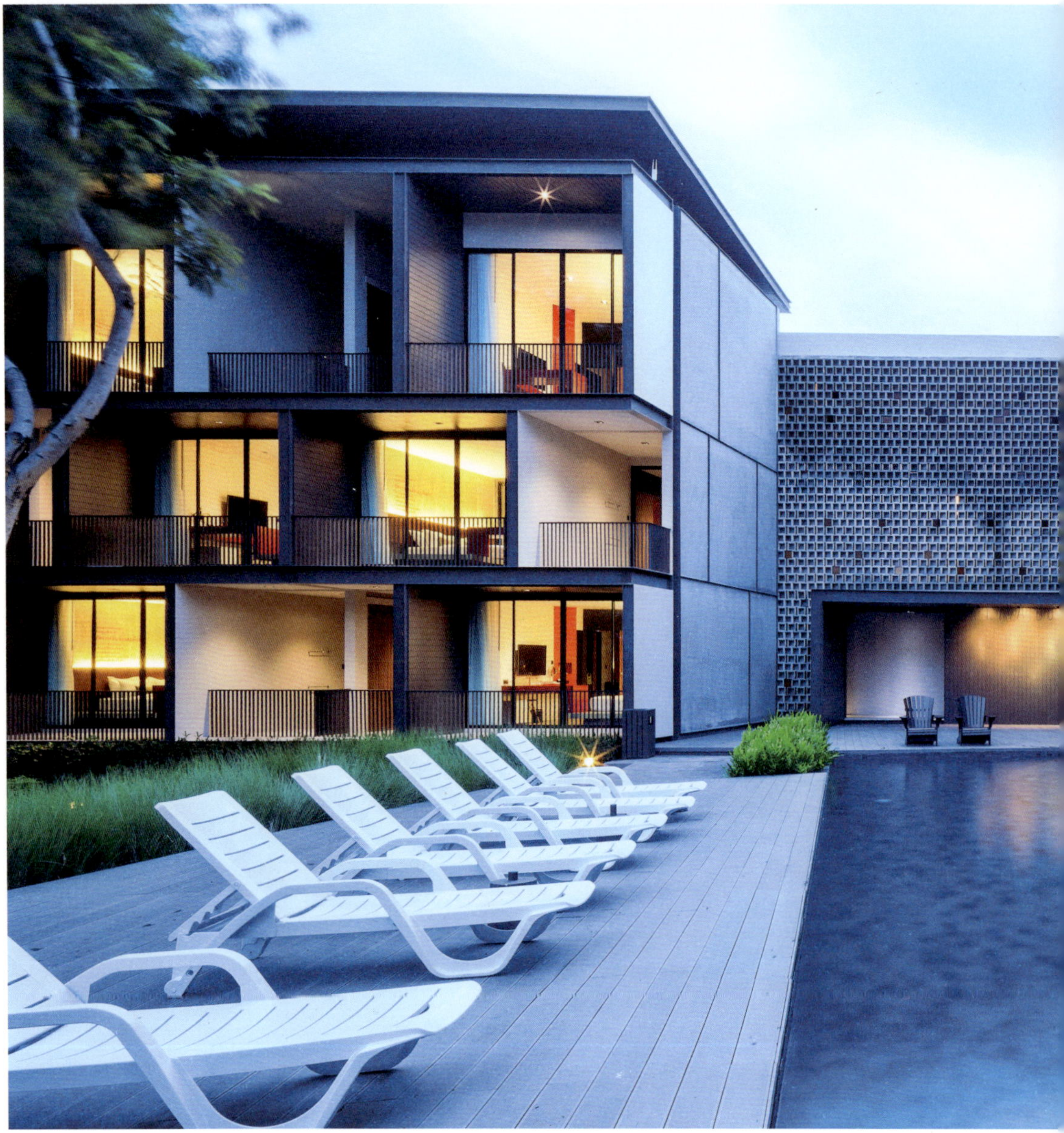

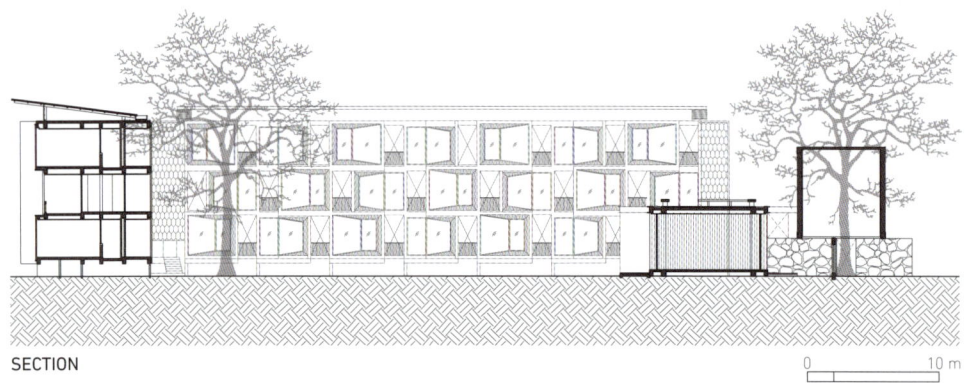

SECTION

0　　10 m

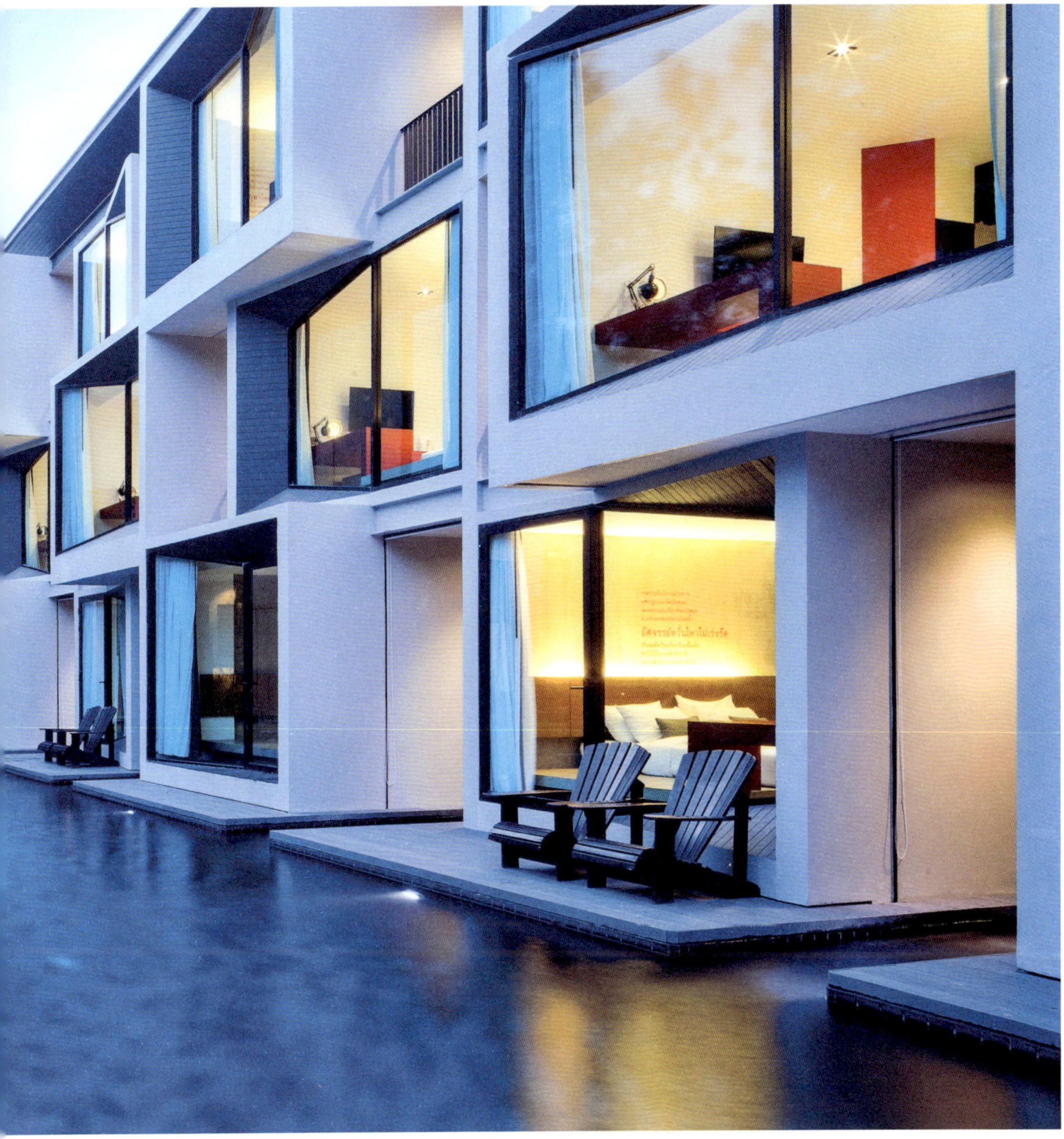

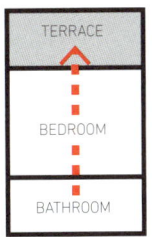

SIMPLE SPACE
ARRANGEMENT

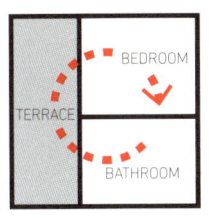

REARRANGED
SPACE LAYOUT

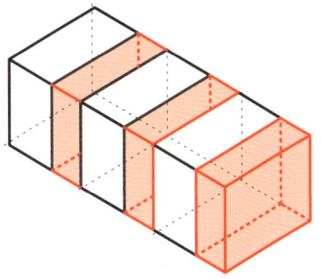

REARRANGING THE POSITION OF THE TERRACE
CREATES PRIVACY AND MINIMIZES NOISE

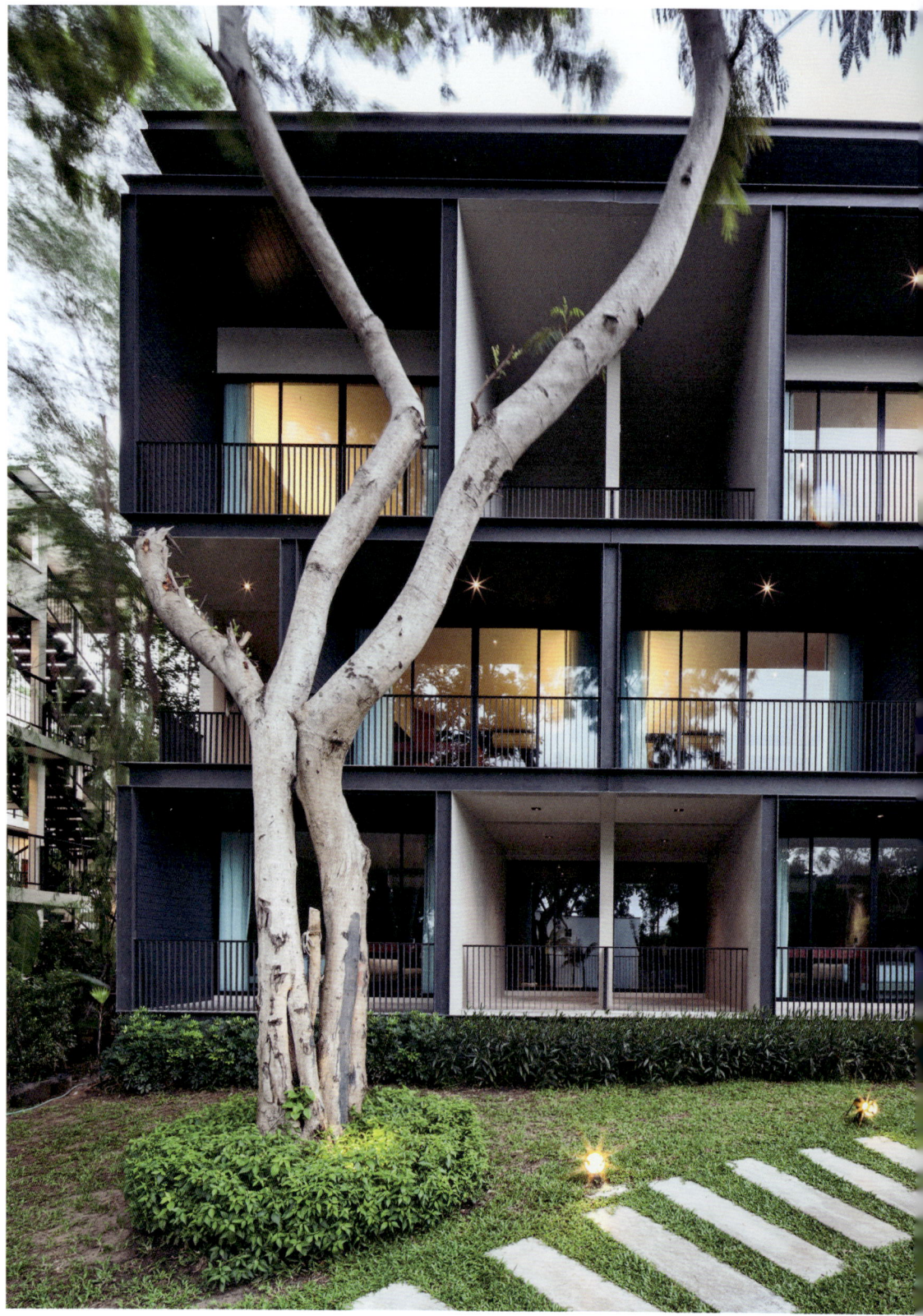

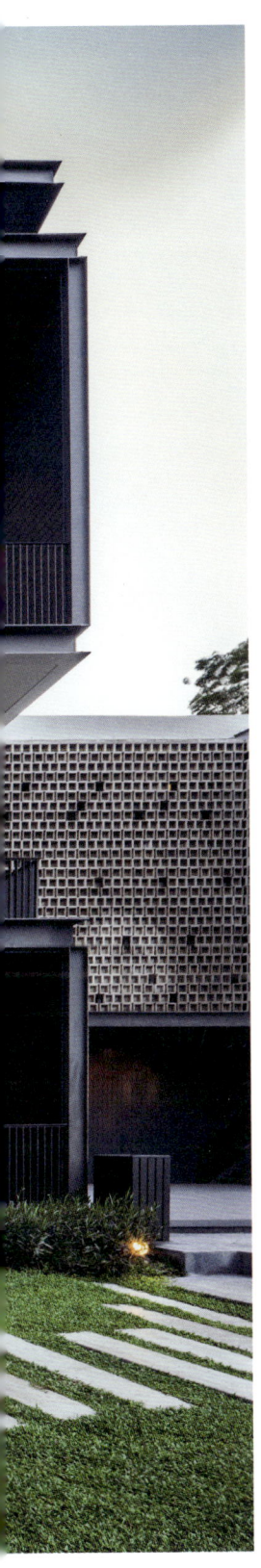

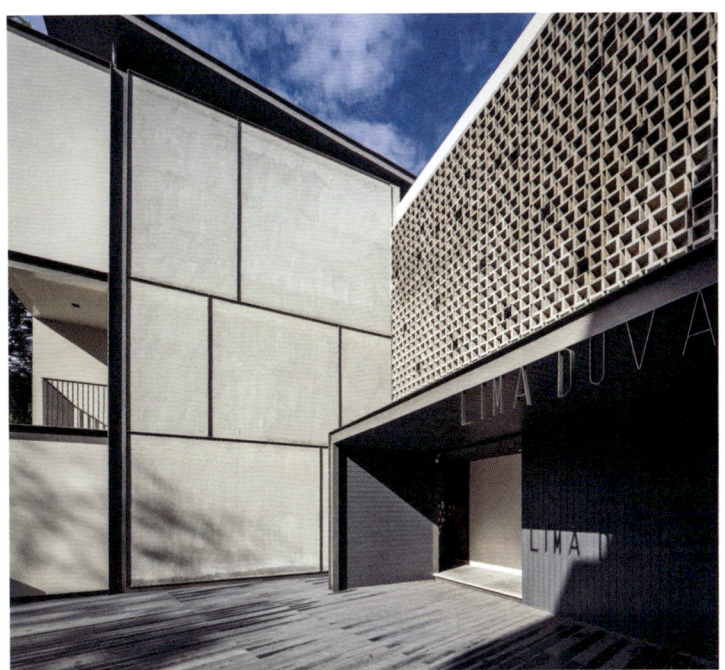

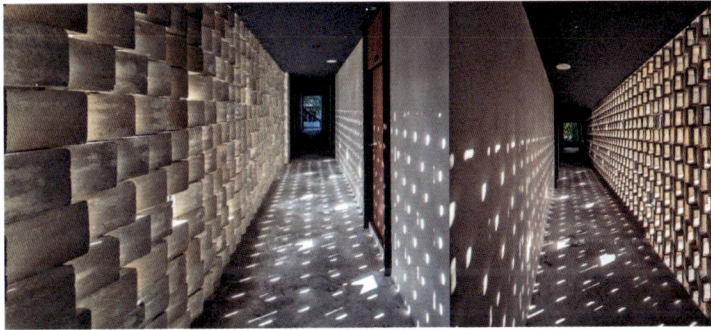

The guestroom buildings adopt an L-shape layout around the main pool; the pool deck connects to a fresh, wide lawn that rolls out to meet the access path for guests from Lima Bella. The restaurant flanks the other short side of the pool in a cozy outfit that reiterates the entrance's masonry detail in its interior, creating a simple, yet striking décor. This repetition of detail also ensures the carry-through of design aesthetics. The area overview depicts an overall U-shape formation, which effectively supports events and activities organized in the inner space. Ventilation blocks along the corridors dapple the sunlight that streams through and create dreamy patterns that vary through the day, so that shuttling about the resort becomes more interesting as guests enjoy nature's many transient art pieces along the way.

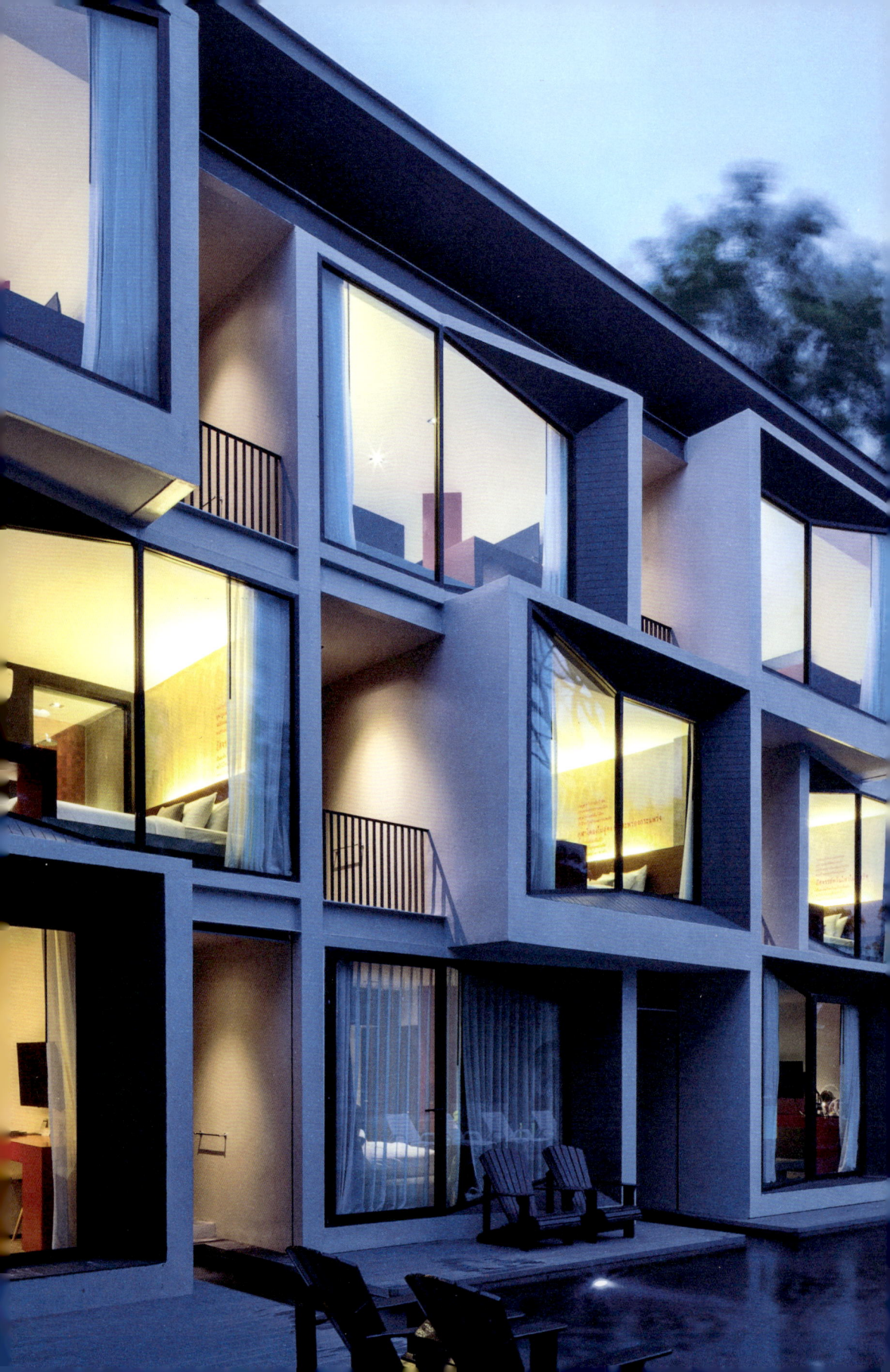

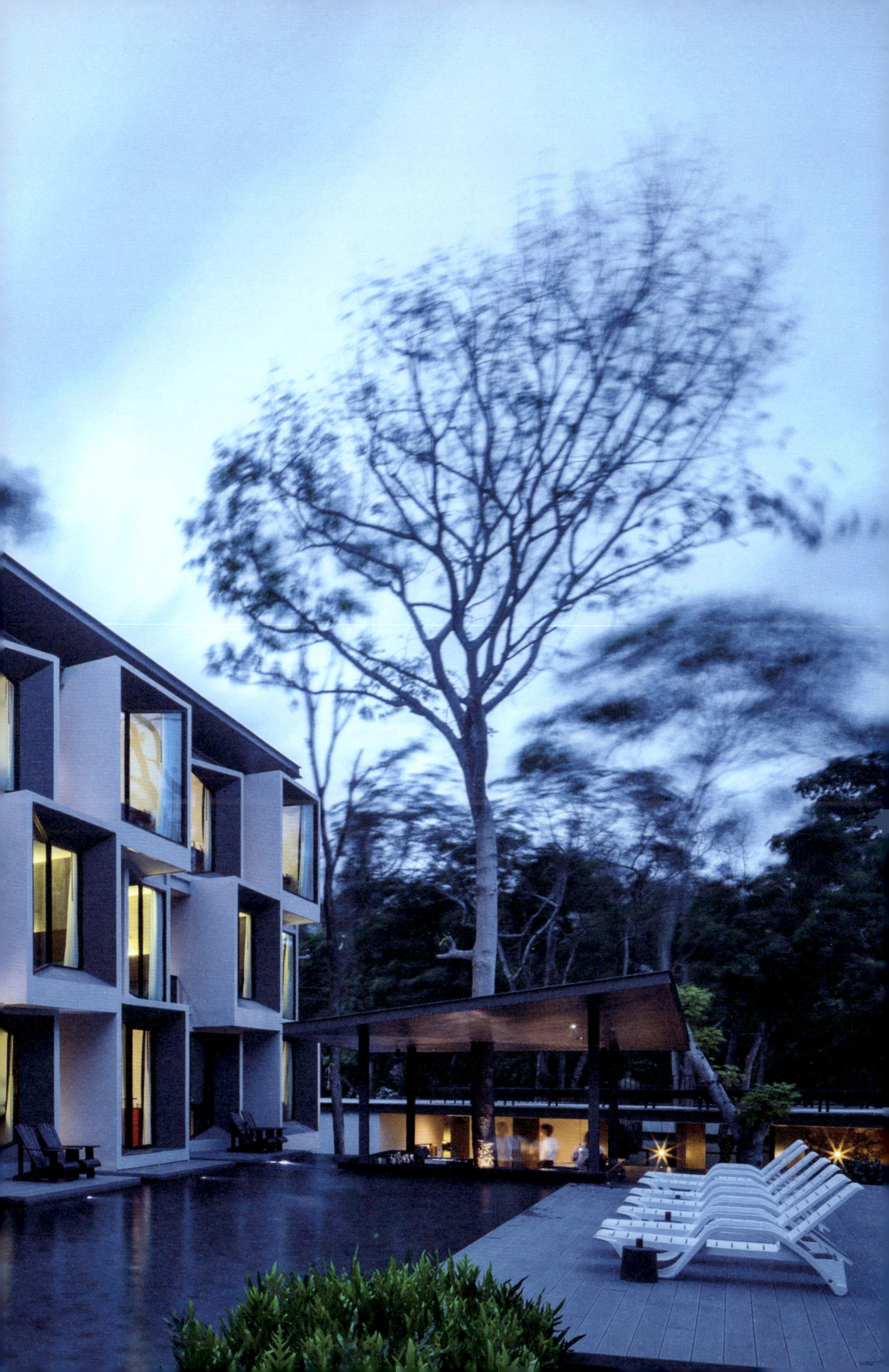

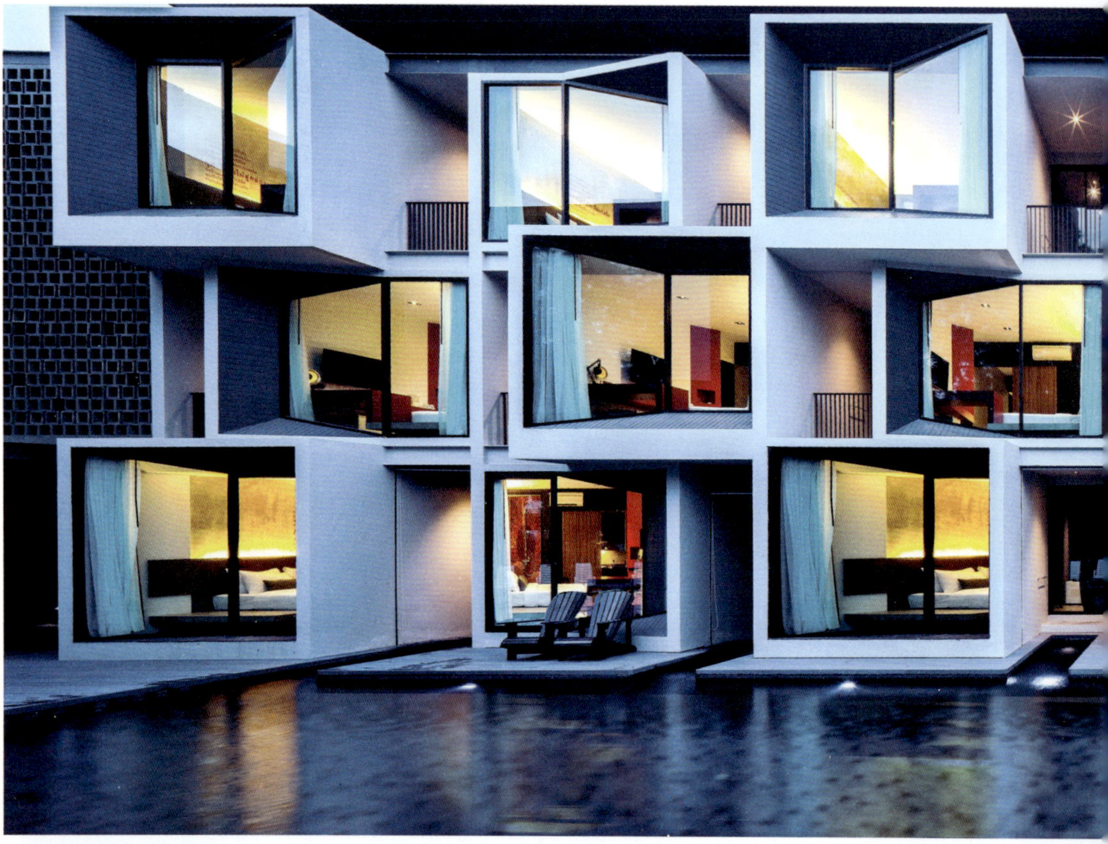

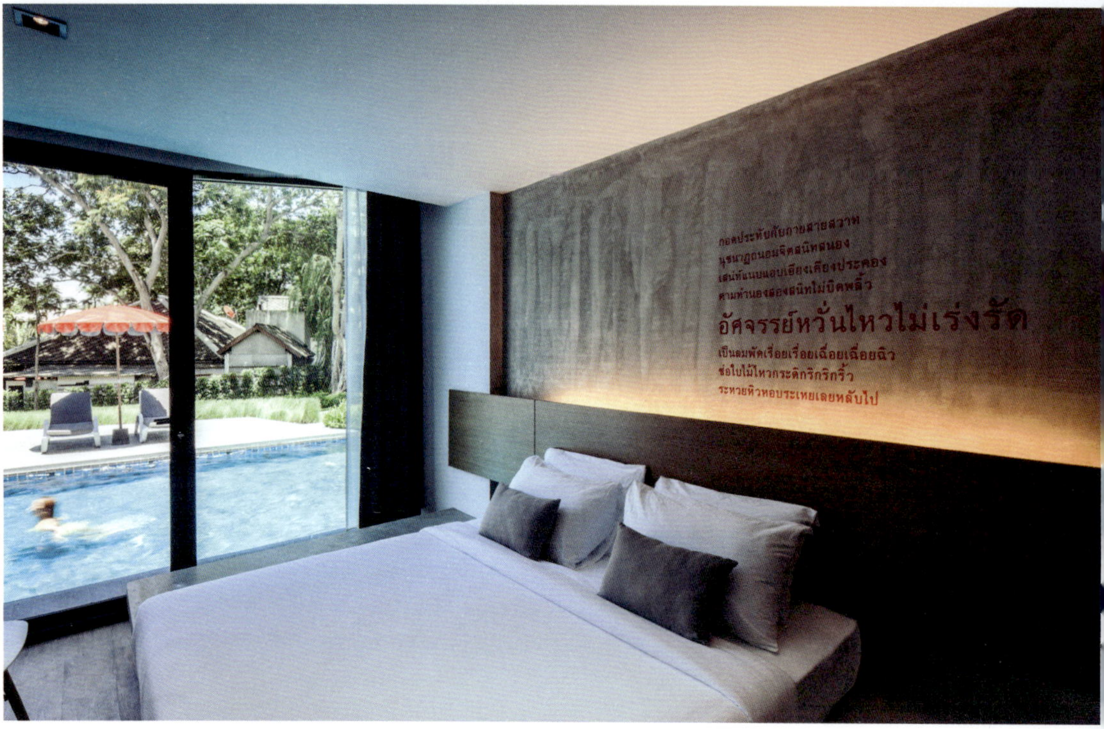

กอดประทับสัยกายสายสวาท
บุระกฏอมยิดสนิทนอง
เอนท์แนบแอบเอียงเคียงประคอง
คมท่านองต้องมนไม่บิดพลิ้ว
อัศจรรย์หวั่นไหวไม่เร่งรัด
เป็นลมพัดเรื่อยเฉื่อยเฉื่อยฉิว
ช่อใบไม้ไหวกระดิกริกริกริ้ว
ระหวยหิวหอบระเหยเลยหลับไป

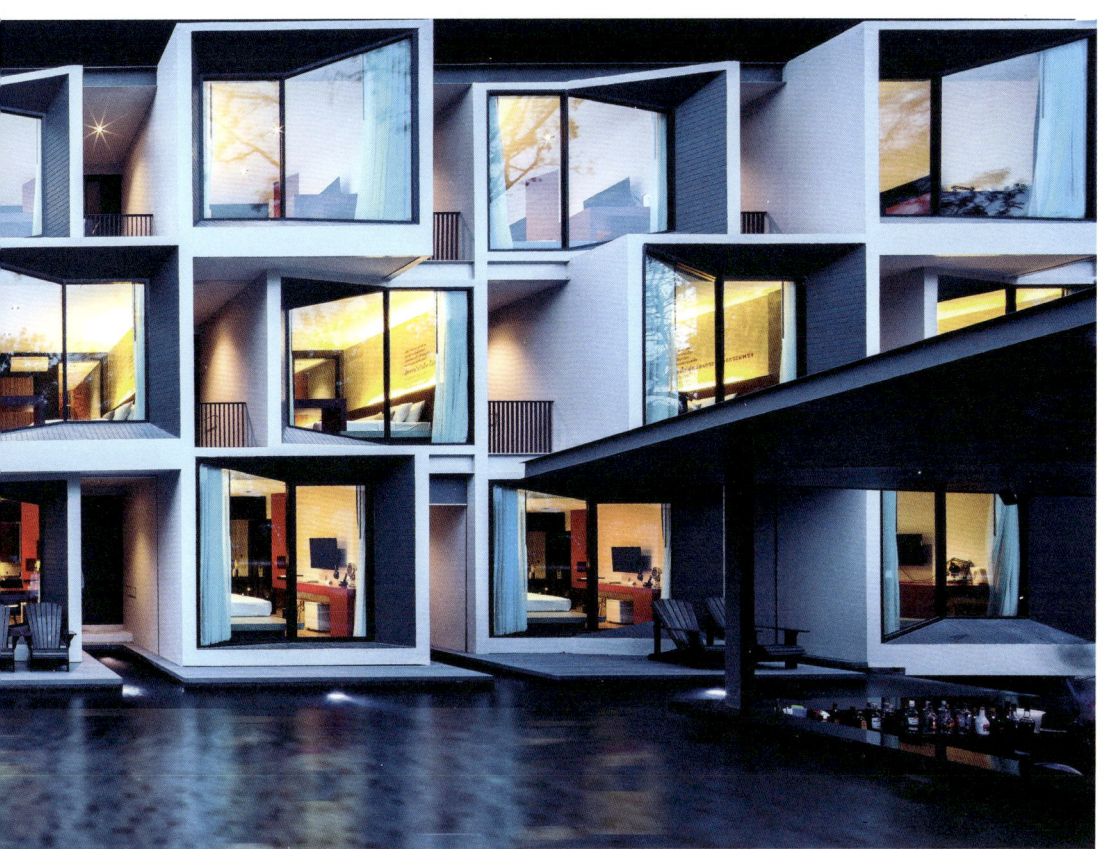

All first-floor units have access to the pool. Nearing the guestrooms, the pool tiles darken to indicate the proximity of the rooms. Between guestrooms, the pool splits into narrow gullies for couples that may want to venture a more intimate, cozy splash. The Jacuzzi area is also located nearer to guestrooms to create visual privacy. All guestrooms are tailored as flexible accommodations and beds can be added when required. On the walls, verses of a *Bot Assajan* (an extract of an erotic scene) from the fable narrate the union of Phra Aphai Mani and the mermaid, bringing home the mood of passion and romance that drifts on Koh Samet.

Mueang, Kanchanaburi, Thailand, 2019

TARA VILLA

Situated along the River Kwai, the small Tara Villa resort is a rest and relaxation sanctuary, as well as an events venue for occasions like weddings, conferences, and seminars. The facilities serve the full spectrum of event programs, and it has been designed with a large area at the rear of the property reserved for future expansion. The number of guestrooms in Tara Villa is small considering its site area, and this inspired the design to pay more attention to the spaces between functional areas, guided by the idea that the journey is more important than the destination.

The concept focuses on experiencing the resort through the senses: feeling different textures; observing scenes of light and shadow; listening to the whistle of the wind; and enjoying the oddly soothing scent of the earth after rain. These instances become an integral part of a user's experience, especially as they move around within the resort.

The main circulation connects with all other common areas, meandering past scatterings of the original trees on-site; care was taken to retain as many of them as possible. The layout is optimized to its fullest, positioning the main building, which houses the lobby/reception and function room, and other primary areas, in the direction of the River Kwai to present the beautiful river view to guests within.

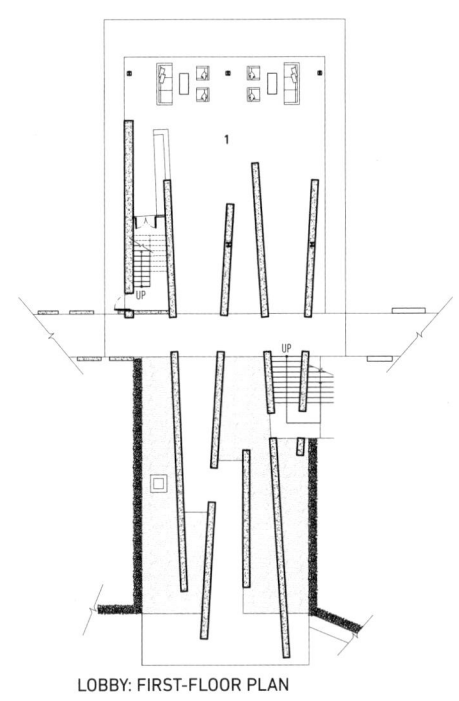

LOBBY: FIRST-FLOOR PLAN

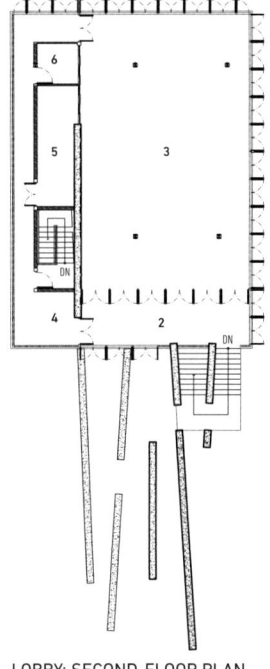

LOBBY: SECOND-FLOOR PLAN

1 LOBBY LOUNGE
2 FOYER
3 FUNCTION ROOM
4 SERVICE CORRIDOR
5 STORAGE ROOM
6 M&E ROOM

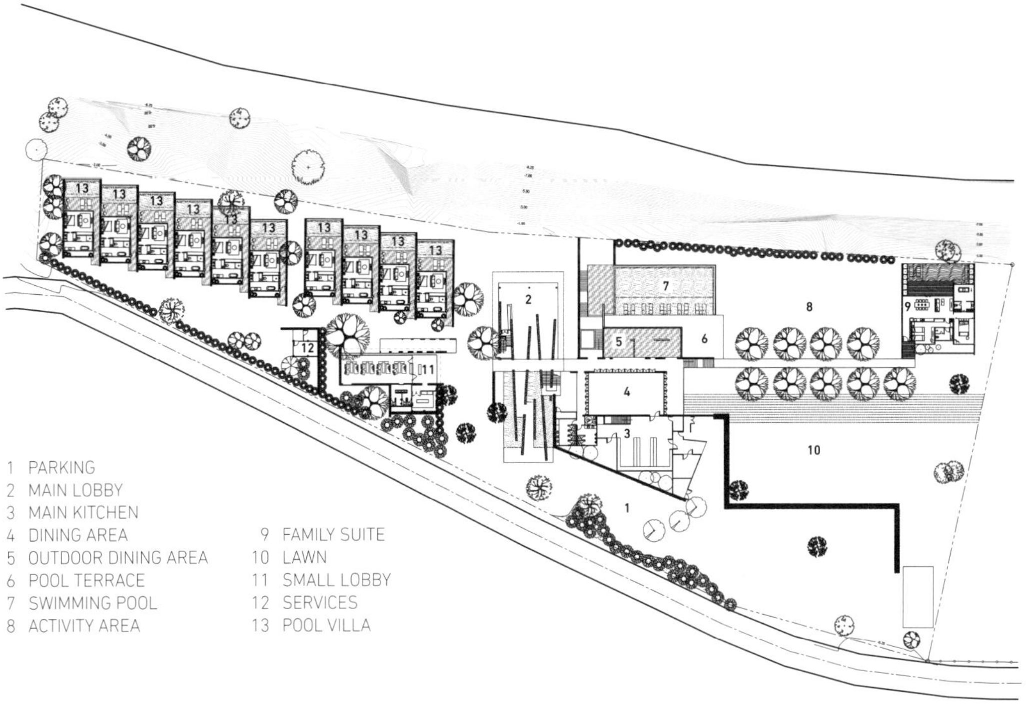

1 PARKING
2 MAIN LOBBY
3 MAIN KITCHEN
4 DINING AREA
5 OUTDOOR DINING AREA
6 POOL TERRACE
7 SWIMMING POOL
8 ACTIVITY AREA
9 FAMILY SUITE
10 LAWN
11 SMALL LOBBY
12 SERVICES
13 POOL VILLA

MASTER PLAN

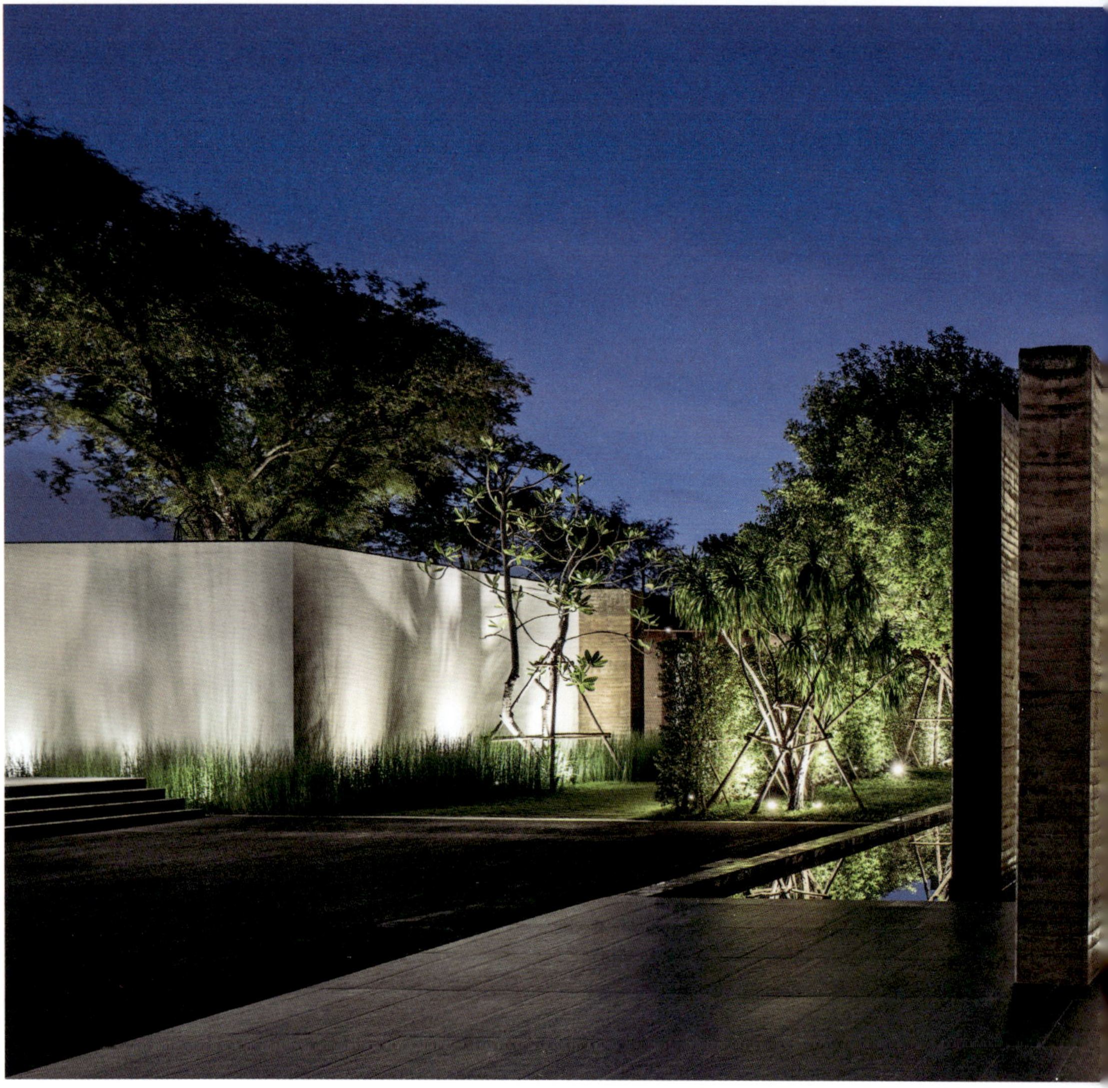

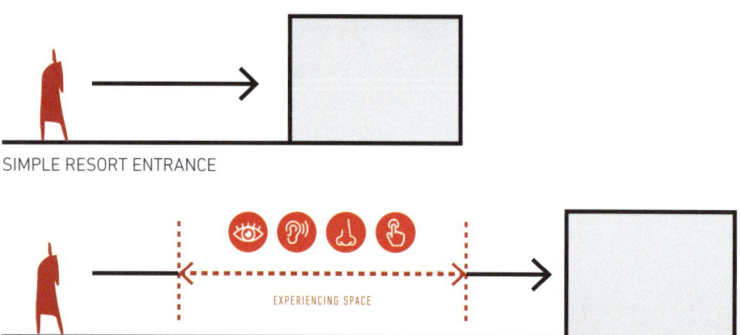

SIMPLE RESORT ENTRANCE

EXPERIENCING SPACE

ENTRANCE EXTENDED TO INCREASE TIME SPENT ALONG THE PATHWAY

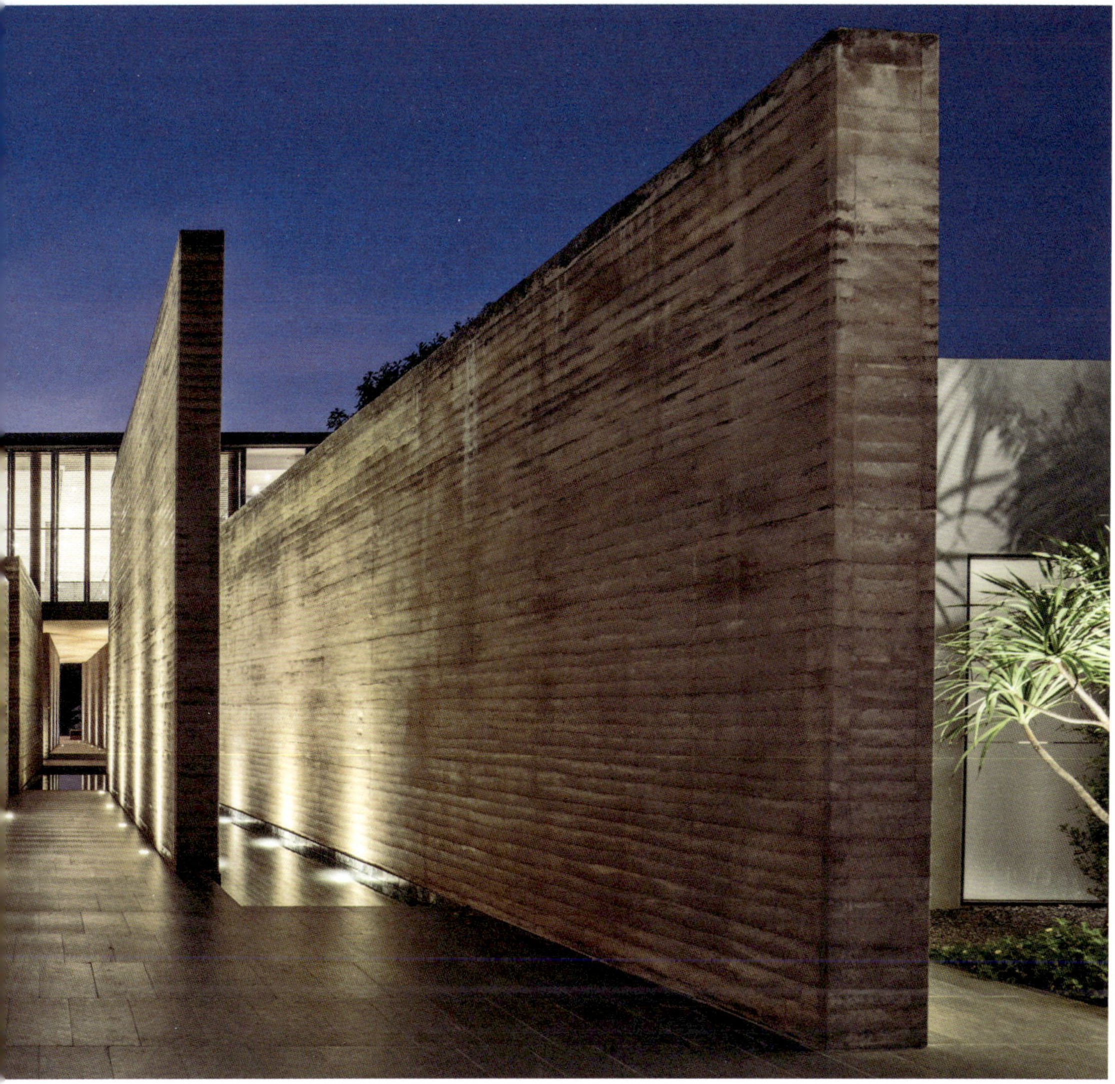

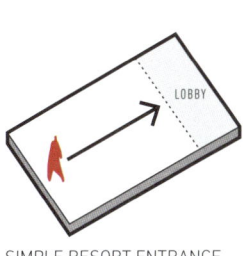
SIMPLE RESORT ENTRANCE

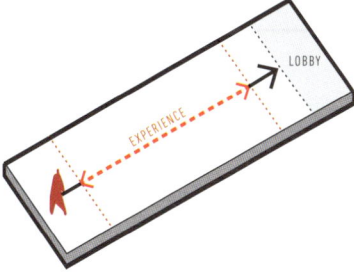
INCREASING TIME SPENT ALONG THE PATHWAY

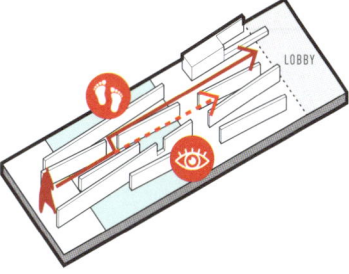
RAMMED-EARTH WALLS MANIPULATE SIGHT LINES AND THE PATH TO THE ENTRANCE

TARA VILLA

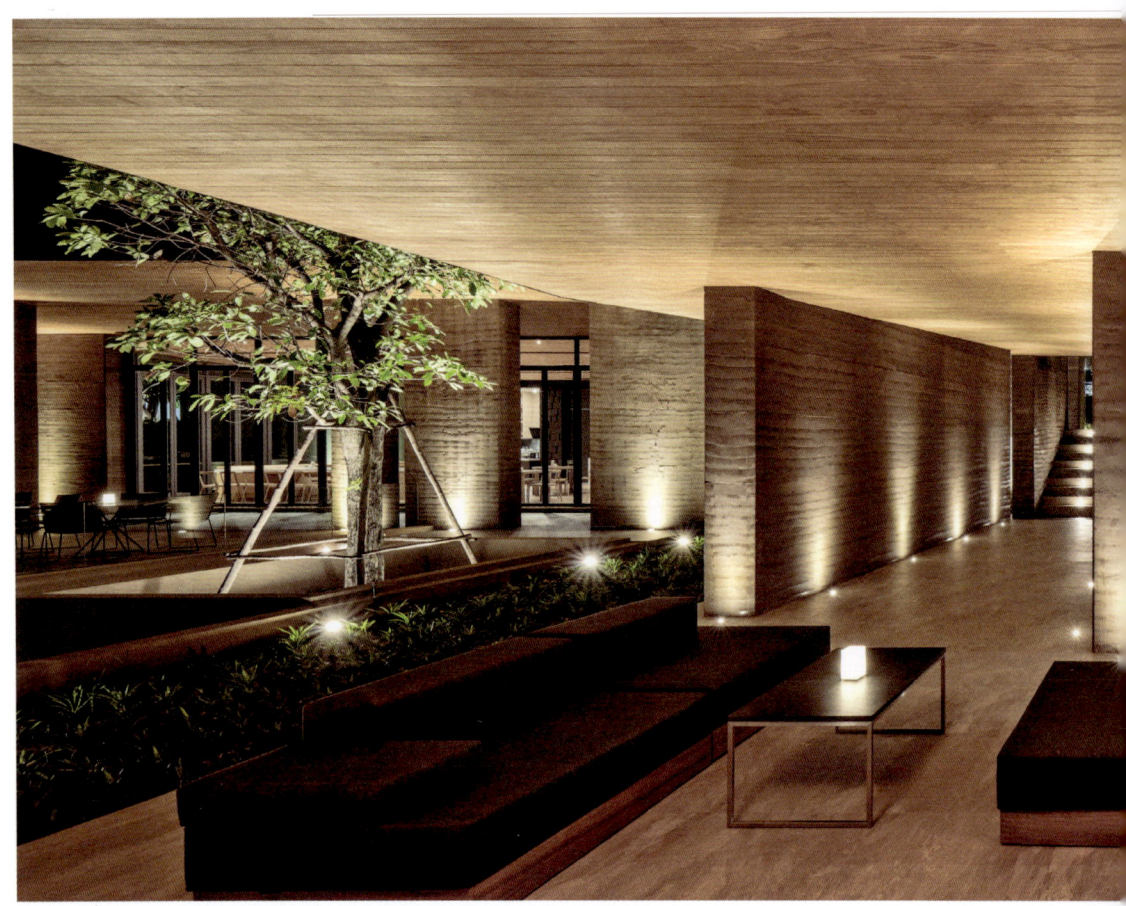

To ensure the proximity of the pool and the courtyard to the River Kwai, the ground level of the land in the right wing is ten feet (three meters) below street level. This reformation removed a large quantity of soil, which is integrated back into the design as rammed-earth walls, in a stroke of inspiration. These eye-catching walls feature a variety of earth layers and lead as the main feature of the resort. They rise as ochre identity monuments and guide the movement of guests through the resort. At the entrance, they play a double role as prologue and epilogue of a user's experience, being the first resort landmark that greets them as they enter, and the last that bids them goodbye as they leave. In other areas, they create accessibility choices that coax guests to take their time along trailing paths. The walls execute the notion of the "journey" as they direct flow in the spaces between functional areas, interacting with users along the way through their prominent texture, color, and magnitude.

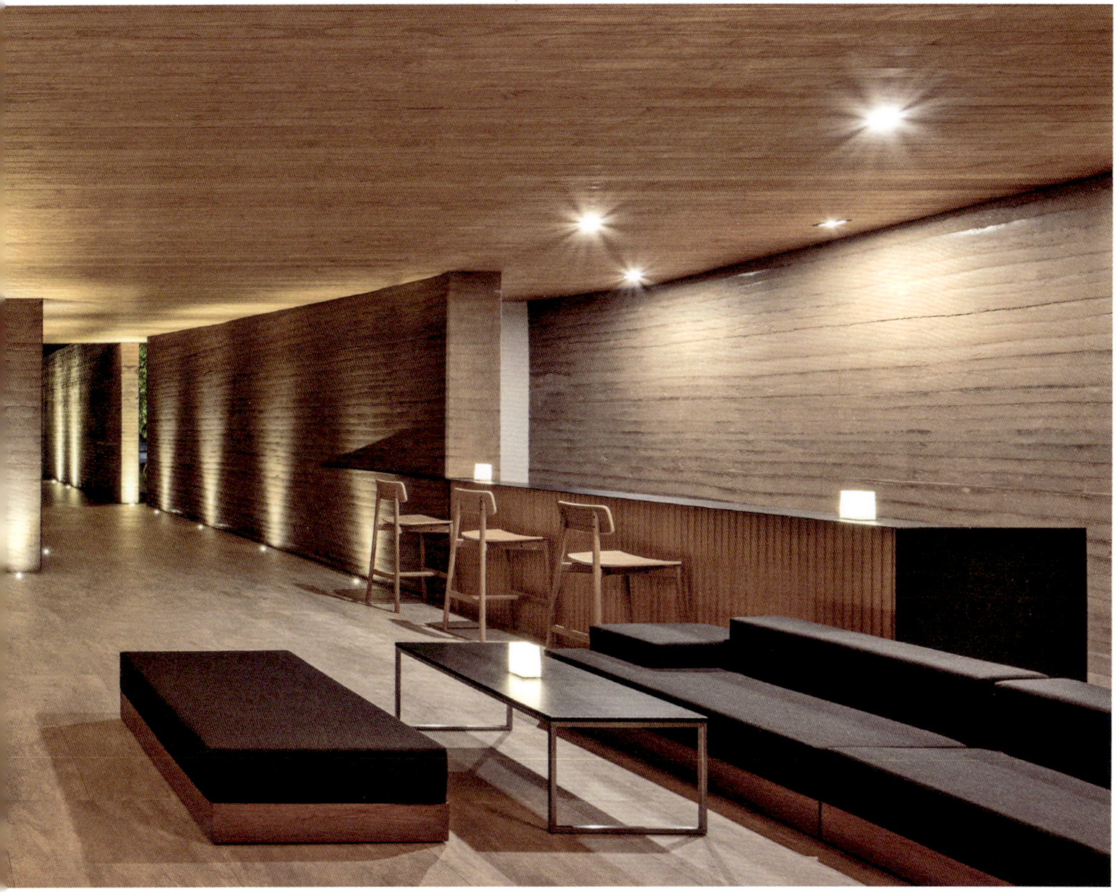

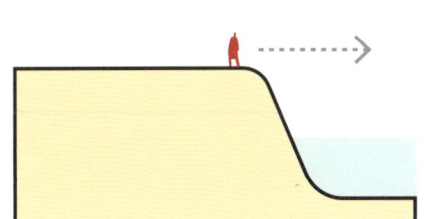

THE PRE-EXISTING LAND LEVEL

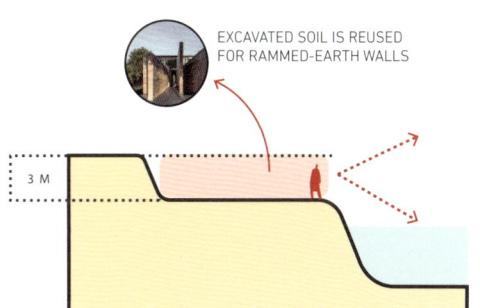

EXCAVATED SOIL IS REUSED FOR RAMMED-EARTH WALLS

3 M

THE OWNER REQUIRED THE SITE TO BE CLOSER TO THE RIVER BY LOWERING THE LAND LEVEL

TARA VILLA

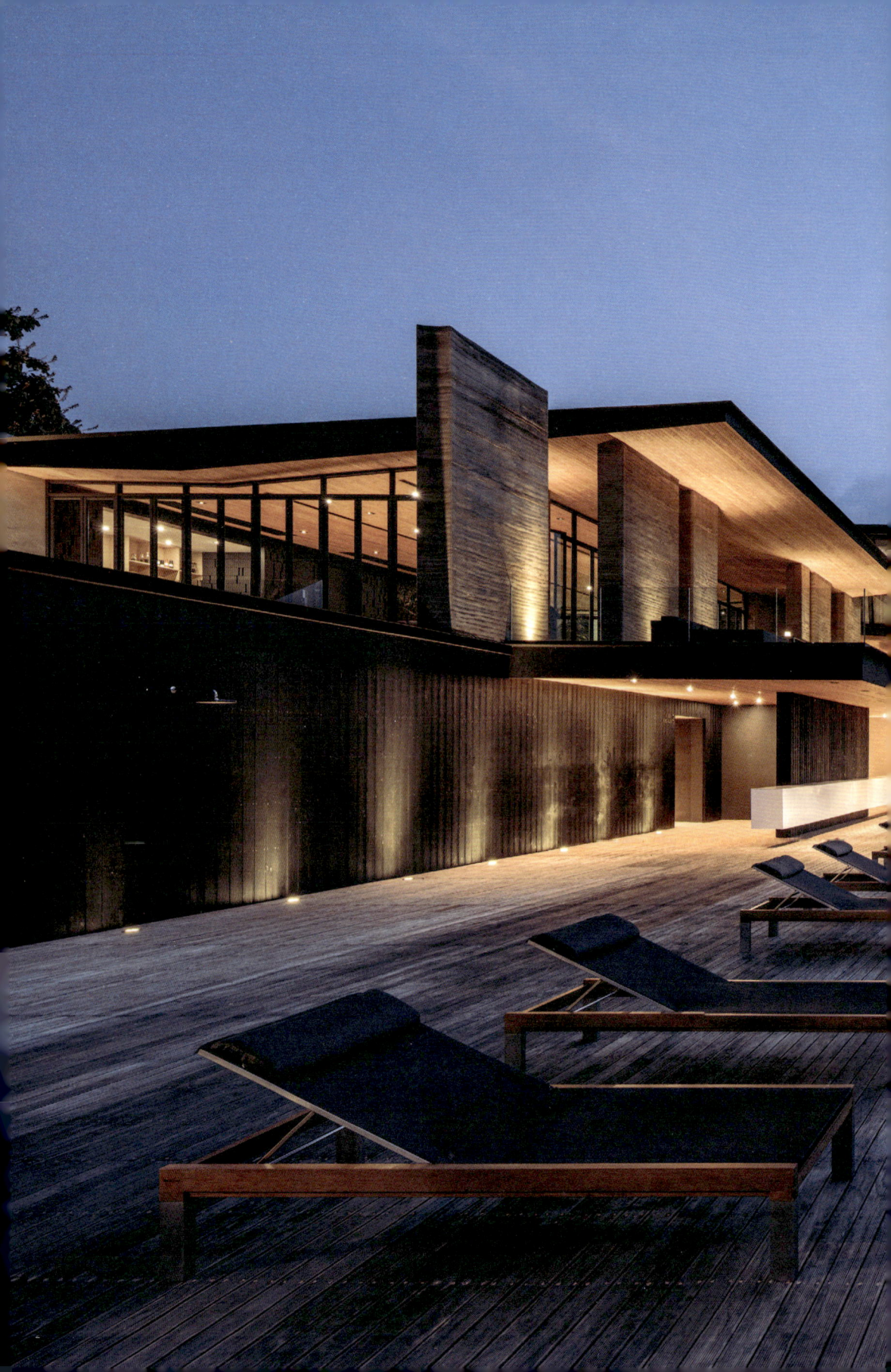

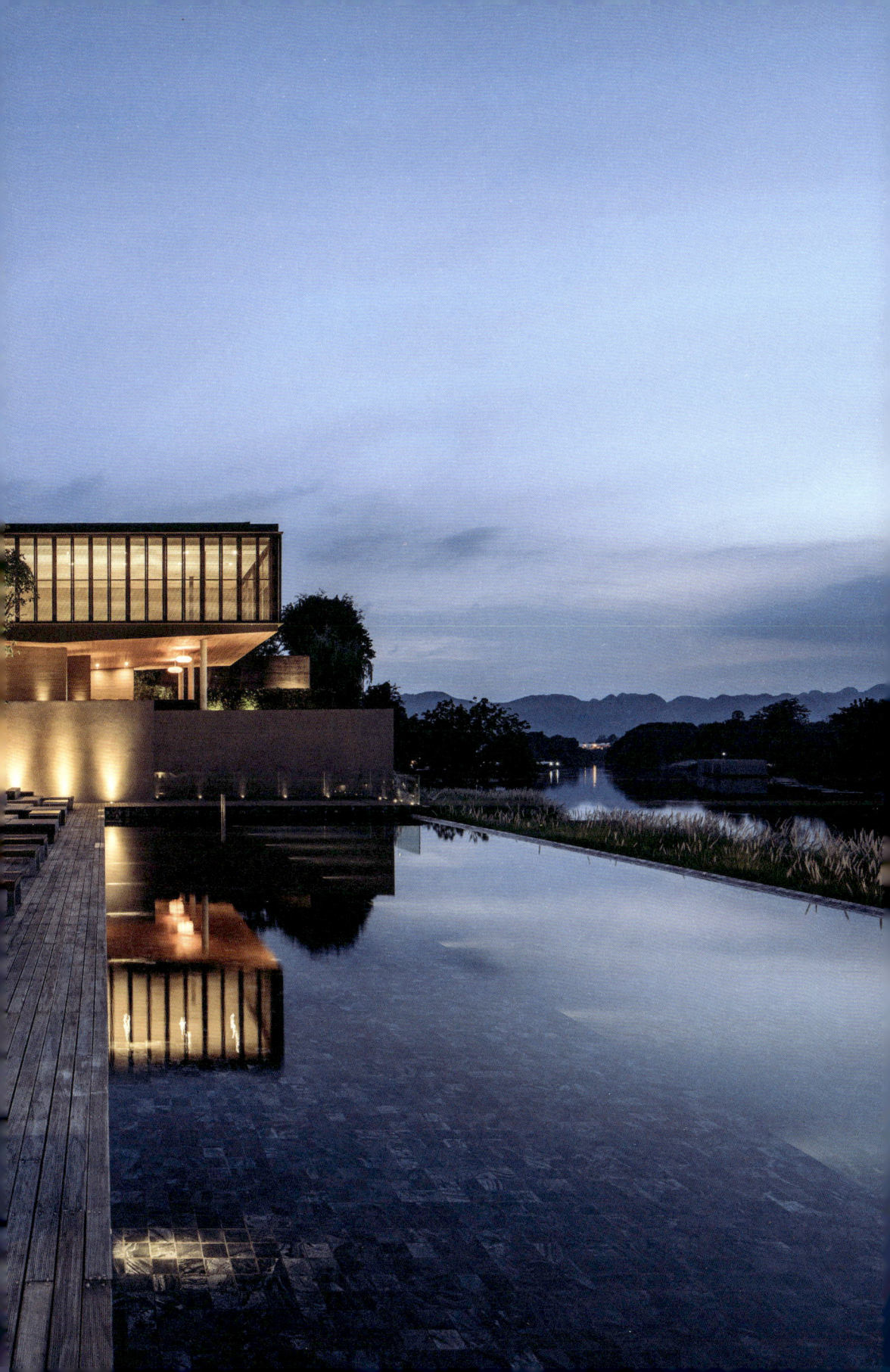

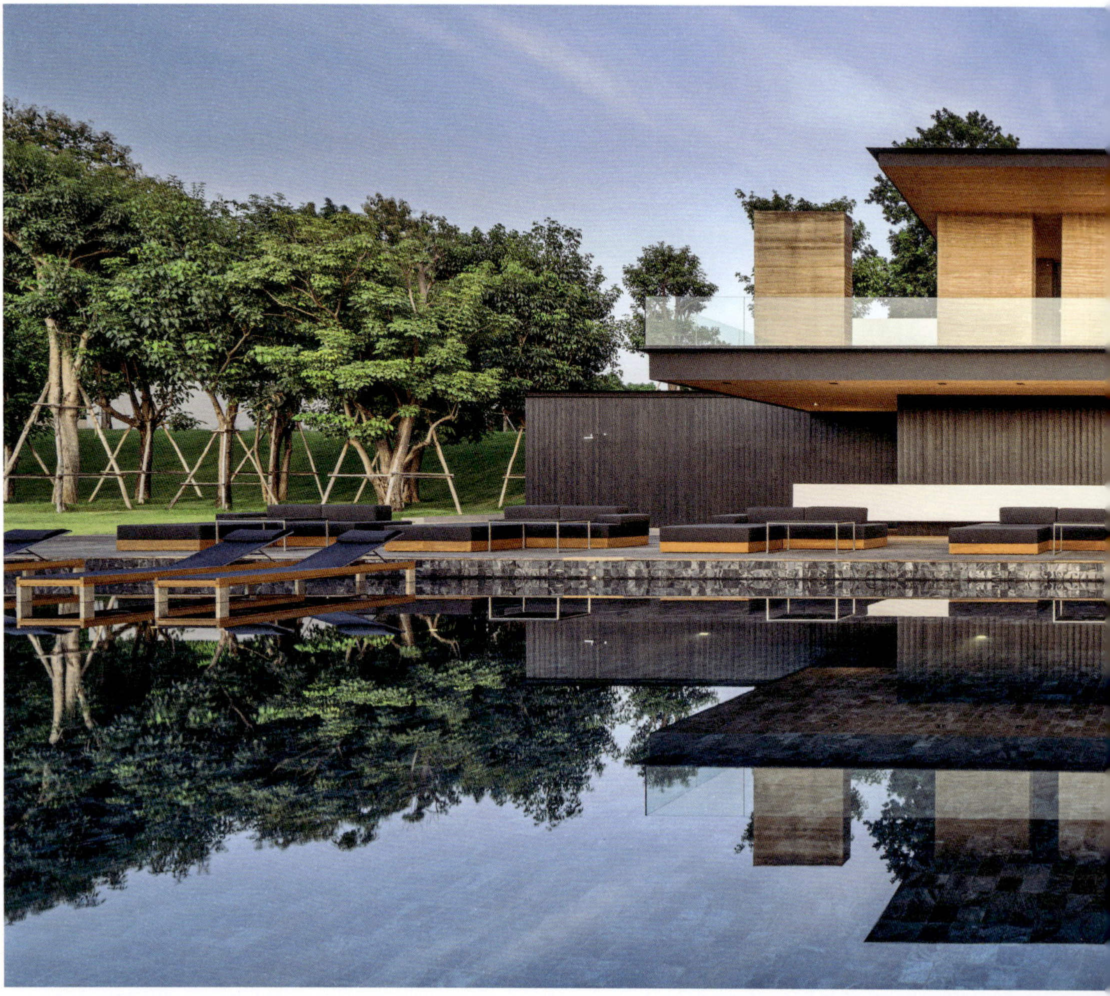

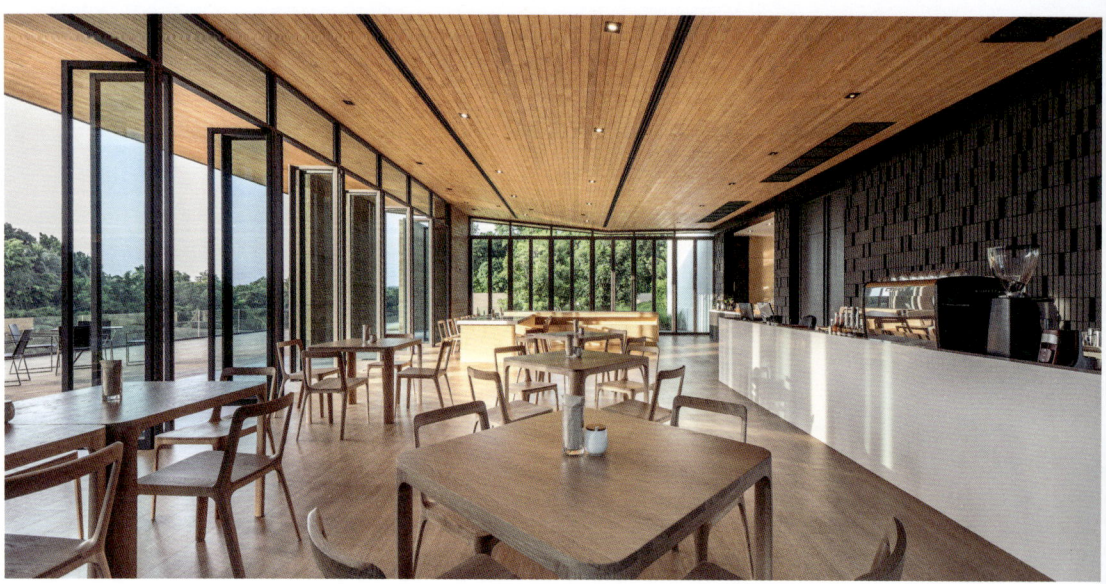

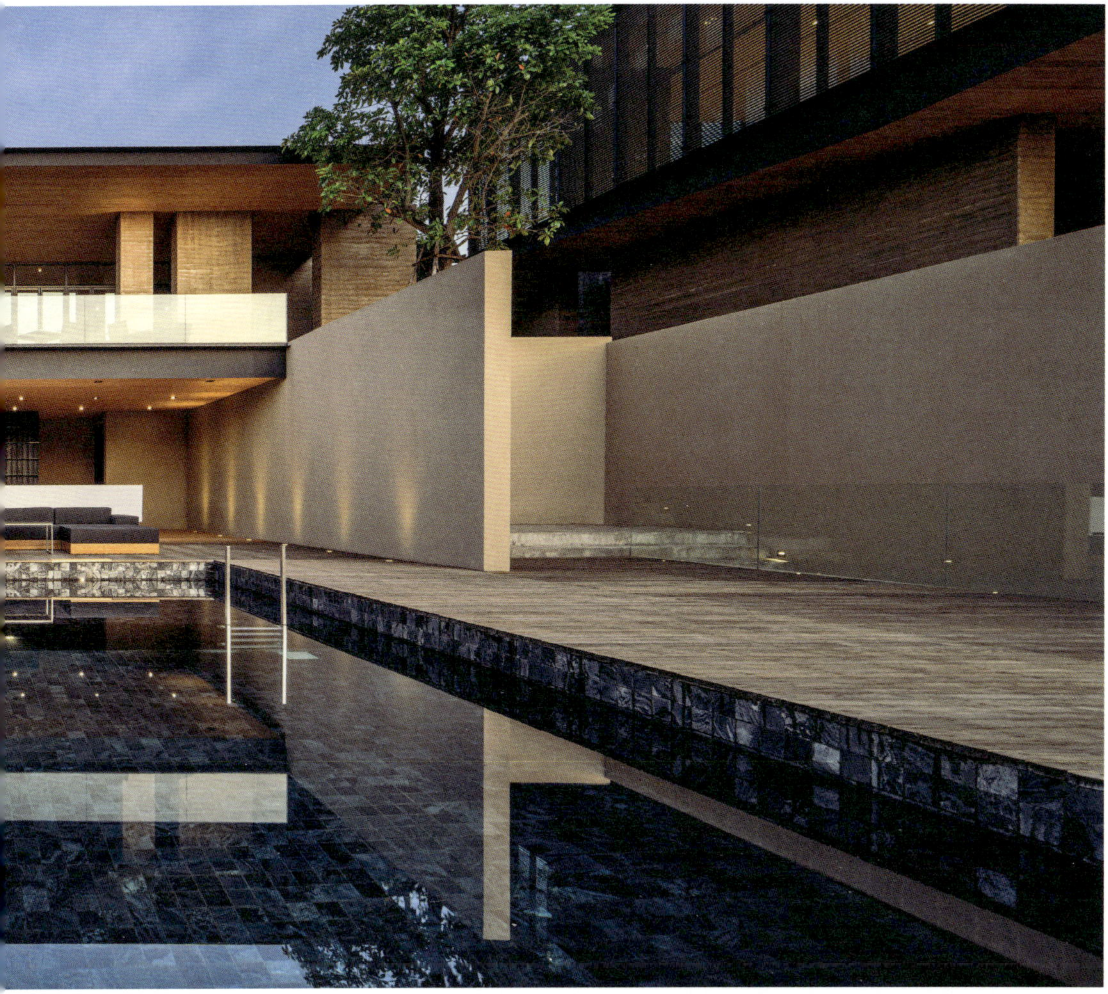

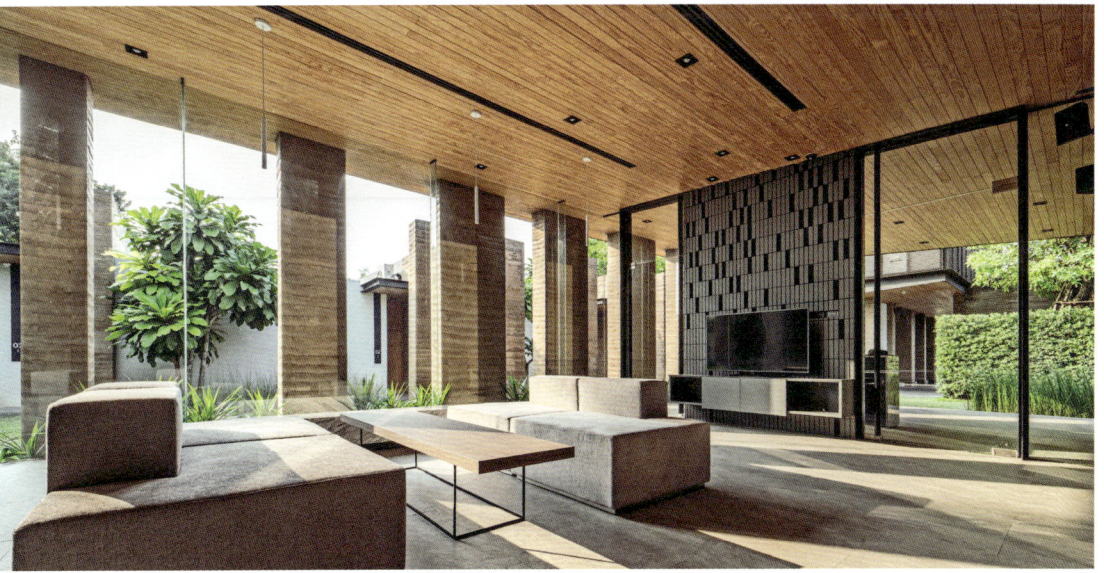

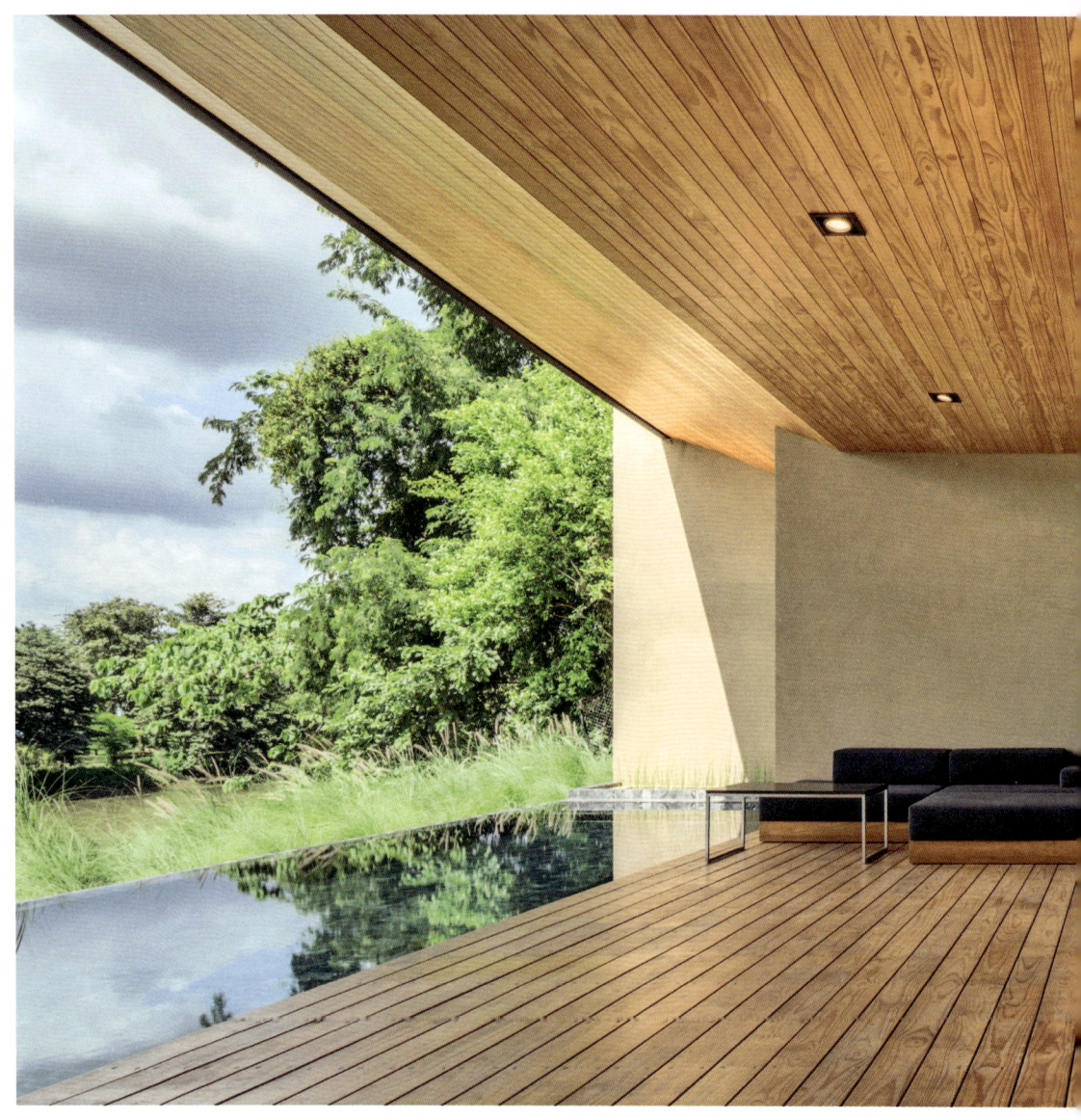

Guests are able to take advantage of the rustic surroundings with the swimming pool and an adjoining courtyard, which sit alongside the river bank. Like the languid ripples in the river, the flow of the space is smooth and continuous, and leads to the family suite located in a segregated area a distance away, to minimize sounds of family activity that might filter out to other guests relaxing by the pool, or dining in the pool terrace. Past family fun time, the villa can be converted into an exclusive honeymoon suite for ardent lovebirds. This accommodates the couple in a spacious area that ranks high in privacy, ensconcing the couple in their personal world of romance, away from other guests.

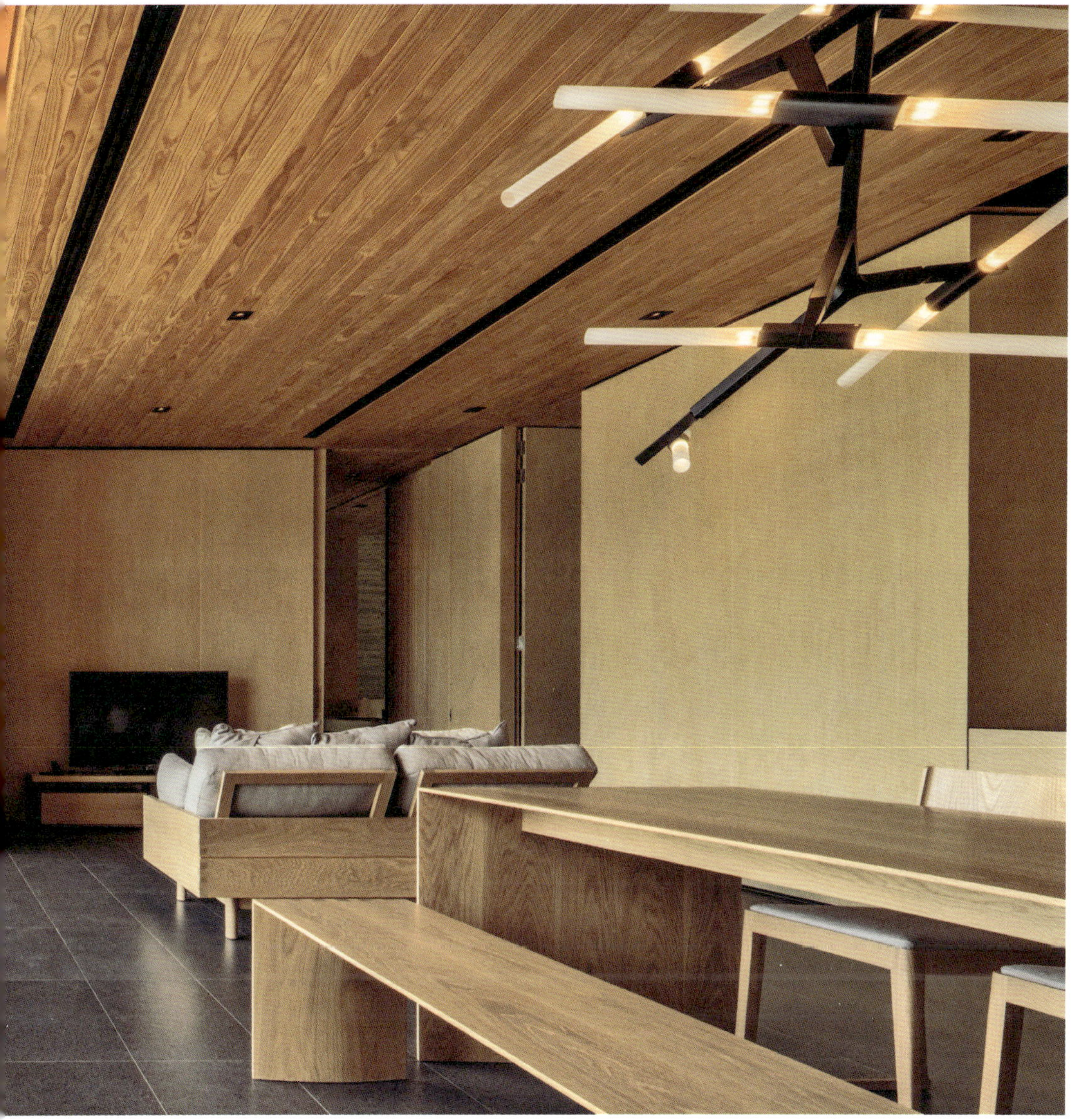

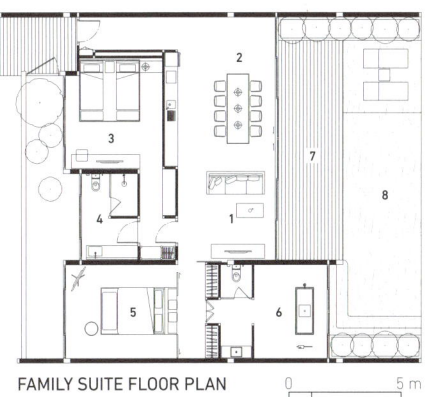

FAMILY SUITE FLOOR PLAN

1 LIVING AREA
2 DINING AREA
3 BEDROOM
4 BATHROOM
5 MASTER BEDROOM
6 MASTER BATHROOM
7 TERRACE
8 SWIMMING POOL

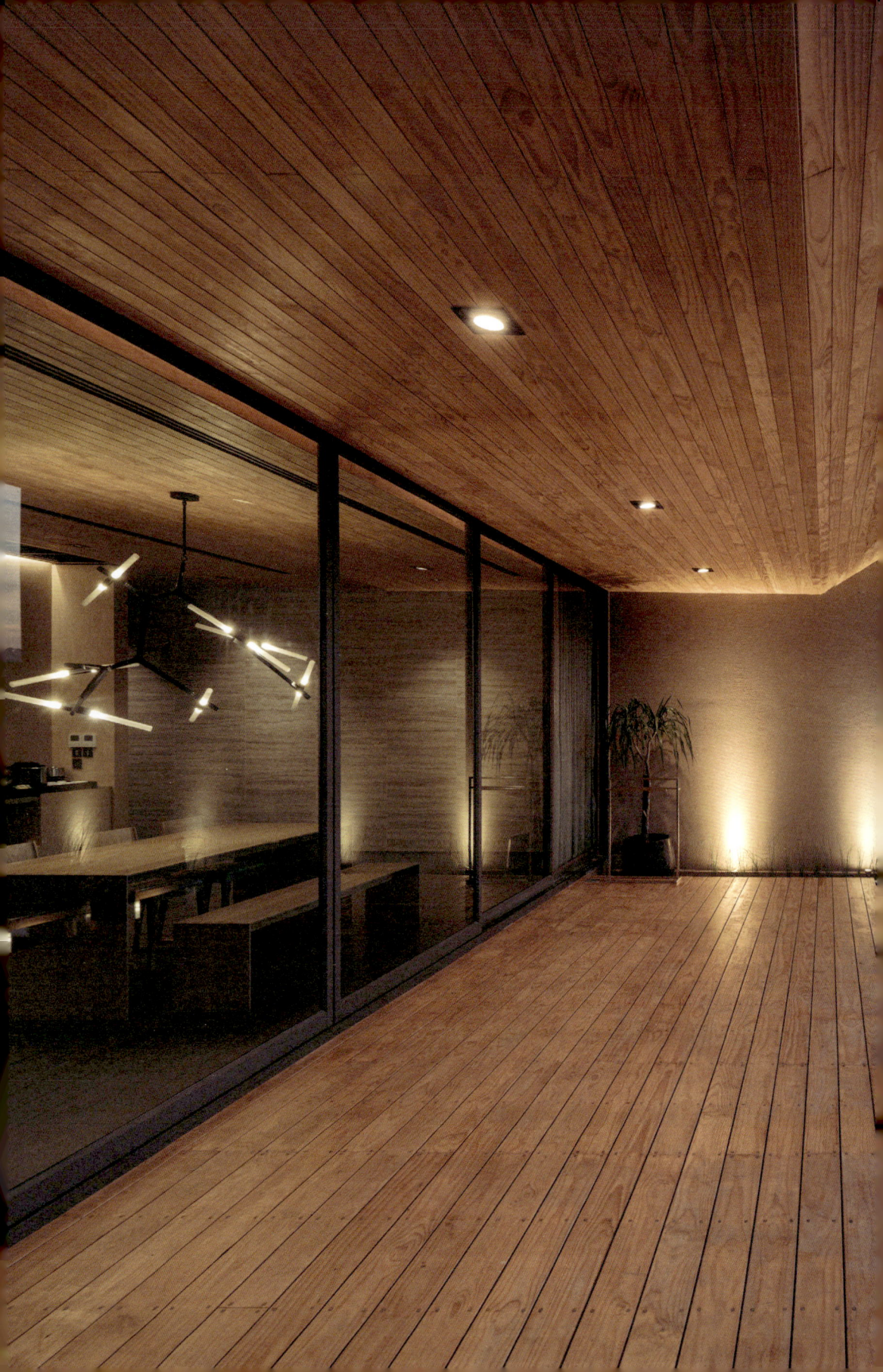

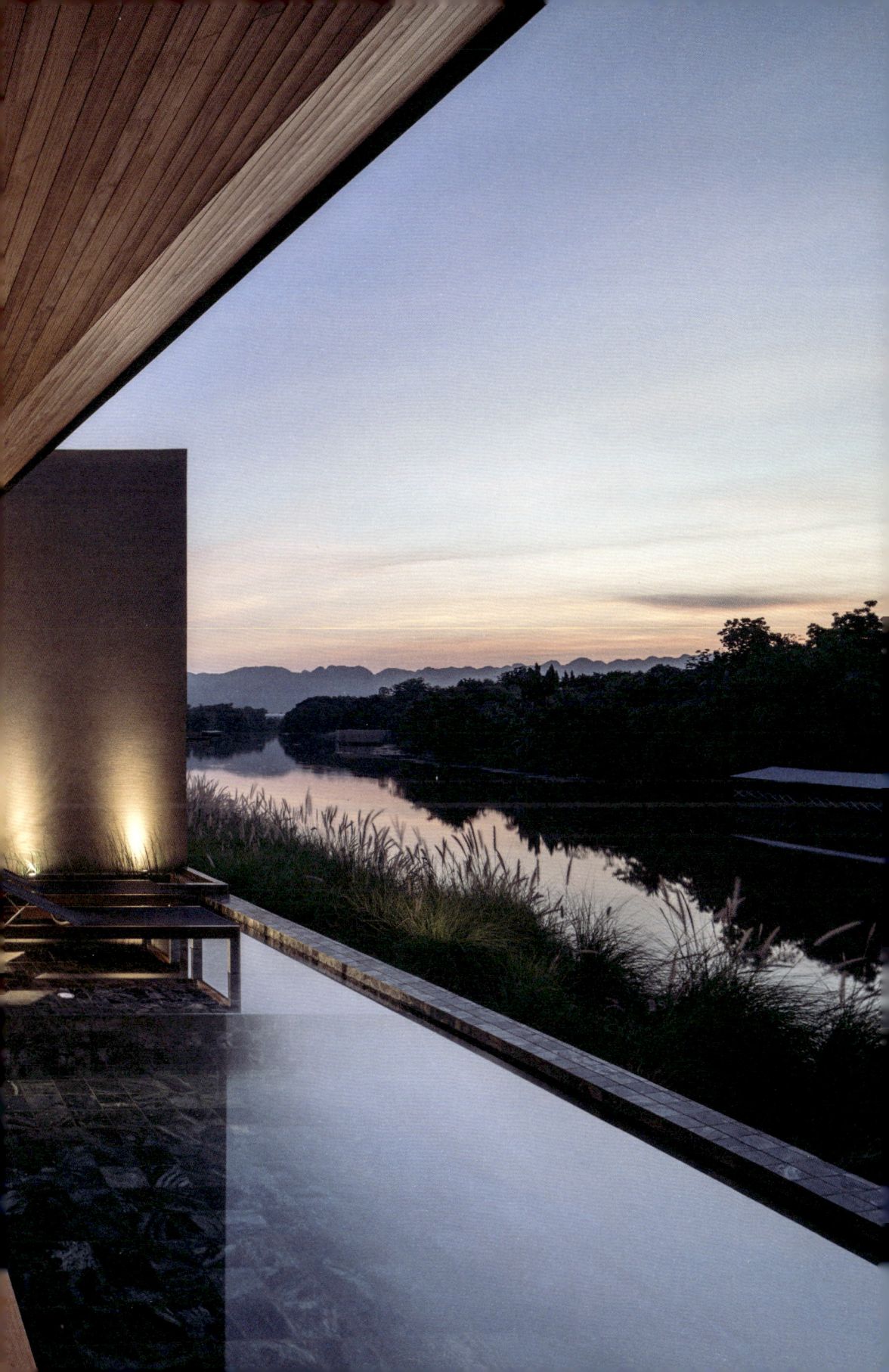

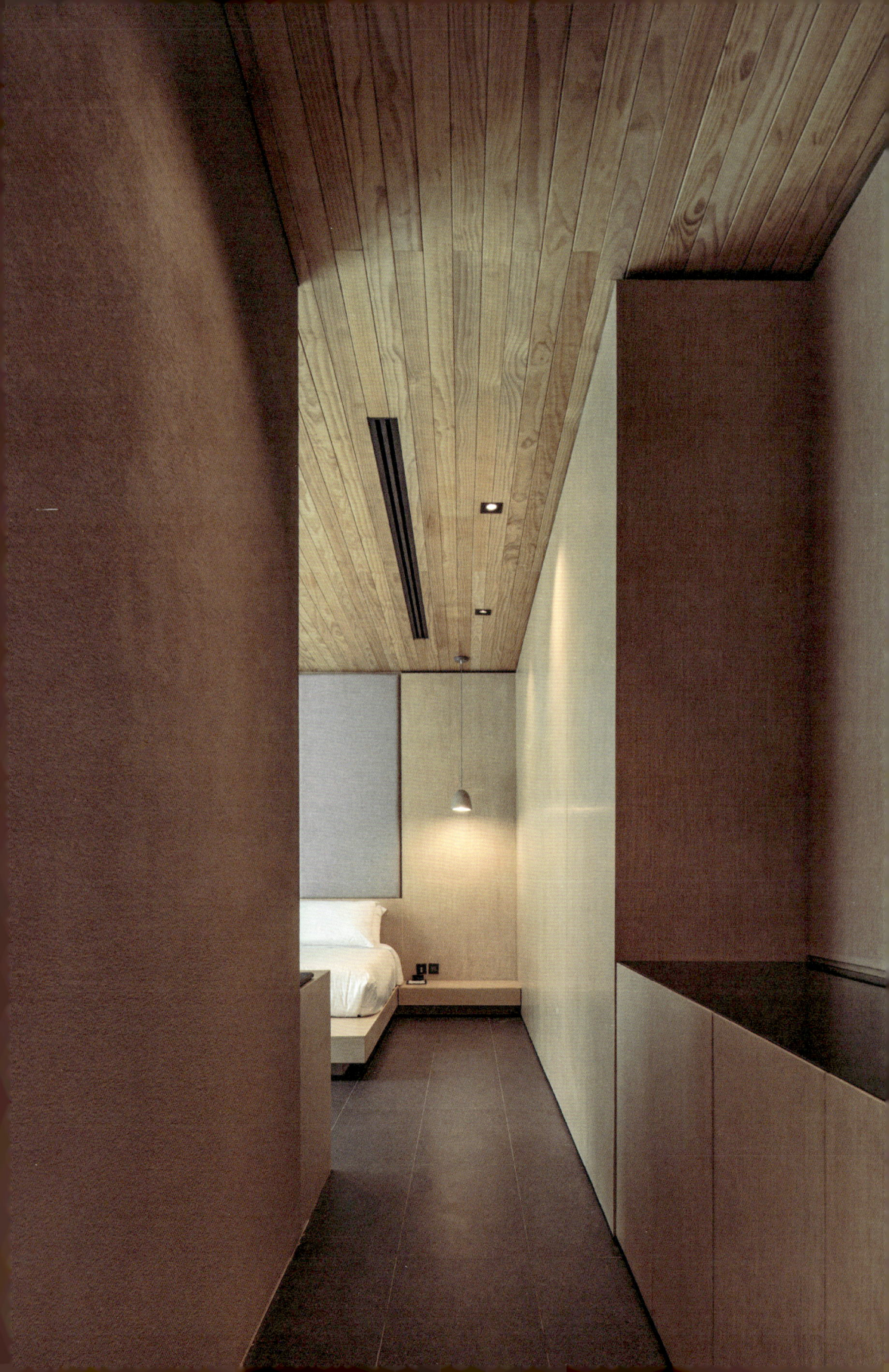

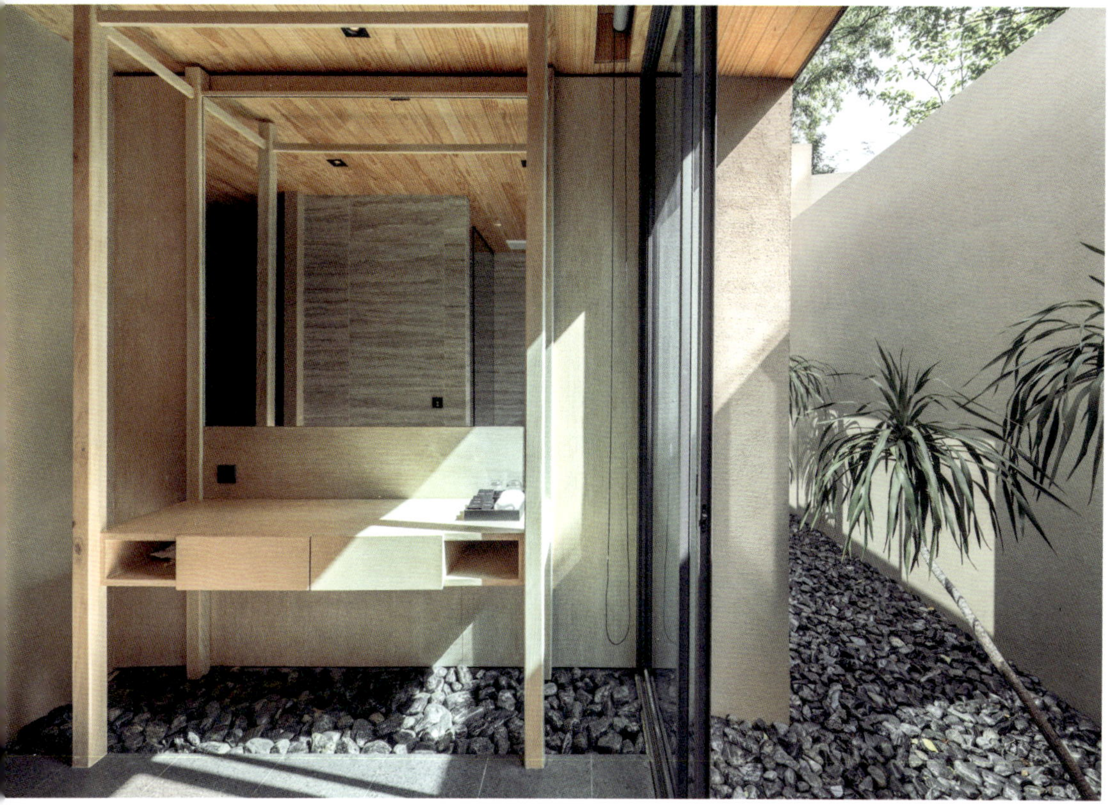

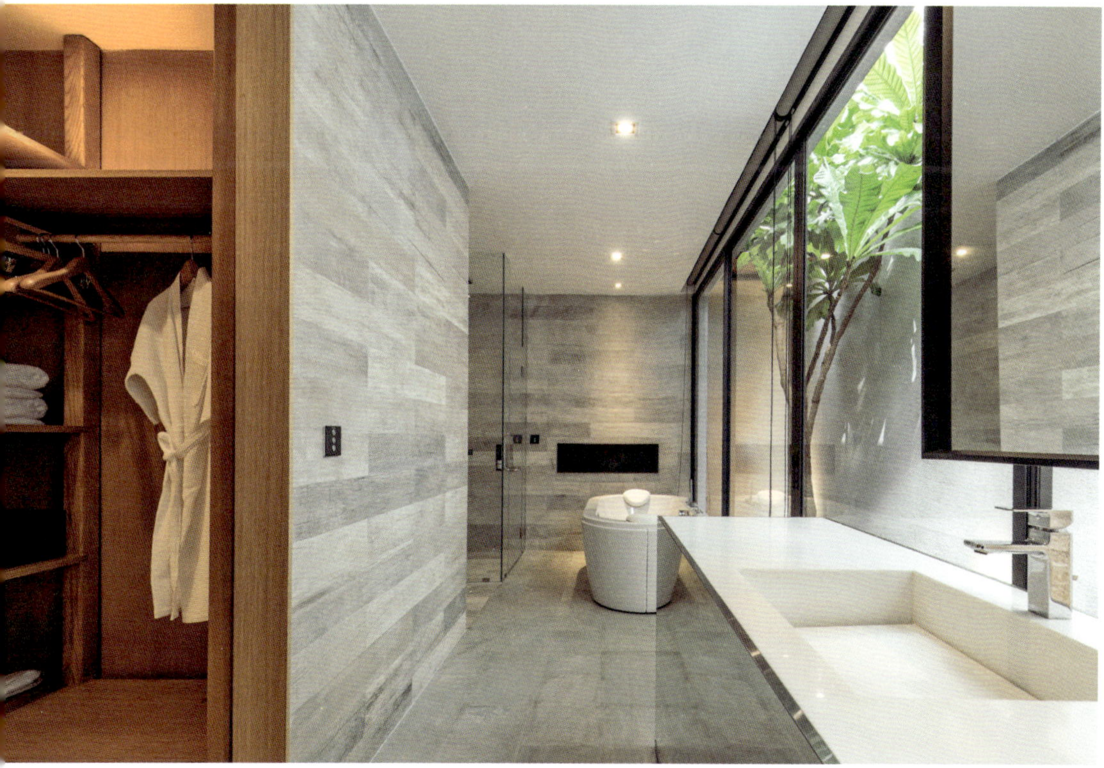

TARA VILLA

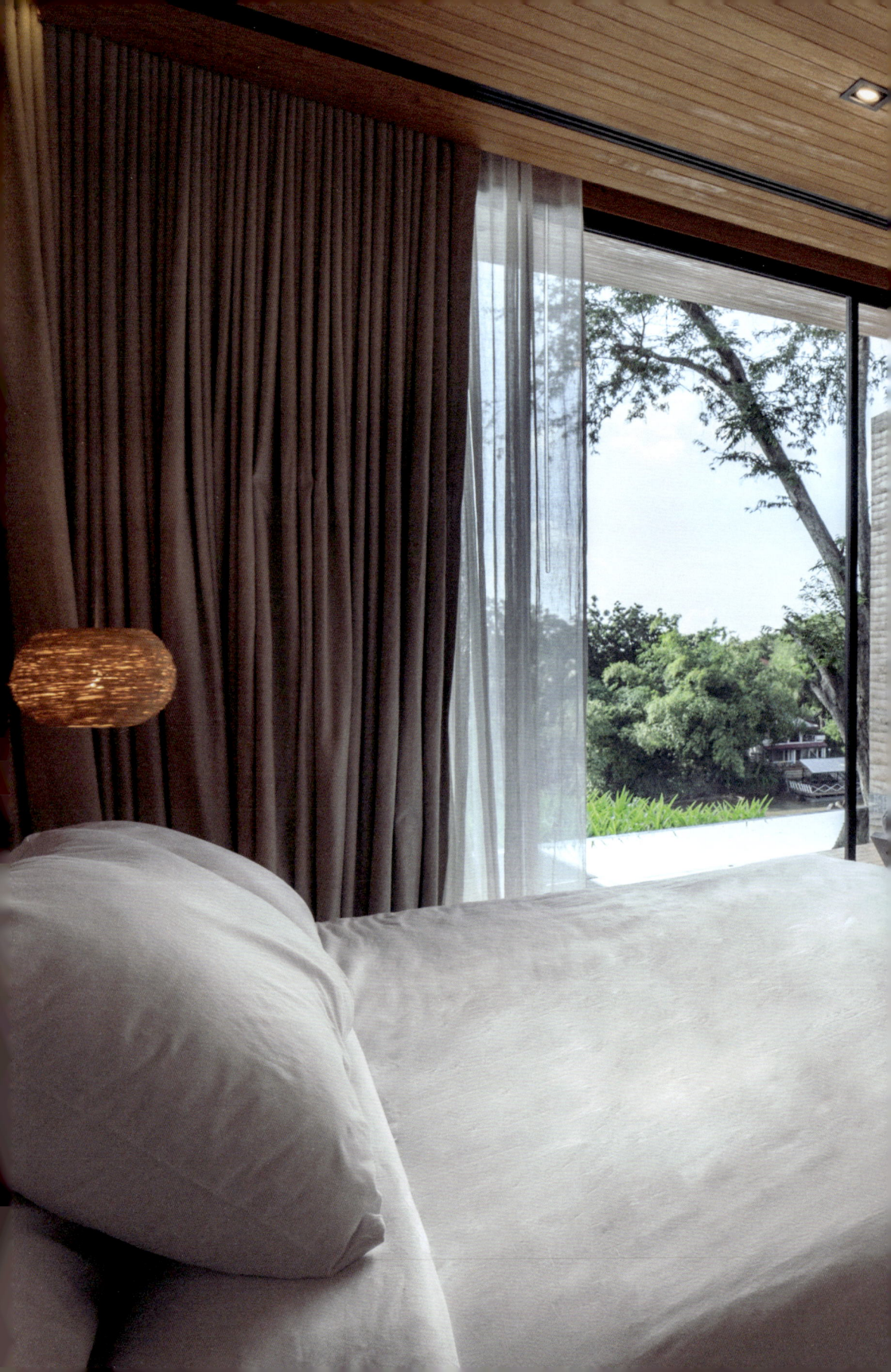

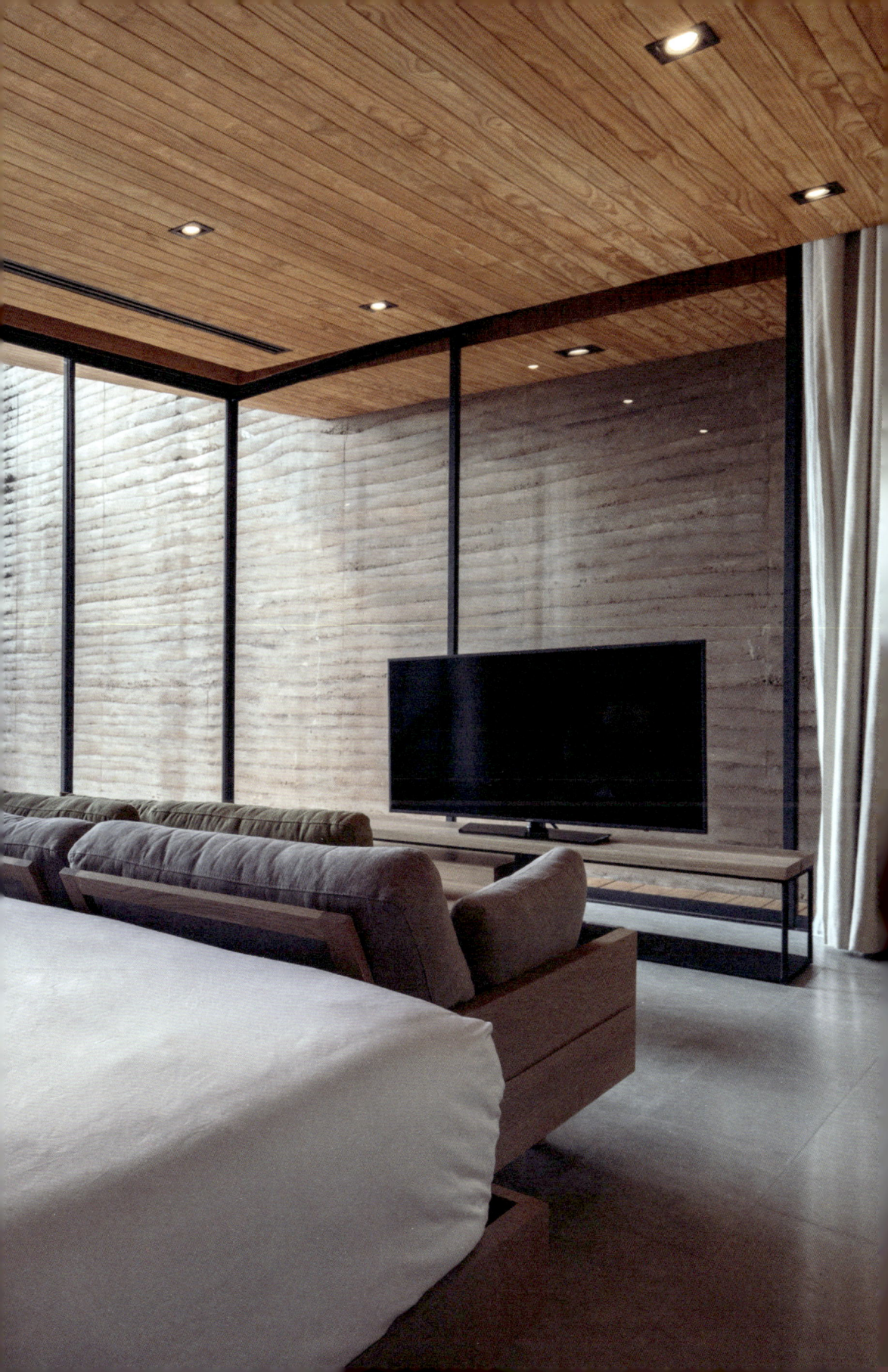

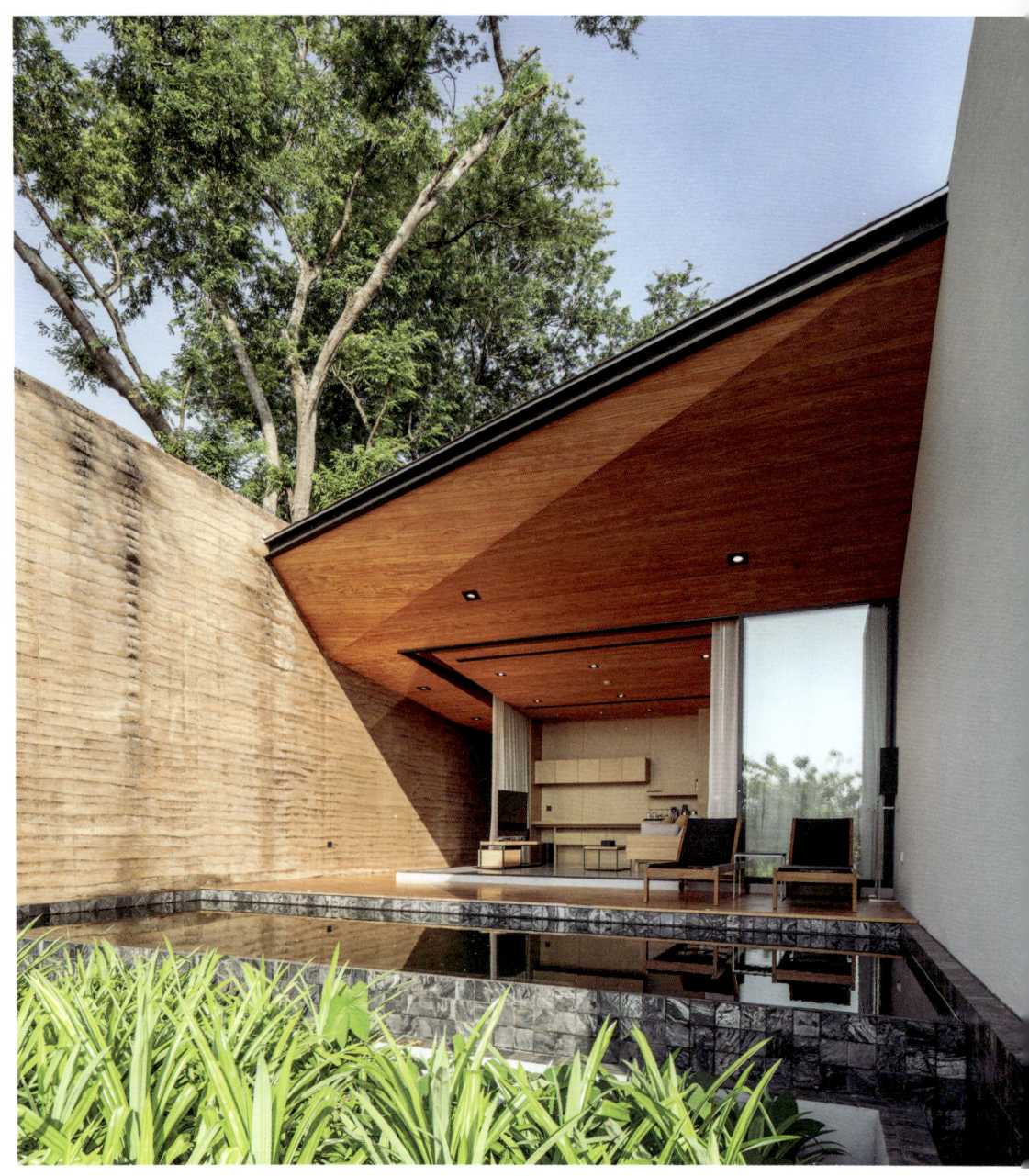

The guest villas are the heart of the resort. Entering the villas, guests walk through a semi-outdoor space, which functions as a transition space before accessing the indoor living area. On a pleasant, breezy day, sliding doors in the villas can be opened wide to merge the indoor and the outdoor areas as one space. This allows for a variety of activities to take place inside, outside, as well as on the terrace near the swimming pool.

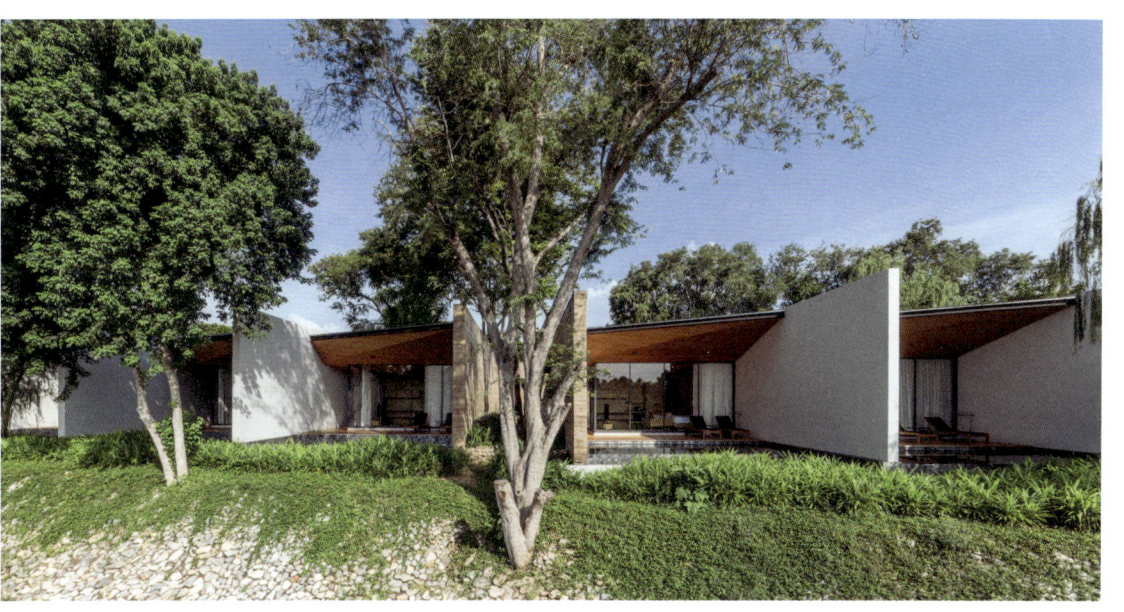

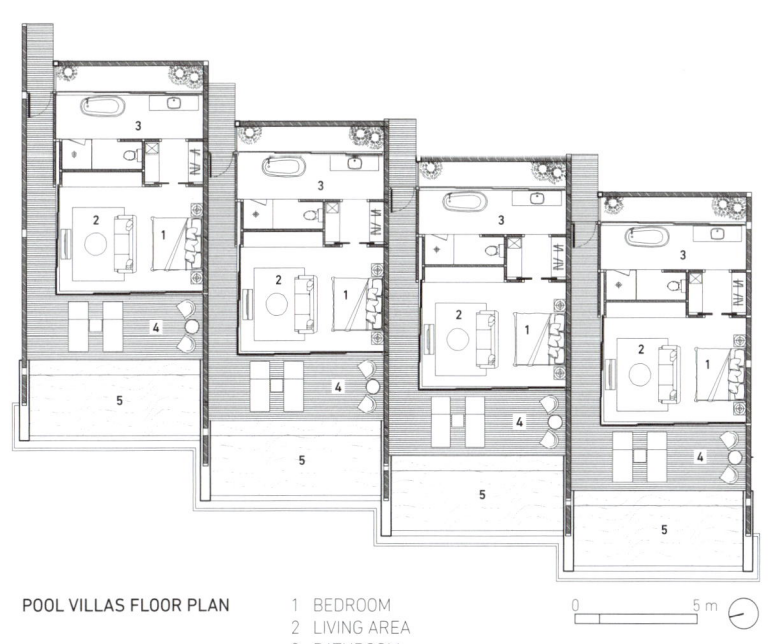

POOL VILLAS FLOOR PLAN

1. BEDROOM
2. LIVING AREA
3. BATHROOM
4. TERRACE
5. SWIMMING POOL

TARA VILLA

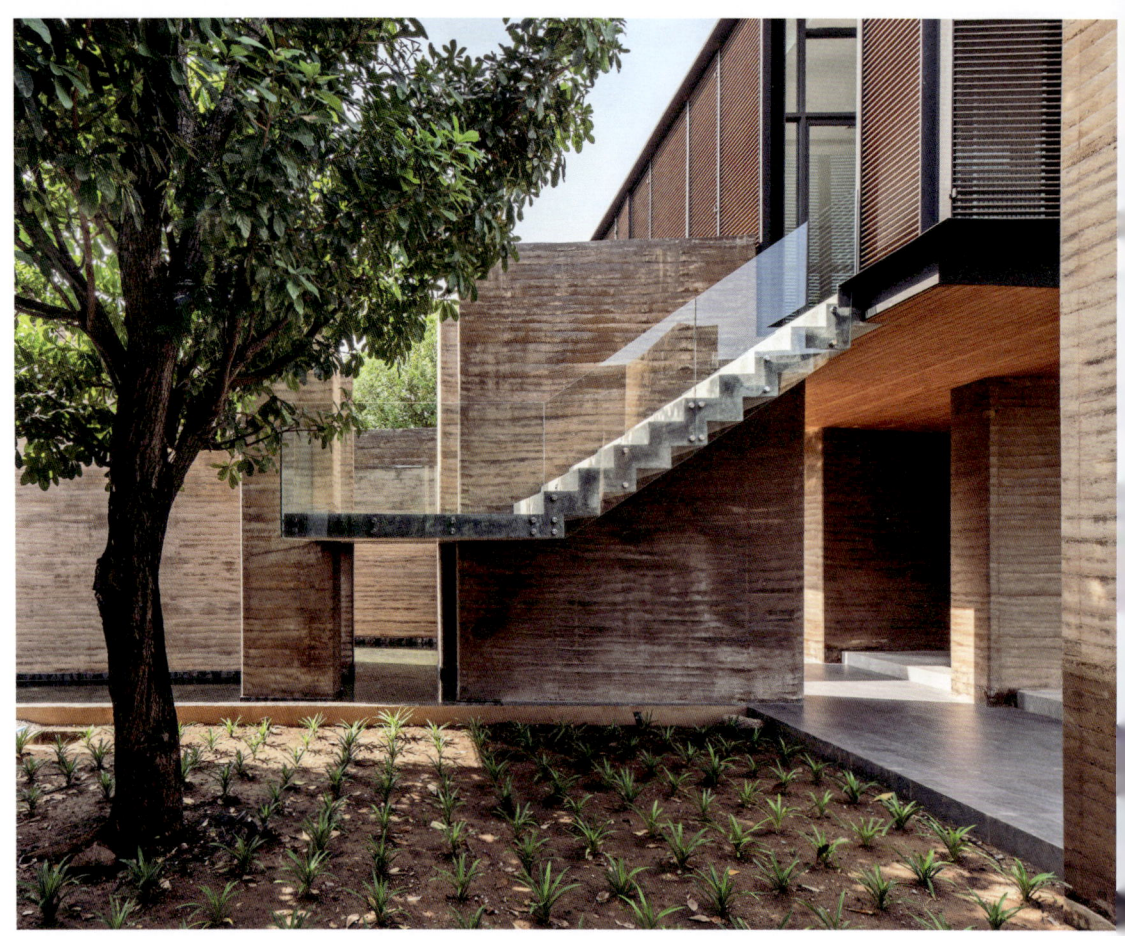

Tara Villa is a project that showcases the value of space between key areas, attributing the words of Lao Tzu (Lao Zi): "We shape clay into a pot, but it is the emptiness inside that holds whatever we want."

The design process of this project gracefully and successfully transforms this well-known expression into a tangible architecture. The construction also attempts to realize the efficient utilization of material. Reusing the excavated soil from the site to construct walls that sit on the very site itself has paid off. The rammed-earth walls not only adorn the resort with a unique character and identity, they also create a physical result that strengthens the design concept and drives home the idea that "the journey is more important than the destination."

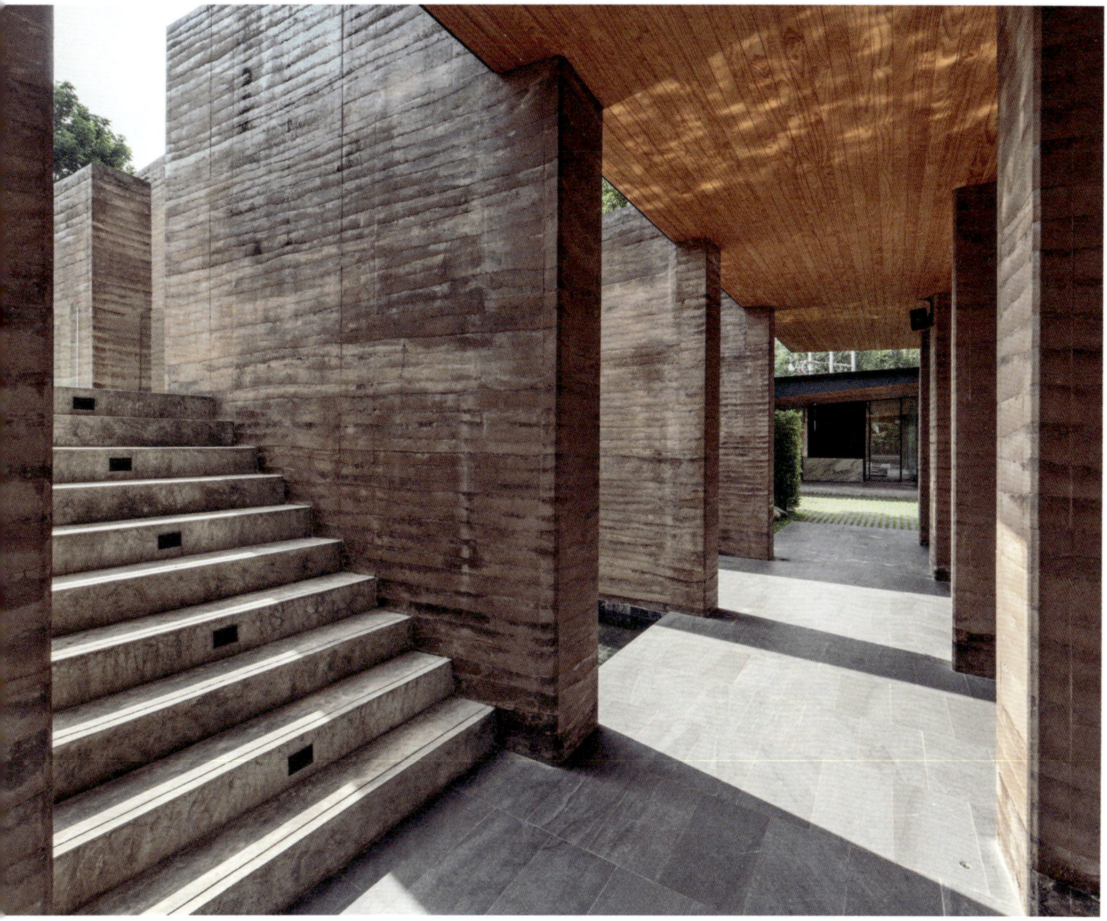

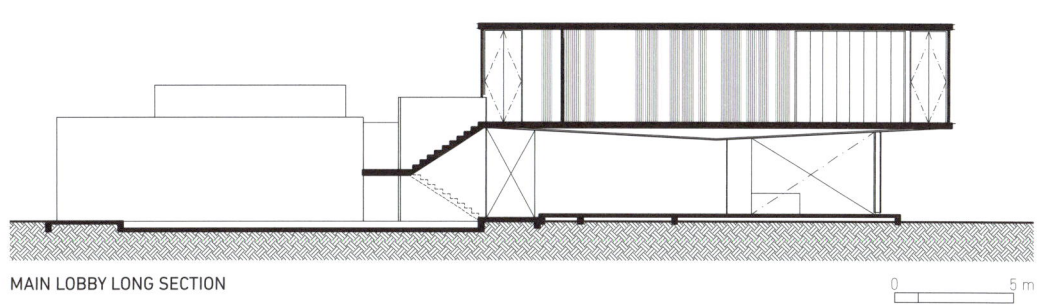

MAIN LOBBY LONG SECTION

TARA VILLA

Sriracha, Chon Buri, Thailand, 2019

ARIZE HOTEL

Targeted at Japanese expatriates, the Arize Hotel brand launched its second establishment in Sriracha, where there is a strong base of Japanese business people. The design of the hotel is attuned to the context and characteristics of the beach city, and accommodates 379 guestrooms. Most of the rooms are tailored for long-stay occupancy and feature additional facilities, including a larger floor area compared to a standard hotel room.

The lobby is positioned to look out at a grand old tamarind tree on the site that backdrops the lobby entrance. Poised in a regal display of nature, the tree creates a riveting contrast against the modern architecture of the hotel with a stately fan of branches that shows its time on the land. Past the lobby, the podium zone beckons guests with a serene courtyard that calms harassed senses as guests step in from the cacophony of the bustling neighborhood outside. Built on the idea of an *engawa*, which is "a terrace connecting people and nature," the courtyard tactfully retains most of the original trees on-site within an eye-catching enclosure of laths. Presented as a feature element in the space, the laths manipulate the streams of light that enter, creating unusual shadow tapestries of shade and light that shift through the day, visually translating the Japanese kanji *ma,* which denotes "the door in the crevice through which sunlight peeps in," being made up of the characters "door" and "sun."

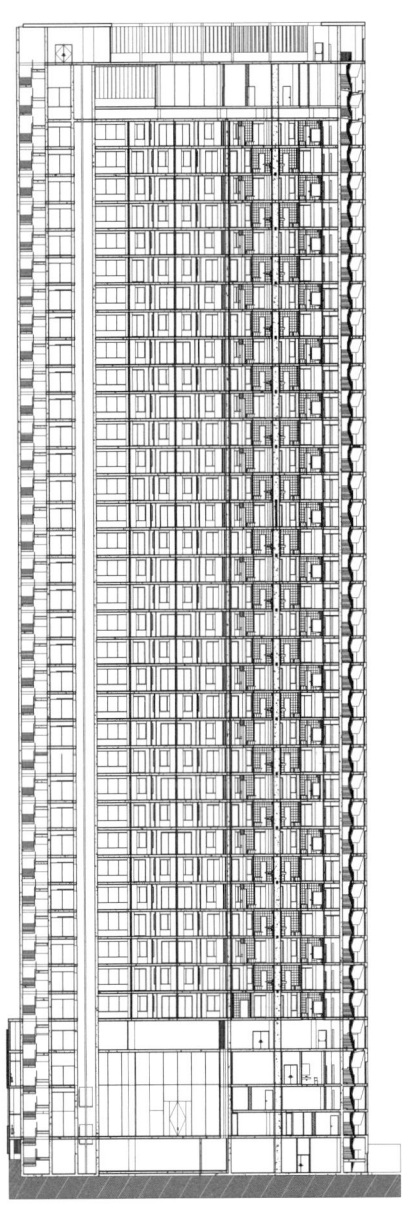

LONG SECTION

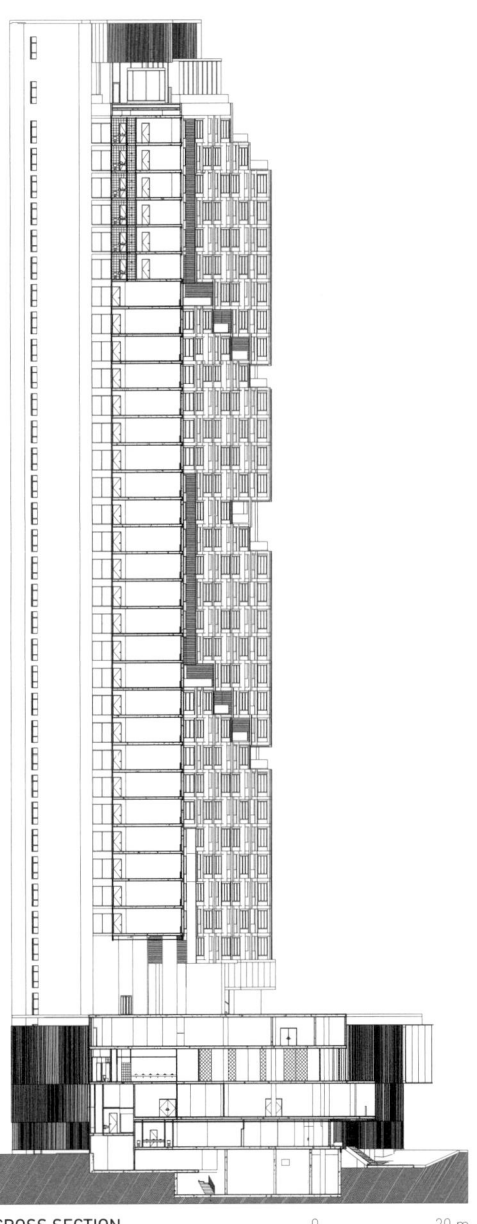

CROSS SECTION   0   20 m

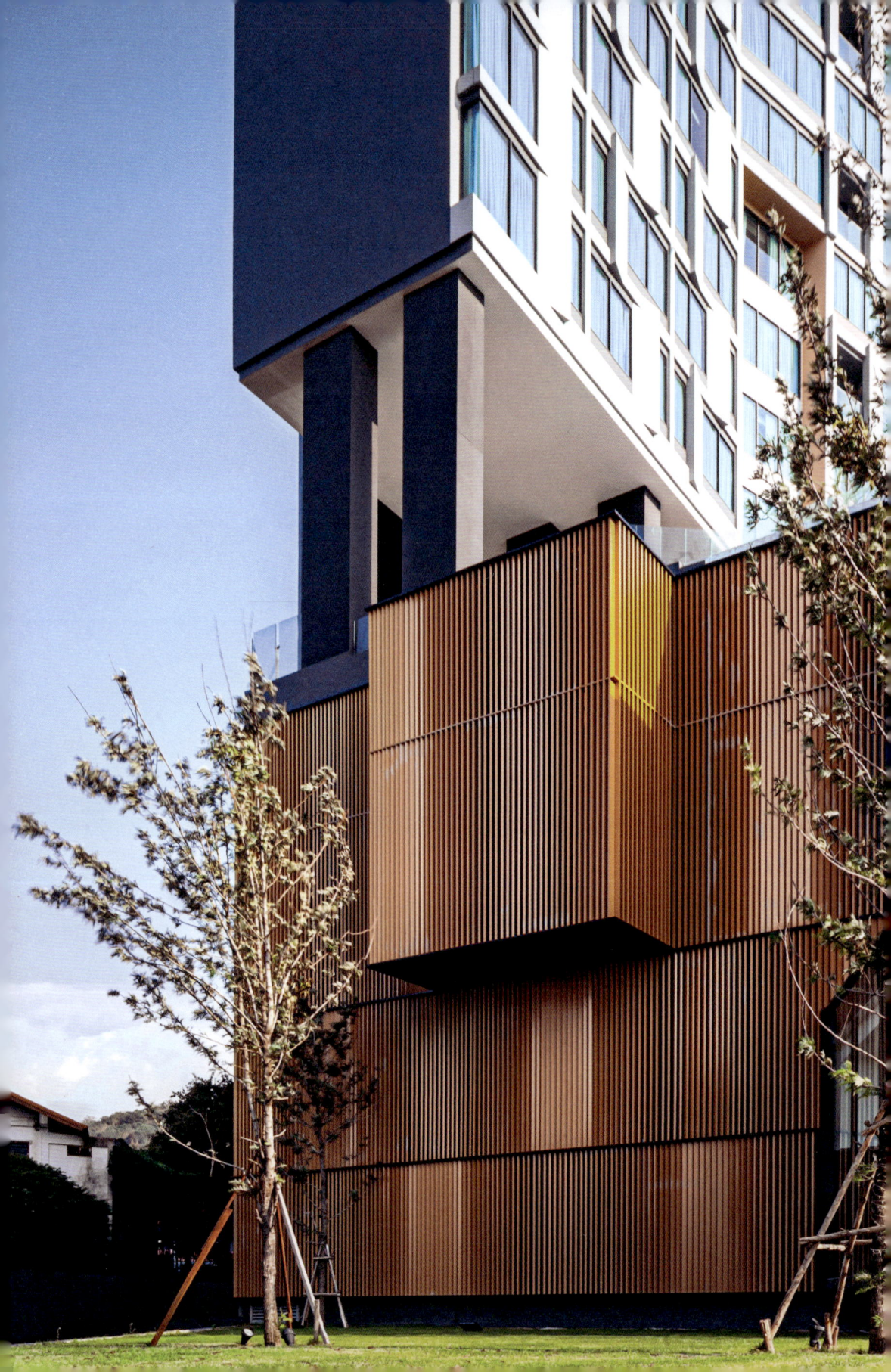

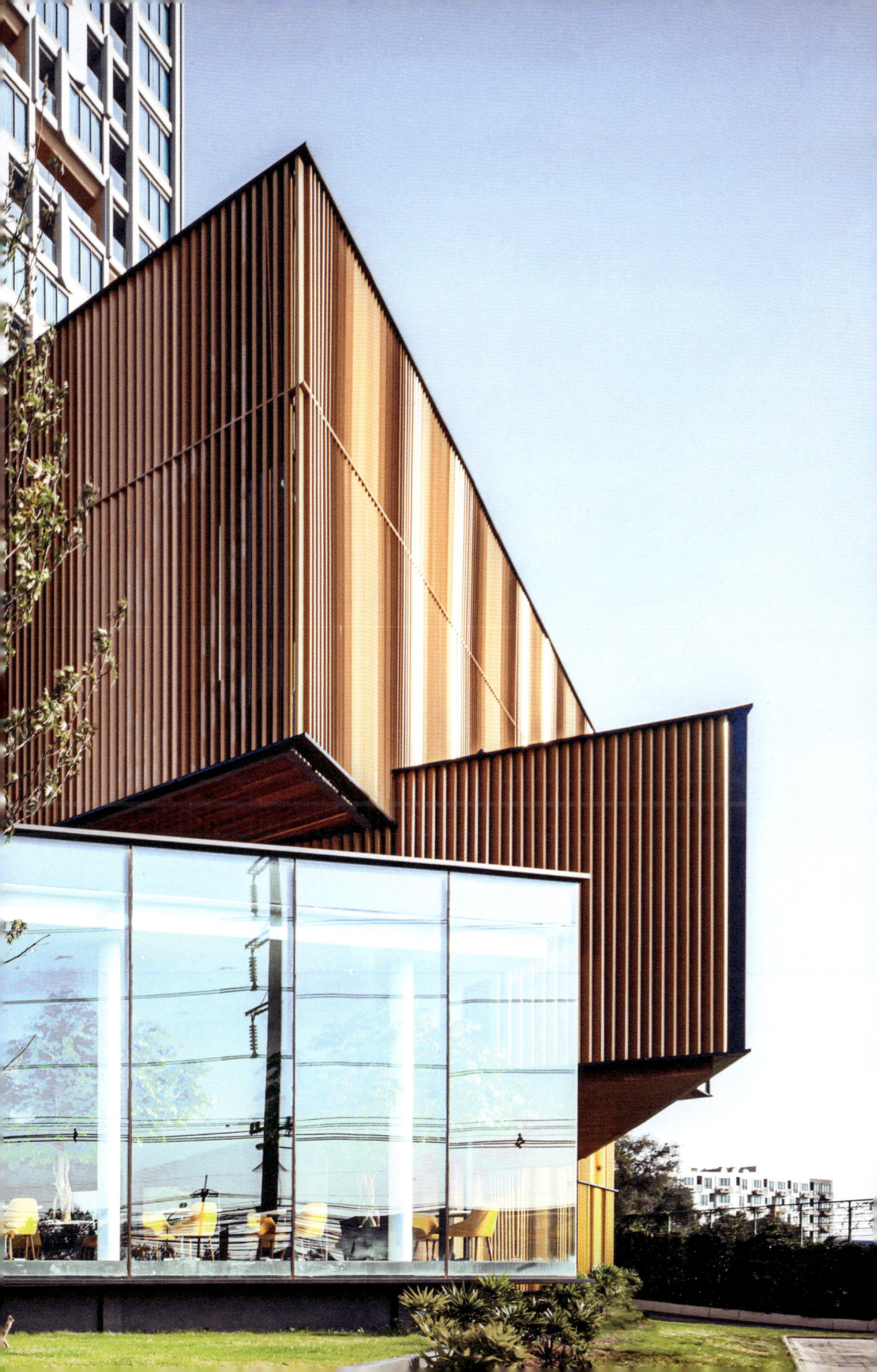

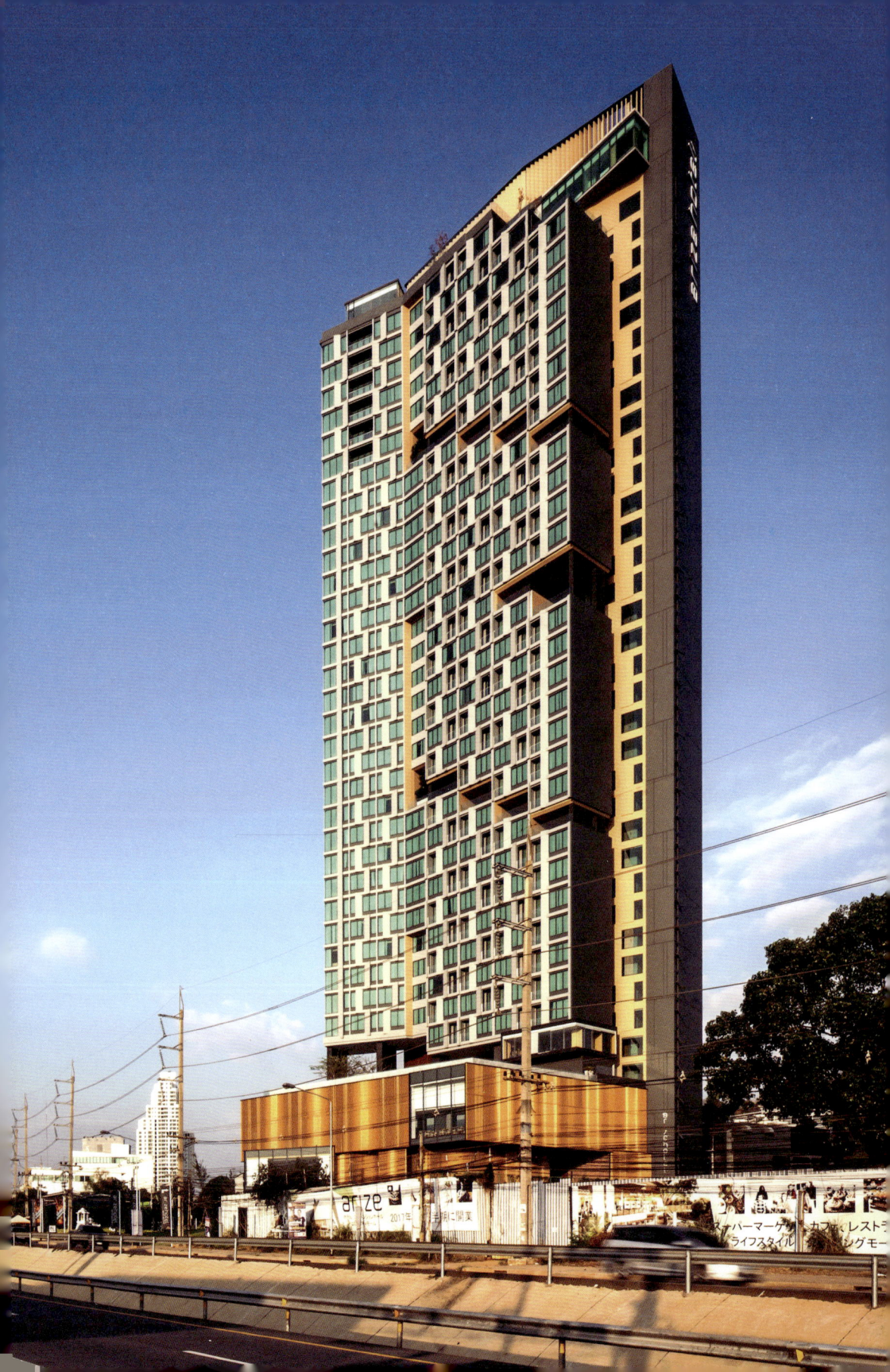

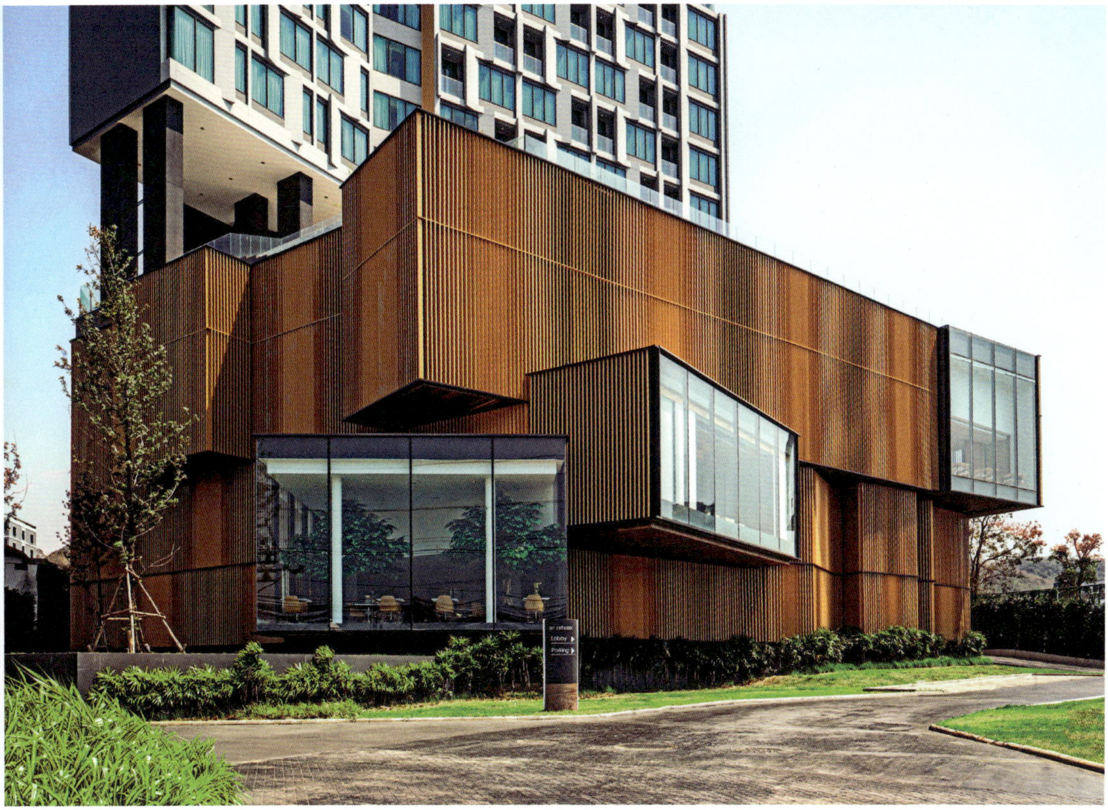

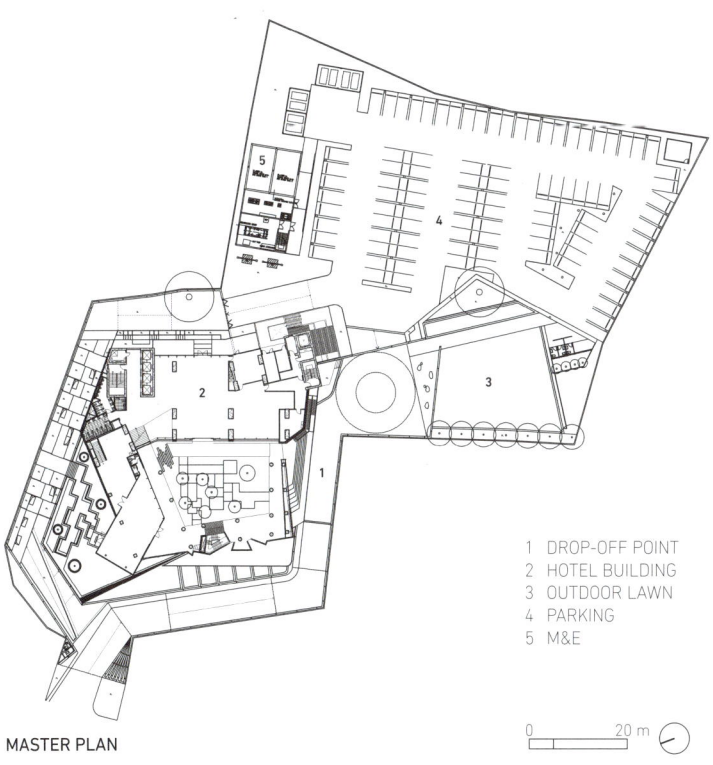

MASTER PLAN

1 DROP-OFF POINT
2 HOTEL BUILDING
3 OUTDOOR LAWN
4 PARKING
5 M&E

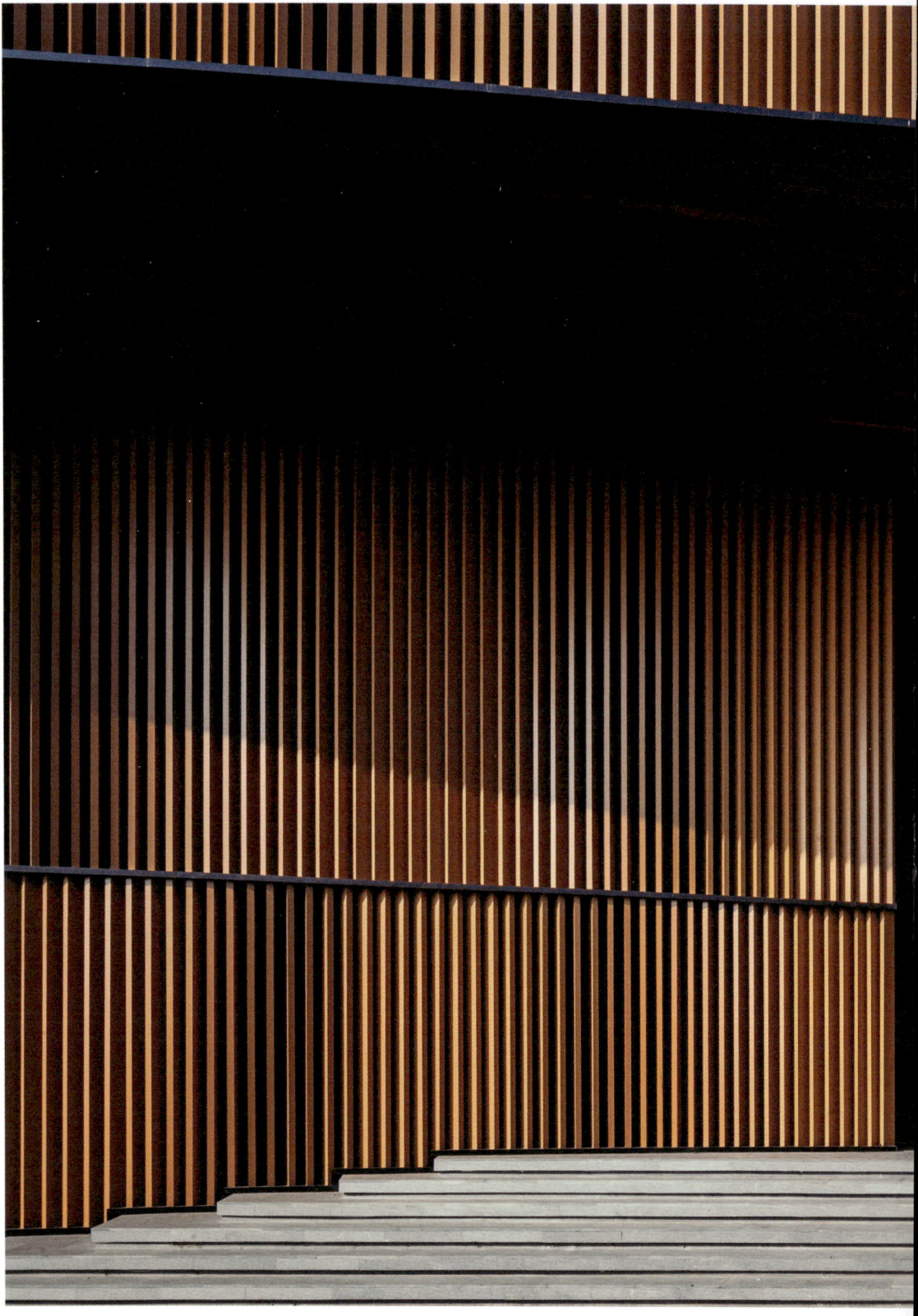

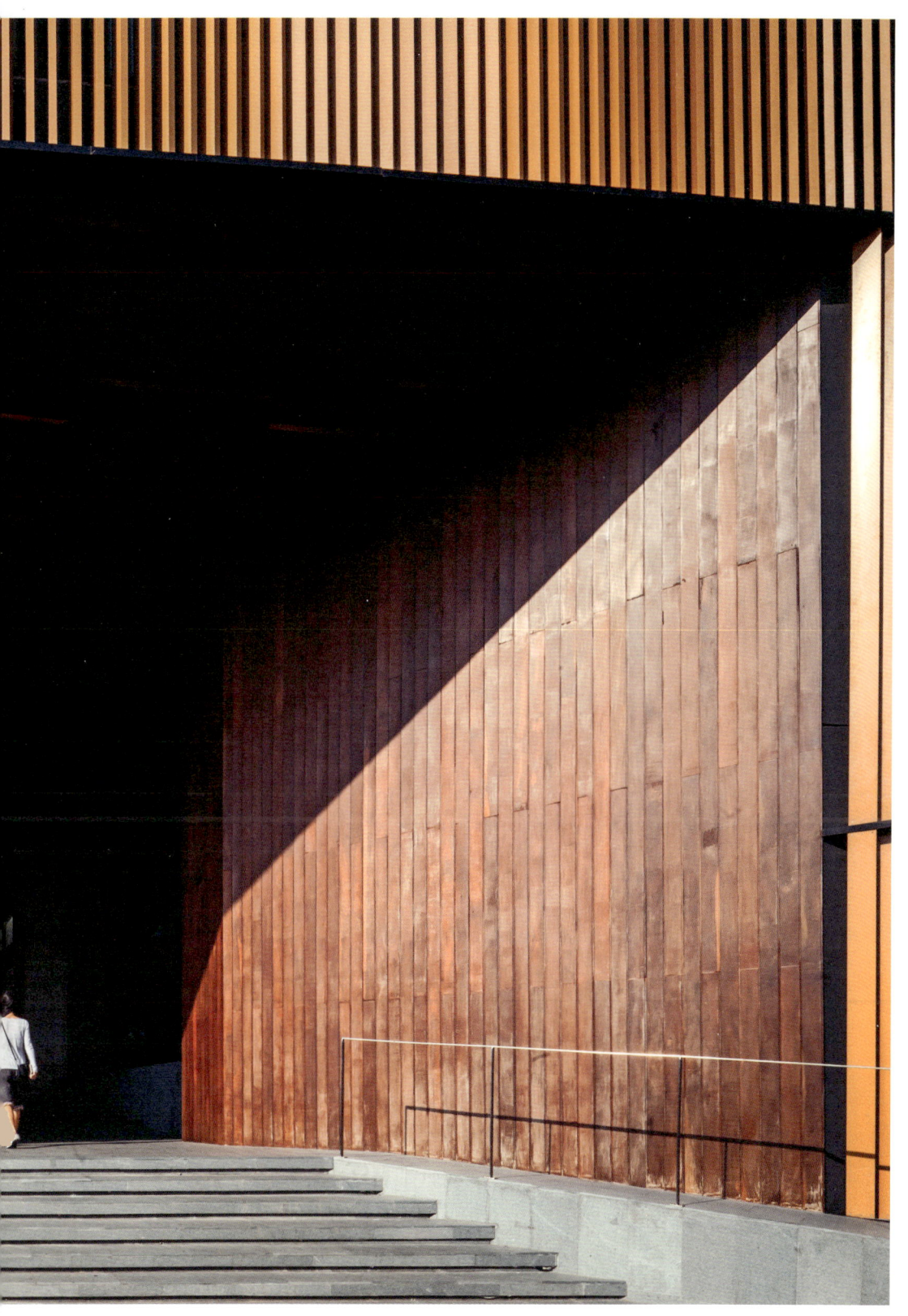

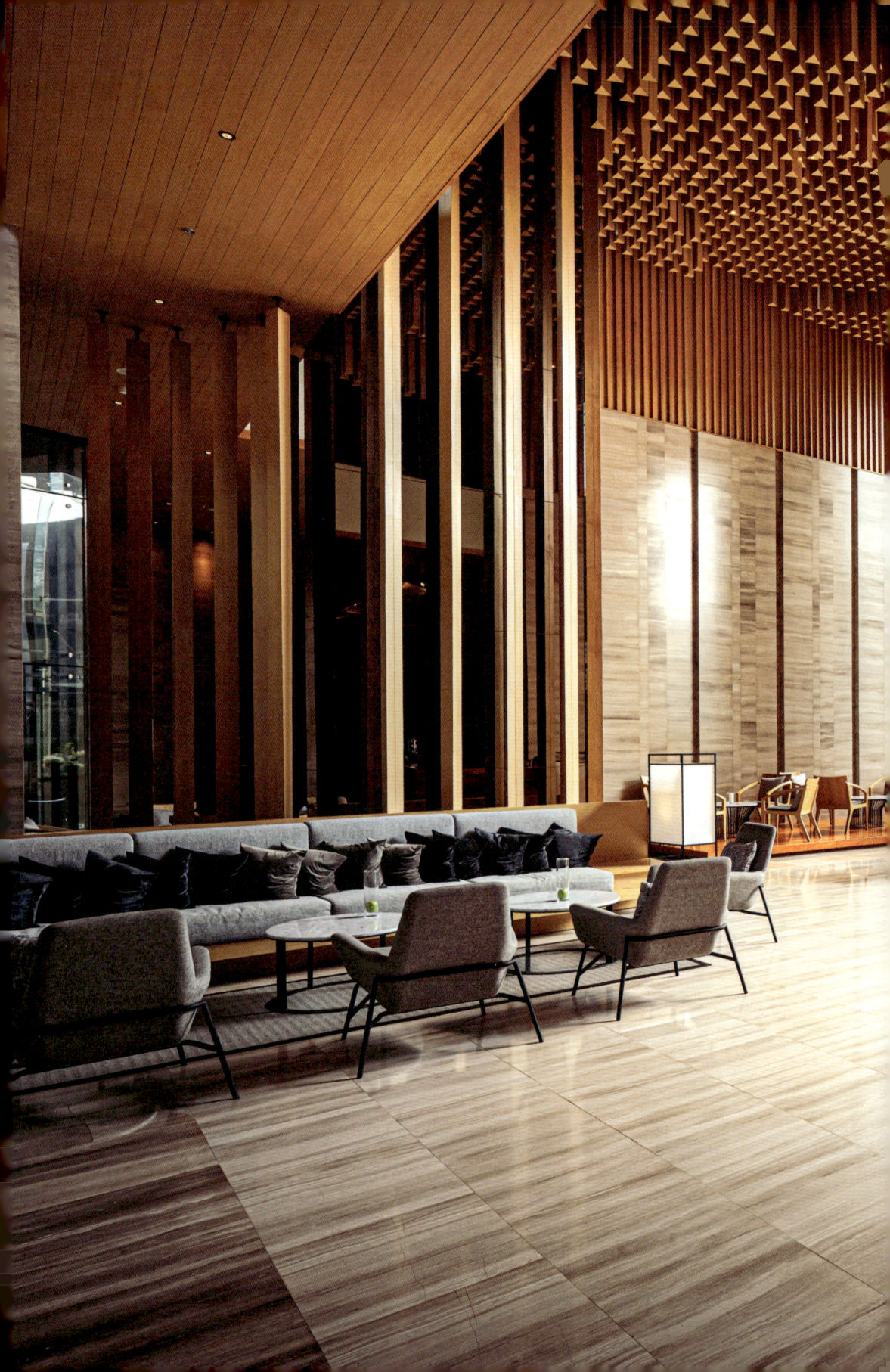

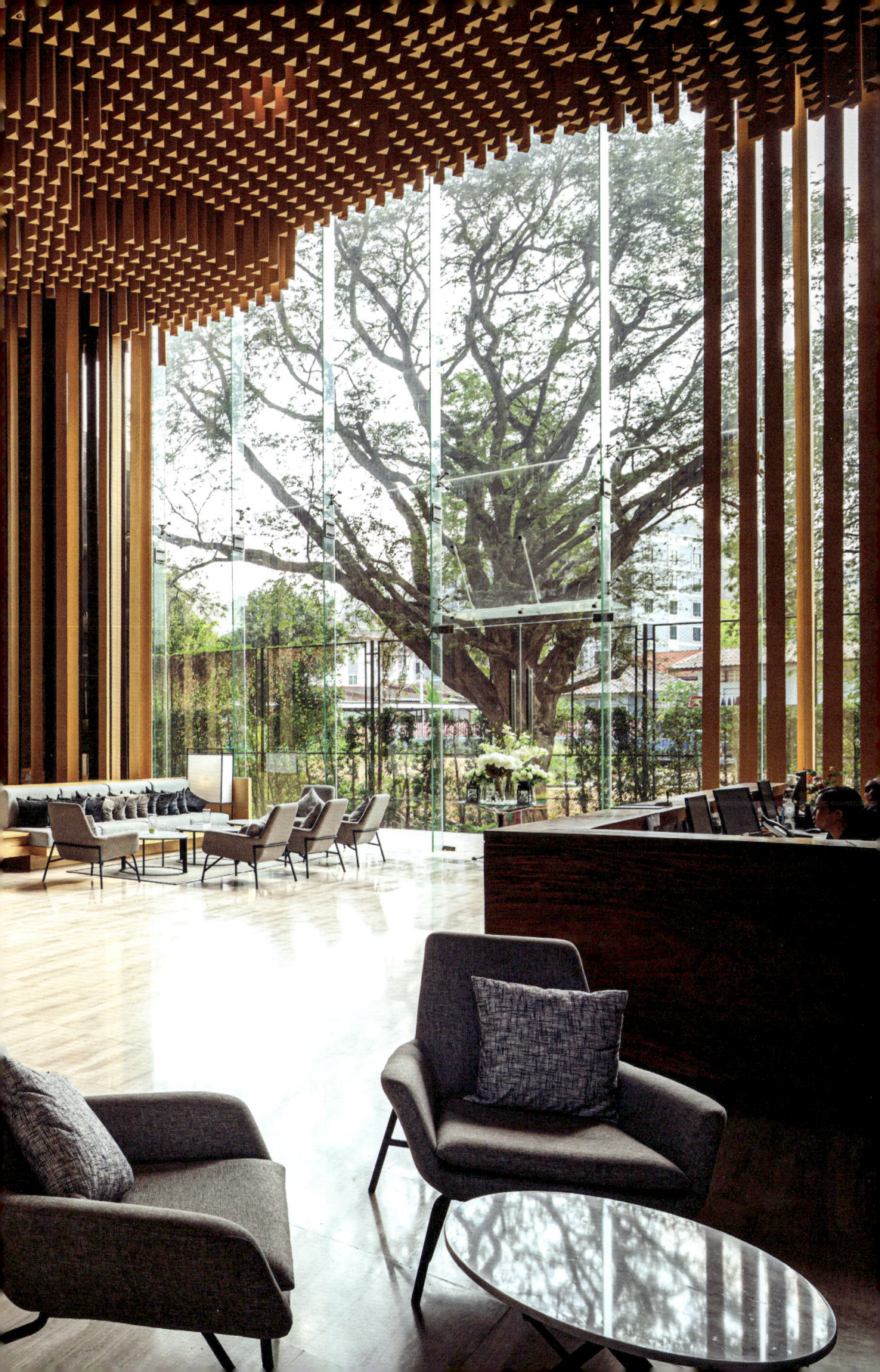

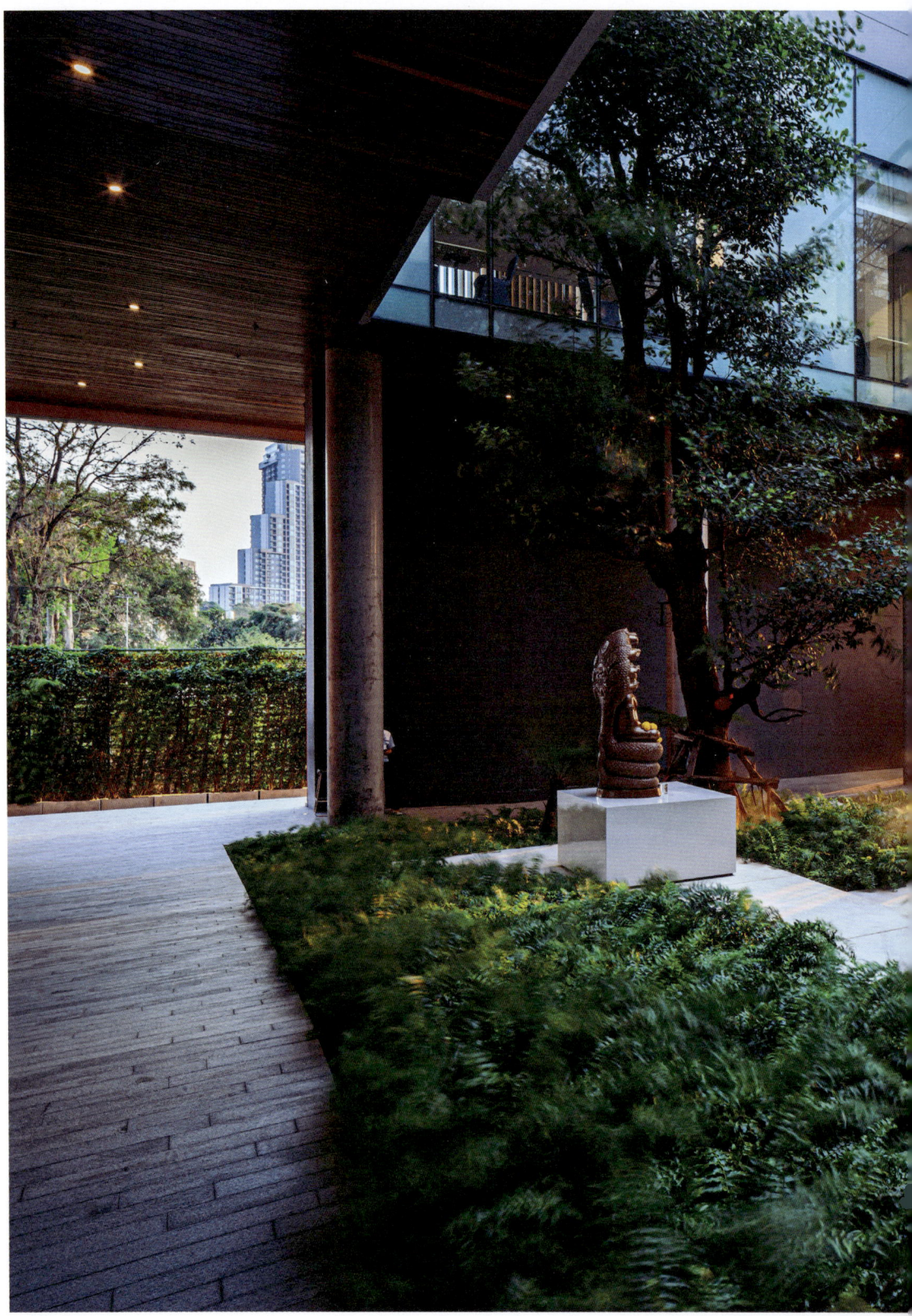

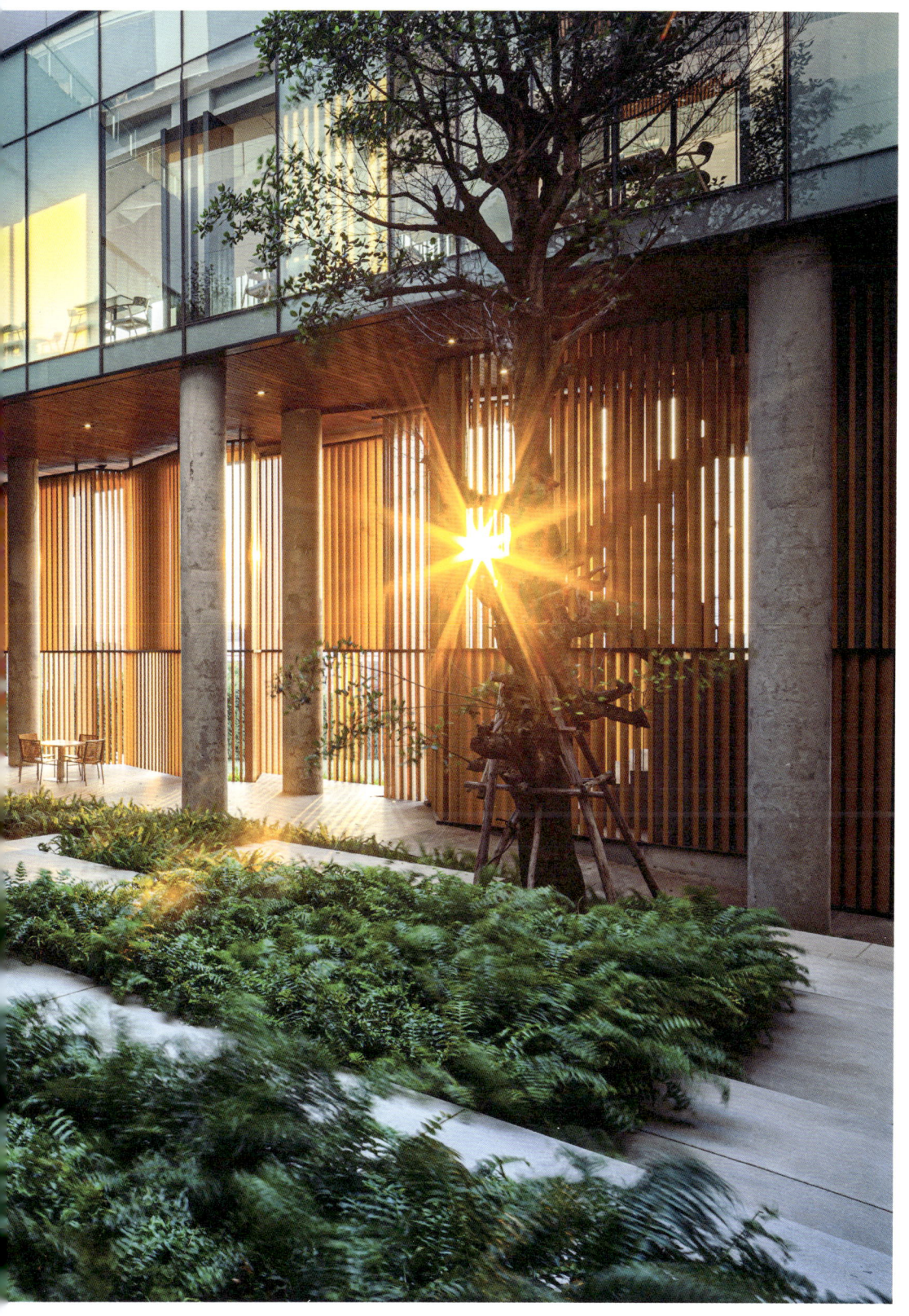

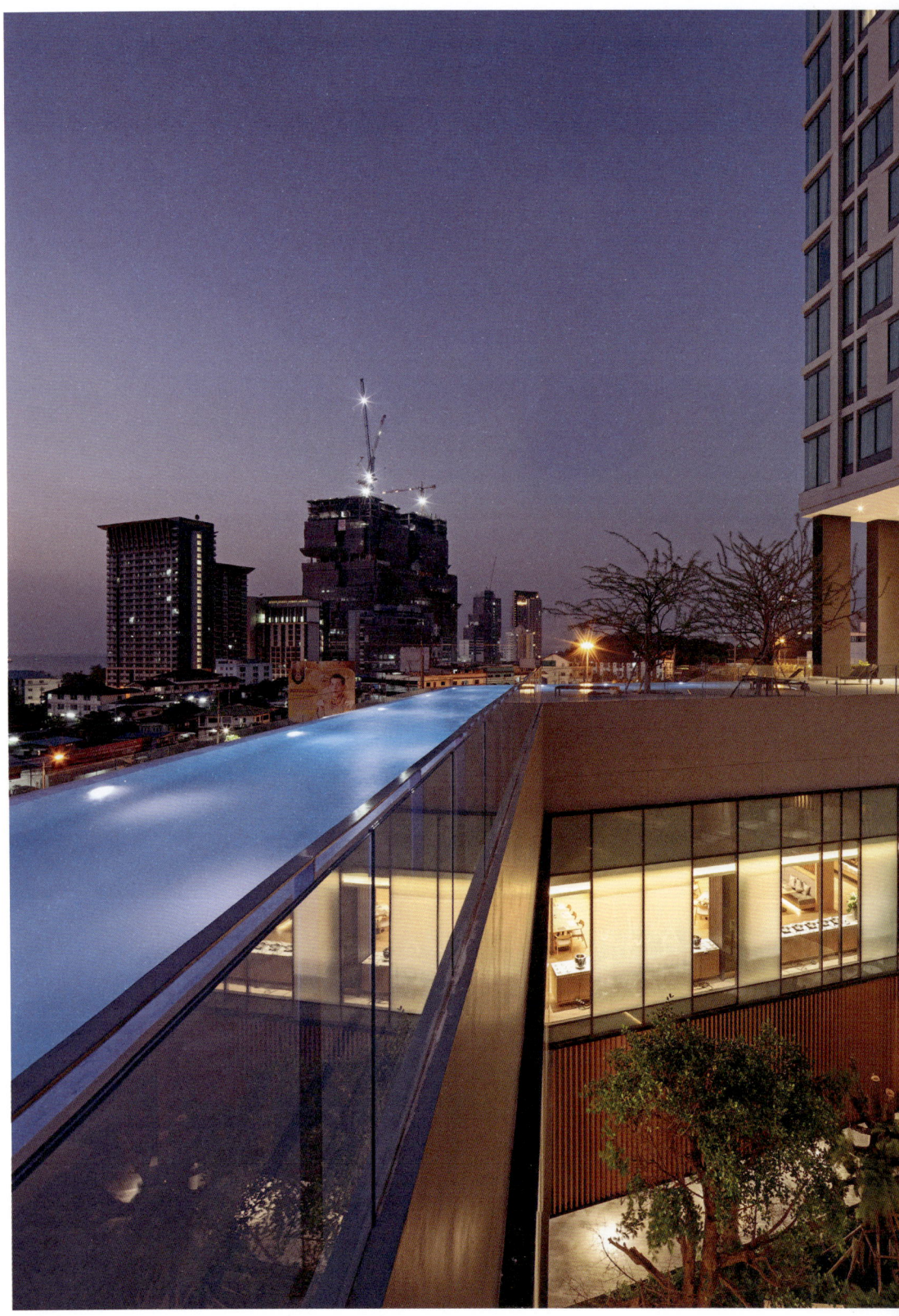

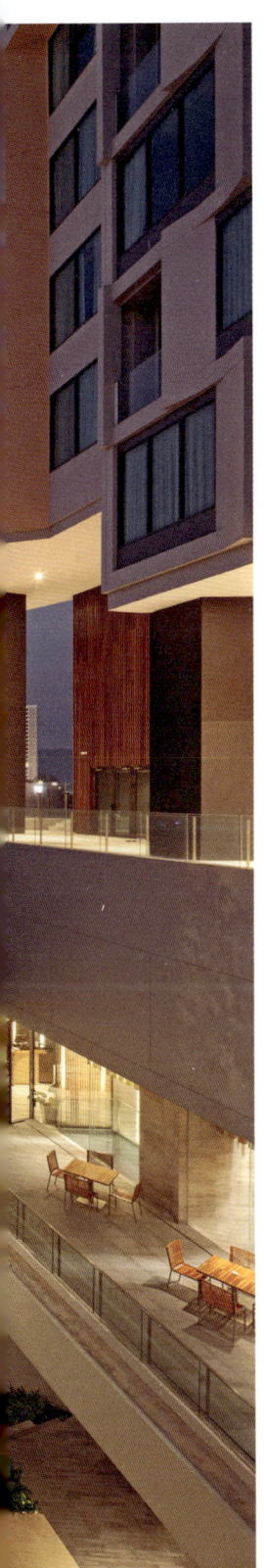
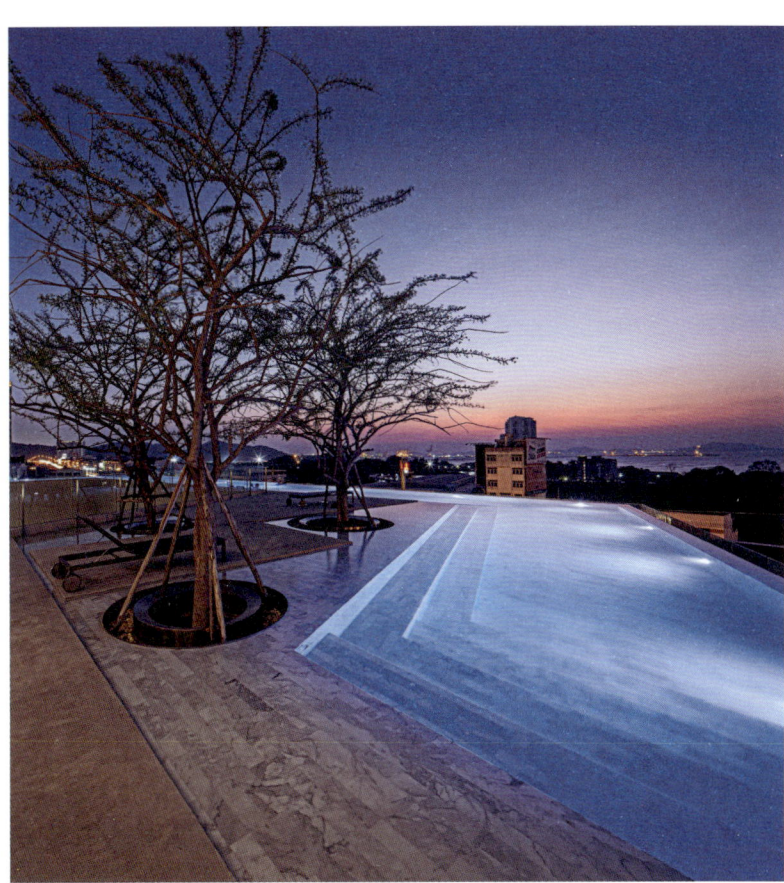

The all-day dining area loops around the second floor and overlooks the courtyard, with options for both indoor and outdoor dining. It is enclosed in glass panels that are semi-transparent at intervals to provide privacy and emulate a Japanese *shōji* (paper screen door) in traditional Japanese architecture. On the top floor of the podium, a crystalline, blue pool wraps around the edge and allows relaxing views of the trees in the courtyard, while indulging in a leisurely swim.

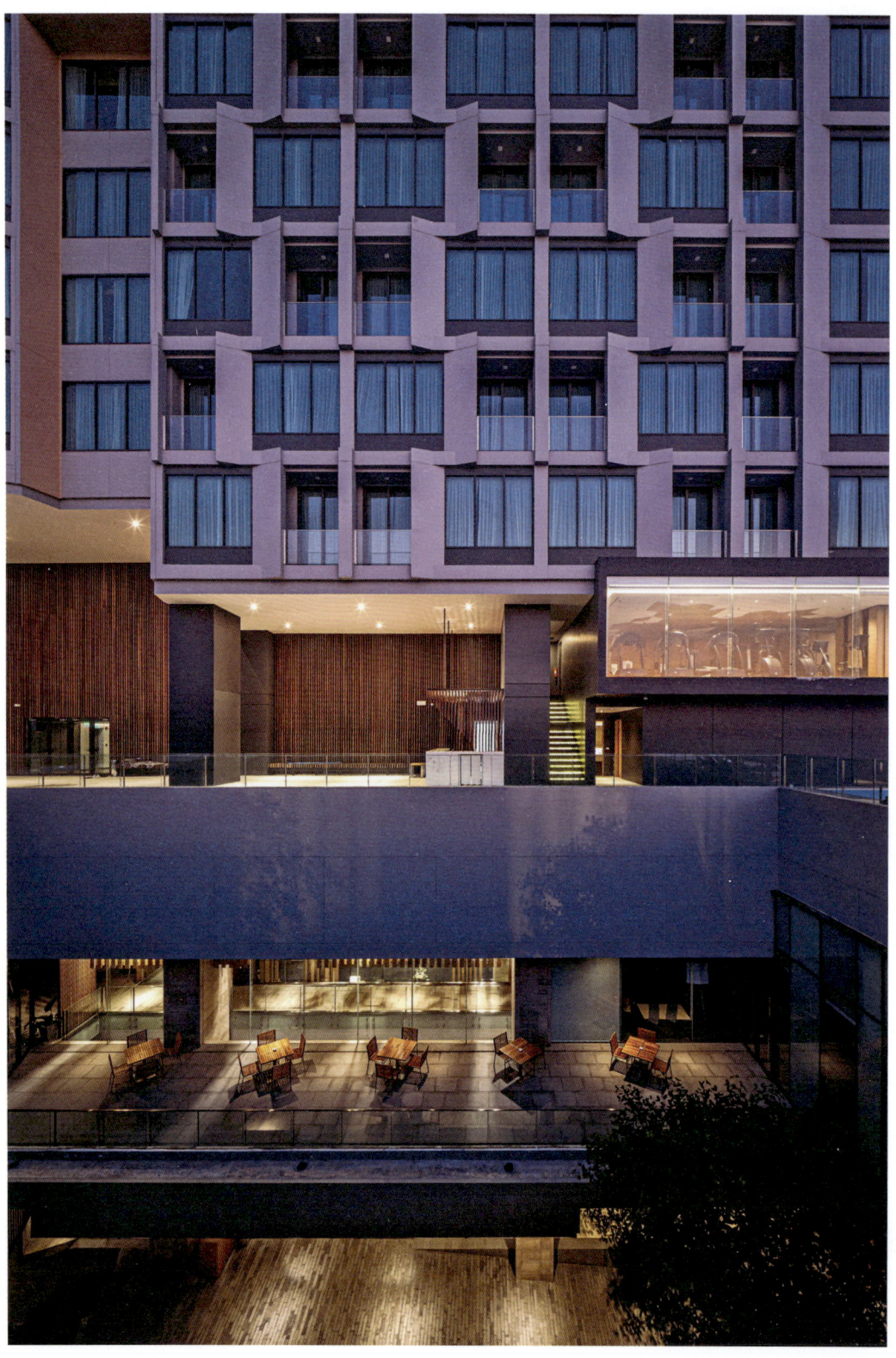

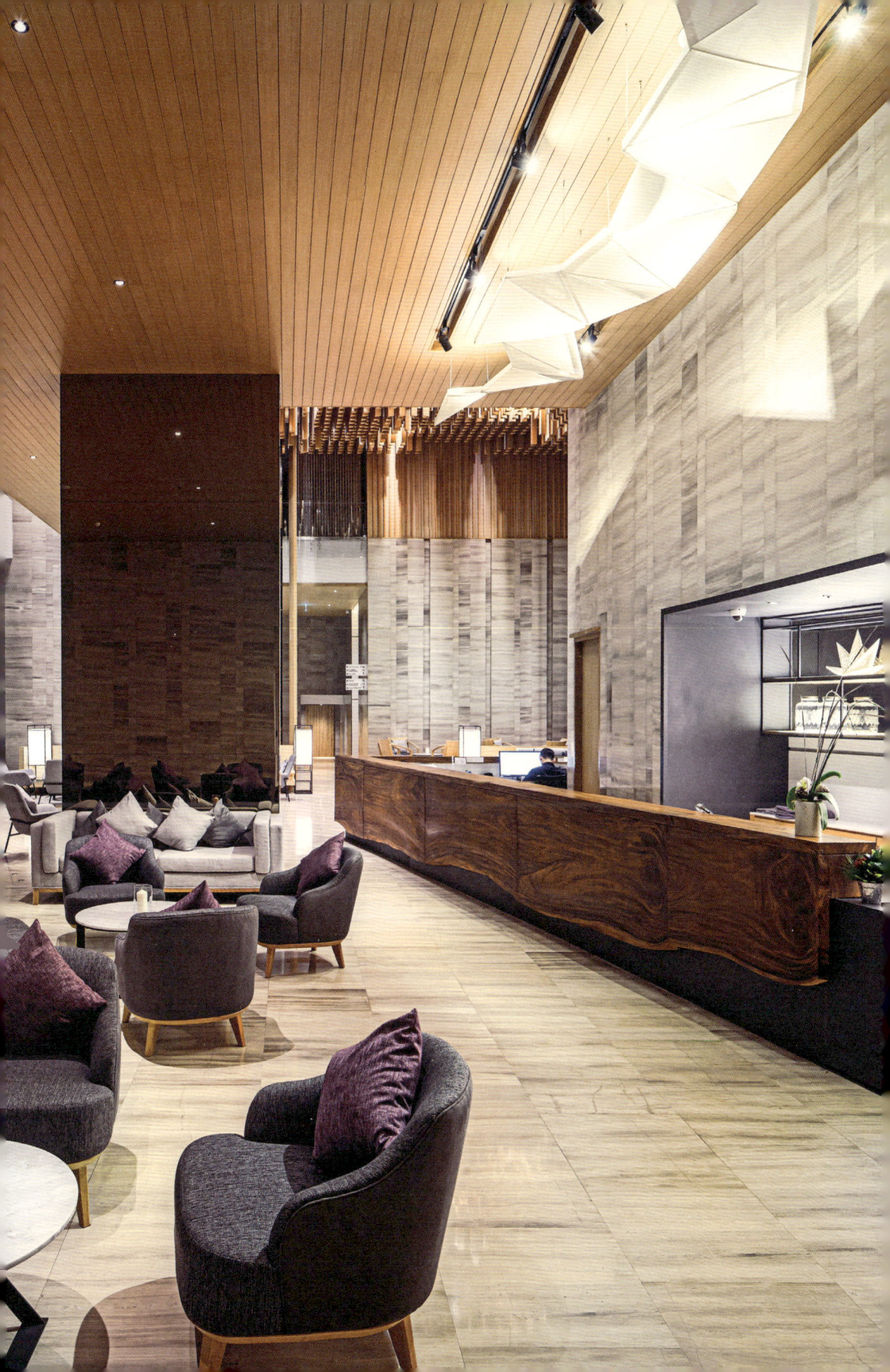

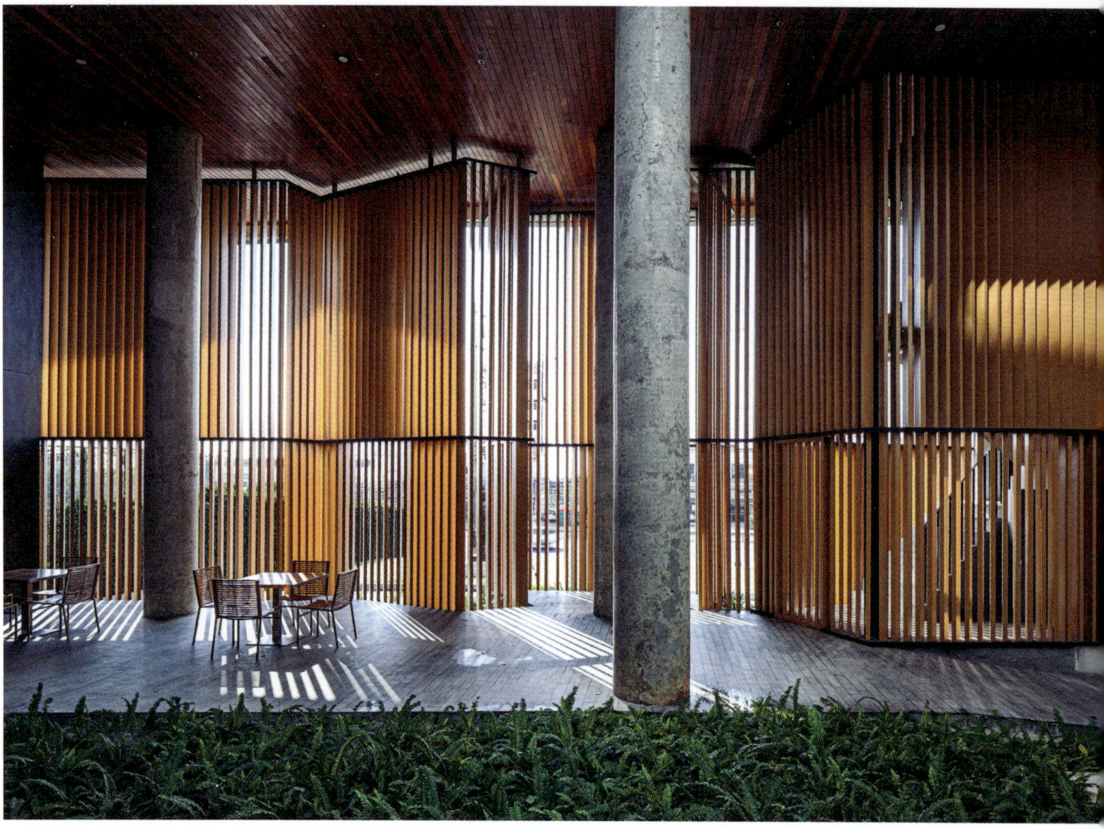

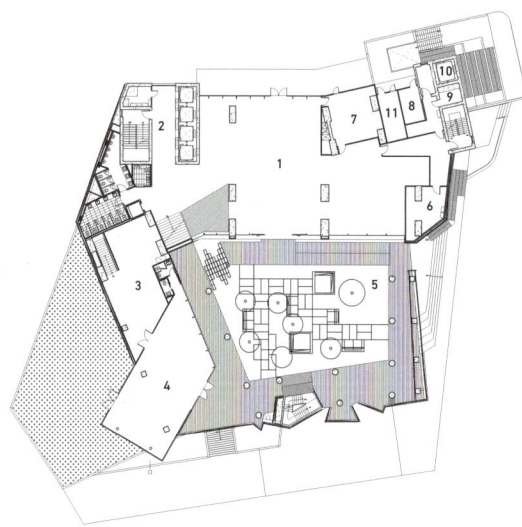

FIRST-FLOOR PLAN
1 LOBBY
2 ELEVATOR HALL
3 KITCHEN
4 RESTAURANT
5 GARDEN
6 LUGGAGE ROOM
7 OFFICE
8 FIRE PROTECTION SYSTEM
9 EE ROOM
10 FIREFIGHTER ELEVATOR
11 FIRST AID ROOM

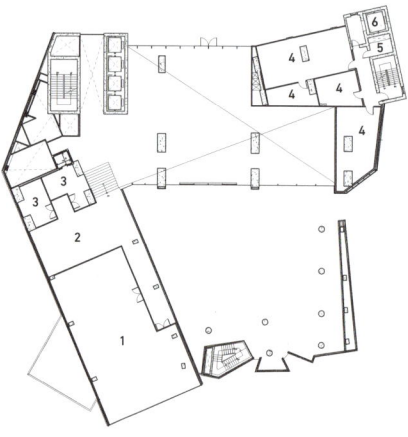

MEZZANINE FLOOR PLAN
1 FUNCTION ROOM
2 PRE-FUNCTION ROOM
3 RESTROOM
4 OFFICE
5 EE ROOM
6 FIREFIGHTER ELEVATOR

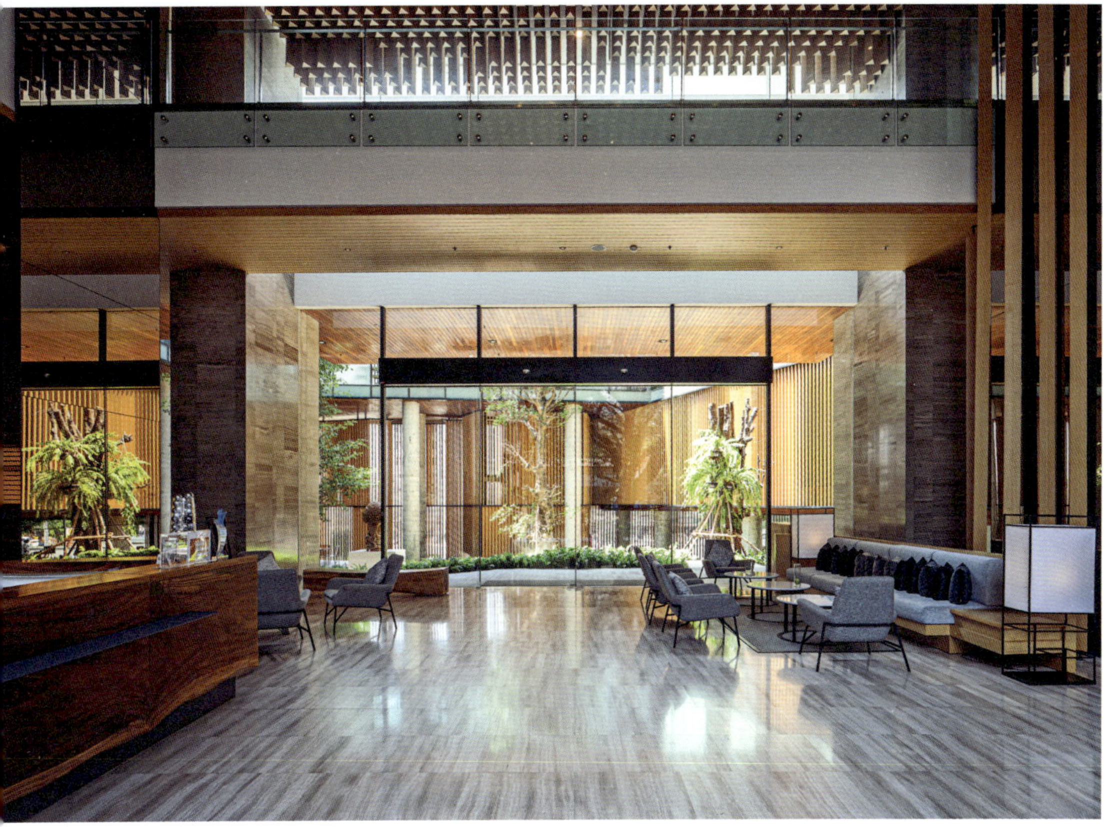

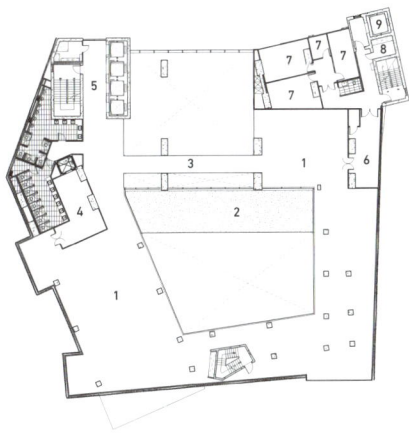

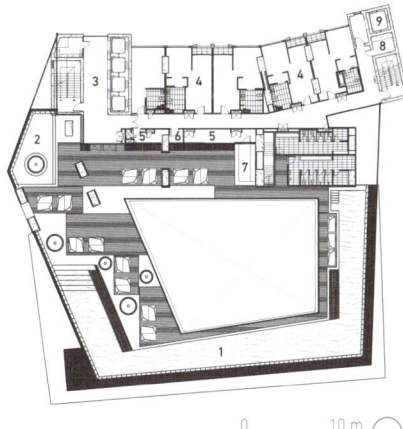

SECOND-FLOOR PLAN
1. DINING AREA
2. OUTDOOR DINING AREA
3. BRIDGE
4. DISPLAYED KITCHEN
5. ELEVATOR HALL
6. KITCHEN
7. OFFICE
8. EE ROOM
9. FIREFIGHTER ELEVATOR

FOURTH-FLOOR PLAN
1. SWIMMING POOL
2. ONSEN
3. ELEVATOR HALL
4. GUESTROOM
5. STORAGE
6. REFUSE DISPOSAL
7. POOL BAR
8. EE ROOM
9. FIREFIGHTER ELEVATOR

ARIZE HOTEL

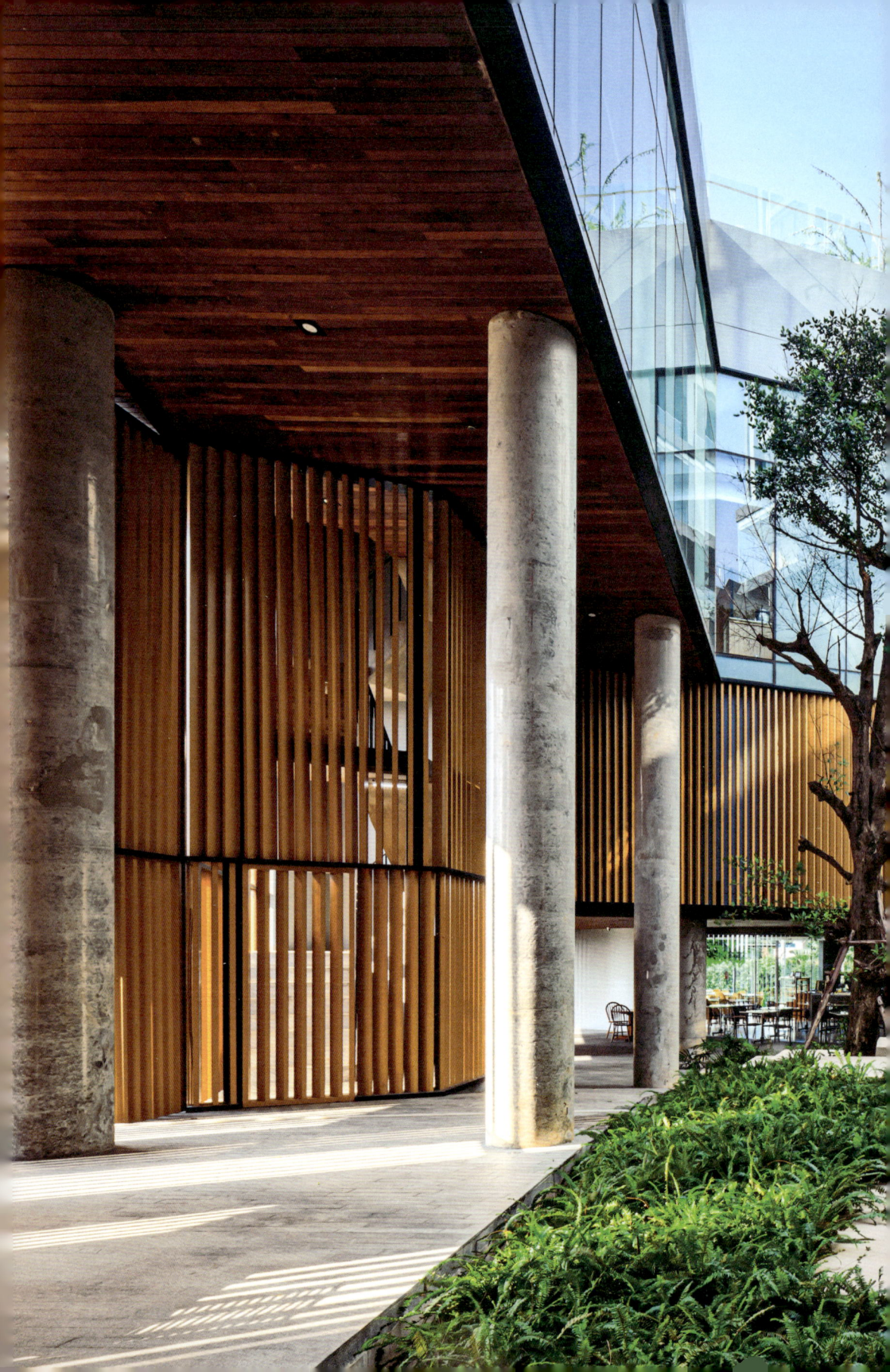

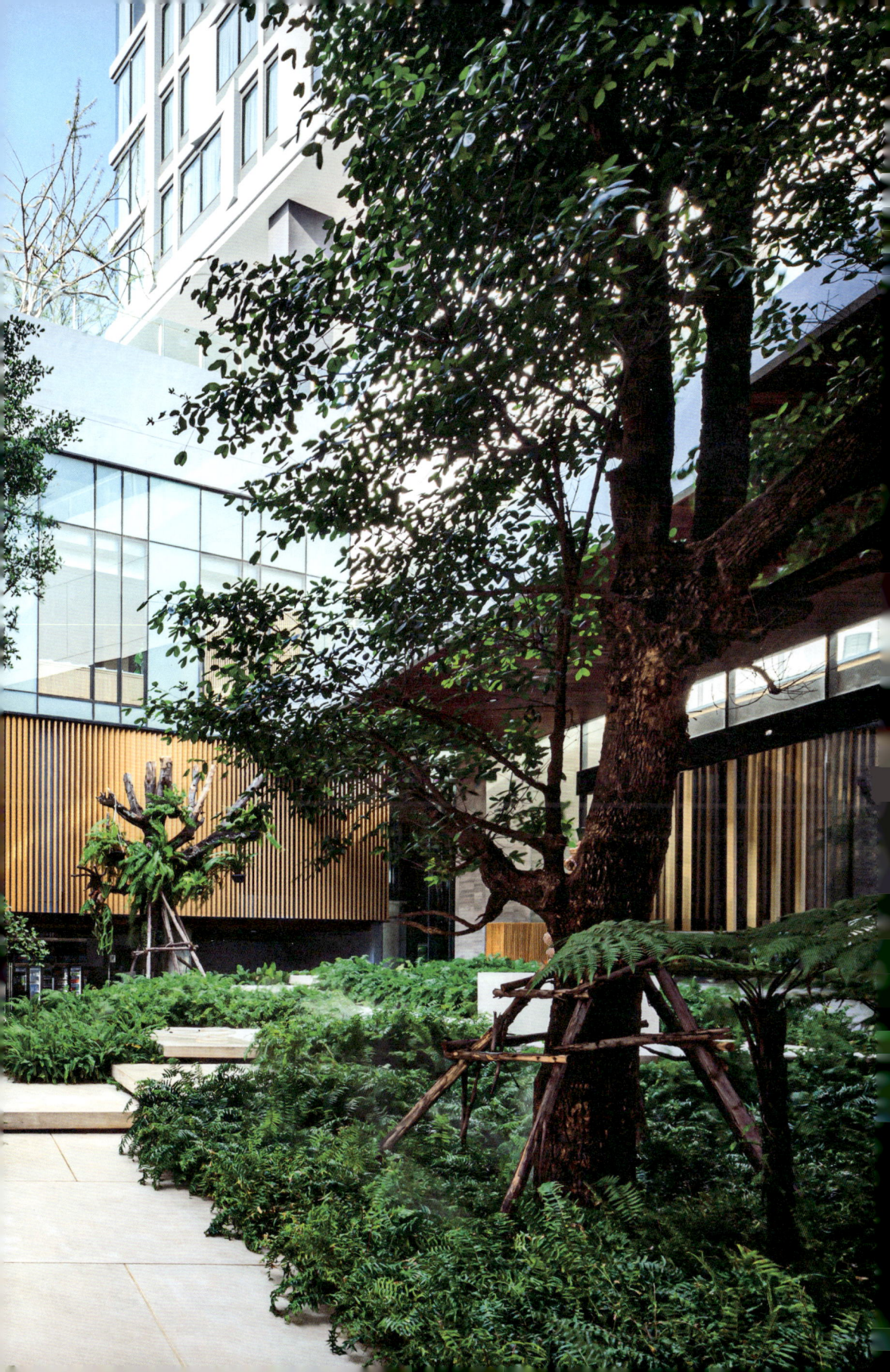

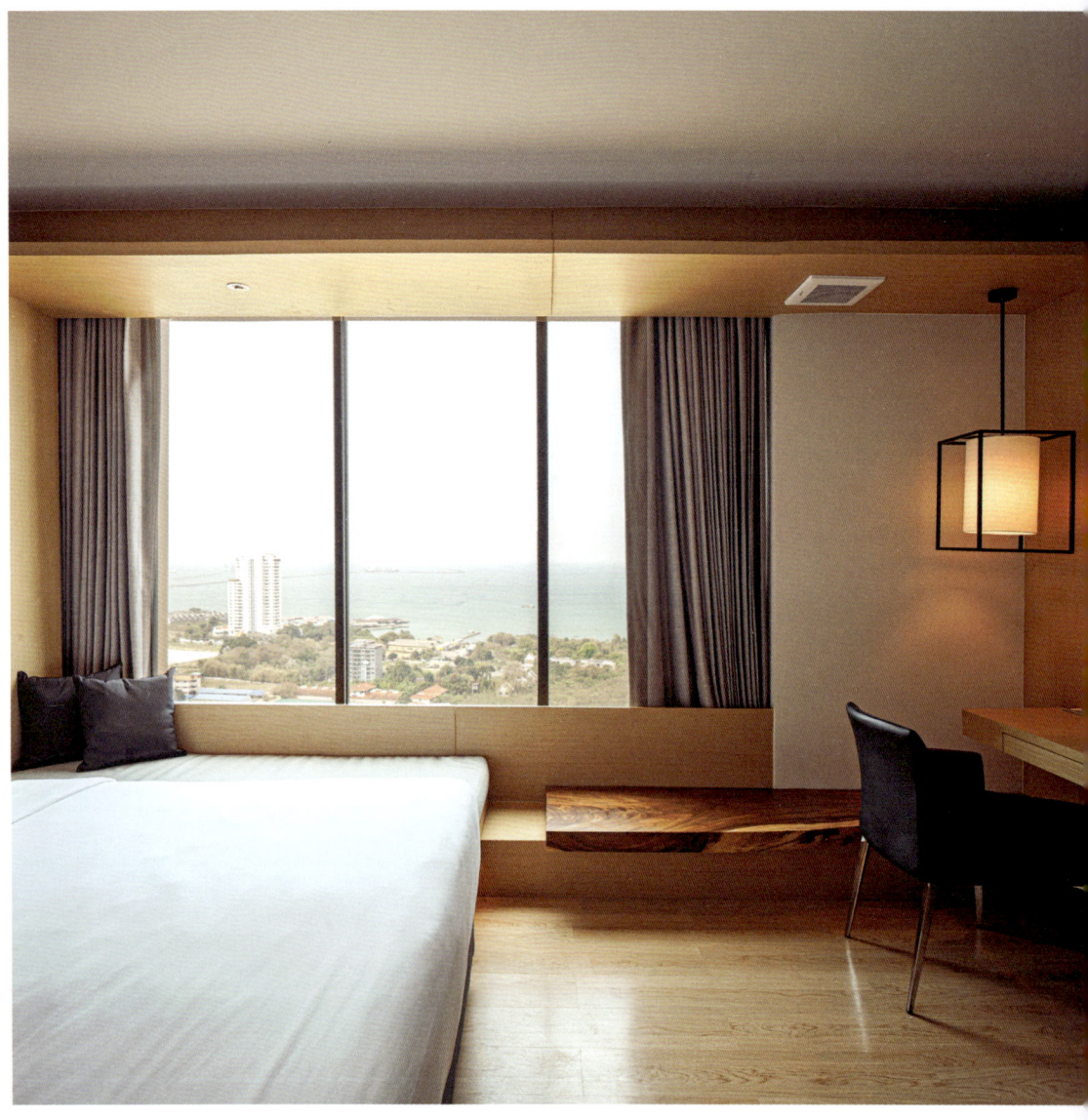

The guest tower employs a double-load-corridor system to minimize the circulation area in the towers. All guestrooms in the guest tower take in beautiful views, with one side of the building facing the gulf of Thailand and the other facing an impressive view of Khao Phra Khru mountain. Every floor is filled with common areas that have been designed as flexible spaces that can also host outdoor activities. On the thirty-seventh floor at the top of the tower, sprawls the penthouse, which accommodates a living area, bedrooms, and a meeting room for the owner to use for business.

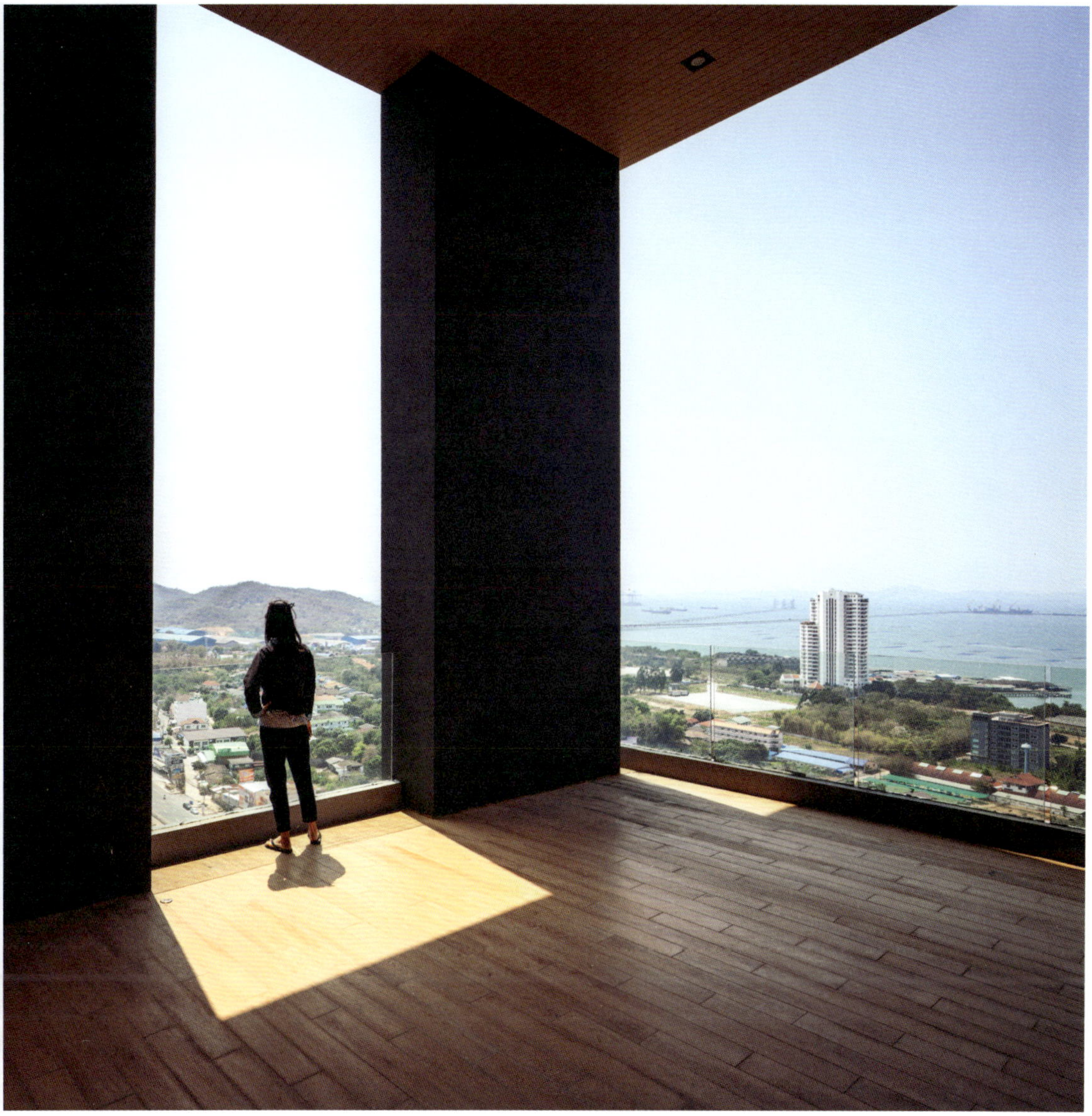

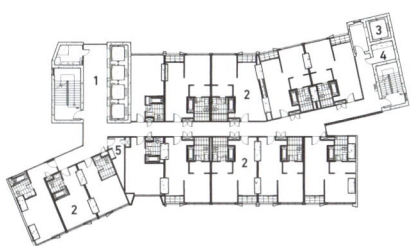
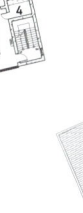

TYPICAL FLOOR PLAN 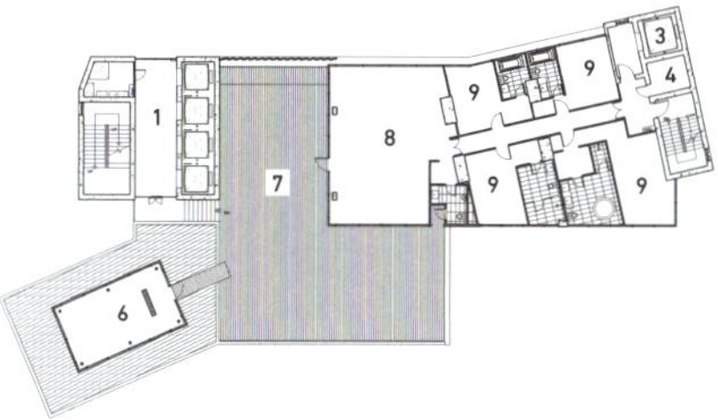 PENTHOUSE FLOOR PLAN

1 ELEVATOR HALL
2 GUESTROOM
3 FIREFIGHTER ELEVATOR
4 EE ROOM
5 STORAGE
6 MEETING ROOM
7 TERRACE
8 LIVING/DINING ROOM
9 PRIVATE BEDROOM

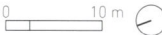

ARIZE HOTEL

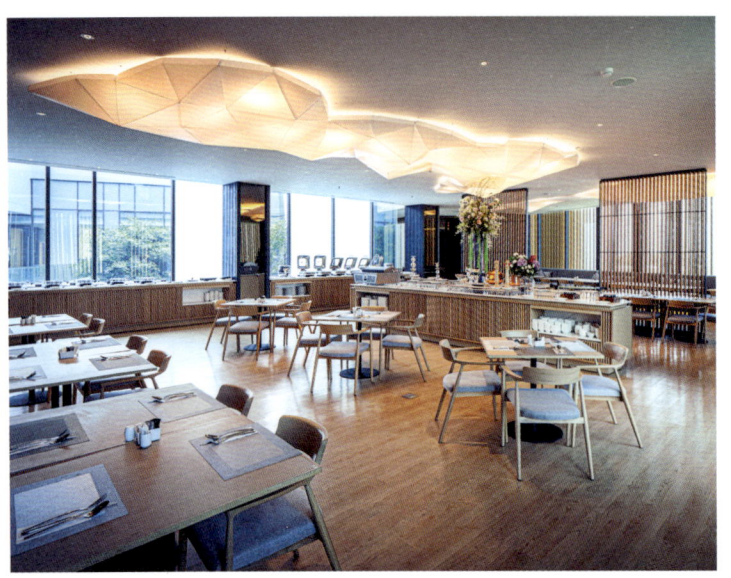

Around the hotel, interior spaces are dressed in a variety of design elements and décor that interpret the late Edo–period Japanese art theme, *Setsu Getsu Ka*, which translates to "Snow, Moon, and Flower." "Snow" takes the stage in the lobby: pillars are covered in reflective glass, and the ceiling showcases an installation of 3,000 wood prisms in varying lengths to mimic snow fall. Reflecting the "falling snow," the glass pillars, consumed by the reflections, present the theme as being "borderless," thereby creating a sense of infinity in the scene. "Moon" shines through in the all-day dining area proclaiming the phenomenon of light and shadow; glowing light features mimic the luminosity of the moon, while daylight, dispersed through decorative screens, dwells in scattered puddles crossed with shadows, painting an image of placid beauty. "Flower" blooms in the conference room, interpreted on the aspects of nature's serenity and movement through a dance of shadows performed by the trees outside.

The more organic concept of *wabi-sabi*, which is to "find beauty in imperfection" (by embracing authenticity without over-ornamentation) finds its place in the décor of the guestrooms with the use of natural wood, its raw texture emphasized to illustrate its imperfect beauty.

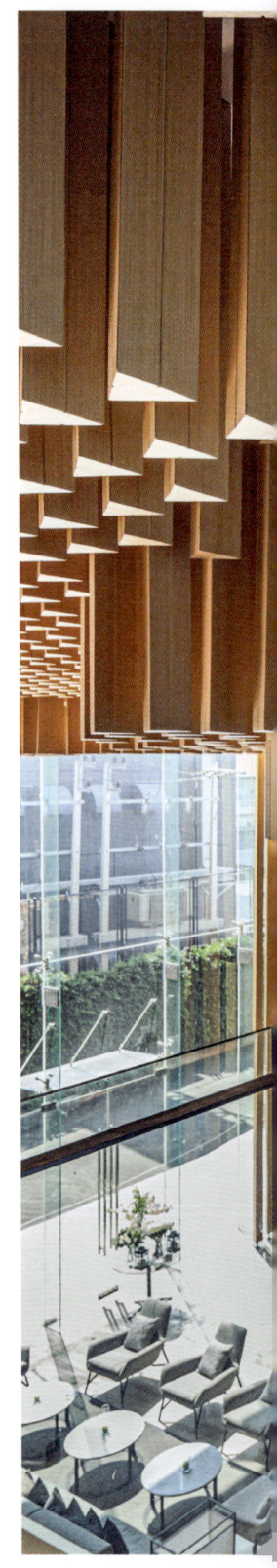

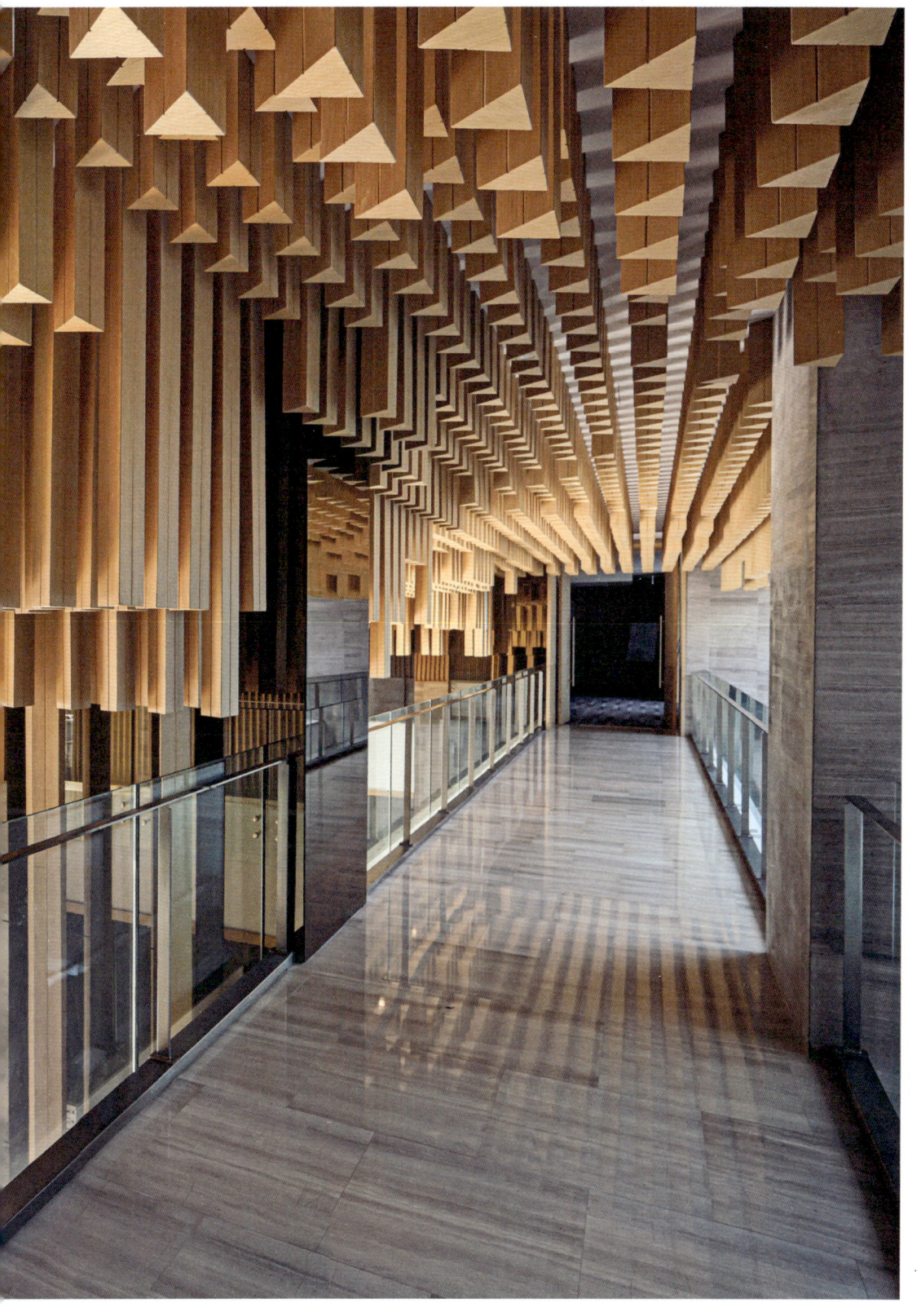

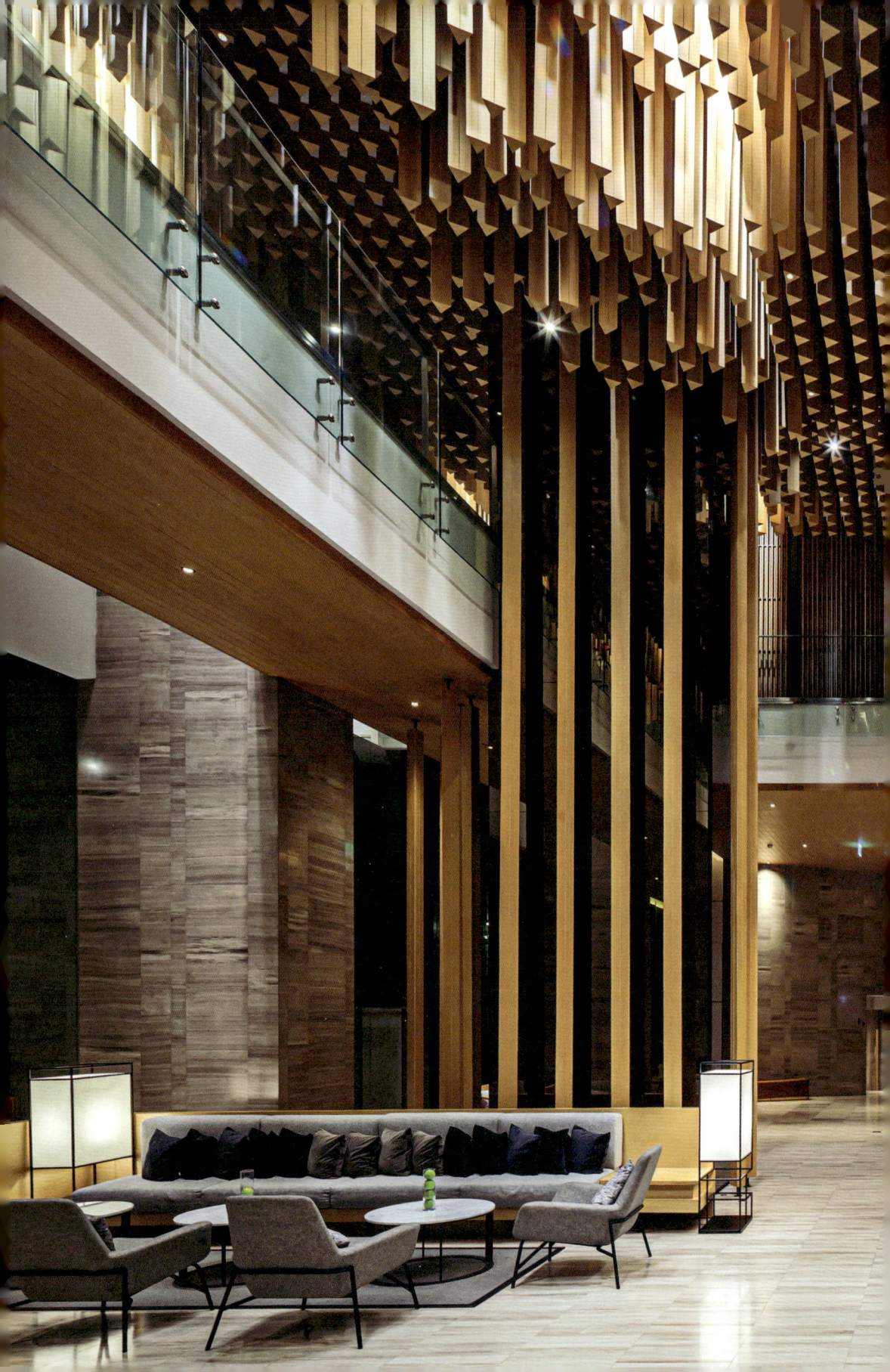

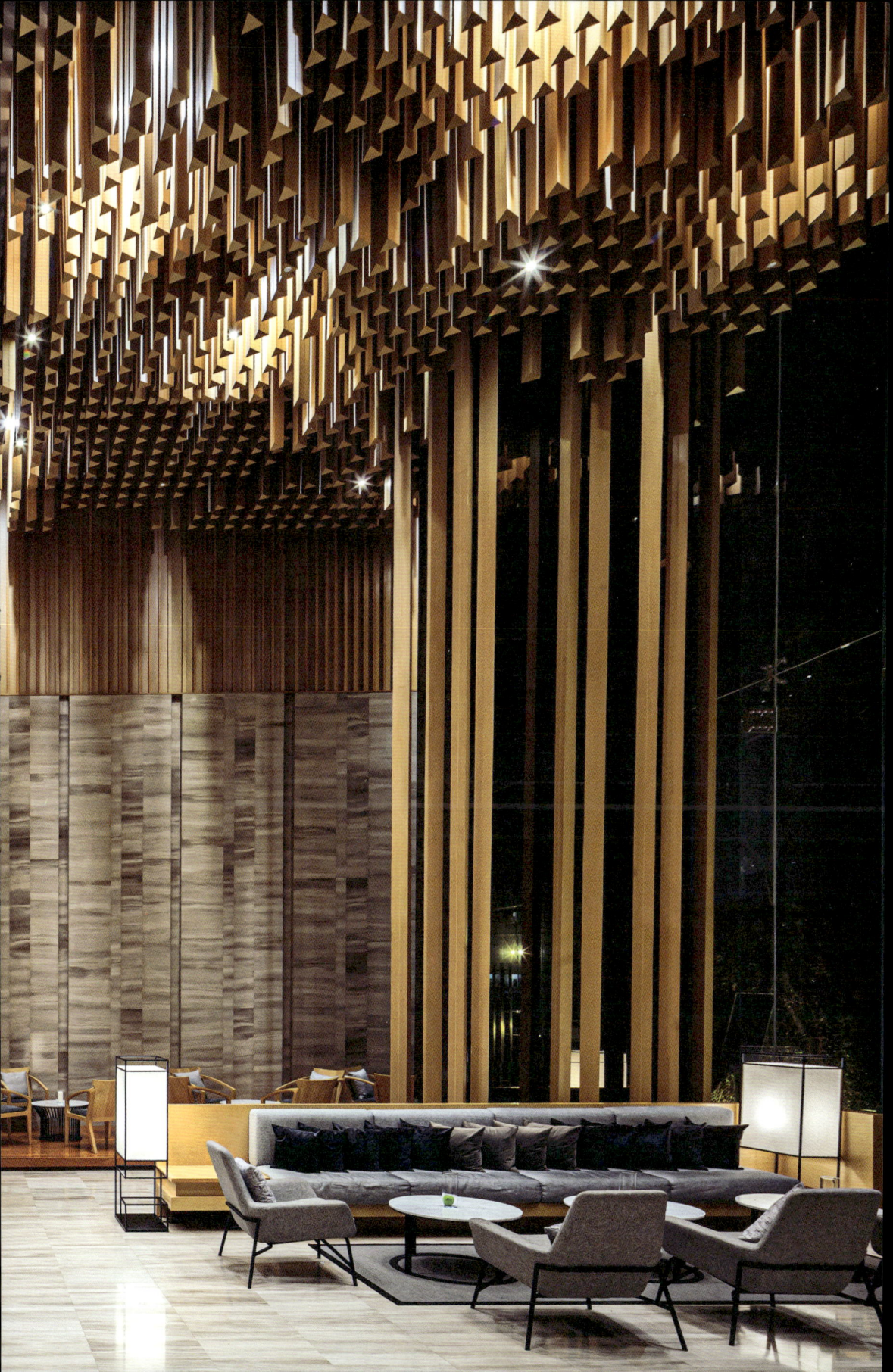

OTHER PROJECTS

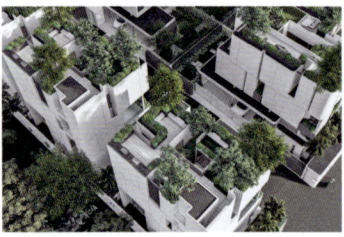

ARQ 10
Category: Residential
Location: Hua Mak, Bangkok, Thailand
Completion: Building in progress

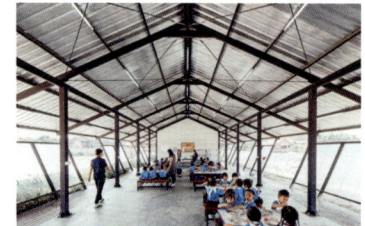

BAAN HUA RIN CHILD DEVELOPMENT CENTER
Category: Public
Location: Mae Prik, Chiang Rai, Thailand
Completion: 2015

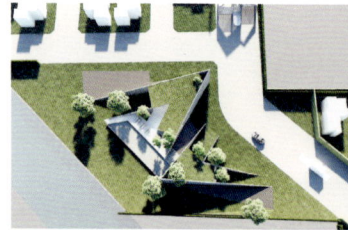

BANGKOK BOULEVARD SATHORN—PINKLAO 2
Category: Public (clubhouse)
Location: Nonthaburi, Bangkok, Thailand
Completion: 2017

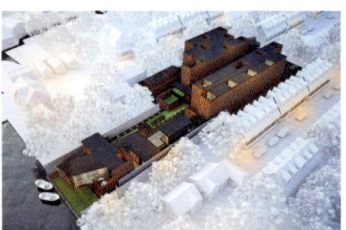

BANGKOKNOI HOTEL
Category: Hospitality
Location: Bangkok Noi, Bangkok, Thailand
Design: 2018

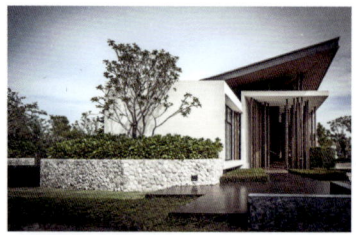

BURASIRI THAKAM RAMA 2
Category: Public (clubhouse)
Location: Thakam Rama 2, Bangkok, Thailand
Completion: 2013

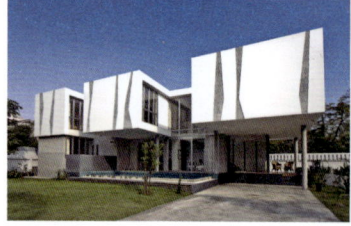

C HOUSE
Category: Residential
Location: Phaholyothin, Bangkok, Thailand
Completion: 2006

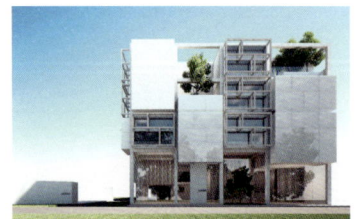

CHAAN HOSTEL
Category: Hospitality
Location: On Nut, Bangkok, Thailand
Design: 2016

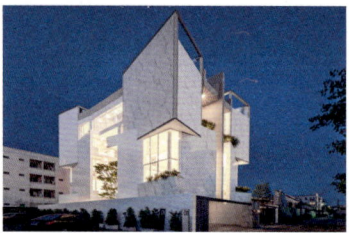

D8 RESIDENCE
Category: Residential
Location: Ladprao, Bangkok, Thailand
Completion: 2019

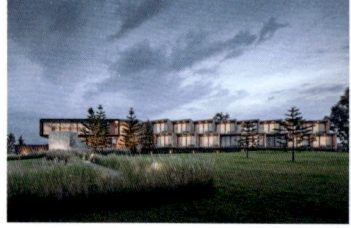

DE CAPOC
Category: Hospitality
Location: Khao Kho, Phetchaburi, Thailand
Completion: 2018

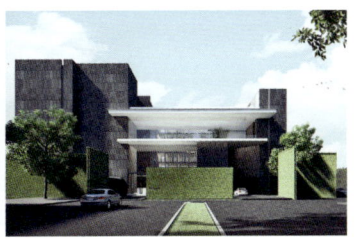

DUSIT D2 HOTEL
Category: Hospitality
Location: Hua Hin, Prachuabkirikhan, Thailand
Completion: Building in progress

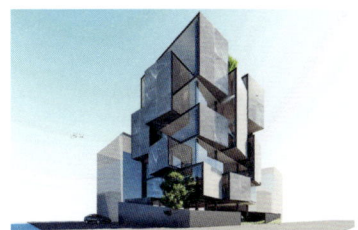

GIO HOME KITCHEN HEADQUARTERS
Category: Commercial/business
Location: Khlong Toei, Bangkok, Thailand
Completion: Building in progress

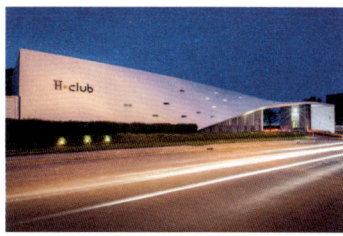

HABITIA PARK THAINTHALE 28
Category: Public (clubhouse)
Location: Rama 2, Bangkok, Thailand
Completion: 2013

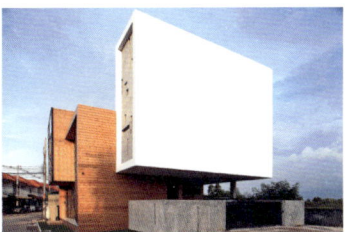

HOF I
Category: Commercial/business
Location: Mak Khaeng, Udon Thani, Thailand
Completion: 2013

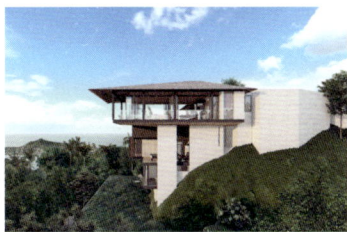

JC HOUSE
Category: Residential
Location: Koh Samui, Surat Thani, Thailand
Completion: Building in progress

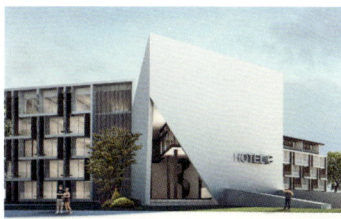

KARON HOTEL
Category: Hospitality
Location: Karon, Phuket, Thailand
Design: 2014

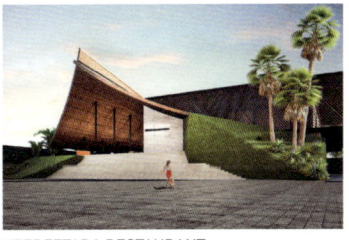

KEEREETARA RESTAURANT
Category: Hospitality
Location: Mueang, Kanchanaburi, Thailand
Completion: Building in progress

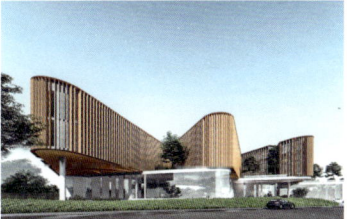

KMITL HOSPITAL (designed by IDIN, DD and AAT)
Category: Public (hospital)
Location: Ladkrabang, Bangkok, Thailand
Completion: Building in progress

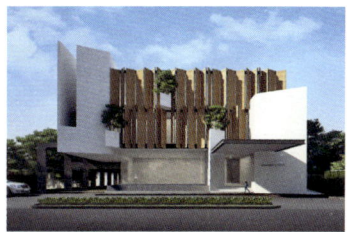

LANNA RESORT
Category: Hospitality
Location: Mueang, Chiang Rai, Thailand
Completion: Building in progress

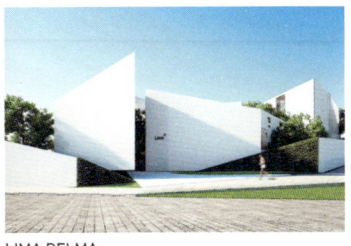

LIMA DELMA
Category: Hospitality
Location: Koh Samet, Rayong, Thailand
Design: 2015

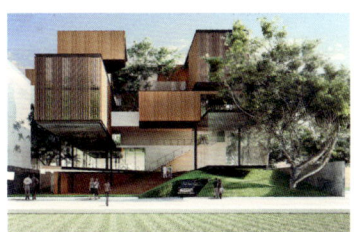

LS COMMUNITY MALL
Category: Retail
Location: Lang Suan, Bangkok, Thailand
Design: 2014

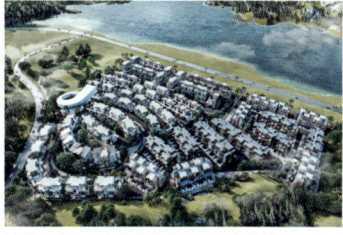

LUXESEA—LOFT AND DUPLEX BUILDING
Category: Residential
Location: Wanning, Hainan, China
Completion: Design in progress

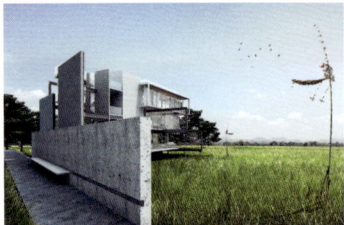
LYN HOUSE
Category: Residential
Location: Nayong, Trang, Thailand
Design: 2018

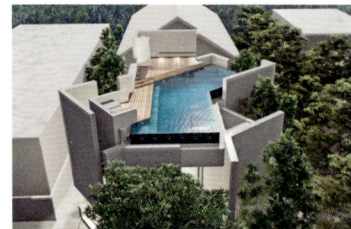
M HOUSE
Category: Residential
Location: Wutthakat, Bangkok, Thailand
Completion: Building in progress

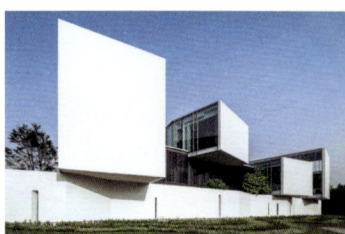
MDC HEADQUARTERS
Category: Commercial/business
Location: Ramkhamhaeng, Bangkok, Thailand
Completion: 2020

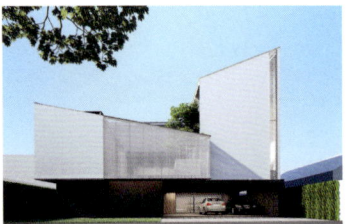
NN HOUSE
Category: Residential
Location: Mueang, Chanthaburi, Thailand
Completion: Building in progress

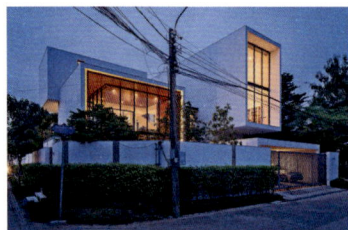
NY HOUSE
Category: Residential
Location: Chatuchak, Bangkok, Thailand
Completion: 2016

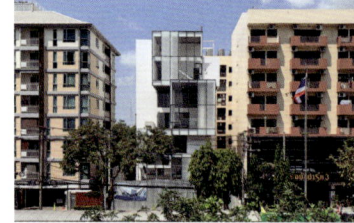
P HOUSE
Category: Residential
Location: Phaholyothin, Bangkok, Thailand
Completion: Building in progress

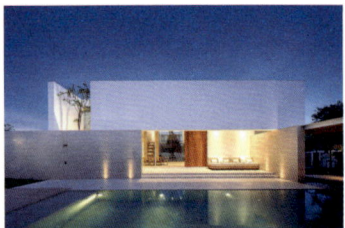
PA HOUSE
Category: Residential
Location: Pinklao, Bangkok, Thailand
Completion: 2017

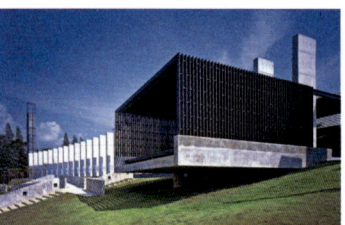
PHUKET GATEWAY
Category: Public
Location: Tah Chat Chai, Phuket, Thailand
Completion: 2007

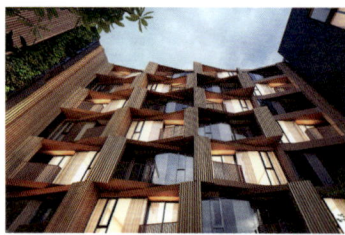
QUINTARA ARTE SUKHUMVIT 52
Category: Residential
Location: Sukhumvit, Bangkok, Thailand
Completion: Building in progress

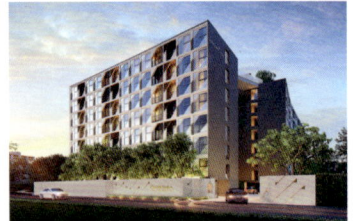
QUINTARA KYNETT RATCHADA 12
Category: Residential
Location: Ratchada, Bangkok, Thailand
Completion: Building in progress

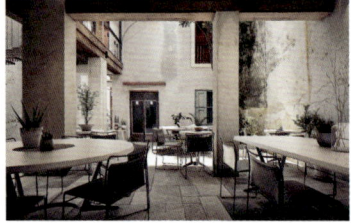
REAL RARE HOTEL
Category: Hospitality
Location: Talad Noi, Bangkok, Thailand
Design: 2018

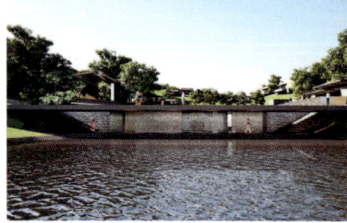
SAMOENG RESORT
Category: Hospitality
Location: Samoeng, Chiang Mai, Thailand
Design: 2014

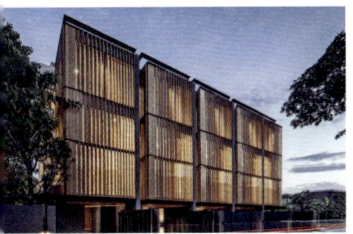

SIGNATURE 51
Category: Residential
Location: Suan Luang, Bangkok, Thailand
Completion: 2019

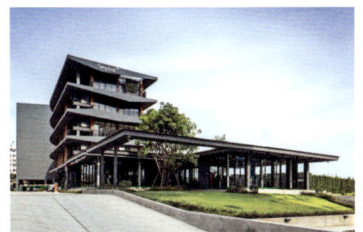

SIRIPHAT DORMITORY
Category: Residential
Location: Salaya, Nakhon Pathom, Thailand
Completion: 2016

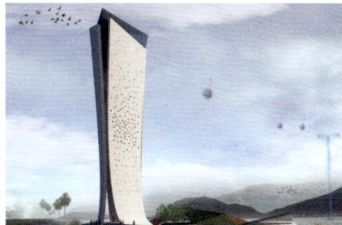

SONGKHLA TOWER
Category: Public
Location: Mueang, Songkhla, Thailand
Design: 2011 (competition winner)

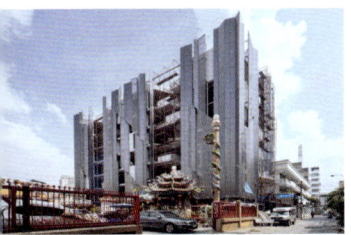

SUANPHLU 9 OFFICE
Category: Commercial/business
Location: Sathorn, Bangkok, Thailand
Completion: 2020

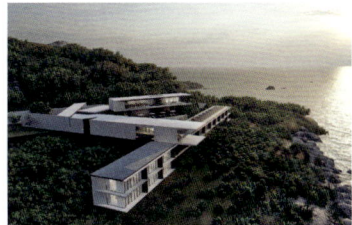

SUGAR OHANA
Category: Hospitality
Location: Mueang, Phuket, Thailand
Completion: Building in progress

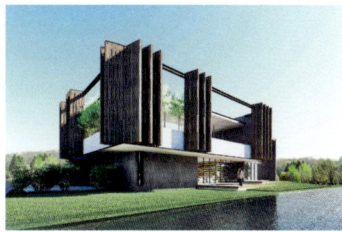

SUNNY VILLE
Category: Residential
Location: Ladkrabang, Bangkok, Thailand
Completion: 2020

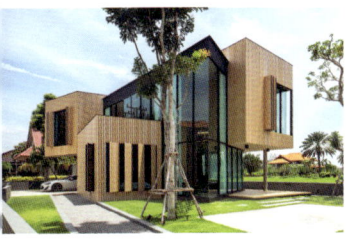

T HOUSE
Category: Residential
Location: Chao Samran, Phetchaburi, Thailand
Completion: 2016

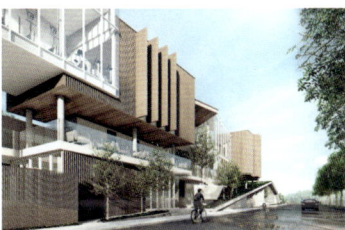

THE MARQ 2
Category: Public (clubhouse)
Location: Talingchan, Bangkok, Thailand
Completion: Building in progress

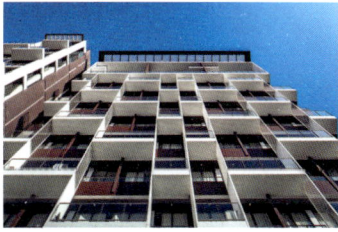

THE ORIENTAL BEACH CONDOMINIUM
Category: Residential
Location: Klaeng, Rayong, Thailand
Completion: 2009

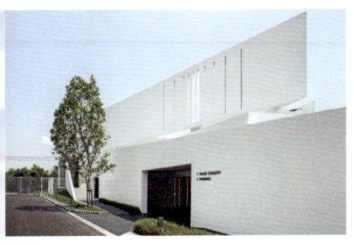

VIVE
Category: Public (clubhouse)
Location: Ramintra, Bangkok, Thailand
Completion: 2019

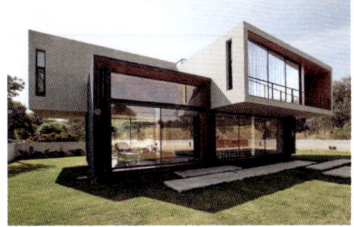

W HOUSE
Category: Residential
Location: Pak Chong, Nakhon Ratchasima, Thailand
Completion: 2010

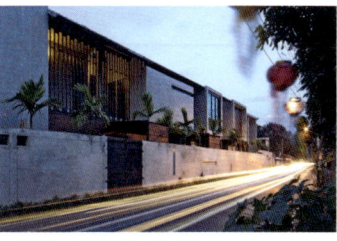

ZENSALA RESORT AND SPA
Category: Hospitality
Location: Mueang, Chiang Mai, Thailand
Completion: 2012

AWARDS

2020

The Plan Award 2020
The Plan Editions
Winner (Hospitality)
Choui Fong Tea Café 2

The Prix Versailles
South Asia and the Pacific 2020
UNESCO and the International
Union of Architects (UIA)
Winner (Restaurant)
Choui Fong Tea Café 2

Architizer A+ Awards
Architizer
Finalist (Hospitality—Restaurant)
Choui Fong Tea Café 2

INDE Awards 2020
Indesign Media Asia Pacific
Honorable Mention (The Work Space)
IDIN Architects Office

Dezeen Awards 2020
Dezeen
Shortlist (Business Building)
IDIN Architects Office

The Plan Award 2020
The Plan Editions
Shortlist (Office & Business)
IDIN Architects Office

INDE Awards 2020
Indesign Media Asia Pacific
Shortlist (The Social Space)
Choui Fong Tea Café 2

DEmark Award 2020
Department of International Trade Promotion
Ministry of Commerce Royal Thai Government
Winner (Interior Design)
Choui Fong Tea Café 2

TIDA Awards 2020
Thailand Interior Designers' Association
Winner (Small Residence Design)
JB House

TIDA Awards 2020
Thailand Interior Designers' Association
Winner (Restaurant Design)
Choui Fong Tea Café 2

DFA Design for Asia Awards 2020
The Hong Kong Design Centre
Silver Award (Hospitality & Leisure Spaces)
Choui Fong Tea Café 2

DFA Design for Asia Awards 2020
The Hong Kong Design Centre
Bronze Award (Workspaces)
IDIN Architects Office

DFA Design for Asia Awards 2020
The Hong Kong Design Centre
Bronze Award (Hospitality & Leisure Spaces)
Tara Villa

2019

Architizer A+ Awards
Architizer
Popular Winner (Commercial—Office Low-Rise)
IDIN Architects Office

2018

German Design Award 2018
German Design Council
Winner (Retail Architecture)
Choui Fong Tea Café

German Design Award 2018
German Design Council
Special Mention (Architecture)
Lima Duva

Arcasia Awards for Architecture (AAA 2018)
Architect Regional Council Asia
Mention (Commercial Buildings)
Choui Fong Tea Café

Arcasia Awards for Architecture (AAA 2018)
Architect Regional Council Asia
Mention (Resort Buildings)
Lima Duva

Best 10 Houses (10 Baan Na Yuu)
Baan Lae Suan Magazine
PA House

2017

American Architecture Prize (AAP 2017)
The American Architecture Prize
Winner (Hospitality Architecture)
Choui Fong Tea Café

American Architecture Prize (AAP 2017)
The American Architecture Prize
Winner (Hospitality Architecture)
Lima Duva

American Architecture Prize (AAP 2017)
The American Architecture Prize
Winner (Residential Architecture)
SIRI House

Architizer A+ Awards
Architizer
Jury Winner (Hospitality—Restaurant)
Choui Fong Tea Café

2A Asia Architecture Award
2A Magazine
Second Place (Commercial)
Choui Fong Tea Café

2A Asia Architecture Award
2A Magazine
Second Place (Residential)
KA House

2A Asia Architecture Award
2A Magazine
Third Place (Old & New)
SIRI House

2016

Arcasia Awards for Architecture 2016 (AAA 2016)
Architect Regional Council Asia
Honorable Mention
SIRI House

Architizer A+ Awards
Architizer
Special Mention
Lima Duva

ASA Architectural Design Awards
The Association of Siamese Architects
under Royal Patronage
Citation Award
SIRI House

ASA Architectural Design Awards
The Association of Siamese Architects
under Royal Patronage
Citation Award
Choui Fong Tea Café

ASA Architectural Design Awards
The Association of Siamese Architects
under Royal Patronage
Citation Award
Lima Duva

ASA Architectural Design Awards
The Association of Siamese Architects
under Royal Patronage
Citation Award
KA House

Best 10 Houses (10 Baan Na Yuu)
Baan Lae Suan Magazine
T House

2015

Best 10 Houses (10 Baan Na Yuu)
Baan Lae Suan Magazine
SIRI House

2011

Songkhla Tower Design Competition
Songkhla Provincial Administrative Organization
and The Association of Siamese Architects
under Royal Patronage
First Prize
Songkhla Tower

2010

ASA Architectural Design Awards
The Association of Siamese Architects
under Royal Patronage
Citation Award
Phuket Gateway

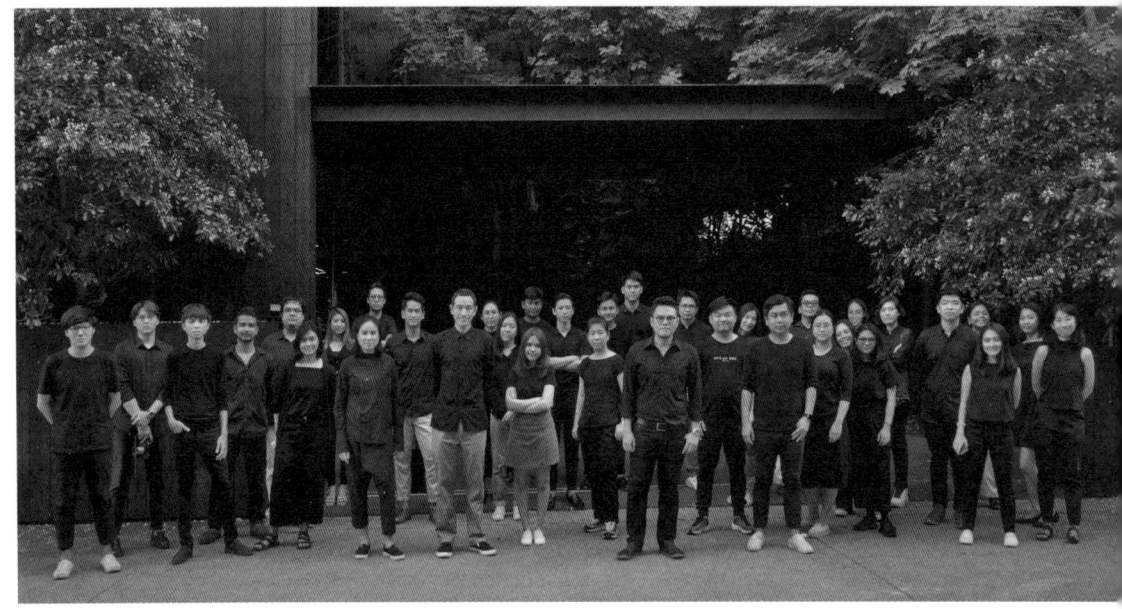

TEAM IDIN ARCHITECTS

Jeravej Hongsakul, Founder and Principal Architect
Eakgaluk Sirijariyawat, Associate Partner

STAFF (2020)

DESIGN TEAM
Naruporn Ngamsritragul, Architect
Sakorn Thongdoang, Architect
Araya Rueangkhongkiat, Architect
Pilanthana Phuawiriyaphan, Architect
Sittipong Wiriyapanich, Architect
Jirapas Leangsakul, Architect
Phennapha Tintamora, Architect
Siravich Pienpitak, Interior Designer
Juthamanee Sawatdeenarumon, Interior Designer
Kantong Wisutthiphat, Interior Designer
Pronnapath Khampiranon, Graphic Designer

ADMINISTRATION
Prapasiri Donlapa, Principal's Assistant
Vilaporn Pongisarawanich, Project Coordinator

FORMER STAFF
Prachya Yothaprasert
Senee Huayhongthong
Pichittra Tantisakunmongkon
Thongsuk Atiwannakul
Sethapong Phisitthawanich
Piyamas Sommapee
Panupong Chinmahavong
Rubporn Memoli
Supachai Piromrach
Wichan Kongnok
Mita Viriyavattanakul
Palathip Chunhasomboon
Boonyawee Tosakulchai
Schyutt Warachatdacha
Nattaphon Nuaksorn
Sarin Rangsikanbhum
Pongpop Narapanich
Chollaporn Ounkomol
Jureerat Korvanichakul
Thuwanont Ruangkanoksilp
Poowadon Siriburanakij
Supinya Chuasongkor

PROJECT CREDITS

IDIN ARCHITECTS OFFICE
Location: Sutthisan, Bangkok, Thailand
Completion: 2018
Area: 8,450 ft² (785 m²)
Architecture and interior design: IDIN Architects
Landscape design: Walllasia
Photography: Spaceshift Studio, Ketsiree Wongwan

CHOUI FONG TEA CAFÉ
Location: Mae Chan, Chiang Rai, Thailand
Completion: 2015
Area: 12,325 ft² (1,145 m²)
Architecture and interior design: IDIN Architects
Photography: Spaceshift Studio

CHOUI FONG TEA CAFÉ 2
Location: Mae Chan, Chiang Rai, Thailand
Completion: 2019
Area: 14,316 ft² (1,330 m²)
Architecture and interior design: IDIN Architects
Photography: DOF Sky|Ground

JB HOUSE
Location: Nakhon Chai Si, Nakhon Pathom, Thailand
Completion: 2017
Area: 1,367 ft² (127 m²)
Architecture and interior design: IDIN Architects
Photography: Ketsiree Wongwan

SIRI HOUSE
Location: Suriyawong, Bangkok, Thailand
Completion: 2015
Area: 8,611 ft² (800 m²)
Architecture and interior design: IDIN Architects
Photography: Spaceshift Studio

KA HOUSE
Location: Pak Chong, Nakhon Ratchasima, Thailand
Completion: 2015
Area: 2,583 ft² (240 m²)
Architecture and interior design: IDIN Architects
Photography: Ketsiree Wongwan

PA PRANK
Location: Phraeng Sanphasat, Bangkok, Thailand
Completion: 2018
Area: 7,804 ft² (725 m²)
Architecture and interior design: IDIN Architects
Photography: Ketsiree Wongwan

LIMA DUVA
Location: Koh Samet, Rayong, Thailand
Completion: 2015
Area: 22,604 ft² (2,100 m²)
Architecture and interior design: IDIN Architects
Landscape design: Pergolar Landscape & Architecture
Photography: Spaceshift Studio

TARA VILLA
Location: Mueang, Kanchanaburi, Thailand
Completion: 2019
Area: 63,507 ft² (5,900 m²)
Architecture and interior design: IDIN Architects
Photography: DOF Sky|Ground

ARIZE HOTEL
Location: Sriracha, Chon Buri, Thailand
Completion: 2019
Area: 355,209 ft² (33,000 m²)
Architecture and interior design: IDIN Architects
Landscape design: TROP : terrains + open space
Photography: Spaceshift Studio

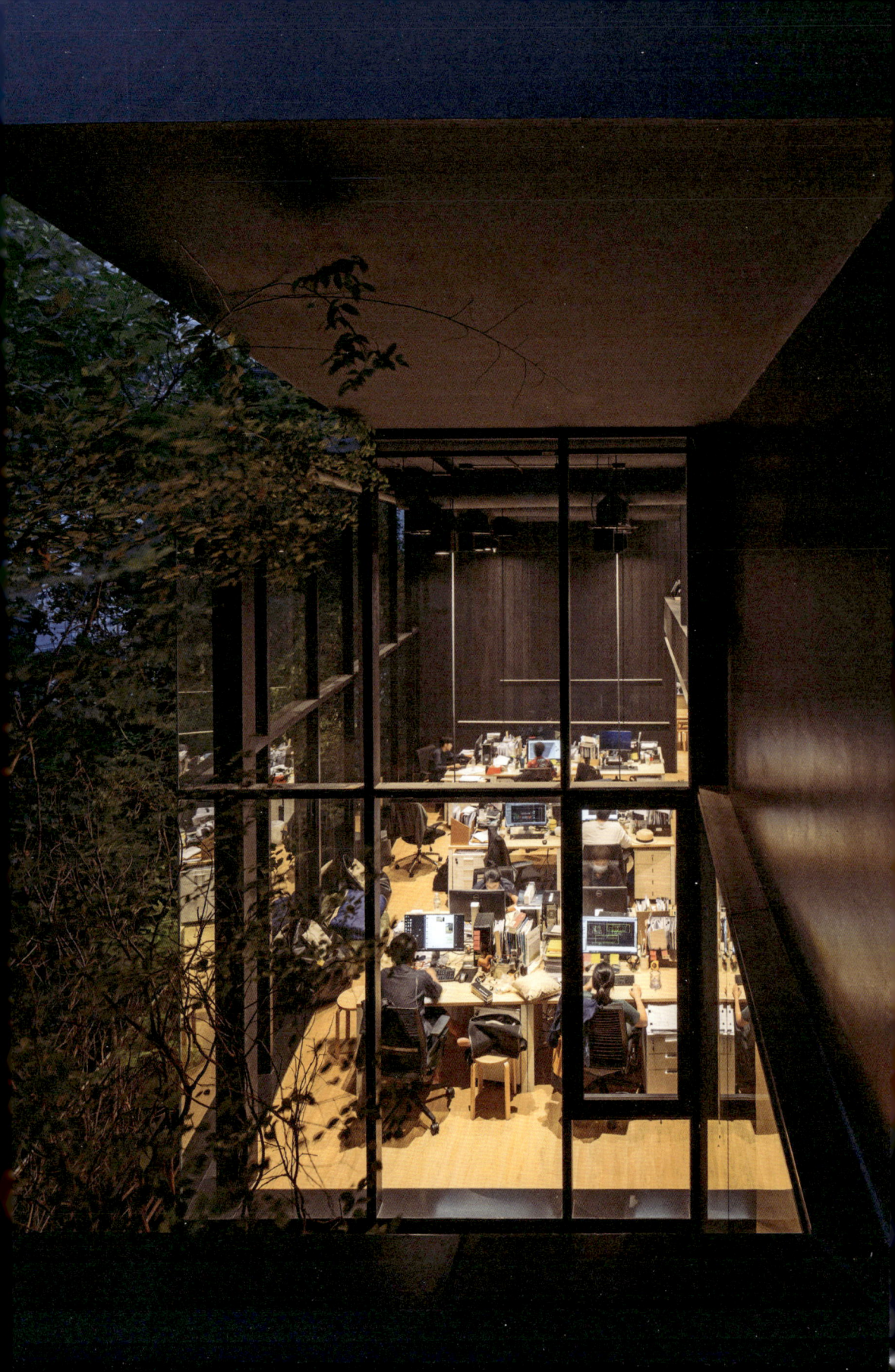